STUDIES IN THE
RELIGIOUS TRADITION OF
THE OLD TESTAMENT

STUDIES IN THE RELIGIOUS TRADITION OF THE OLD TESTAMENT

PETER R. ACKROYD

Professor Emeritus of Old Testament Studies
University of London (King's College)

SCM PRESS LTD

British Library Cataloguing in Publication Data

Ackroyd, Peter R.
Studies in the religious tradition of
the Old Testament.
1. Bible. O.T.—Criticism, interpretation,
etc.
I. Title
221.6   BS1171.2

ISBN 0–334–01560–X

First published 1987
by SCM Press Ltd
26–30 Tottenham Road, London N1

Phototypeset by Input Typesetting Ltd
and printed in Great Britain by
Richard Clay Ltd, Bungay

CONTENTS

III TOWARDS THE CANON

INTRODUCTION

The essays in this volume all stem in some degree from the theme of continuity within the religious tradition of the Old Testament. They represent various ways in which, over the past twenty-five years or so, I have endeavoured to explore the nature of that continuity, the degree to which continuity and discontinuity, unity and diversity, operate within a tradition which believes itself to have coherence and yet shows everywhere the evidences of difference and pluriformity. The problem (and this is one which is given some wider context in the final essay) is how in the end it is proper and possible to describe the tradition as forming a whole, and what may be said to constitute that which its adherents in the period of its formation and which its successors in Christian and Jewish tradition have regarded as that to which they belong. That the claim to belong may be expressed in more conservative and in more radical ways constitutes yet another facet of the interrelation between unity and diversity.

A division has been made into three sections. In the first group of essays the wider questions of continuity and discontinuity have been explored. In the second, what might be termed the more practical aspects of this are considered in relation to the prophets, and more specifically in relation to the Isaiah tradition. In the third, another broader question, that of the canon, is dealt with from various related angles. The final essay offers not conclusions but some reflections on historical and theological aspects of these issues.

With the exception of this final essay, all these studies have been published previously, and the bibliographical details are set out in the notes. My thanks are due to the original publishers for their willingness to allow them to be reprinted in this collected form.

The essays have not been revised, though some few corrections and changes appear, partly to use a single style for references and the like, but also (by means of material included in square brackets) to add either comments or references to more recent discussions. Cross-references between the various essays have also been added where this seemed helpful, though it will be apparent that there are many interlinkages of theme throughout the collection.

There is, perhaps inevitably, some degree of overlap in the contents of these essays. My endeavour has always been to keep a close association between the discussion of general principles of interpretation of the Old Testament text and the examination of particular passages – some of which appear more than once as the questions that they raise continue to invite renewed reflection. Such a balance is essential to a real approach to the material. It derives for me in part at least from my teaching, and in particular for what has always been the most rewarding part of that work, the examination, in class or seminar, of passages of Hebrew text. The way in which the text itself, and not infrequently the same text repeatedly over a period of years, invites questions and provides a corrective to generalization, has been the practical aspect of the consideration of texts as literature, that is, writings which engage author and reader in a complex dialogue. With an ancient text, which has its own history deducible in so far as it may be within itself, knowledge of the author remains always problematic, even in the few cases where to speak of an author may appear to be proper; but the interrelationship between text and reader or user – and particularly here where appropriate in the context of religious use, in worship or in reflection – is richer by reason of the recognition that the text in its known form or forms has been shaped not simply by an author but by the users and interpreters themselves. It is for this reason that terms such as preaching, homiletic, exegesis appear, perhaps with too little precision, at numerous points: the lack of precision, whatever its disadvantages, may serve as a reminder that it should not be assumed that modern practice corresponds to ancient, but also that the processes of use and interpretation do not necessarily fit into neat definitions. The more detailed study of this whole area, now so skilfully furthered by Michael Fishbane in his *Biblical Interpretation in Ancient Israel* (Clarendon Press, Oxford 1985), has revealed the richness of the interpretative tradition, and enabled the recognition that what used to be thought of too much in terms of pedestrian editing is in fact part of a creative process. Inevitably, the evaluation of particular elements will vary, partly in accordance with the presuppositions of the later users of the now more developed text. The carrying of this through into the history of exegesis, both Christian and Jewish, down to our own time is again an area in which differences of viewpoint mean differences of assessment. But we have come to respect our predecessors, even where we think them wrong, and may perhaps hope that our successors, however they judge us, will seek to understand what we have been doing.

Much of what appears in this volume would benefit from being reworked in the light of more recent studies. In particular, more recent commentaries, and discussions of the nature of Old Testament religion and theology, offer much that continues to open up the topics here discussed. But the reader can turn to these, and it does not seem necessary to list them: in some few instances, suggestions have been made, but the modern commentary series and the bibliographies in the Book Lists of the Society for Old Testament Study and elsewhere will provide what is needed. If my original thought in accepting the suggestion that these essays should be gathered into a volume was that I would have to revise them all, I am grateful to those who persuaded me that it was more appropriate, as well as more practical, to let them stand and simply to make them more readily available. In this context, I would wish to express my gratitude in particular to Dr John S. Bowden of the SCM Press, to Dr Robert P. Carroll of the University of Glasgow, and to my former colleagues at King's College, Professor Michael A. Knibb and the Revd. Richard J. Coggins. If a dedication of the volume is in order, it is to these last two that I would like it to be, in gratitude for their support and the critical stimulus of their thinking over the years in which we worked together.

ABBREVIATIONS

AASF	Annales Academiae Scientiarum Fennicae, Helsinki
ABR	*Australian Biblical Review*, Melbourne
ALUOS	*Annual of the Leeds University Oriental Society*, Leeds
AnalBibl	Analecta Biblica, Biblical Institute Press, Rome
ANEP	*The Ancient Near East in Pictures*, ed. J. B. Pritchard, Princeton UP 1954, ²1969
ANET	*Ancient Near Eastern Texts relating to the Old Testament*, ed. J. B. Pritchard, Princeton UP 1950, ³1959
ANVAO	Avhandlinger utgitt av Det Norske Videnskaps Akademi i Oslo
AOAT	Alter Orient und Altes Testament, Neukirchener Verlag, Neukirchen-Vluyn
ATD	Das Altes Testament Deutsch, Vandenhoeck und Ruprecht, Göttingen
BAL	Berichte über die Verhandlungen der sächsischen Akademie der Wissenschaften zu Leipzig. Philologisch-historische Klasse, Akademie-Verlag, Berlin
BASOR	*Bulletin of the American Schools of Oriental Research*, Jerusalem and Baghdad
BET	Beiträge zu biblischen Exegese und Theologie, Peter Lang, Frankfurt and Berne
BHS	Biblia Hebraica Stuttgartensia, Stuttgart 1976–77
BiblRes	*Biblical Research*, Chicago

BK	Biblischer Kommentar, Neukirchener Verlag, Neukirchen-Vluyn
BRL	*Biblisches Reallexikon*, ed. K. Galling (HAT 1.1), 1937 [rev. ed. 1977]
BZ	*Biblische Zeitschrift*, Freiburg, Paderborn
BZAW	Beiheft zur *ZAW*, W. de Gruyter, Berlin
CAT	Commentaire de l'Ancien Testament, Delachaux et Niestlé, Neuchâtel
EvQu	*Evangelical Quarterly*, London
ExpT	*Expository Times*, Edinburgh
FRLANT	Forschungen zur Religion und Literatur des Alten und Neuen Testaments, Vandenhoeck und Ruprecht, Göttingen
HAT	Handbuch zum Alten Testament, J. C. B. Mohr, Tübingen
HUCA	*Hebrew Union College Annual*, Cincinnati
IB	*Interpreter's Bible*, 12 vols., Abingdon Press, Nashville 1951–57
ICC	International Critical Commentary, T. & T. Clark, Edinburgh, and Scribners, New York
IDB	*Interpreter's Dictionary of the Bible*, Abingdon, Nashville 1962
IDBS	*IDB* Supplementary volume, Abingdon, Nashville 1976
IEJ	*Israel Exploration Journal*, Jerusalem
IJT	*Indian Journal of Theology*, Calcutta
JANESCU	*Journal of Ancient Near Eastern Studies* of Columbia University, New York
JBL	*Journal of Biblical Literature*, Philadelphia, Missoula, Mont.
JJS	*Journal of Jewish Studies*, London
JNES	*Journal of Near Eastern Studies*, Chicago
JQR	*Jewish Quarterly Review*, London, Chicago

JSJ	*Journal for the Study of Judaism*, Leiden
JSOT(S)	*Journal for the Study of the Old Testament* (Supplements), Sheffield
JSS	*Journal of Semitic Studies*, Manchester
JTS	*Journal of Theological Studies*, Oxford
KBL	L. Köhler and W. Baumgartner, *Lexicon in Veteris Testamenti Libros*, Brill, Leiden 1953, ³1967ff.
KAT	Kommentar zum Alten Testament, Leipzig, Gütersloh
NAB	The New American Bible, Kenedy, New York, and Collier-Macmillan, London 1970
NEB	The New English Bible, OUP and CUP, 1961–70
NF	Neue Folge
NS	New series
NZST	*Neue Zeitschrift für Systematische Theologie*, Berlin
OTL	Old Testament Library, SCM Press and Westminster Press, Philadelphia
OTS	Oudtestamentische Studiën, Brill, Leiden
OTWSA	Die Oud-Testamentiese Werkgemeenskap van Suid-Afrika, Pretoria
PEQ	*Palestine Exploration Quarterly*, London
RB	*Revue biblique*, Paris
RSV	Revised Standard Version of the Bible, Nelson, London and New York 1952
SBLDS	Society of Biblical Literature Dissertation Series, Missoula, Mont., Chico, Cal.
SBLMS	Society of Biblical Literature Monograph Series, Philadelphia, Missoula, Mont.
SBS	Stuttgarter Bibelstudien, Katholisches Bibelwerk, Stuttgart
SBT	Studies in Biblical Theology, SCM Press and Allenson, Naperville, Ill.
SEÅ	*Svensk Exegetisk Årsbok*, Lund

SJLA	Studies in Judaism in Late Antiquity, Brill, Leiden
SNVAO	Skrifter utgitt av Det Norske Videnskap Akademi i Oslo
StTh	*Studia Theologica: Scandinavian Journal of Theology*, Universitetsforlaget, Oslo
TBC	Torch Bible Commentaries, SCM Press
TDNT	*Theological Dictionary of the New Testament*, ET of *TWNT*, Eerdmans, Grand Rapids, Michigan 1964–76
TGUOS	*Transactions of the Glasgow University Oriental Society*, Glasgow
TLZ	*Theologische Literaturzeitung*, Leipzig
TU	Texte und Untersuchungen zur Geschichte der altchristlichen Literatur, Hinrichs, Leipzig, Akademie-Verlag, Berlin
TWAT	*Theologisches Wörterbuch zum Alten Testament*, ed. G. J. Botterweck and H. Ringgren, Kohlhammer, Stuttgart 1973ff.
TWNT	*Theologisches Wörterbuch zum Neuen Testament*, ed. G. Kittel, Kohlhammer, Stuttgart 1932–79
UP	University Press
UUÅ	Uppsala Universitets Åarskrift, Uppsala
USQR	*Union Seminary Quarterly Review*, New York
VD	*Verbum Domini*, Rome
VT	*Vetus Testamentum*, Leiden
VTS	Supplements to *VT*, Brill, Leiden
WMANT	Wissenschaftliche Untersuchungen zum Alten und Neuen Testament, Neukirchener Verlag, Neukirchen-Vluyn
h10.5*ZAW*	*Zeitschrift für die alttestamentliche Wissenschaft*, Giessen, Berlin
ZDPV	*Zeitschrift des Deutschen Palästinavereins*, Wiesbaden
ZST	*Zeitschrift für Systematische Theologie*, Gütersloh

I

CONTINUITY

Continuity: A Contribution to the Study of the Old Testament Religious Tradition

There is a story told in the opening chapters of the first book of Samuel which may be taken as symbolic of the basic problem of continuity. It tells of Elkanah and his two wives, Hannah and Peninnah, of their domestic situation and their pious observance of religious custom. It shows what we may reasonably regard as a typical family, travelling year by year to the shrine of the Ark at Shiloh (I Sam. 1.3, 21), to engage in the celebration of the annual festival there. It describes vividly how Hannah offered her own private prayer in the shrine, her faith, her willingness to dedicate the son for whom she longed so ardently to the God in whose power to give she had such deep confidence. It reveals the depths of her religious devotion, the sensitiveness of her spirit. And subsequently we are shown the fulfilment of her desires, the birth of a son, his dedication at the shrine, and the continued blessing of God upon Elkanah and Hannah (I Sam. 2. 18–21).[1]

Now all this centres around the religious shrine of Shiloh, the shrine of the Ark, itself the symbol of the presence of God in Israel, a symbol which instils awe into the hearts of Israel and terror into the hearts of her enemies (cf. I Samuel 4). If we are unsure about the details of Israelite tribal organization, we may nevertheless realize that here is the centre of the tribal association, the amphictyony, and that the priest of Shiloh appears, therefore, as a leading figure in the people's life. We have indications of the movement of the Ark from one shrine to another,[2] possibly as the centre of gravity in the amphictyony shifted, possibly on some system by which the claims of different traditional centres of divine revelation and action were adjusted. Of the predecessors of the priest of

Shiloh we have little precise information. Are they to be found in the so-called Minor Judges of Judges 10 and 12?[3] Of successors too we have no clear picture. The hereditary principle was evidently recognized, but was found in practice to be unsatisfactory.[4] Samuel became the true successor, but the portrait of Samuel has been painted by more than one artist, and the amalgamating of his diverse characters into one composite personality is on the whole a less edifying occupation than the recognition of the wealth of the tradition and its value in itself. The ultimate succession to the priests of Shiloh is to be found in the establishment of the Zadokite dynasty under Solomon,[5] and this succession is one of the themes, running parallel to that of the royal succession, with which the books of Samuel are largely concerned.

But although there is much that is nebulous here, there are certain points which emerge quite clearly. It need not trouble us that there are literary levels in which differing judgments are expressed,[6] points at which we may discern the richness of the tradition and the skill in the handling of tradition which is to be associated with so much of Old Testament literary composition.[7] The different levels together make up a pattern, and it is a recurring pattern within the Old Testament. Side by side with the picture of idyllic piety, of personal faith and acceptance, typified in Hannah and her husband, no less devout than she, we have another picture of the religious situation in Shiloh. The administration has passed, with Eli's old age, to his sons. They are described as having 'no regard for Yahweh' (I Sam. 2.12) disobeying the sacrificial laws so as to get sacrificial meat as they liked it (I Sam. 2.15), and also as engaging in immoral practices – possibly cult-prostitutional practices – with the women attendants of the shrine (I Sam. 2.22). The devotion and piety of people like Hannah and Elkanah was being practised at a shrine whose priests were scoundrels.

We may also observe that in the Elkanah/Hannah tradition itself there is an indication of an unsatisfactory feature of the festival celebration. When Eli admonishes Hannah for drunkenness in the shrine (I Sam. 1.14), we can only conclude that such drunkenness was a not infrequent feature of the festival worship. If, as seems most probable, the festival was the autumnal one, it was the time of the grape harvest, and the nature of the celebration is in part indicated by the parallel in the story of Abimelech, when the Shechemites celebrated their grape harvest 'in the house of their god' and make it evident by their behaviour that they were far from sober (Judg. 9.27–29). The context of the pious acts of such people as Hannah and Elkanah is a festival of riotous feasting and excessive drinking, the kind of celebration familiar from later prophetic condemnation (so e.g. Hos. 4.11, 18; Isa. 5.11f.).

The juxtaposition of faithful worship and riotous celebration, personal piety and worthless priesthood, poses the problem. It is a problem raised more sharply by the tirades of the prophets[8] against the religious observances of their time, and in particular against the importation of alien practice and alien thinking about God. How is there to be found continuity of belief? How were the great truths of Israel's experience preserved? What guarantee was there that those truths would not be lost with all the hazards of a religious and political situation in which unworthy priests and prophets and kings are all singled out for special condemnation. There appears to be an unbridgeable gulf between the true faith and piety of good men and women and the religious pattern indicated by prophets and lawgivers and psalmists and wise men as being prevalent.[9] Nor does there seem to be any truly idyllic period, much as the devoutness of piety has been projected into the patriarchal narratives, for here too the blameworthiness of men cuts across the pattern.[10]

The problem is, in fact, a wider and deeper one. One of the perpetually odd facts about the Old Testament is its lack of cross-reference. The interrelationship between one aspect of its life and another has often to be assumed because evidence is lacking. The affinities between Jeremiah and the circle of thought which produced the Deuteronomic works are sufficiently evident to suggest a close relationship at least between the processes by which the book of Jeremiah and these other books were compiled, and probably too a relationship between his personality and teaching and that of those who stand behind that tremendously influential movement of thought. Yet the book of Kings, so close to him in spirit, in its final summing up of the kingdom of Judah, does not even name the prophet most involved in the events.[11] And this is in spite of the fact that the latter part of the book of Jeremiah reads at many points like an elaborated extract from the historical work.[12] We in our own day are, of course, familiar with the reprehensible practice of authors who utilize the work of others without acknowledgment. Yet the complete silence about Jeremiah[13] at the moment of greatest crisis, the fall of Jerusalem, is one of the oddest pieces of omission we could imagine.

This is only one very striking example. It is a reminder that within the life of the Old Testament there is not simply one circle of life and tradition, but many. It is proper that we should be reminded[14] that the life of the people centred around not one shrine but many, and even when centralization of worship did take place, the local factors continued to operate.[15] Later Judaism knew its various schools and traditions, its Shammai and Hillel, its Pharisees, Sadducees, Essenes and the like, its eastern and western Masoretes, its Tiberias and its Nehardea and Sura. Uniformity of religious life appears as the less natural form; pluriformity, complexity in the interrelationship of differing groups as the normal. And even where the attempt is made at enforcing rigid uniformity, as for example in the reform of Ezra, the human spirit appears to express itself with such forcefulness that even that uniformity is always under pressure and modifying itself.[16] Perhaps we ought rather to say not the human spirit, but the divine spirit. For one of the best arguments, if arguments there are to be, in favour of belief in God is this very diversity in human behaviour and outlook. To argue from uniformity to God would be, I should imagine, much more difficult because uniformity would raise no questions, though some of the more rigidly minded would seem to think this preferable to our present complexities, as if any certainty were better than none.[17]

The people of the Old Testament formed many groups. In different centres differing codes of law, differing forms of the tradition, differing emphases, were fostered. We hesitate nowadays to look for the exact lines of literary linkage between one centre and another, between one 'school' and another, between one form of a story and another. Traditio-history provides us with a less rigid formula – though its presentation has often been artificially rigid in its opposition to certain of the more obvious processes of transmission of material and the almost pathological reaction of some of its exponents to the term 'literary criticism'. We may be encouraged to think more broadly, less rigidly. We can picture the differing groups. At the end of the Old Testament period, they appear in more sharply defined form, and we may not unreasonably look within the Old Testament for some traces of their antecedents. The antecedents of apocalyptists, of Zealots, Qumran nationalists and the like, of Pharisees, Sadducees and others, are to be traced in the rich life of earlier times. Prophetic and priestly circles, the circles of the wise and of the scribes, and within these a much richer and less uniform pattern, so that the dividing lines are not to be sharply drawn, provide us with indications of the diversity of thinking out of which there grew the whole wealth of the Old Testament. In one form or another, diversity was always present.[18]

But the more we stress this richness and diversity, the more perplexing does the problem of continuity become. It is the problem which underlies the study of Old Testament theology, for that very term as normally understood implies that there is continuity. The attempt to make the whole intelligible, as distinct from the understanding of this or that part of it, demands the discovery of an underlying principle. Yet the attempt to discover such a principle normally results in a one-sided picture, for it is found that this or that feature of Old Testament life and thought does not fit easily into the pattern. So the emphasis on *Heilsgeschichte*, on the great saving acts of God seen as a decisive pattern of events, leaves us in uncertainty as to where wisdom is to be placed,[19] and equally takes no adequate account of Israel's inherited and developed understanding of God as creator.[20]

The problem of continuity is a parallel one to this. If we could trace completely the interrelatedness of different aspects of Old Testament thought, we should be able to see more clearly how it does belong together. If we could see how the pattern of faith is maintained, the tradition perpetuated from one period to another, one place to another, we should be able to see more clearly what are the essential features of the faith, what makes for that vitality which keeps it in being. My intention here is briefly to point to some of the indications of continuity which may help to illuminate and to order the richness of the tradition, and so contribute to that understanding of the totality of Old Testament thought, which is always necessary as background to the minutiae of commentary and exegesis. There are three lines of thought which I should like to indicate.

1. *The Credal Pattern*

The first of these begins with the now familiar credal pattern, worked out in detail by von Rad. The work of this great scholar is

now at last beginning to be available in English,[21] though the
immense two-volume *Theology of the Old Testament*[22] is yet to
come.[23] The discovery of an Old Testament equivalent to the New
Testament Apostolic *kerugma*,[24] traceable in such confessional
statements as Deuteronomy 26 and Joshua 24,[25] with their four-
point formulae: forefathers to Egypt, oppression, deliverance,
promised land, provides an exciting linkage between the prophets
and psalmists on the one hand, and the historians on the other.
For not only do certain passages in the prophets[26] and certain
psalms[27] depend upon this *confessio fidei*, but the whole sweep of the
Tetrateuch – representing the culmination of diverse presentations
of the same faith[28] – is bound together within this pattern. The
Deuteronomic History and the Chronicler's History exemplify the
working out of the same pattern, seen in the light of a historical
development which knew of many events since the conquest and
understood the success and failure of the later periods in terms
primarily dictated by the ancient forms, though in each case there
is incorporated into the presentation an interpretation of the newer
elements in Israel's experience, primarily that of kingship, but also
the multiplicity of ideas connected with the temple in which the
central religious focus of the tribal era has come to be largely
enshrined.[29] In the same way, the presentations at least of J and P
incorporate the creation concept as prolegomenon to the events of
the *Heilsgeschichte*.

But side by side with this are other indications of the moulding of
Old Testament thought according to certain well-defined patterns.
Essentially the same process of the moulding of later thought on
the patterns of earlier experience can be found in the transmission
of the material of law, formed on the basis of the twofold source of
Israel's law – its ancient semi-nomadic practice going back to
Aram-Naharaim and beyond, and its absorption of the common
legal inheritance as it must have been embodied in the law of
Canaan at the time of the settlement. The corpora of law represent
the clarification of this in terms of the differing needs and outlooks
of different periods and communities. Essentially Israel's law is
the expression of a conservative process, the holding of the old
laws as the norm, and the evolution of newer legal forms to meet
the developing situations of a more complex society.

The conservatism is also expressed in the wisdom material,
whether this is pictured primarily in terms of a professional activity

confined to the circles of the wise who appear as a group alongside priest and prophet as mediators of the divine will (cf. Jer. 18.18), or considered on a somewhat wider basis as belonging also to the elders of the village communities, a sphere of activity for those who cherish the sayings handed down from the past. Here too, no doubt, there will be some members of a community who have greater facility in remembering and greater ingenuity in the turning of an original phrase based upon the ancient forms.[30] The occurrence of the same proverb in a variety of forms, with differing parallel members (e.g. Prov. 9.14; 24.6; 13.9; 24.20), suggests that different localities had their own forms of the tradition, in which, however, the ancient pattern was always preserved.

The transmission of prophecy also reveals the blend of conservatism and innovation which is so characteristic of Hebrew thought. The occurrence of the same prophetic oracle in more than one book suggests the growth of a body of familiar material, ready to hand.[31] Jeremiah complains of prophets who borrow one another's oracles, having no original and direct word from the Lord to speak (23.30). But it is clear that we cannot simply dismiss all 'plagiarizing' prophets as false and claim that newness is the only test of the reality of inspiration. For Jeremiah himself appears most evidently deeply influenced by the thought-forms of Hosea, and the recent study of the prophetic literature suggests that so far as forms and methods are concerned it is to be placed within the context of a wider prophetic tradition.[32] The point at issue is the reality of inspiration,[33] not the form in which it comes; the re-use of older forms is not necessarily an exclusion of the newness of religious experience.[34] Indeed one might well imagine the horror of a prophet who was accused of innovation when he was in fact presenting what he knew to be the age-old realities of God as seen in the life and experience of his people. New and old stand side by side. And the continuity rests in the realization of the traditional element within the newness of presentation related to the immediate historical situation in which the prophet works, as well as in the realization of the new element which is presented within the age-old familiar patterns.

Credal pattern, legal pattern, wisdom, prophecy – and we might equally well have added psalmody[35] – all provide us, at literary and oral level, with evidence of a continuity in which new ideas are enshrined within the familiar forms and so can themselves become part of the inheritance.[36]

2.   *The Context of Continuity*

The second line of thought concerns the context in which the continuity is maintained. Here we may return for a moment to the story of Hannah and Elkanah. One of the features of the story which we rather naturally pass over is the indication that when the child was taken to the shrine to be dedicated to the service of God, the fulfilling of the vow was accompanied by the sacrificial killing of a bull. It is to the accompaniment of the slaughter of beasts and birds, with blood and entrails and their attendant flies, that Hannah makes her declaration: 'For this child I prayed; and Yahweh has granted me my petition which I made to him. Therefore I have lent him to Yahweh; as long as he lives, he is lent to Yahweh' (I Sam. 1.24f.). To this the narrator, or the editor, or perhaps some pious scribe, added a psalm to express what seemed to him the appropriate sentiments on so great an occasion as this, significant both in the life of the child and still more in that of Israel.[37]

The context of continuity is here shown to be the twofold formal religious life – cult and piety, the worship of a great national festival and the prayer and praise of individual or family. It is important that we should hold these together. In certain circles it is still fashionable to decry the cult – understandably, because it is not easy to enter sympathetically into the practices of sacrificial worship if our imaginations are at all vivid – and to endeavour to discover within the Old Testament a growing tendency to 'de-culticize', a movement away from the elaborate rituals of sacrifice towards the purer religion of the heart. One result of this tendency has always been the depreciating of the post-exilic period,[38] for it is impossible to understand that period rightly without giving due weight to the elaboration of priestly order and of sacrificial practice, reflected in the later Pentateuchal strands and in the Chronicler, expressing the same convictions about the re-ordering of the community's life which are to be found in the last chapters of Ezekiel, in substantial parts of post-exilic prophecy, and in Ezra's reform. Such depreciation is linked with the prophets' condemnations of the cult as it was in their day. The extreme view which interprets the prophets – or significant representatives of them – as totally anti-cultic in outlook, may be regarded as based on a forced interpretation of the texts in question.[39] Their condemnation of the cult is based in reality on their belief in a God who requires holiness in his people, and on their realization of the people's unacceptability, and this means essentially that they adopt what we might for convenience call a cultic viewpoint.[40]

The other line of thought has been to suggest too rigidly that religion in the pre-exilic period was entirely corporate, bound up in the formal acts of worship, which expressed the whole religious relationship of people and God, but lacking in that personal element which appears to us to be so essential a part of the religious response. Here too it is in part the prophets who have provided the evidence which enlarges our understanding. The intensity of religious experience which so evidently underlies the activities of such men as Amos, Hosea, Micah and Isaiah of Jerusalem, makes it impossible to speak as if there were no reality of personal religion in the earlier period. The same point may be made with regard to some earlier figures[41] but less readily since our narratives concerning them are of later origin and may impute to them ways of thinking which they did not know.[42] Here care has to be taken too that the sense in which the expressions of piety and religious experience are couched corresponds with ancient usage.[43] Yet there are clear indications of the antiquity of what we term 'personal religion'. In fact personal religion is not to be seen simply as a new element which cuts sharply across the experience of belonging within a religious community.[44] A full appreciation of religious experience demands both the sense of immediacy in relationship with God and the sense of belonging within a community whose relationship with God gives context and meaning to that immediacy. In the tension thus engendered lies a fruitful source of deepening of the understanding. The great men of faith of the Old Testament are men whose immediacy of experience and whose consciousness of their place within their people are both at once obvious (cf. e.g. Isa.6.1ff.) The tension is not one of conflict, but of the realization of the incompleteness of both aspects of experience. It is at its clearest in the words and experience of Jeremiah, of Second Isaiah, of the author of Job. But the fruits of its deepening of man's understanding of his own being and of the nature of the people to which he belongs, may be seen throughout.

This tension is a persistent element in Hebrew thought and experience.

We may go neither to the extreme of emphasizing the individual nor the corporate. But the consequence of this, when we are thinking in terms of the continuity and preservation of Israel's faith, must be that we hold together the religious practice and experience of both cult and piety. In so far as the cult degenerates into an artificially manœuvred procedure benefiting no one but the priests and others who derive material support from it, it will find its condemnation in those who realize what it should be. In this we naturally see the prophets as the foremost critics. Hosea condemns priests (Hos. 4.4–9) and so does the book of Malachi (Mal. 2.1–9): the condemnation is based on the recognition that they are *not* priests, that is, they are not performing the function of priests and consequently the people suffers. In so far as the cult comes to be regarded as a means of manœuvring the deity into favourable attitudes, it will also be condemned by those who are sensitive enough to realize that God is one who does not change (cf. Mal.3.6), that he stands above the cult, and is free of it. 'If I were hungry, I would not tell you; for the world and all that is in it is mine' (Ps. 50.12). When he chooses, he withdraws himself, and no amount of ritual searching according to the prescribed forms will avail if he does not will to reveal himself (cf. Hos. 5.6). On the other hand, the Old Testament never becomes narrowly individualist in outlook. With all the intensity of the personal experience to which it bears witness, this is in the broader context of worship, of the cult which represents the God-given means by which the channel of divine blessing is kept open.[45] The personal vow, the personal prayer of distress, the personal thanksgiving, are in that broader context, and rest not upon some single person's realization of God, but upon the people's affirmation of the divine action, the divine self-revelation (cf. e.g. Ps.106.4–5). Israel's cult, like the other aspects of her life, is closely bound up with the practice of the ancient Near East as a whole. Many of its forms derive from Canaan, though these were grafted on to the already existing forms which Israel possessed in the pre-Canaanite period.[46] Yet Israel, as a result of that tension between the personal and the corporate, was always in some measure aware of the inconclusiveness of the cult, or, perhaps we should say, of its dependent position, dependent upon the prior action of God and so ultimately resting upon the experience of divine election by which Israel became the people of God.

In this respect, the continuity within the Old Testament is found in this dual aspect of religious life and practice, and in the tension between them and in the consciousness of their incompleteness in themselves, there is the realization of an underlying continuity which is not dependent upon them.

3. *The Canonical Principle*

The continuity within the Old Testament thus rests on the one hand upon the conservatism and adherence to tradition which is to be found exemplified in so many aspects of its life and thought, and on the other hand upon the continuing tension, seen at its clearest in the great personalities of the prophets, but discernible too in those who stand behind the great historical surveys and within the wisdom literature and the psalms, a tension between the realization of the knowledge of God in the cult and the realization of incompleteness which derives from the experience of direct confrontation. But to these points we must add a third, that of the canonical principle.

Both in the conservatism and adherence to tradition, and in the realization of the inadequacy of religious forms, there is an expression of the desire to preserve the ancient faith, to see its relevance to new situations, to trace how the one God whose action is attested in historic experience continues to make himself known in the changing pattern of Israel's subsequent career and in the immediate dilemmas of day-to-day life. But with this goes a conscious and deliberate endeavour to provide a fixed norm, to clarify and lay down a standard which can be preserved, a canon in which the tradition is definitively enshrined. The history of the Old Testament canon begins, as has been recognized,[47] not with the decisions of Jamnia, or with the choices which we may suppose the Maccabean martyrs to have made when faced with the alternative of allowing their sacred books to be destroyed or of dying for them.[48] Nor does it begin with the definition of a particular law as standard, attested in the two great moments of Israel's history at which this can be seen happening datably, namely the reform of Ezra and the reform of Josiah. It begins imperceptibly in the recognition of certain utterances of men as representing in reality the word of God,[49] and in the acceptance as binding of such single utterances or groups of utterances. Thus a group of laws becomes normative for a particular area or a particular sanctuary. It is recognized that the requirements of God may be made precise in a particular form which continues to standardize the understanding and presentation of subsequent developments of belief. In so far as these are in written form – as is clearly likely to be the case with laws[50] – continuity finds something of a hold in the fixity of the written document.[51] The traditio-historian's view of the use of writing as an expedient in moments of crisis[52] may be generalized into the recognition that writing down constitutes an attempt at establishing a fixity, a continuity which can otherwise be lost.

The formulation of the ancient *credo* not only provides a basis for the statement of the faith, it provides also a standard, a pattern, into which later ideas are to be fitted.[53] The patterns of distress and deliverance, of promise and of fulfilment, are to be found again and again within the Old Testament itself, with the interrelationship of the two pairs of ideas made closer as subsequent history shows promise frustrated by human failure, and distress and deliverance the divinely appointed means by which both the realization of the failure and the consciousness of divine action lead to the ultimate fulfilment. The formulating of the law codes, the provision of a standard law which is eventually elaborated into the collected laws of the Pentateuch, provides a similar fixation.[54] These partly conscious, partly unconscious attempts at defining the nature of the religious tradition show that the search for continuity is not in fact a new problem.

The realization of continuity came already with the Old Testament period in the experience of discontinuity. The earlier prophets and psalmists were aware of the continuity of faith in that they saw the present situation as a departure from a norm which they and their contemporaries could equally recognize. To that norm they made their appeal (cf. Amos 2.9ff. etc.). There was no agreement between them and their contemporaries as to the nature of the departure from it, for this could be labelled by the one side as apostasy and by the other side as progress.[55] The seal to prophetic judgment in the disaster of destruction to kingdom and temple produced a crisis of thought which necessitated rethinking, though this need not be regarded as the only moment or crisis. It is not without significance that the great prophet of the exile, the Second Isaiah, so much harks back to the past (e.g., 51.1f., 9–11; 52. 3–6, 11f.), and that Zechariah, shortly after the exile, reminds his hearers of the words of the 'former prophets' (Zech.1.4; 7.7) – a term destined to become technical as the description of the major part of that great Deuteronomic History which expressed Israel's acknowledgment of the pattern of continuity in judgment and disaster.[56] At the same time, this History portrays continuity in terms of promise, as for example in the succession themes, both royal and priestly, as set out in I and II Samuel and the opening of I Kings and as indicated in the final note of hope in the release of the last Davidic king from prison in the year 561 BC.[57] It was the Chronicler who carried the pattern further, seeing the detail of the interweaving of prophetic word and historic event. He saw the period of the exile not simply in terms of judgment – too simplified a view of the events.[58] He saw it as the land 'keeping sabbath for seventy years' (II Chron. 36.21), and in this he was to be echoed two centuries or so later in the Danielic interpretation of that sabbath pattern.[59] The restoration and the destruction are all of a piece; discontinuity is resolved in the discovery of a continuity within it.

The climax – for we are not here to enter into detailed discussion – is reached in the formulation of the canon, not now considered as a process whose contributory factors are to be described, but the canon as it is seen by those to whom it is complete, the norm, the established and unified whole to which the community may look. The period of prophetic inspiration of Josephus' understanding – from Moses to Artaxerxes[60] – the unity of dictation by an Ezra acting under the divine guiding hand (II Esdras 14.24–48) – these are descriptions after the event, but significant in that they are designed to make clear the continuity within what is seen and experienced as a rich entity, sometimes so rich as to appear contradictory. Subsequent debates on the value of the canon, the relation between canonical and non-canonical works, are a proper recognition of the thinness of the dividing line.[61] At the same time we recognize that the drawing of the line is an attempt, proper though always to be qualified, at resolving the uncertainties for minds such as our own which cannot fully fathom the richness of divine self-revelation.

The consideration of this problem provides a warning, so

necessary in any statement about the Old Testament. To oversimplify the pattern is to miss its full significance. To attempt to fit together in a precise and easily definable manner the various aspects of Old Testament thought is to destroy the richness of their variety. The search in the writing of Old Testament theologies for the unifying principle is a vain one. The selection of one particular principle – especially if this be one which is of central import in Old Testament thought and experience – may well result in a vivid illumination of much that the Old Testament has to say.[62] The coherence of von Rad's treatment owes not a little to its picturing of the whole in terms which readily draw the material together and to his attempt at seeing it as it was seen by the differing generations and groups of the people themselves, as well as in its relationship to subsequent, Christian, developments.

But the real unity of truth is not so readily defined. Our attempts at defining it precisely lead inevitably to the elevation of one or another exclusive principle with a resulting irresolvable conflict of opinion.[63] The ultimate continuity lies not in the defined systems of human thought but in the reality of God.[64] To say that is to appear platitudinous and to seem to suggest that the search for truth is illusory. It is really to emphasize the abundant richness of what the Old Testament has to say, in its covering of so long a period and so wide a range of human experience.

2

The Theology of Tradition: An Approach to Old Testament Theological Problems[1]

In my inaugural lecture at King's College in 1961,[2] I raised certain questions about the nature of the Old Testament tradition and in particular the question of 'continuity', which was the title given to the lecture. The discussion included some consideration of the diversity within the Old Testament, and warned against oversimplification of the discussion of theological questions. It is from this point that I begin this discussion.

The use of the term 'continuity' inevitably has some dangers inherent in it. It seems an entirely proper term to use by way of clarifying the interrelationship between aspects of the Old Testament which might be thought to point to disruption. The maintenance of what – for convenience' sake – we may term the central religious tradition in the Old Testament (and that is a way of speaking which needs to be further looked at) presupposes a continuity within the life of the community by which, whatever changes are introduced as a result of modifications in the political or social structure, or as a result of pressures and influences from outside, it may be recognized that it is the same faith which is being handed on. And it is within this continuity that we can appreciate the preservation and elaboration of the thought of the main exponents of the faith.

The complex nature of the 'continuum' is brought out in N. W. Porteous' 'The Prophets and the Problem of Continuity'.[3] He is concerned to stress the prophetic element in this, and to point to the danger of an overemphasis on the cultic aspect. He is also concerned to suggest that the 'quiet in the land', the ordinary pious people, may be regarded as of primary importance, and to see the prophets in part at least as spokesmen not only of God, but also of these humble and faithful folk. Yet it would be a mistake to emphasize any one area at the expense of the others. Prophet and priest, psalmist and wise, official and ordinary person, can all have their place both in the maintenance of continuity and also in its undermining.

I

1. But the very concept of continuity has its meaning only in so far as we set it over against its reverse: *discontinuity*. And to define the latter is in some ways even more difficult than to define the former. It has both a negative and a positive side. As an example of the more extreme type of its negative aspect, we may clearly cite the moment of the exile. The destruction of the temple and the abolition of the Davidic monarchy as a ruling force in Judah may be seen as the clearest historical example within the Old Testament of a break with the past. There is a finality about this which cannot be gainsaid. That the temple was eventually restored and that continuity of religious tradition was both argued and contrived is clear. But the very emphasis which appears increasingly in later material on this continuity – for example, in the stress on the theme of the temple vessels, given prominence in Jeremiah 27–28, in II Kings 25, in Ezra 1, in Ezra 8,[4] or later still on that of the ark and the temple fire in II Maccabees 1–2, or again on the priestly line and its genealogies – itself shows the anxiety lest there should have been an irreparable break in the Jerusalem cult and religious tradition. The divergent approaches to this matter in Jewish and Samaritan presentations reveal both an element of polemic and also a deep and understandable concern with the continuity of the faith.

At the same time, the break of the exilic age is clearly not absolute. It can be regarded rather as a large-scale historical expression of a repeated pattern of discontinuity. It may be held that certain psalms which appear now to express concern at such a great moment of disaster – e.g. Psalms 74 and 79 – may have originated not in historical experience in that larger sense but rather in the ever-present need to maintain continuity of religious life and practice in a shrine, a continuity which can be broken accidentally by some infringement, some impurity, some defilement.[5] Such a view brings out the point, whether or not we accept the detail of the explanation, that, within the religious life and practice of any particular centre, interruptions which are bound to occur require a procedure by which continuity may be restored. The well-being of the community depends, in the Old Testament view, ultimately upon a deity whose willingness to bestow blessing and life can be frustrated by human failure. The withdrawal of the divine word from Saul because of Jonathan's infringement of an oath is pictured as automatic; its restoration can only be effected when the cause is discovered and the appropriate action taken, whatever in a given case that might be (I Samuel 14). The story of the return of the ark from the Philistine area shows the same kind of thought; recovery for the Philistines equally is possible only when the cause is removed and order is restored (I Samuel 6).

2. But there is another aspect to discontinuity which is not to be seen so simply in negative terms. The Old Testament narratives point to this in their various descriptions of religious reform, and within this in the distinguishing between *reform* and *regression*. In the judgments on Hezekiah and Josiah, an element of break with the religious tradition is indicated which is regarded as good; praise is therefore assigned to these particular kings. Equally, certain other kings are associated with retrogressive or improper action – the restoration of alien elements which had been removed by the reformers or the introduction of new elements which were seen as improper innovations in the correct cultus.[6] We may follow common practice and designate the great prophets as 'reform prophets', recognizing that reform is constituted by a welding together of new and old and that it is so designated by reference to some agreed or supposed standard. These may be contrasted with other prophets who are said to be 'false', whether this be for their support of religious policies which are associated with evil rulers, or for their maintenance of immoral practice, or for their failure to recognize the nature of divine action in a given situation. The criterion most often adduced for discrimination here is that of fulfilment or non-fulfilment of the particular prophetic pronouncement, a criterion which immediately comes up against the difficulty both of determining fulfilment and of elucidating non-fulfilment. But in both these examples, we need to recognize that the precise determining of what is true and progressive and what is false and regressive is not easy. Other factors need to be

taken into account in the assessment of the kings and their policies; restoration of high places may be seen as a revival of practices alien to the religion of Yahweh, but also as an act of piety and a restoration of balance over against a too great measure of centralization; the provision of a new altar by Ahaz, on Assyrian or other pattern, may be understood by the king himself and also by good Yahwists, as being expressive of devotion and religious zeal. The word of a prophet may, in a given historical context, have an emphasis or a basis which is inadequate or even false; the same prophetic word – e.g. 'Babylon shall be overthrown' – may in another context be true (cf. Jeremiah 28 and 50). A divine word of judgment given by a prophet may, in new conditions, be reversed and replaced by one of promise (so Jer. 32.28, 36f.; 33.10f.).

3. The nature of continuity and discontinuity is seen again when we consider the relationship between a particular prophet and the religious tradition in which he stands. If emphasis is laid upon his re-statement of ancient truth, ancient covenant law, ancient interpretation of historic experience, then the prophet may be seen as the upholder of the tradition, the exponent of the old ways. The term 'reform prophets' allows this backward-looking element. At the same time, it also serves to draw attention to that experience of the prophet, that encounter with the God of the religious tradition, which enables him to clarify his position *vis-à-vis* the past, to claim for his message a newness, an independence over against the past. His position is one both of continuity and of discontinuity. The most complex example of this, for the Christian theologian, lies in the delicate question of where, in regard to the New Testament and to the life and teaching of Jesus, we must speak of continuity and where of discontinuity.

4. Another way in which we may express the same point is to underline the more personal aspect of any particular individual's experience, the particular way in which his own personality, his own upbringing and natural gifts and disposition contribute to the precise way in which he presents his view both of the tradition in which he stands and of the contemporary situation to which it is directed. In regard to Old Testament characters, the problem of elucidating this is even greater than it is in regard to more modern ones. The relationship of these factors, even where in a modern instance the external circumstances are well known and the special influences and contacts may be established, is still a very difficult

one to define, and the variety of biographies which may, with greater or less justice, be written about one outstanding person is an indication that the contributory factors may be differently assessed and that the perspective of distance, while not necessarily enabling any new facts to be taken into account, may nevertheless allow a more balanced judgment than that which belongs to a near contemporary or a close associate. The situation in regard to the great creative personalities of the Old Testament is both more complex and at the same time apparently more simple. On the one hand, we have the clearly impossible task of extracting from sources which have relatively little interest in biography such information as will enable a reasonable picture of man and situation to be drawn;[7] on the other hand, the very lack of information, or its very limited extent, may encourage simplified judgments which we have no means of correcting but which may be quite inadequate. In a partial study of the Jeremiah tradition[8] I have drawn attention to the advantage of our possession of a divergent series of sources of information for the one prophet, an advantage which is not immediately apparent if the interest is in simple biography; the tradition, with its richness and variegated presentation, offers us insights which are not easily co-ordinated into one. But rather than oversimplify, we must at least see that the tradition is such that we can say of it, as has been suggested we should say in regard to the New Testament traditions: 'What must the truth have been if it appeared like this to men who thought like that?'[9] Behind the richness of the tradition lies a real personality, from whom it stems. But it will be clear that the tradition (or the traditions) is more than the deposit left by the personality, for it adds also the interpretation of those who handed it on.

5. Thus it is rare indeed that we have anything approaching a direct contact with a creative personality, and it may be doubted if the right approach to the complexity of the tradition is that of trying to remove the glosses and expansion and other interpretative material which has become associated with a supposedly recoverable original. This is an error into which the New English Bible translators have fallen in certain instances. Thus they have omitted from the text what is virtually certainly a gloss in Hag. 2.5: 'the word which I established with you when you came out from Egypt'. This phrase has been put in the footnotes with the comment: 'Heb.

Continuity

adds'.[10] But it is not clear why this should be done in cases where – on textual or other grounds – a gloss may be clearly discussed, why in other cases a phrase is bracketed,[11] and why it should not be done in other cases where it is equally plain that the 'original text' or 'original word' may be seen to be overlaid with subsequent applications. The search for *ipsissima verba* is itself, for the most part at any rate, not only a frustrating occupation, since there are no certainties at the end of the search, but also a somewhat misleading one: the prophet or the other speaker, of whatever kind, is visible only in the tradition. Yet this recognition of uncertainty and of interpretation should not be regarded as suggesting any lack of concern for the reality of the personalities behind the tradition, or any supposition that the whole explanation lies in it. The reality of the more personal impetus is part at least of the reason why, tradition notwithstanding, Isaiah does not look like Jeremiah, nor Ezekiel quite like the compiler of the Holiness Code. With all the pressures towards uniformity, the Old Testament still gives clear evidence of the diversity within the tradition, the separate strands of the tradition themselves witnessing to the existence of personalities and groups in which the theology develops.

II

1. The evidence of diversity in the tradition is not difficult to find. At the lowest level – that is to say the textual, though the division between textual and other types of deviation has become increasingly blurred as textual criticism and the history of exegesis are seen to be interwoven areas of study – we have alternative texts of the same passage. It may be that we can reduce the alternatives here by the observation, based on the particular points of evidence, that one text is more primitive, more evidently the basis of another. But even where this is possible – and it may rarely be expected to be more than a working hypothesis – the differences between the texts have still to be explained. The more obvious deviations due to the characteristic errors of scribal transmission may be eliminated. But even with some of these – where a difference may be due to the similarity of one letter with another – we may still wish to ask the often unanswerable question: why did the scribe misread? Was he just inadvertent – and this may be likely where the resulting text is evidently meaningless – or was there some

other factor which affected his mind? Were his own cultural or theological presuppositions such that he read the text as he did because he believed it to mean something other than the plain sense of the words? The double occurrence of the same psalm or prophecy or narrative most often confronts us with a problem of interpretation. Isa. 2.2–4 (5) is almost equal to Micah 4.1–5; but the two contexts in which this oracle occurs must be expected to shed some light on the ways in which it was understood in two different prophetic traditions. The textual deviations may be expected to provide some clue to the alternative lines of interpretation which have been followed. The closeness of the text of Psalm 18 to its other occurrence in II Samuel 22 must not be allowed to conceal the fact that as soon as a psalm is placed in a narrative context, it is given a meaning which is more sharply defined than that which it has in the context of a collection of psalms, where order and arrangement may be examined but where inevitably the principles underlying the order and arrangement are much less easy to discover.

The position which obtains with such virtually identical texts is a small-scale example of the major problems of the diversity of the tradition which confront us with books such as Samuel and Jeremiah where the textual traditions in the Hebrew and the Greek are so offten strongly divergent. A similar position obtains in regard to the alternatives found within the transmissionof the text of Tobit. The existence of doublet narratives, so often a clue to literary analysis, points to alternative ways in which particular traditions have developed. Where they are used side by side or interwoven, they reveal something of the complexity of the growth of tradition; where they appear in relation to different characters or situations, they show a greater degree of deviation and the study of the evolution of the various traditions is assisted. On a larger scale, the alternative presentations of the Deuteronomic History and the Chronicler's Work, or the differences of J and P, provide us with a more readily examinable picture of theological difference – as well as cultural and historical difference – which illuminates the changing life and thought of a community whose literature extends over more than a millennium.

The precise division between these various examples of different levels is impossible. The important point is that they indicate ways in which the diversity within the tradition may be discerned, a

diversity which must be taken fully into account in the consideration of theological interpretation and in the construction of any
kind of theological statement related to the biblical material. A
simplistic 'The Bible says' is not simply inadequate as an argument
in favour of a particular theological view; it just does not bear any
satisfactory resemblance to the nature of the biblical material
itself.

2. As a further aspect of diversity, though not unrelated to this
more textual one, we must bear in mind that of social structure.
The community is not all of one piece. The older tendency, for
example in psalm criticism, to discover evidence of sharply divided
parties within the community, and to define the contrasts drawn,
for example, between wicked and righteous, poor and rich, humble
and ruthless, in terms of precise social divisions, was clearly
defective. But that we must recognize social divisions is clear; they
are evident within the history, and at certain points the contrast
between opposing or divergent views is apparent. A typical case
is that expressed in the division of opinion over Jeremiah set out
in Jeremiah 26. But we may also see the divergence expressed
within what would otherwise be thought to be the orthodox centre;
the major historical surveys alone indicate a difference of emphasis,
expressive of groups concerned about particular aspects of life and
faith. A similar division brought about the Samaritan-Jewish
conflict. The history of the priesthood, incomplete as the evidence
for it is, strongly indicates pressures and stresses. The sects, so-
called, of a later period are the partial expression of these tensions;
their titles, as the evidence shows, conceal a sometimes wide range
of diversity within them, and this has been particularly confirmed
by the difficulty of placing the Qumran community, which appears
by turn to be Essene, Pharisee and Zealot.

3. Two further considerations need to be taken into account
before we turn to look at the nature of unity as it may be discerned
in the biblical material. (*a*) The first of these is what we may term
the 'non-evidence' of diversity, the illusion created at certain points
of a uniform tradition. Where we are confronted by divergent texts,
divergent forms of the same narrative, we may adopt various
methods to resolve the problems they create, just as from an
early stage we may observe such methods as harmonization,
interweaving and the like; but at least we recognize, as the earliest
exegetes did, that there is something here which needs resolving.

Where, however, we have a single text, and no divergence of any substance, we have all the time to be sensitive to the possibility that the alternatives may have existed and be lost to us; that they may have been so subordinated as to leave little more than the barest trace – the odd motif which, it is rightly seen, does not in itself provide sufficient evidence of an alternative version. The text as we have it represents already something of the process of selection, harmonization, reinterpretation which belongs to the making of the biblical literature.

(*b*) The second point concerns the very nature of text and canon itself. Barr describes it as 'the written crystallization of one great tradition';[12] it is not the tradition itself, it is a crystallization of it in writing which inevitably involves limitation. The description needs, however, to be still further qualified. John Bowker speaks of the ongoing process of targumic interpretation, of the development of the targums themselves, and says that 'The written Targums can best be understood as a sort of cross-section of that process, a point at which the developing tradition has been frozen for a moment and committed to writing'.[13] This is what may be said also of the biblical text. It is not a uniform and neatly ordered text; it has its unevennesses, in spite of the measure of processing to which it has been subjected. For reasons which we can only very partially deduce, we have *this* selection of books in *this* particular text form, which we may place alongside other examples of selection and other examples of text. The community eventually appears through this: it is our primary, and in large measure our only, source of information, basis of judgment.

III

1. The degree of attention so far given to the existence of diversity may seem to be out of proportion. But it appears to be a necessary precaution against an all too natural tendency to look for unity, and often in doing so to confuse unity with uniformity. There is a simple level at which this is the case. The opinion is often voiced that the multiplying of modern translations of the Bible does not serve the cause of bringing together those who see in the Bible the foundation documents of their faith. At one moment in recent years it looked as though there had been a break-through in the production of a Roman Catholic edition of the Revised Standard Version: admittedly, the very fact that an RSVCE was felt to

be necessary indicated that there were certain points at which agreement on a translation could not be reached, but the deviations could be rightly seen to be very small by comparison with the major area of agreement. Surely now, it was felt, Douai and Knox could be put on one side, and the growing use of RSV in Protestant churches – apart from that area in which King (or Saint!) James retained his authority – would mean that discussion about doctrine could proceed on the basis of the same text being used by all parties. The cause of ecumenism could not but be aided. But within a very short space, a further change has come; the Jerusalem Bible on the Roman side has become immensely popular with Protestants also, and rightly so, and the Protestant side now has the complete NEB which has still to establish its place but, in spite of criticisms which can be made, must certainly be seen as a major attempt at utilizing modern research in the elucidation of the text. A closer look, however, reveals how much more complex the matter is, and how easily the acceptance of an agreed text, whether an original or a translation, while clearly of great import and very convenient for liturgical purposes and for convenience of quotation, conceals the differences in interpretation which belong to the varied traditions in which we stand. An agreed text can, in fact, be a dangerous threat to real unity in that it can resemble those formulae which are evolved in the course of discussion, formulae to which each party can put its name and assent but which in fact each party is interpreting in its own particular way. Unity at the expense of ambiguity of statement is not unity.[14]

2. There is another aspect of this pressure towards uniformity which is more subtle. It may be summed up in the declaration, sometimes made explicitly but more often assumed: 'The Bible is its own best commentary.' It must be clear that there are levels at which this will clearly have considerable force. If I wish to know the meaning of a Hebrew word, then I have two sources of information. On the one hand, there is the philological evidence, from cognate languages, from ancient and more modern translations, from the root from which the particular word is derived. On the other hand, there is the evidence of usage within the Old Testament and beyond in the related literature; here the process by which meaning can be deduced is inevitably complex but necessary. It involves a consideration of every passage, and of the interpretation of each passage in the context in which it belongs.

From the possibly wide range of meanings which have to be assigned to a word, we may be able then, by a process of elimination, to arrive at perhaps only a small group of equivalents which eventually come up for consideration. The method can be not unlike that which I have myself used in translating from German when I have been unable to discover readily the proper equivalent for a particular term; the German-English dictionary – if it contained the word at all, though often it would not! – would provide a number of renderings, and it was often in the process of eliminating the unsuitable ones that what appeared to be a good equivalent would appear, sometimes from among those offered, sometimes not. But it is clear that in the defining of biblical words and their meaning, this can never satisfactorily become a process by which we limit our search to biblical usage alone, nor one in which we can assume that a word once defined can be so defined in all its occurrences, even within the writings of one author or within one theological tradition. A criticism made of the NEB – this was of the New Testament alone – that it did not always render the same Greek word with the same English one, in other words, the criticism that it was a translation and not a crib, was indicative of a supposition castigated over recent years by James Barr in a number of studies, the supposition that words are counters.[15]

This particular view of words derives clearly enough in part from a faulty linguistic technique; it also, so far as the Bible is concerned, derives from a particular theological bias. If the Bible is believed to be a unity in an artificial sense, then there will be a tendency to suppose that its words continue to carry the same meaning, that different statements are eventually reconcilable, that apparent contradictions can in the end be shown to be illusory. The discovery of 'what the Bible says', of the 'Bible view of this or that', is another expression of that same conviction, though such studies may be carefully set out to make clear the differences of understanding which appear in different sections. Nevertheless, the titles automatically suggest that a unitary view can ultimately be established.

Much of the process by which the text itself has evolved, and much of the exegetical work, particularly in the early centuries, was devoted, implicitly or explicitly, to such an end. The selective process by which certain passages are designated as crucial – printed in red, or listed in an introduction under appropriate headings, or simply appealed to most frequently – expresses the same concern. The imposition on the biblical material of a norm of interpretation which thereby enables or encourages the reading of every part with an eye towards certain determinative themes, limits the understanding. As we have seen, the very expression 'The Bible says' – not this or that passage says – undercuts the recognition of diversity by imposing a spurious uniformity.

3. A similar effect is produced by the assumption that there is an orthodox line, a single true tradition, from which all else deviates. There are, of course, points at which we may perfectly reasonably see what we may describe as 'mainstream Old Testament religion'. When Deuteronomy (13.2–6) analyses the problem of truth and falsity in prophecy, and recognizes that a sign given and fulfilled offers confirmation of a prophecy, it adds the qualification that if the utterance is in terms of 'Go and worship other gods', it is clearly not to be obeyed despite its apparent confirmation; it runs so contrary to the very nature of Old Testament religion, that it can at once be recognized for the false injunction that it is. But to generalize from such an example is hazardous. Where is the line to be neatly drawn between the worship of other gods – which is 'out' – and the delineation of the nature and function of Yahweh in terms which also belong to other gods? When is it right to call Yahweh *ba'al* and when not? Why is the title *'adon* legitimate, in spite of its alien connections?[16] What constitutes right theological interpretation of particular institutions, of high places, of particular forms of sacrifice, of particular aspects of human behaviour? There are certain religious and moral requirements which have a central place; the precise mode of their application, the precise interpretation placed upon them, are not so defined as to exclude variety of understanding.

4. The too ready assumption that there is such a clearly discernible central 'orthodox' line is yet another of the ways in which the complexity of Old Testament theological truth may be obscured. That appeals are made to a human and accepted religious tradition is clear. It is evident in the appeal to experience in acts interpreted as divine deliverance; it may be seen in the assurances of divine help in the psalms, patterned sometimes in terms of history, but equally often in a more generalized form. The wisdom teachers express the knowableness of God and his action in set forms, forms which are, however, especially in Job and Ecclesiastes, subject to

careful scrutiny and criticism. But a closer examination of these various pictures of what constitutes 'orthodoxy' reveals that in detail there is considerable variation, and the variation expresses itself more generally, as we have seen, in the main distinguishable lines of Old Testament thought – Priestly, Deuteronomic, Prophetic (in all its various forms), Wisdom, Psalmic. An inter-relatedness which is also discernible is not readily defined; if it consists in something like the formula 'Yahweh God of Israel; Israel people of Yahweh', the explication of this in detail involves many different points of emphasis. As has been observed, such a statement is really no different from 'Chemosh God of Moab, Moab people of Chemosh' so that the basic form becomes platitudinous unless it is given its fuller but multifarious exposition. (Could we perhaps say the same of what might pass for a New Testament equivalent: 'Jesus is Lord', on which all New Testament writers could agree? But would they all expound the phrase in the same way?)

IV

My concern in this discussion has been first to emphasize the nature and range of the evidence of diversity, and second to show how easily spurious assertions of unity may be made. Is there then any unity other than a hypothetical underlying one? Can we unify without reducing? Granted a 'centre' which is unsatisfactorily defined, is it essential, or important, or even desirable, to extend the area of unity?

I recall a lecture which I heard in Chicago some three years ago by Mr M. M. Thomas of Bangalore – it was on Paul and his handling of the practical problems of early church life. Thomas drew from this discussion his realization of the need for us to have 'more things a matter of indifference in a pluriform society', 'less convention and rigidity, more variety and acceptance where there is no issue of right or wrong or of principle involved'. (He went on to stress the relevance of this to the life of the church.)

Pluriformity in theology – as evidenced by the Old Testament itself. But to this there is something important to add. G. K. Chesterton once commented that if one elephant had a trunk it would look like a joke; but since all elephants have trunks, it looks like a conspiracy!

Can we twist this a little? If all biblical documents said the same things, would it not look like a conspiracy? (That silly man John Allegro tried to explain the New Testament as the result of a conspiracy designed to obscure the truth; but if it were, it would be a very poor attempt!) The very diversity – of emphasis, of presentation, of interpretation, points to a reality which they all attest, but which – at different periods and in different places, in different persons and areas of life – is attested in a variety of ways; a reality whose nature cannot be disclosed with any adequacy unless we are prepared to take account of *all* the evidence.

3

Continuity and Discontinuity:
Rehabilitation and Authentication

The existence of major strands of thought, traceable over long periods of the life of ancient Israel, is witness to the degree to which, in spite of all the political hazards, particular lines of belief and particular styles of expression continue to be effective in the community's life. O. H. Steck[1] has clarified some of these strands of tradition, presenting them as the contexts within which particular elements in the literature may be understood. Such a presentation rightly stresses the continuity in tradition. But the element of discontinuity is a political reality, and the doubts which are raised by major or minor disruptions in life must affect the attitudes of those who experience them and in turn have repercussions upon the way in which they understand the traditions, and upon the way in which they express them.

The purpose of this present study is to examine the nature of the breaks in continuity and the ways in which attempts are made to overcome them, and to suggest the effects that these processes have upon the formation of the literature and the modification of the thought. To a large extent the attempt is made to incorporate the discontinuity into coherent thinking, and to find means of authenticating the re-established sense of continuity. It must, however, be evident that there will remain a measure of uncertainty, a question mark put against the validity of the tradition, which may in the end lead to more radical questioning of it.

That questioning is a theme which is taken up in the study by J. L. Crenshaw.[2]

I.   *Breaks and Bridgings*

When Saul attempted to consult the deity after the battle in which
Jonathan had infringed the oath the king had laid on the army, he
was met with silence (I Sam. 14.37). The contact between man
and God, essential for the ordering of public as of private affairs,
was broken. To re-establish contact was a matter of urgency, and
necessitated the appropriate inquiry, the obviating of the offence
by the appropriate mechanism. Then, and only then, the continuity
of relationship could be assured. The example is but one of many;
it concerns public policy, in this instance a matter of warfare and
its successful pursuit. It illustrates a principle expressed in many
areas of life, that of the need for a continuing relationship between
man and God, and that of the danger to life which must follow
from discontinuity. Continuity and discontinuity are correlative;[3]
the need to maintain relationship is cut across by the mischances
which introduce breaks into it. Such a break may be at a relatively
trivial level, although this will not be unimportant to the one who
experiences it; it may derive from some temporary impurity which
debars a man from full participation in religious life (so, e.g.,
Leviticus 13–14, the law governing *sāraʿatʰ*). It may be the result of
a major calamity, a total political collapse, such as the Babylonian
conquest and the exile of the sixth century BC. In each case there
must be found ways of overcoming the break in continuity, and it
is evident that some of the situations will be more readily and
simply met than others.

The two extreme examples just cited represent the two major
subdivisions of discontinuity. The one may be termed *cultic*, not
simply because it is clear that a problem immediately connected
with cultic observance is involved, but also because, while the
particular instance will have an historical setting – the affliction
will affect this man at that moment in time – this setting is less
important than the provisions which govern cultic observance and
continue to operate over a long period of time. So long as these
particular provisions exist, there will be countless examples of
infringement and of consequent break in relationship. The other
may be termed *historical*, since it belongs to a particular moment
of political change and adjustment. It will for that reason be unique
in that the particular moment of time at which it happens is
unrepeatable. But a closer examination of the examples shows that

the distinction between them is less precise than this. We may, in relation to the first type, recognize that, while the origins of such practices and beliefs are so remote that we can hardly now hope to describe them, they are nevertheless rooted in precise experience; and when, as in Leviticus 13–14, we get a long catalogue of instances, believed to be related because of a certain external similarity, we may detect something of the historical process by which a law applicable to one type of condition – say a skin condition in men – may be understood to be relevant also to other types of condition, which we would not, in our culture, associate at all, namely, the condition of mould in materials and mildew on building plaster. We cannot say just how the development of the legal descriptions proceeded; we may simply recognize a degree of ordering, of correlating and harmonizing, which serves not only to provide satisfying methods of diagnosis and action, but also, by the ordering together of apparently unrelated experiences, makes them more manageable, more comprehensible, and therefore more easily resolved and less a matter of anxiety. To classify, as sociological and anthropological studies have made clear, is in itself a procedure which aids security; it is the anomalous which appears dangerous because it does not fit into known categories.

Similarly, we may observe that while, in some instances at least, we may see the precise historical context for a particular moment of break, a merely historical approach is less than adequate to understanding the way in which such experiences are regarded. There will, inevitably, be some degree of change in the points at which external military and political pressures bring disaster to a given community. To some extent we may perhaps be right to recognize, in the men and women (prophets or others) who forecast such moments of disaster, those who by that very forecasting assist the process of meeting the emergency when it comes.[5] To foretell an earthquake (and is this perhaps how Amos 1.1 'two years before the earthquake' was understood by whatever editor gave us the reference?) will not prevent it happening, but it may well serve to reduce the shattering effects which it must have on those whose understanding of seismology is limited to cosmological conceptions of insecurity and beliefs in divine anger which could, momentarily at least, allow the firm pillars of the earth to move. To speak of national disaster in terms of divine judgment provides a comment on the contemporary situation and invites reform; it also makes possible a handling of the disaster when it comes by those for whom the prophecy of it is accepted as genuine. Once this is accepted, even the unexpected, the unprophesied disaster, may be fitted into a known pattern, recognized for what it is, and thus become less terrifying; it ceases to be anomalous.[6]

What is true of the external disaster will be seen even more clearly in internal affairs. Changes which bring a break in continuity will acquire a pattern and therefore be both recognizable and manageable. When dynastic kingship is accepted as the system of government, as it was for roughly four centuries in Judah, the death of the king will be an unforeseen event; illness, battle, old age have some measure of predictability but not absolute precision.[7] But the event will also be anticipated in the sense that it is inevitable, and provision can be made for it by the designating of a successor (so I Kings 1) or by the appointment of a regent (so II Kings 15.5, where Jotham acts for Azariah/Uzziah). Thus a dangerous break is handled. There will be occasions, even in so orderly a dynastic system, when the process will be broken; Amon son of Manasseh was assassinated, for reasons not known to us, but whatever the assassins had in mind was presumably frustrated by the placing of Josiah on the throne by 'the people of the land' (II Kings 21.23–24). We may readily see that such changes of ruler as normally take place within a dynasty will have a pattern, a form; there will be particular procedures to be carried through, although we may only project these from the information given us about the exceptions (e.g., the coronation of Joash in II Kings 11 after an interregnum).

The break involves the relation between deity and people; for whatever the precise religious status of the king is believed to be, there is no doubt of his functioning in religious matters. The recognition that there are psalms concerned with the king and his function (e.g., Psalm 72), and prophetic oracles equally so concerned (e.g., Isa. 11.1–9 [10]), carries with it the possibility of using such words in association with the transfer from one king to his successor of the status and functions which eventually may be seen to belong to the whole dynasty and be projected back into its origins (so in the final complex form of II Samuel 7). Then the particular break at the death of a king becomes only one in a series. It is not to be viewed casually, for we can see how, particularly in the Northern kingdom of Israel, the death of a ruler is on a number of occasions taken as an opportunity for breaking the dynastic principle;[8] indeed in terms of political overlordship, the death of an Assyrian ruler could be a moment for revolt and the regaining of independence. But there is, nevertheless, a subordinating of the particular instance to a known scheme. Only when, with 722 in the North and 587 in the South, kingship comes to an end, is the pattern irrevocably broken. We shall note subsequently some indications of attempts to recover it.

Just as these particular historical instances acquire something of a cultic dimension – although irregular, they are nevertheless susceptible to order – so too we may detect an interchange between the historical and the cultic in other circumstances too. The exposition of Psalm 74 by F. Willesen[9] relates this and other comparable psalms to a cultic background, illuminated by Babylonian and other examples, in which disaster to shrine and city, as the dwelling place of the deity, is depicted in military terms – siege, destruction, and the like – where it may be held in reality to concern a cultic situation, a moment of defilement, of loss of communication with the deity, which is, for the community, just as disastrous as the destructive event which appears to be described. It is probable that the matter is more complex; the imagery of disaster derives from experience or knowledge of actual destructions, and the interrelationship between event and cultic form is subtle. But the point that Willesen makes is valid insofar as he sees that what is described in such political language need not have that particular quality. So, even if Psalm 74 and others like it derive their present form in part at least from some particular historical moment – although commentators have never been able to agree absolutely which moment it is – their significance is not limited to such a moment, nor is it limited to a series of such moments; it has meaning for other situations, less outwardly drastic but nevertheless serious for the continuing religious life and well-being of the community.[10]

There is a clue here to the methods adopted by the community for the *overcoming of breaks* in continuity. The more commonly experienced internal emergencies provide a basis for the meeting of the more urgent but less frequent major crises. That this is so becomes important for the understanding of the overall, as distinct from the more particular, purposes of such compilations as the Holiness Code (Leviticus 17–26) and the Priestly Work. Here we may observe how an endeavour is made at clarifying the nature of the community and the ways in which it is to be re-established and preserved as the true and holy people, partly by the reinterpretation of older traditions and the giving of a wider and more coherent portrayal of the past as a normative period, from creation to the entry to the promised land, partly also by the stress upon purity and its maintenance, in the gathering into a coherent form of the great mass of legislation, now viewed as related to the overall purpose and not merely to the particular needs. For our discussion at this point, the relevance of the occasional internal breaks is that they provide indications of the mechanisms which are available, as well as providing a basis for their reapplication to wider concerns. Particular rituals, of which some are clearly known to us in the various purificatory requirements laid down especially in the books of Leviticus and Numbers, provide the means by which the individual who is cut off for some specific reason from full participation in the community's life may be restored and recognized to be restored. The two aspects are important; for it is not simply a question of carrying through a specified mechanism – the offering of particular sacrifices, the undertaking of particular recitals of formulae, the passage of a certain fixed period of time – but also one of certification that the break has been overcome, a re-acceptance into the life of the community which is acknowledged.

When this is considered in relation to the experiences of the whole community in major moments of crisis, we may see how the attempt is made at placing the particular event and experience in such a context of interpretation that it becomes meaningful and capable of resolution. Thus, without specifying the precise relationship between event and celebration in such an instance as the defeat of Sisera, described in Judges 4 and hymned in Judges 5,[11] we may observe that the presentation in the poem of the moment of disaster overcome gives it a universal or a typical quality: 'So may all your enemies perish, Yahweh' (Judg. 5.31). The break in religious continuity which is presented in the poem (e.g., vv. 6 f.) is seen to be overcome by the direct delivering action of God, through the agency of his faithful. 'But let those who love him be as the sun when he rises in might' (v. 31) underlines the re-establishment of the relationship and the blessing which is the appropriate concomitant of it. The particular historical event, now only partly discernible, becomes significant for other moments of disaster in that it provides the reassurance which enables men to meet them.

The point just made lays the stress on the one aspect of the overcoming of the break – that of the action, both divine and human, which is essential for it to be achieved. Both the laws and customs governing warfare and the provisions for purificatory rituals presuppose that both deity and people are involved in the restoration of order: the deity by his willingness to act, to restore relationship, as well as by his recognized responsibility for the laying down of the mechanisms which open up the way to restoration; the people by their response to the situation, their recognition of responsibility, or their fitting the experience into a context which points to the particular actions needed. There is, as we have seen, another aspect involved. Restoration is not simply a matter of experience; it is also a matter of *authentication*. In theory at least – and here we move into an area which touches on the whole problem of truth and falsity in religious interpretation – restoration, the apparent renewal of contact with the deity, could be an illusion. When the prophet Hananiah (Jeremiah 28) speaks of the speedy overthrow of Babylon and the restoration of exiled king and leaders, he is giving an assurance of the overcoming of the break which Jeremiah declares to be non-genuine. In another context, Jeremiah says: 'They have healed the calamity (*šeber*) of my people lightly, saying "All is well (*šālôm šālôm*)"; but there is no well-being (*šālôm*)' (Jer. 6.14). The belief may exist in men's minds that all is well, when in fact all that has taken place is a restoration of outward security, apparent blessing from the deity. Authentication of the restoration requires the assurance that the break really has been overcome, that relationship really has been restored.

Now this, it is clear, is a point on which views may differ. With the collapse of the kingdom of Judah in 597 and 587, it is evident that there was not one single view of what would constitute restoration. There was even, so Jeremiah 44 relates, a segment of the people which claimed that the disaster was due to the neglect of the worship of the Queen of Heaven, and that restoration could only be possible with a due acknowledgment of her status and claims. For them, the break in religious continuity lay not in a loss of contact with Yahweh, but in a relatively long-standing loss of contact with another deity, perhaps understood as his consort. For them, the assurance of re-established relationship would be made

in terms of her renewed favour, her blessing, the bestowal of life
and well-being deriving from her resumption of her proper place.
For others – and their position is now largely obscured in our texts
– rehabilitation lay with the appointment of Gedaliah as this is
described in the longer texts of Jeremiah 40–41. The willingness
of Jeremiah to stay with him and his unwillingness to go to Egypt
argue for a positive evaluation of this particular political set-up,
although in fact it was doomed to failure. A vivid picture is drawn
in Jeremiah 40. 7–12 of a renewed community, a gathering of
scattered Jews to join the remnant (š*'ērît*) with Gedaliah. There is
no precise information, and our sources are limited in scope,
but we may legitimately suppose that there were those (and
presumably including Jeremiah) who were prepared to authenticate this as the point of rehabilitation.[12] We have no means of
determining the sequel. Our sources provide no direct information
about what went on in Judah after the assassination of Gedaliah,
beyond a possible inference in Jeremiah 52.30 that a further exiling
of Jews in the twenty-third year of Nebuchadrezzar (583/2) could
be one aspect of this. That there were many who remained in
Judah – although how many must be quite uncertain – is clear
enough. That they thought of themselves as the true and continuing
community would seem very likely, but nothing that has survived
indicates this clearly. That some of the problems of fifty years later
derive from conflicting claims to true continuity is again probable,
without our being able to specify just who made what claims. What
we do observe is that eventually any claims that were made
to continuity in Judah were overshadowed by those made for
continuity through the exiled group in Babylonia. Both the
Deuteronomistic writers and the Chronicler claim this; it is less
certain, but probable, that the same is true for the Priestly writers,
though conceivable that some Palestinian material from this period
may be incorporated in their work.

The problem of authentication becomes acute in the early
Persian period. The purpose of this discussion is not to investigate
the alternative views of different groups, although it is important
to recognize the problems that are created by the existence of
differing claims.[13] What we need to observe is the *processes* involved.
At the moment when restoration is brought about, its validity is
claimed on the basis of lines of succession to the past. The
rebuilding of the temple and the rehabilitation of Jerusalem in

themselves constitute endeavours to reactivate the past. When the rebuilding was initiated it is said that many of those 'who had seen the first temple, when the foundation of this temple was laid before their eyes, wept with a loud voice, and many shouted aloud for joy' (Ezra 3.12). It is often assumed that the weeping was in distress at the comparison between the impoverished post-exilic temple and its earlier and richer form. The basis for such an interpretation is found in Haggai 2.3 ('Who among you is left who saw this temple in its former glory? and how do you see it now? is it not as nothing in your eyes?'). But this latter passage is making a different point: it is in reality contrasting the new temple, less rich than the old, with the glory that is about to break out (Haggai 2.4, 6–9). The passage in Ezra 3 shows a community weeping and rejoicing, responding in the forms of worship to the reality of the rebuilding of the temple which brings back again the reality of the former temple.[14] It is the recognition that in this rebuilding the link is re-established; continuity is recovered.

Closer examination of the Chronicler's presentation reveals how this is elaborated. The theme of the temple vessels provides a bridge.[15] Priestly genealogies[16] provide another link, and this is taken a stage further with the direct association of Ezra with his immediate pre-exilic ancestor Seraiah (Ezra 7.1).[17] This theme of priestly genealogy is in fact used a great deal in the post-exilic period, and particular elements now to be found in the Chronicler's work take us further in tracing the differing claims to true continuity in priesthood with the past. The Samaritan high priestly lists offer a comparable claim to authority.[18] In another area, appearing at the end of II Kings and reflected subsequently in hopes centred on Zerubbabel, there is raised the question of the revival and hence the continuity of the Davidic dynasty. The claim at the end of II Kings 25 (vv. 27–30) is clear, but no consequences are drawn. Deutero-Isaiah, whose reflections on the servant figure may have some link with the royal line and perhaps more particularly with the (recently) released Jehoiachin,[19] at one point expresses confidence in the 'sure mercies (*ḥasdê*) of David' (Isaiah 55.3). It must remain uncertain how far such a reference is to be understood in political terms, but it is clear that there is here an expression of confidence that the restoration to which the prophecies point involves a link back to the Davidic covenant, just as so much of what Deutero-Isaiah envisages is expressed in terms of a new

exodus, and hence, by implication, a new entry into the land.
(For this latter, see especially Isaiah 35 and also the further
developments of the theme beyond Deutero-Isaiah in such passages as Isaiah 62.1–5.) The subsequent repercussions of hopes of
a restored Davidic monarchy may be detected in passages in
Jeremiah and Ezekiel which are probably later additions (e.g.,
Jeremiah 33.14–26 [not in LXX]; Ezekiel 37.24 f.). Attempts have
been made to find the theme in Nehemiah, although this is very
uncertain.[20] It is evident in later writings still, in the Testaments
of the Twelve Patriarchs (especially Levi and Judah), the Psalms
of Solomon (especially Psalms of Solomon 17 and 18), the Qumran
texts and the New Testament (cf., e.g., Matthew 1.1; 20.30;21.9),
and in some rabbinic writings.[21]

These are some of the mechanisms used to bring out the claim
for the re-establishing of continuity with the past. They may clearly
be used in the interests of different groups, and it is characteristic
of the post-exilic period that, after the extreme break of the exilic
age, there should be indications of rival and conflicting groups,
even though these do not become fully articulated until the second
century BC, in the various parties within Judaism and in the
Samaritan community. But it is there again important to observe
how, for example, such a theme as that of the true Zadokite line
appears to be employed by more than one group in its endeavour
to demonstrate itself to be the true succession. Rival claimants to
status will perhaps most readily appear after a break. Thus it is
no surprise to find that the break brought about in the period of
Antiochus IV Epiphanes is followed not only by the restoration
effected under Judas Maccabeus, but also by a gradually sharp-
ening conflict between various claimants to be the true community.
We may observe the same again in the first century AD, not only
in the various groups which appear within Judaism itself, including
the Christian group, but also in the attempts at establishing the
claims of Jewish and Christian communities, particularly in the
period after the disaster of AD 70.

II. *Implications for Literature and Theology*

What has been said so far has concentrated on the nature of the
breaks in continuity and the means which may be employed to
overcome them, with some comment also on the effects that such

breaks may have on the internal life of the community and particularly on groups which may emerge within it. We must now turn to another aspect of this and attempt to define more closely the literary and theological handling of these breaks and bridgings, asking how they may be reflected in the literature, and what kinds of effects are produced in the thought by moments of crisis, major or minor. Again it will be clear that our limited knowledge of the history means that we can only postulate certain of the effects, generalizing in some degree from the moments in which a clearer picture of the literary and theological developments may be obtained.

It is not possible in such a survey as this to discuss more than a few examples of the procedures and effects. They may serve as pointers to the thorough discussion which is needed for a more adequate assessment.

We may begin with a relatively simply example. The debates of many years concerning the dating of the psalms have eventually shown up the weakness of discussions which centre upon trying to pinpoint the moment of origin. Indeed we may properly suppose that the origins of Israel's cultic poetry lie far back in her prehistory, and we may further consider it likely that, together with sanctuaries and festivals and rituals already existing in Canaan, Israel took over the concomitants of religious worship such as psalms and prayers, making perhaps only slight modifications to qualify them for inclusion in the Yahweh cult (Psalm 29 is often held to be a good example of such a takeover.)[22] So too we must recognize that from a very early date such religious poetry was used and re-used, and in the process came to be charged with new meanings corresponding to the current trends of thought and practice.[23] It is a matter of debate how far such changing use produced modifications in wording; at some points, where precise allusions appear to be made, we may naturally suppose a particular adjustment. More often we may see the re-use itself providing a re-interpretation, not in itself necessitating change of wording, or requiring only such relatively small adjustments as might better fit contemporary usage. Where this becomes clearest is, of course, in psalms which refer to the king. It is no longer necessary for commentators, set on a post-exilic date for all psalmody, to argue for a late Maccabean, Hasmonean date for such royal psalms; but equally, while a pre-exilic date may rightly be claimed, it must also be observed that use extends beyond the boundary imposed by the end of the monarchy. Whatever adjustments of wording took place, the references to the king remained, and in one way or another were re-interpreted. This process – and clearly it may be illustrated more broadly – has two effects relevant to our present discussion. On the one hand, the retaining of older wording and of older references, here to an outmoded politico-religious institution, may serve to stress continuity where the realities of the situation point to discontinuity. There is no longer any king; but the references to the king are not dropped, and their very preservation provides an automatic recall of the days of the past with which continuity needs to be preserved.[24] On the other hand, it is clear that the use of the same wording in widely different periods – different not only in time, but in political order and religious organization and outlook – conceals the degree to which there has in fact been change. The preservation of the older material may be deceptive in its suggestion of continuity; in actual fact, the difference between the point of earlier and more literal use and the point of later and re-interpreted understanding, may be so great that there is more of discontinuity than of continuity in thought. And when the community endeavours to articulate its beliefs in contemporary language, it will hardly be surprising if there are some for whom the evidence of change will appear to imply an abandonment of older belief. We may, in the light of contemporary discussions of doctrinal formulation in Christian circles, the better appreciate the problem. We may wonder how far the contemporaries of Hosea could accept the use of what appears to be 'fertility cult' language for the re-statement of Yahwistic faith, and we may the better understand the debate between 'Hellenizers' and 'traditionalists' in the second century BC.

The moment of crisis which brings to an end certain familiar patterns of life and established institutions must by its very occurrence raise questions about the validity of received ideas. If certain central elements of religious thought turn on the existence and meaning of a temple, established as linked to the ruling dynasty and to the life of the kingdom, and expressive of the reality of the divine presence in the people – we need not here attempt to make more nearly precise the particular styles of interpretation hinted at – then the destruction of the temple immediately puts a question mark against what has been held and done. Insofar as the very existence of the temple is held to guarantee the presence of the people's deity, the reality of this presence must at the very least be regarded as less than sure.[25] One way to meet this may be the simplest, that of rebuilding the destroyed shrine; the Jews of Elephantine, faced with such an emergency, sought both authorization and support in carrying through just such a rebuilding. But even this cannot fail to leave open the anxious thought: if this has happened once, can it not happen again, and if so, what becomes of the assurance of divine presence and blessing? Another way, and here we may instance the reaction of Jews and Christians after AD 70, is to argue either that the particular significance which the temple had is maintained in another form (for Christians this could be associated with sayings about the destroying and rebuilding of the temple attributed to Jesus himself and understood of his own person, thus focusing on him sentiments otherwise directed to the temple); or alternatively (though not to the exclusion of the first) that the destroyed temple, though lost, points to a future and ultimate rehabilitation, a final temple, not susceptible to the chances which may destroy an earthly building. The last chapters of Ezekiel (40–48), in an earlier situation (though precisely what situation remains uncertain), and the 'heavenly temple' ideas, found, for example, in the Revelation of John (cf. Revelation 21 for the heavenly city in which the presence of deity and Lamb constitutes the temple), illustrate such projection. In the interim, regret for the loss of the destroyed temple may be replaced, in part, by anticipation of the final temple; continuity of sentiment concerning the temple may find a different focus in piety, seeing such forms as prayer and almsgiving as substitutes for the sacrificial worship characteristic of temple practice.[26]

If, as has been argued, the writing down of traditions is particularly linked with general crises of confidence,[27] it may also be seen that the written product of such a process is not identical with the traditions which it replaces. It inevitably possesses a different character, and in particular a different kind of authority may come to be attached to it.[28]

The natural sequel to this is to recognize in this process of fixation in writing an attempt at guaranteeing a continuity which might otherwise be lost.[29] But a further effect is that of showing more clearly inconsistencies within the tradition which may create difficulty and uncertainty. While we may observe

how, in the transmission process itself, some inconsistencies will
be smoothed out – differing versions of the same story will tend to
be dovetailed, as if they were one – it is only when the texts appear
in written form that the more detailed comparison can be made
and the inconsistencies adjusted, either by an editorial process,
with the texts emended to conform, or by an interpretative process,
by which what are quite evidently discordant elements are
explained as being in reality in accord.[30] Insofar as it is at moments
of break that the rethinking takes place and the gathering of the
materials associated with the tradition is undertaken, we may
recognize this harmonizing process, incorporated in the text or
superimposed upon it, to be an after-effect of discontinuity, and
itself in part a literary and theological procedure by which a single,
intelligible tradition is shown to be present, linked in the rehandling
of the earlier materials with what is regarded as an earlier
orthodoxy.

But such harmonization may conceal the more basic problem,
that of knowing where the true tradition, the true theological
interpretation, is to be found. Stress upon the different theologies
within the Old Testament is an important aspect of its study;
critical analysis has made this possible. But for centuries it was
possible for both Jews and Christians to read the Old Testament
as a coherent theological document, assuming or demonstrating
the unity of its theological witness. The issue between the two
religious communities must always be defined in part as being a
difference of view in regard to what was the correct understanding,
and whether the discontinuity which appears in the major breaks
of the last centuries of the pre-Christian era is to be regarded as
bridged by the continuity claimed for Christian or for Jewish
tradition.

At a much earlier stage we may see the same kind of problem
posed, after the division of the kingdom, by the undoubted claims
of both kingdoms to represent a true succession. The charge of
apostasy levelled at the Northern kingdom cannot be satisfactorily
substantiated; we are dealing with a polemical situation, in which
the story of Jeroboam's setting up of golden calves is understood
in terms of religious disaster from the viewpoint of a later Judean
writer, but could undoubtedly be seen in terms of the upholding
of the religious succession by those who saw in them the symbols
of continuity with the God 'who brought Israel out of Egypt' (I

Kings 12.28). It would appear probable that the story of the golden calf in Exodus 32, in which Aaron has a central place and which now points to religious failure even on his part, could have been differently related by those who would seek in the ancient traditions – and perhaps with propriety – a basis for current Northern practice.[31] What eventually became of the Northern religious tradition is a matter, in part at least, of hypothesis; the preservation in the South of prophetic traditions associated with Hosea and Amos, directed to the Northern community, shows that at some point endeavours were made at drawing together into one the broken elements of what was believed to have been one community, however much of separateness may be traceable even in the earlier stages. And the same is true of the significant Elijah and Elisha traditions with their emphasis on the preservation of true Yahwism in the North as well as their elements of critique directed against Northern apostasy.

If discontinuity must be the experience of any community, political or religious, then the problem of what constitutes the true succession will always be present. Whatever changes, political or social, come, there must be some means for recognizing and authenticating the handing on of the true tradition, what is acknowledged to be the same faith.[32] But in this there is no simple shortcut. The very richness and diversity within the tradition, its pluriformity, mean that, however much particular groups may wish to claim a direct and clear link between their own position and what they, with some selectivity of outlook, regard as the true faith of the past, there will be other groups for whom that particular link is not valid. It is in such a context easier to see the unsatisfactory nature of claims for a simple succession than to define where true continuity lies. An adequate theological understanding must go beyond that to the recognition that the religious tradition is rich enough to allow of more than one development, and that in assessing the validity of particular aspects of that development, regard must be paid both to the richness of the tradition and to the degree to which particular political and social pressures lead to the stressing of this particular claim or that. If the ultimate reality underlying the religious tradition is to be described, it must be in terms which allow for the element of the unknown and the unknowable which must be present in any valid theological statement.[33]

4

The Temple Vessels: A Continuity Theme

The concern of this discussion is not with the nature of the vessels or with any aspect of their description such as may be found in biblical dictionaries or *Realenzyklopädien*; nor is it intended to attempt a survey of the development of such vessels with an examination of the uses to which they were put in such a way as to draw out – if that be possible – the changing beliefs and attitudes of the worshippers and officiants. This latter, assisted as it might be by archaeological evidence, would, if the task proved to be a possible one to undertake, perhaps point towards the relationship between practice and belief in a way which might illuminate some of the many problems in the history of Israel's religious life and thought.

These two aspects of the subject, with which we shall not be concerned, offer the one an important part of the reconstruction of actual life and practice, and the other a potentially valuable contribution to wider questions of thought and belief. For their full study it is unlikely that there is anything like sufficient evidence in the Old Testament and in the archaeological finds. But there is a third aspect of the subject which is capable of some investigation. This is the more general question concerning the relationship which is believed to subsist between the actual existence of the objects themselves and the continuing religious life of the community. It is for this reason that the subtitle of this discussion is 'A Continuity Theme', for I believe we may see in some of the statements which are made about the temple vessels indications of certain aspects of the concern, which belongs to any religious community, that there shall be no break within its life which will

irremediably cut it off from the source of life and blessing which is
believed to rest in the deity. The idea that at a certain point in
time all links with the past may be cut and that we may begin as
if we had no predecessors whether in knowledge or in faith, is quite
devoid of any reality. We may, of course, resolutely set our faces
against the past, and attempt to produce a pattern of belief and
practice which entirely denies what has previously been said and
done; but in this case, we are inevitably formulating a new position
on the basis of the old, even in the process of repudiation. The
more natural and more common method of reform is a subtle
combination of rejection and acceptance. We are more prone in
the contemporary situation to suppose that we can cut ourselves
off from the past; the inhabitants of the ancient world were certainly
not. And more than this, they were conscious of a need, which has
its parallels too in contemporary thinking, that, whatever breaches
with the past might occur, there should be a demonstrable link
between the later and the earlier stages of a community's life. It is
clear that they could consider the past as indicating failure and
misunderstanding which must be denied if the life of present and
future was to be stable.[1] But the failure and misunderstanding of
the past were themselves seen as reactions against a known
standard, an already existing pattern. In rejecting the reactions,
they were endeavouring to restore continuity with a true past, and
by this to maintain their own religious life and practice in the
consciousness that it must cohere with what was already known
and experienced.

Some aspects of this question of continuity were raised in my
inaugural lecture in London on that subject.[2] Recently, in an
endeavour to clarify the nature of the diversity within the Old
Testament tradition, while still seeing the nature of continuity, I
have concerned myself with the evidence for discontinuity.[3] And
it is from this point that the present discussion may be said to take
off, since it will have as a central theme the consideration of how
the temple vessels are connected with the problem of maintaining
continuity between the moment which lies before a disaster and
that which comes after.

But there is also a more positive aspect of this. The description
of the vessels themselves, the cataloguing of them as they actually
existed at a given moment or as they were believed to have existed
at some particular point of importance, provides an indication not

simply of practice but also of order, the continuing order which is traced back into the past and which provides authentication for the present. Hence the first part of the discussion will be devoted to considering some aspects of this more descriptive material; in the second part we shall consider how the temple vessels appear as a theme concerned with the establishment of continuity across a break in the tradition; and as a third part we shall briefly note some of the indications which are to be found in still later writings of the persistence of this same theme, to bridge other moments of discontinuity or to establish authority for the beliefs and practices of later generations.

I

There is a remarkable fact to be observed concerning the long descriptive passages in the Old Testament which deal with the temple vessels. It is that when these passages were incorporated into the works in which they now stand, the objects described can no longer have existed; the descriptions are quite evidently of past conditions. Although at the time of compilation there probably were in use comparable objects to those described, yet all this loving attention to detail is devoted to the past. This is true whether we consider the description of the temple of Solomon in I Kings, incorporated in the Deuteronomic History which took more or less its present shape in the mid-sixth century BC, after the destruction of the temple in 587; or whether we consider that of the Chronicler in II Chronicles which is incorporated into a work whose final shaping can hardly be earlier than the fourth century BC. The same may be said of the description of the tabernacle and its contents in Exodus. Here the problem is complicated by our uncertainty as to what kind of tent-shrine may have existed in the pre-settlement period, how far the descriptions bear a relationship to such a tent-shrine as may have existed, and how long such a shrine continued to exist into the settlement period – and indeed how far the tabernacle theme is to be seen as a projection back of the temple theme. The tabernacle theme is itself a continuity theme, and might appropriately be examined alongside that of the vessels it is supposed to have contained. This is particularly clear for the Chronicler. In his account, the tabernacle existed at Gibeon in the time of David and Solomon and was only then subsumed into the temple. But whatever the precise interpretation of this particular theme may be, it remains the case that the eventual compilation of the Tetrateuch, the Priestly Work, took place when all this lay in the distant past.

Two points of reservation must be entered here. On the one hand we may quite properly argue that, however much these descriptions are of objects belonging to the past, they have their counterpart in contemporary practice. This is in fact an important pointer to the significance of the descriptions being preserved. On the other hand we may observe that both in this respect and in many others the later compilations preserve a great deal of material which belongs to the past, describing conditions which no longer exist – as an occasional scribal note indicates (cf. I Sam. 9.9) – and that it has always been necessary to emphasize that the older material acquired a degree of what will eventually be called 'canonicity,' an authoritative status, which made it impossible (or at the very least rather difficult) for the later editors to excise what was in fact no longer relevant. But on this we might comment that an examination of the two forms of the same material which we have in Samuel-Kings and in Chronicles shows that one compiler at least could show both a remarkable degree of respect for his sources and a very considerable degree of freedom in handling them. If at times he quotes verbatim or virtually so – though perhaps a few such passages are due to later insertion by a scribe who added what was missing from the earlier text – at other times, and this most evidently in the whole survey of the period of the monarchy from Rehoboam to Zedekiah, he could so rewrite and re-present that we have difficulty at times in recognizing that he is dealing with the same rulers. (Think of Manasseh!) He did in fact substantially modify the material concerning the temple vessels in I Kings, except for one passage which is of this verbatim kind and which is for various reasons suspect (II Chron. 4.11–5.1; cf. I Kings 7.40–51). But the inclusion of this passage, whether due to the Chronicler or to his commentators, still has its significance within the matter with which we are concerned.

For it is not simply the fact that these descriptions are preserved which is important. It is the extent and the detail of them. It is a very substantial part of Exodus which is devoted to the tabernacle, and not only that, but virtually the entire material appears twice, once as command to do and once as description of what is done. It is a substantial part of the descriptions in I Kings which is devoted to the equipment of the temple, even though this is a relatively small part of the whole work in which it belongs; the same is true for II Chronicles, though to this we should really add the large preparatory sections in I Chronicles.

The very setting out of the lists and descriptions of the vessels does much more than provide points of comparison or contrast with contemporary usage or, at a lower level, indications of the way in which lost or damaged vessels might be replaced. It provides an overall picture of what belongs essentially to the true cultus, to the existence of a proper relationship with the deity; and we may note that some emphasis is laid on the enumeration of vessels, a concern with the completeness of their provision. In this respect, this kind of description must be placed alongside the delineation of buildings. Here again we may see that such plans and measurements could possibly provide a basis for reconstruction. But in the case of the Old Testament the details are never quite sufficient and the older reconstructions which lacked any correlation with the evidence of archaeology were inevitably in danger of being fancy rather than fact, and even with archaeological evidence there remain substantial differences of view among the experts. But blueprints for building is hardly what they are really intended to be; they are directed rather towards exemplifying, in the process of description, that belief in the pattern to which temple buildings are supposed to conform, the pattern which, in the case of the tabernacle (e.g. Exodus 25.9), of Ezekiel's temple (chs. 40ff.) and of the Chronicler's temple (e.g. I Chronicles 28.19), is believed to have been divinely given. For such divinely given temple plans we have examples from other ancient cultures.[4] The temple vessels as essential component parts of the temple itself would then have the same function, that of depicting the order to which practice must conform, the order which is itself linked to what the deity himself ordains. So, as in the tabernacle sections, and as by implication in the temple descriptions – and more explicitly in the Chronicler's form of these – what is being provided is not simply the necessary objects for religious use, but what corresponds to the divine command.

The temple vessels, seen in this way, take their place within that larger area of thought in which attempts are being made at defining the relationship between the divine and human spheres in terms of temples which have a correspondence to the divine dwelling or to the cosmos seen as expressive of the divine dwelling. The larger aspects of this need not concern us here; they have been the subject of numerous studies, among which we may note particularly that of R. E. Clements.[5]

The theme of making such vessels, or the emphasis on their provision, or on their purification (cf. II Chronicles 29.18) and guarding (cf. I Chronicles 9.28 f.), equally provides points at which we may detect the concern with the continuing in proper form of the religious observances which are seen as necessary to the well-being of the community.

These more positive aspects of the materials concerning the temple vessels may well conceal something of the more negative side. Just as we may reasonably see in the enactment of a law against a particular offence some evidence that the office is liable to be committed, so in this care and concern we may see an anxiety lest the vessels be neglected, lest their proper care be not undertaken, lest there be some disaster occasioned by a break in the proper procedures. And what belongs to preserving continuity may also be seen as the most appropriate mechanism for re-establishing that continuity once it has been broken.[6]

II

With this, we reach the second part of this discussion and here the element of discontinuity comes to the fore. We may preface this by the general comment that discontinuity is something which may be the result of some quite minor lapse, some accident, some unforeseen incident which disrupts normal procedures. Some aspects of this less drastic interruption – though serious enough for the community when it is observed in such an example as the narrative of I Samuel 14 – have been discussed in the article already mentioned on 'The Theology of Tradition'.[7] The great breaks, such as that of the exile, deserve fuller attention, and they receive it in the Old Testament in regard to the larger questions of political existence, of restoration to community life, of temple rebuilding and the like. In this context there belong also those many themes which are connected with showing the relationship between the older and the subsequently established mechanisms of political and religious life. But such concern with rehabilitation and its nature shows itself also in regard to what we might consider the smaller details, and it is here that we may place the concern with the temple vessels.

When we examine the evidence, however, we observe that this theme is given considerably more attention than we might expect it to receive. This points to its importance. It will therefore be our next task to examine some aspects of the material which sheds light on this concern.

There are three main sections of material to be considered: II Kings 24–25 with Jeremiah 52 as a parallel to part of the text, together with the related material in Jeremiah 37–44; Jeremiah 27–28; II Chronicles 36 and Ezra 1–6 and 7–8.

(*a*) II Kings 24.13 is quite categorical. All the gold vessels of the temple of Yahweh which Solomon had made were broken up by the king of Babylon 'as Yahweh had spoken.' This destruction is associated with the first capture of Jerusalem in 597. The last phrase 'as Yahweh had spoken' links this aspect of the disaster with a particular divine word, though it is a divine word which we cannot satisfactorily identify. The evidence which we shall see, that these and other verses concerning the temple vessels are probably not part of the original narrative, may well point to the inclusion of such a precise authentication of the destruction as a result of later correlating of various tradition elements. But to say, as John Gray does, for example,[8] that it has been drawn from Jeremiah 27. 22 is to overlook the fact that the divine word here purports to refer to a foretold destruction of vessels, whereas the word ascribed to Jeremiah is concerned with their being carried to Babylon and there preserved (on the questions of the text of Jeremiah 27. 22, see below). It may be that there is a loose link to the Jeremiah message, and we may observe that the Chronicler uses Jeremiah with greater precision in his very different account of the fall of Judah; but it is more likely that we have an extension to this particular part of the temple furniture of the prophecies of destruction of the temple which are to be found not only in Jeremiah and Ezekiel but also in Micah 3. 12. The prophecy and fulfilment pattern forms one of the important bases for the Deuteronomic account of the fall of the two kingdoms.[9]

II Kings 25. 13–17 associates a further destructive action with the period of the second capture of Jerusalem in 587. Verse 13 relates that the bronze pillars, the stands, the bronze sea were broken up and their material carried to Babylon. Verse 14 adds a further list of vessels which were taken; it is not stated that these were broken up. Verse 15 adds yet another detail; a further series of vessels, both of gold and silver, was also carried away. The meaning here is not absolutely clear, but it is most probable that it means that the metal of which these objects were made was carried away.[10] The implication of this would seem to be that the same is really intended also for the vessels of v.14.[11] The point is further suggested by the emphasis in v. 16 on the incalculable amount of bronze contained in the larger pieces.

The parallel text in Jeremiah 52. 17 ff. provides the same information; its account is in some respects more detailed, suggesting a greater emphasis on the totality of the disaster. Here is added too a reference to the twelve bronze bulls under the sea (v. 20); that these bulls had been removed by Ahaz and replaced by a stone base – and the bronze presumably used for other purposes as is indicated by the reference to the breaking up of some other vessels (II Kings 16. 17) – is either overlooked by the writer of this form of the text,[12] or the sea is deliberately included in the interests of completeness.[13]

The difference in detail between these two texts need not here be examined; what we observe is that the emphasis on even greater destruction and an even more final disaster in Jeremiah 52 fits well with its more negative attitude towards the situation in Judah,[14] which may also be seen in the absence of any reference here to the governorship of Gedaliah.[15]

We may note in regard to these two passages in II Kings 24 and 25 (Jeremiah 52) that they interrupt the course of the narrative. Significantly, no mention of the temple vessels appears in the closely parallel text of Jeremiah 39. It is probable that one or both of them is a later insertion in the text.[16] But for our present purpose, we may observe the longer and shorter forms, and consider the value of each. At whatever stage the narrative took on its present form and by whatever processes its various elements were woven together, as we have them in II Kings, the final effect is to stress that temple and vessels were brought to an end. There is no room for restoration.[17]

It is in the light of this that we may see the significance of the emphasis on the vessels and their description in I Kings. As is well known, the Deuteronomic History holds out no easy hope of restoration, though it contains a number of passages – and not only its last verses – which point beyond disaster. But in the contrast between this picture of total loss and the description of vessels in detail we may see a discreet way of suggesting that there can be restoration; it must be by way of recovery of the past, by way of a repetition, in some sense, of the events of the past. The writers, tracing through the history from the wilderness (in Deuteronomy) to the building of the temple under Solomon (before the first moment of disaster) are inviting their readers, to whom the loss of the land is a part of their experience, to set what hope for the future they can have in the reality of the divine action which led them into the land in the first instance and through to the moment when, in rest from their enemies (cf. Deut. 12. 10; II Sam. 7.1), they were able to establish the central shrine. To a community transported as it were again to the wilderness beyond Jordan, the descriptions of past experience are both a warning against the repetition of failure and a promise of the possibility of restoration.[18]

(*b*) Jeremiah 27–28 contains two passages which dwell on the theme of the temple vessels, viz. 27. 16–22 and 28. 1–9. The latter passage may conveniently be taken first, since it relates a specific incident in which this theme is a detail on which some emphasis is laid, whereas the former passage is entirely devoted to the temple vessels as a theme.

The message of the prophet Hananiah in 28. 2–4 makes three points.[19] First, that God has broken the yoke of Babylon, a statement which provides the verbal commentary on the symbolic action performed by this prophet (28. 10) by way of controverting the action of Jeremiah in wearing the yoke. Second, that the temple vessels carried to Babylon will be returned within two years. Third, that Jeconiah (Jehoiachin) will be restored to the throne of Judah and the exiles brought back. The latter two points provide the positive counterpart to the negative of the overthrow of Babylon; they envisage a twofold restoration, that of temple and worship and that of the Davidic king still regarded, as witness Ezekiel and the Weidner tablets, as the legitimate ruler, together with a rehabilitation of the community. It has, of course, been pointed out that the statement about the bringing back of the temple vessels is a direct contradiction of II Kings 24. 13 in which the only statement concerning the vessels in the first capture of Jerusalem relates their breaking up.[20] But such a comment misses the real point. We are dealing with a variety of traditions which do not necessarily all coincide. To attempt harmonization is unsatisfactory; more important is to see what particular point is being made by the presentation with which we are concerned.[21] Clearly restoration of the vessels implies re-establishment of that continuity of the cultus which was in some measure interrupted by the disaster of 597. The vessels are a symbol of this. The comment on this oracular pronouncement attributed to Jeremiah (28. 6–9) repeats the main part of Hananiah's prophecy, with emphasis on the restoring of temple vessels and of exiles; but it further indicates by implication that there is room for an element of doubt concerning the validity of the pronouncement which has been made. The sequel in vv. 10–17 elaborates this in the complete word of rejection of Hananiah.

The other passage (27. 16–22) takes its start from the same basic theme, but develops it differently. It makes a general utterance concerning 'prophets' (in the plural) who proclaim restoration of worship, the re-establishment of continuity, in terms of the bringing back of the vessels taken in 597. This contains the same point as we find in 28. 3, and clearly it depends on the same type of tradition. It should probably be regarded as a doublet of the specific Hananiah incident. The same theme is then continued in a mocking word concerning these supposed prophets, who if they really exercised the function should intercede with Yahweh so that he would not permit the remaining vessels in the temple to be transported. We may see here another line of thought, not precisely the same as that of ch. 28. The taking of the vessels is regarded as happening in two stages – first in 597, second in 587. But there is to be no withdrawing of the divine word of judgment. Instead, there is a pronouncement 'concerning the pillars and the sea . . . and all the other vessels' (v. 19).[22] They are to be taken to Babylon. But to this the passage adds a significant point, namely that these vessels are to remain in Babylon until they are brought back by Yahweh himself and restored to the holy shrine. It is to be observed that this form of the text is considerably longer than that of the Septuagint[23]; there the phrases which speak of the return of the vessels are absent, and we read simply: 'They shall be brought to Babylon, says the Lord.' According to Rudolph[24] the restoration words have been added on the basis of Ezra 1. 7 ff. But the dissimilarity of the texts – except in the reference to Nebuchadrezzar as the king who took the vessels away (an obvious point) –

is such as to suggest that the expansion of the Jeremiah text is due rather to a certain kind of understanding of the temple vessel theme, an understanding expressed also in the Chronicler's narrative but not in identical form.

Thus we have two types of statement here. If we follow the MT – and for our present purpose the important point is the existence of a certain kind of interpretation, not the unravelling of the textual history – then we have a theme of restoration built into a theme of exile; the idea of continuity with the previous temple is maintained by the promise of the restoration of the temple vessels. This may be seen to build in effect on a reversal of the Jeremianic word of ch. 28 and to accept in a modified form the rejected oracle of Hananiah. An examination of the whole section Jeremiah 26–36 reveals that such restoration themes are commonly to be found there. It is true that at a number of points the restoration element is not in the LXX where it appears in the MT, and we can therefore argue that a more uncompromising form of this Jeremiah corpus also existed alongside the more hopeful one. Yet the existence of the more hopeful form is attested by the MT, and is to be seen as an important witness to the transformation of the prophetic word, even to the extent of a direct reversal of earlier and more obviously Jeremianic sayings.[25]

(*c*) The most consistent continuity theme connected with the temple vessels is found in the writings of the Chronicler. We have already noted the presence there of both the preparatory work for the temple under David and the description of the carrying through of the work under Solomon. This in itself provides a basis for the subsequent emphasis upon the vessels in the exilic age and after. There are also some intervening passages which have the effect of emphasizing continuity in a slightly different form, namely as expressed in the votive gifts of rulers who thereby preserve continuity: Asa in II Chronicles 15. 18, which speaks of his father's and his own votive gifts in the form of temple vessels; the provision of vessels after the restoration of the true Davidic line under Joash in II Chronicles 24. 14; and the purification of the vessels under Hezekiah in II Chronicles 29. 26 f. The obverse to these is to be found in Amaziah's loss of the vessels to Samaria, recorded in II Chronicles 25.24, and the destruction of vessels by Ahaz in II Chronicles 28.24. In II Chronicles 36.7, we are told that some of the temple vessels were removed when, as this narrative relates,

Jehoiakim was taken captive to Babylon. (As in other cases, the Chronicler's account differs sharply from that of Kings.) We may perhaps see here a link between the Chronicler's account and the Jeremiah material which defines the removal of the vessels in two stages, as indeed we observe that the Chronicler makes precise reference to Jeremiah and his prophecies three times in this chapter. In II Chronicles 36.10 the removal of Jehoiachin to Babylon is accompanied by the taking of the choicest temple vessels. In 36.18, the removal of all the temple vessels is associated with the final disaster to Jerusalem; the emphasis on the total removal, 'vessels great and small' – surely a formula of complete-ness – is in line with the Chronicler's view, made clear in this passage as elsewhere, that nothing was left in Judah which could permit a true worship; everything had gone to Babylon so that the land was left empty.

In Ezra 1, the full reversal of this is indicated. Verses 7–11[26] do not merely state that Cyrus produced the temple vessels and committed them to Mithredath and hence to Sheshbazzar; we are also informed that an inventory was made and that what was restored represented the totality of the vessels.[27] Thus the resto-ration of the temple includes the bringing back of the vessels, and with them the guarantee that there is a direct link with the earlier worship of the community. The point is further developed in Ezra 5.14 f. and 6.5, where it is also said that Nebuchadrezzar had placed the vessels in the temple in Babylon. Of this passage, Galling writes: 'In regard to the temple it is not *de jure* a matter of a new building' (we may note that Galling there neatly sidesteps the unanswerable question as to how far it was a new building *de facto*; it would be nice to know, but theologically speaking this is relatively unimportant[28]) 'but of a continuation, and for this reference is made for evidence to the building edict of Cyrus and to the handing back of the cult objects to Sheshbazzar the commissary.'[29] We may note also in this form of the material, where the reference to the placing of the vessels in a temple in Babylon appears, that a further motif has been introduced, which finds its counterpart in the adventures of the Ark in I Samuel 4–6. What may be seen as a perfectly normal procedure – for where else would such objects be placed but in the shrine of the deity who has shown himself superior in power?[30] – is in fact a witness to the continuing efficacy of the temple vessels as associated symbols of the divine power and presence. For the power of Babylon has fallen, and as the Second Isaiah so vividly expressed it, the gods of Babylon have bowed in submission (Isaiah 46.1). The breach of the exilic age is healed.

The point is carried a stage further, as in the similar passages in II Chronicles, by the inclusion of a reference to yet further temple vessels for the renewal of religious life under Ezra – 7.19 in the royal commission, 8.26–28, with an emphasis on the care given to their preservation on the journey, and 8.33f. at their handing over and the checking and recording of the whole supply of vessels. Here various themes associated with the temple vessels are drawn together. Ezra (and behind him the Persian king) are furthering the worship of the temple; they are also engaging in a restoration of true worship which stands in a line with that established at the very outset under David.[31] The same point is underlined in Nehemiah 10.40 (EVV 39) at the end of the covenant document which is probably also to be associated with Ezra. The Nehemiah story, which at so many points runs parallel with that of Ezra[32] has a comparable emphasis in Nehemiah 13.5, 9, where Nehemiah acts to restore the vessels to their proper place of safe keeping.

Now it is clear that these various passages in which the temple vessels are discussed cannot simply be harmonized into a neat and coherent pattern. We need to consider the purpose and emphasis of each. We have seen (1) that the theme can be used to underline total destruction and loss, as it is in II Kings and Jeremiah 52 and in one form of the texts of Jeremiah 27–28; the continuity element in the theme is here provided, not by any suggestion that somehow the vessels were preserved and restored, thus re-establishing an earlier form, but by the emphasis laid upon the original provision of the vessels in the temple description; (2) that the theme can be used to underline continuity, by preservation through the period of exile, as this is done by the MT in Jeremiah 27 and by the Chronicler with a much greater logic. The Chronicler indeed utilizes the temple vessels theme as one of those by which, alongside other kinds of institutional description, he endeavours to establish the reality of the link between his contemporaries and the original establishment; and by implication and sometimes by statement right back before that to the Exodus period.[33] Thus across the disaster of the exile, in which the loss of the temple might seem to mark an irreparable breach, there is a continuity established which enables the later worshipper to know, through the actual vessels in use, that he stands with his ancestors in the faith. This theme makes its contribution to the wider one of continuity in priesthood and in worship as ordered by the levitical officials of various kinds.[34]

III

This is not the end of the story, and some references to the subsequent use of the theme may be briefly noted. Daniel 1.2 describes the carrying away of the remainder of the temple vessels at a siege of Jerusalem in the third year of Jehoiakim (a siege not otherwise attested and hardly historical); and Daniel 5 picks up the story of the vessels by showing how their use for improper purposes by Belshazzar provides the moment for the word of judgment against Babylon. I Esdras, in addition to repeating the material found in the book of Ezra, adds a theme of restoring the vessels to the story of Darius who is reminded by Zerubbabel of the vow that he made to restore the vessels set aside by Cyrus (4.43–46), and its fulfilment is related in 4.57.II Esdras 10.21 f. gives a description of the disaster in terms which underline the loss of the temple and its worship – the lamp is out, the ark has gone as spoil, the holy vessels are defiled. Loss and restoration are expressed in I Maccabees in the same terms: 1.23, the vessels are taken as booty by Antiochus; 4.49, they are renewed, and so too 14.15. II Maccabees 1–2 uses not this theme but its near counterpart, in that it purports to tell how continuity was preserved by recovery of the sacred fire hidden by pious priests and brought back by Nehemiah; and also by the hiding of tent, ark and incense-altar by Jeremiah which are to remain hidden so that at the final moment of the gathering of the scattered people there will be a true restoration of the shrine, as it was in the time of Moses and in the time of Solomon. The theme of the vessels is also used in Baruch 1.8 f. The relevance of such material to later disasters will be evident, not least to that of AD 70.

IV

The problem of the temple vessels is often posed in the form of a discussion about what happened to them; were they destroyed or preserved in captivity? Were they lost to sight entirely or kept and produced again at the moment of restoration? It may be doubted

if a satisfactory historical answer is to be found, though we may
certainly observe that the earliest of our sources most naturally
suggests the breaking up of the vessels for the sake of the valuable
metal they comprised.[35] Furthermore, insofar as such vessels are
seen to be intimately related with the worship and hence with the
life of the people, their removal from use can be seen as one part
of the action of the conqueror against the conquered.

But the historical answer, whether it can be given or not, is of
relatively little significance. What is important is to see the way in
which this apparently minor theme is given a prominence which
suggests that it was anything but unimportant to the later
community. The community which sought to re-establish itself
after the exile, deeply conscious of its ancestry in faith, but also
aware of the problem of continuity with that faith, made use of the
theme of the vessels, as it made use of other themes, to make good
its claim to be the true successor (perhaps thereby to invalidate
the claims of others), to be directly linked with those who stood on
the other side of the exilic gulf. What they could see to be validated
in spite of the historical break, their successors could see to be true
also in later situations of distress. It is the same people of God
which lives on in consciousness of its ancestry of faith.

5

The Vitality of the Word of God in the Old Testament: A Contribution to the Study of the Transmission and Exposition of Old Testament Material[1]

It is my purpose to draw a picture of some of the processes involved in the shaping of the Old Testament material, not by the pens of authors and editors, but by the living application of the recognized word of God – whether in prophecy or psalm, law or story – to the ever new needs of a community sensitive to the vitality of that word. It is a *picture*, and does not therefore at every point depend upon full and reasoned arguments. Indeed there are inevitably many uncertainties in our describing of Old Testament processes, and the gaps can only be filled in imaginatively. Yet some such picture is necessary if we are to understand both the shaping of the Old Testament material, and the place that it has continued to occupy in the nurturing of men's faith.

I

I propose to begin with an illustration of the problem, and so to sketch the first outlines of the picture.

Three times in the first book of Kings, there appears the same prophecy of judgment uttered against a ruler of the Northern kingdom, Israel. Set out in its rhythmic form it runs thus, as it appears as its first occurrence:

> He who dies belonging to Jeroboam in the city
>   the dogs shall eat;

and he who dies in the open country
the birds of the air shall eat;
for the LORD has spoken
(I Kings 14. 11; 16.4; 21.24).[2]

In the first passage, the pronouncement is made by Ahijah, the prophet of the division of the kingdom, to the wife of Jeroboam I on the occasion of her inquiry concerning the illness of her son. In the second, it is said by a prophet, otherwise unknown, named Jehu ben Hanani, against Baasha who overthrew the dynasty of Jeroboam I. In the third, it is said by Elijah against Ahab, the best-known ruler of the dynasty which replaced that of Baasha.

This curious feature of the narrative, all within the space of a few chapters, may be explained in various ways. We may pass over the first possible explanation as being highly improbable, namely that three prophets all quite independently thought of precisely the same picture and uttered their judgment in exactly the same wording (apart from an enclitic *lô* in 16.4 and the necessary change in the name of the ruler condemned). Admittedly the saying may have been a popular proverb; but in that case the idea of independent inspiration lies in the use of the material, and this is closer to one or other of the alternative explanations.

The second possibility is that we have here a simple literary connection which may be described in various ways. When almost identical oracles occur in two different prophets, the solution sometimes proposed is that one quoted from the other, or that both utilized a common source. Such an explanation has often been given, for example, for the double occurrence of the oracle which begins 'It shall come to pass in the latter days . . .' in Isa. 2. 1–4(5) and Micah 4. 1–4(5). Few Old Testament scholars would wish to maintain a strictly literary view of such quotation, as if prophets had available to them books of earlier material to which they had recourse when inspiration failed or when they wished to illustrate a point, as when a preacher quotes the poets. Insofar as the idea of quotation represents the handling of a tradition, it approaches, though it does not coincide with, the third view to which we shall come in a moment. Yet the attempt to establish quotation, whether from literary source or fixed oral tradition, is still much in vogue, and is still frequently employed as a criterion for the relative dating of Old Testament passages, in spite of the fact that actual quotation is often difficult to prove and the direction of quotation even more difficult.[3]

Psalm 1.3 and Jer. 17.7 both use the same image of the tree planted by streams of water. This has suggested that psalmist has quoted prophet, or prophet has quoted psalmist. But the discovery of the same metaphor in Egyptian wisdom literature[4] makes quotation seem considerably less probable.[5] Quotation may indeed only be claimed with certainty where re-interpretation is evident. Such reinterpretation indicates dependence upon an earlier form of the same material, and its rehandling with a distinctively new point in mind, as when Job (7.17f.) uses similar words to those of Ps. 8. 5f., but gives a sinister twist to their meaning.[6]

The oracles in I Kings have often been treated simply in terms of quotation, but also in terms of free but unimaginative composition by an author who had so little real ability in the creation of original material that he merely repeated himself three times over. Thus R. H. Pfeiffer in his *Introduction to the Old Testament*[7] comments:

'Whenever possible, the author *gratuitously* attributed the rooting out of a line of heretical kings of North Israel to a divine sentence' (p. 382, with reference to I Kings 14 and 16. Italics mine).

'The end of the story (of Naboth's vineyard) has been supplemented with a sentence against Ahab . . . written by the first Deuteronomist' (p. 405).

'The style and language of this oracle prove that it was written by the author of Kings. He reproduces it with slight changes when the sentence is carried out by Jehu (II Kings 9. 7–9); he refers in both passages to similar oracles *from his pen* against Jeroboam I and Baasha' (p. 406. Italics mine).

The process is thus described as an artificial literary device, from an author lacking in imagination.

A more positive view concerning prophetic sayings in the books of Kings is taken by von Rad in his *Studies in Deuteronomy*. He says that 'the sources of the quotations are in general to be traced to genuine prophetic words',[8] and points to the rhythmic form and non-deuteronomic pictorial phraseology[9] as indications of their genuineness. Yet even von Rad considers that 'the sources available to the Deuteronomist cannot have been very abundant'[10] otherwise he would not have quoted this saying three times. In other words, von Rad too describes the handling of the prophetic material in terms of a conscious literary process. Since insufficient illustrative material was available to the compiler, he found himself compelled – rather unimaginatively we may think – to use the same saying three times over. Why, we may wonder, did he not use this saying twice, and duplicate another oracle, instead of using one three times? Was he really so unimaginative as all that?

Yet only a few lines earlier in his book, von Rad had stated that 'we tend to overestimate the freedom with which ancient writers handled traditional material', which suggests that he expects to find some reluctance in the Deuteronomic historian to invent, or to treat traditional matter with any degree of freedom. Is there not then a possibility that the historian knew what he was doing when he presented this oracle three times over? May not the solution be found in a third, more positive, view of the material?

This view would be that we are dealing neither with spontaneous and independent inspiration, nor with conscious and deliberate literary usage, necessitated by paucity of material. We are dealing with the creative handling of what is seen to be the word of God. This is not 'gratuitous' insertion of a divine sentence of judgment, nor is it unimaginative repetition. It is the recognition of a pattern in events, and of the vitality of the word of God delivered by the prophets. The question is not: Did one of these prophets originally utter this oracle, and has it then been wrongly, even if not altogether inappropriately, attributed to both the others? It is rather: Is there not here a divine judgment, proclaimed by the agency of a prophet, a word of God, which has its validity not only in relation to one event but to several? For the message delivered from God to man cannot be of merely limited application; it belongs to the divine will, however much its expression is conditioned by the human agent through whom it comes and the historical moment to which it belongs. The element of truth within it cannot but be of enduring value.

Thus we may see, when a divine utterance appears more than once, that each occurrence has its own validity. As so often, theological truth may be expressed in the words of Lewis Carroll; as was said by the Dodo at the conclusion of the caucus race: 'Everybody has won and all must have prizes.'[11] In each case, the divine oracle has its message, and the application of one word to three different situations proves not the versatility of the transmitter, certainly not his threadbare imagination, but rather his sense of its vitality and meaning as comment on the pattern of history. The fundamental theological premise here involved is one of those which underlie the whole Deuteronomic history, namely that the kingship of the Northern kingdom is apostate, illegitimate. If this be granted, then the appropriateness of this threefold judgment, whether already found in the traditional material which the historian utilized, or creatively fashioned into it by the historian himself, is immediately apparent. The three dynasties of that kingdom, up to the moment of the prophetic revolution under Jehu – that of Jeroboam I, that of Baasha, and that of Omri – all fell under the same divine condemnation and came to the same bitter end. To each of them the same judgment was proper, though the historian expounded it differently and made an appropriate setting for it. The dynasty which followed these – that of Jehu – is differently treated by the historian, for this dynasty was brought into being at divine command through the agency of the prophet Elisha, though too late for any radical change to be made in Israel's apostate life.[12]

Such a tracing of the theological motive underlying the handling of his source material by the Deuteronomic historian reveals something of his methods. It also suggests a sharp contrast between the unsympathetic extremism of literary criticism and this more positive appraisal of the homiletical method of editors and glossators. The drawing of such a contrast is, of course, unjust to much that has been said and written in Old Testament commentaries. Yet the popular notion still persists in many circles that an editor must be heavy-handed, and that a glossator, a copyist, an interpreter, must inevitably have less spiritual apprehension than the original prophet or psalmist or other religious teacher whose works he 'contaminates' with his own pedestrian comments. If I draw this caricature, it is because such views are often laid to the charge of Old Testament scholarship, in many cases with little justice. It is true that terms like 'genuine' and 'non-genuine' are used to distinguish between what a commentator regards as the original, authentic words of a prophet, and what he regards as later elaboration. Such terminolology is not, however, to be understood as expressing a value-judgment; it is simply a convenient description. That the elaborator may be a creative personality ought to be immediately apparent to anyone who considers, for example, the generality of ancient Near Eastern mythology and compares it with the theological elaboration of that material and its reinterpretation in the opening chapters of Genesis and elsewhere in the Old Testament.[13]

Such a harsh judgment on interpreters and editors is applied with particular frequency to the Deuteronomic historians. They have not infrequently been depicted in rather uncharitable terms, accused of rewriting the history of their people for their own ends. They are said to have boosted up a reform which was to the advantage of their own party – the reform of Josiah. Somehow, though it is not easy to be sure how, they were hand in glove with the Jerusalem priests who wanted all the local sanctuaries closed down so that they could enjoy all the benefits of the sacrificial system for themselves.

Yet surely Köhler in *Der hebräische Mensch*[14] was nearer the mark when he pointed to the homiletical tendencies of the Deuteronomists. Were they not in this sense the successors of the eighth-century prophets, in that they preached the law in Deuteronomy itself, and preached the history in the books that follow?[15] To them the word of God delivered to the prophets, the word of God delivered through whatever agency, was of enduring validity. It was applicable not to one situation alone, but to many. Nor was it merely a case of taking an old prophetic saying and applying it to a new situation, any more than the Deuteronomic handling of the law meant the mere bringing up to date of ancient law codes. These men had inherited the creative principle which underlies prophecy. To them the word of God was alive, full of meaning, vitally important to every generation. They dared to say to their contemporaries:

Not with our fathers did the LORD make this covenant, but with us; who are all of us here alive this day (Deut. 5. 3).

So law was preached, and prophecy became the text of sermons – of which the three passages in I Kings 14, 16 and 21 are but examples, with the prophetic saying not just a text on which to hang a homily, but a living word of God which could not but have meaning in a new situation, and indeed as indicating the unity within the whole course of Israel's history.

II

Now it is most improbable that this way of regarding the word of God was entirely new with the Deuteronomists. Köhler indeed remarks on the developed technique which we there discover. 'Where we meet with it, the sermon style is already mature and fully developed. It must therefore have come into being earlier'.[16] It is worth while to ask whether we can discover whence this creative handling of the divine word was derived, and we may best begin by looking at the prophetic material in the Old Testament, since it was with the exegesis of prophecy that we began our discussion.

We may first consider the evidence provided by a famous passage in Jeremiah 36, recognizing that in its present form it is not far removed in date from the Deuteronomic history, though its evidence may nevertheless be of interest in determining the exegetical method. This is the story of the dictation by Jeremiah of a scroll of prophecies, which was then read in the temple by Baruch and subsequently burnt by King Jehoiakim.

It is my intention merely to point to one aspect of the story and the information which it provides. At a certain date, namely 605/ 604 BC, when Nebuchadrezzar, the crown prince of Babylon, had defeated the Egyptians at Carchemish, had taken his father's place on the throne, and was soon to receive the submission of 'all the kings of Hatti' – Syria and Palestine[17] – Jeremiah was moved by God, by what precise impulse we do not know, to dictate a scroll of 'all the words that I have spoken to you against Israel and Judah and all the nations, from the day I spoke to you, from the days of Josiah, until today' (36.2). Now it is idle speculation to ask what precisely were the prophecies written in this scroll, though it seems not unlikely that they included words of judgment and exhortation, speaking of the foe from the North that was to come, and warning the people of the desperate state in which they were living. The message included an appeal for a change of heart (36.3). Idolatry and social and personal evils find a large place in the opening chapters of the book of Jeremiah, and judgment by an enemy from the North (cf. 1. 13–15) is prominent too. This is the kind of material the scroll contained.

We are, however, given a further clue to the contents of the scroll in ch. 36 itself. When Jehoiakim had burnt the scroll and Jeremiah prepared to dictate it afresh, he was told to add a specific oracle against the king, and here it is recorded that Jehoiakim had said, concerning the scroll whose words he had had read to him:

Why have you written in it that the king of Babylon will certainly come and destroy this land, and will cut off from it man and beast? (36. 29).

Thus it appears that just at this precise historical moment – we cannot be sure whether it was before or after Jehoiakim had made his submission to Nebuchadrezzar along with his fellow-princes in Palestine – Jeremiah dared to reiterate his earlier words of judgment, and proclaimed it to be plain now that Babylon was the instrument of divine judgment.[18] In other words, he saw that there was a pattern in events, and that the word of God which he had spoken earlier was now vitally relevant.[19] The new situation demanded the restating in new terms of a message already delivered.

Thus the exegetical method which we have seen in I Kings is to be found not merely in the book of Jeremiah, but as a clear element in his prophetic method. Whereas in other prophetic books we may infer that such an exegetical principle is operative, here it is quite plainly indicated. We may plausibly suggest that Ezekiel too, after the fall of Jerusalem, expounded afresh the message he had so vigorously given before the disaster; for the judgment itself changed his perspective and brought a new need for a statement of the purpose of God towards his people. Something of the homiletical material in the book of Ezekiel may with reason be attributable to the prophet's own exegesis.[20] We may infer that the same method underlies the presentation of the prophecies of Zechariah, with visions expanded with the aid of other prophetic material, some of which may well be of earlier origin.[21] But these are inferences rather than statements of what can be fully documented in the actual accounts. They, together with Jeremiah and the Deuteronomic history, suggest that the homiletical tendency was growing, and that during the exilic period it became particularly strong. This is important for the study of the evolution of Hebrew worship and for the eventual appearance of the synagogue, and it offers a clue in the tracing of that otherwise so obscure development.

We may, however, trace the process of exegesis further back. As

far as the eighth-century prophets are concerned, we have few
indications of the processes which underlie the formation of their
books. Here I want to point to two important passages, both in
Isaiah. The first is in Isaiah 8 (fully and usefully discussed by D.
R. Jones[22]) where v. 16 runs:

$$\text{ṣôr } t^e \text{ 'ûdāh} \qquad \text{ḥ}^a \text{tôm tôrāh } b^e \text{limmūdāy}$$

perhaps to be rendered as:

> 'Bind up the testimony,
> seal the teaching among my disciples'.[23]

This has its own special significance to which I wish to return in
a moment. The second is in Isaiah 28, where we find in vv. 1–4 an
isolated oracle concerning the drunken leaders of Ephraim, living
in Samaria (as is clearly indicated by the imagery), brought into
close relationship with words against the rulers of Jerusalem
(vv. 7ff.). That this may be due to the editors of the prophetic
material cannot be denied, but it is significant that a similar
collocation of ideas is to be found in Micah, where the opening
chapter points the warning of disaster to Jerusalem, because of the
disaster which overtakes Samaria (1.5–9). Only twenty years
elapsed between the fall of Samaria and Sennacherib's siege of
Jerusalem in 701; the earlier prophecies of both Isaiah and Micah
upon the people of Samaria would find ready application to the
situation which then faced Judah. Micah foresaw an equally
complete disaster (3.12). What Isaiah's message was, is less easy
to discover, and I do not propose to attempt a discussion here of
the complex issues involved.[24] That he saw a relationship between
the two events there seems no good reason to doubt.[25]

The suggestion may not unreasonably be made on the basis of
this, that some at least of the prophets viewed their message as
having significance not for one moment alone, and saw it as
applicable to new situations as they occurred. The impetus to
exegesis lies in the prophet's own handling of the word of God.[26]

III

Here we have then a clue to the processes of Old Testament
transmission. But we must take the point a stage further, to draw
from these passages their full significance. Birkeland has written:

> '. . . only what somehow found a hearing, what showed itself in

the course of time to be effective and relevant in the life of the community, was handed on till the time of written fixation'.[27]

I should be inclined to put this in a somewhat less rigidly oral form than he does, but I have no doubt that such an unconscious process is involved. That which is transitory, applicable only to one moment, is lost; and of the prophet's words there survives but a fragment.[28] But to that unconscious principle must, I believe, be added a conscious, positive principle. The prophet himself is to be viewed not simply as the great creative personality to whose impulse a line of thought and a tradition of sayings is due. He himself in some measure may be held consciously to direct the handing on of this message. He may – as Isaiah is described as saying – commit his words: 'bind up the testimony, seal the teaching' (Isa. 8. 16), among his disciples. This may or may not refer to a written document. The metaphor is evidently from the written document, sealed and tied. That Isaiah could use a similar method of attesting his words for future reference is seen in 8. 1–4. But what I propose to say in a moment about oral methods of teaching seems to me to argue for 'oral committal' and the injunction to preserve a tradition rather than a document, though this does not exclude the possibility that written collections of prophecy could also have existed.

It would be possible to illustrate this also from the New Testament tradition, by suggesting that Jesus' special training of his disciples – expounding to them in private all that he taught in public (Mark 4.34) – constitutes a most important element in the formation of the gospel tradition.[29] We may consider rather two or three other indications in the Old Testament of this deliberate transmitting of teaching. We have Jeremiah's dictation of a second scroll, with its extra oracular material. Was this perhaps handed into the safe keeping of Baruch the scribe (cf. also Jeremiah 45)? We have the commissioning of Elisha by Elijah, to carry out the tasks which were to be undertaken after Elijah's death (I Kings 19. 15ff., cf. II Kings 2). Here we have perhaps an element of a testamentary kind, as in David's last words to Solomon in I Kings 2, and paralleled by the death-bed blessings of Old Testament patriarchs (e.g. Genesis 49).

There is other evidence which is relevant to the question. Too often a rigid separation has been made between different types of

Old Testament material. We have suffered from the unwholesome separation of prophet and priest – and largely because of a too literal interpretation of the violent denunciation by certain prophets of priestly failure. We still suffer from the isolation of Old Testament wisdom; it does not fit readily into the pattern of *Heilsgeschichte* which has come to dominate so much Old Testament theology, and is therefore often left on one side. Yet we ought to be warned by the statement in Jer. 18.18 (cf. Ezek. 7.26) where prophet and priest and wise man appear side by side, mediators of the divine will, and recognize the intimate interconnections of the various agencies both for receiving the divine word to men and for instructing and exhorting obedience to it. For the functions of all three are essentially one, and all derive from the early-felt need to establish blessing and well-being and to keep the supernatural powers favourably disposed. They all contribute to šālôm.

The aspect of the wisdom literature which is here relevant is that of 'education'. It belongs to the form of wisdom where we meet it as early as the middle of the third millennium in Egypt, directed towards instructing men in the way they should go:

Then he said to his son:
  Let not thy heart be puffed up because of thy knowledge;
  Be not confident because thou art a wise man.
  Take counsel with the ignorant as well as the wise.
  The full limits of skill cannot be attained,
  And there is no skilled man equipped to his full advantage.[30]

> My son – says the wise man
> Hear your father's instruction,
>   And reject not your mother's teaching
>   (Prov. 1. 8; cf. 2. 1–2; 3. 1 etc.)

The form is ancient: the method of instruction essentially oral. The injunction to hear and receive the words of the wise, to preserve them, to treasure them – all these are indications of the deliberate process by which the word of God may be preserved. It is the method still used centuries later by the Jewish rabbis, whose words were remembered in the form: Rabbi N. said . . ., for thus it had been heard and learned.

This educational method, in which repetition plays a part, is marked especially by the strongly moralizing tone in which much of it is couched. There is here no dry-as-dust account of behaviour, manners, good morals, but an exhortation, strongly accented by warning, example, and with indications of the blessings which follow from obedience and the dangers which attend the unwary.[31] In the opening part of Proverbs, the whole process is vividly maintained with a picture of Wisdom as the expression of God's activity as counsellor,[32] directing aright the steps of the young man, and guarding from the evil seductress whose ways are described in terms reminiscent of a bawdy tale and of the alien religious practice to which Israel was so exposed.

When we find an association of wisdom with the period of Hezekiah,[33] the king who figures so prominently in the Isaiah tradition, it does not seem unreasonable to see this particular period as a moment at which the drawing together of the homiletical tendencies of the prophetic schools and of the wisdom movement resulted in the fostering of that process of exposition of the divine word, so clearly to be seen in the sermonizing words of the Deuteronomists and later in the equally homiletical Chronicler.

IV

In the development of the Old Testament tradition we may see creative personalities – of whom the prophets may be most plainly depicted – and their successors, the disciples, the preachers, the exegetes, the educationists. The word of God, spoken in law and prophecy, in wise precept and in psalm, becomes the subject of the sermon. To quote Köhler again, who describes the sermon as 'the greatest and best form of human instruction', we may see that the 'sermon follows on the prophets and prepares the way for the transformation of life according to the ideas which the prophets were sent to formulate. It spreads abroad among the population the gold of the revelation, in small change and not always without a certain lowering of value'.[34]

That a 'lowering of value' may take place is evident enough. Yet, as I have already suggested, the reapplication of a divine word to a new need or situation does not necessarily involve this. In so far as it arises out of a sense of the vitality of that word, and so of its continued significance, there may be not a lowering of value but rather an extension of meaning. For the application itself reveals not only something about the vitality of the word of God as declared by its first exponent, but also something of the personality and faith of the 'preacher'.

Moreover, this reapplication has a certain point in common with the original prophetic utterance, namely its vital apprehension of the historic moment at which the word of God is found to be relevant. The Old Testament awareness of history as the sphere of divine activity is to be found not only in the way in which a prophetic word belongs in a historic setting, but in the way also in which a prophecy or a law or a psalm may be seen to illuminate some new moment of history.[35]

The study of the Old Testament involves us in much more than the attempt to discover what its ideas are; and more than an attempt to say who were the authors of particular books. It also goes far beyond the form-critical attempt to discover to what situation in life a particular passage may be assigned. It involves the illumination of a living process, the life of a real community in which the word of God has been not merely handed down, but creatively applied. Each point in the process is historically conditioned, and, though the full description is clearly not possible, ideally we ought to be able to say of a particular passage not only that it came into being on such and such a historic occasion, whether national or personal, but that it was re-used and elaborated, annotated or expounded, in such another situation or situations, by men who were real people and whose faith has itself contributed to our understanding of the nature of God and his purpose.

Inevitably our knowledge is too limited for such full-scale description. Such reconstructions as we make are tentative and conjectural. We may generalize, but cannot particularize. We may see that the words of Isaiah have been reapplied to the fall of Jerusalem in 587, and see their reinterpretation in the light of that event. Yet we cannot depict with precision those whose faith made that reinterpretation possible.[36] We may suggest that the words of Haggai and Zechariah have been reapplied to the urgent problems of the Samaritan schism, and yet hesitate to say just what is the relationship between this reapplication and the Chronicler's approach to the same problem.[37] We may see that a psalm, originating perhaps in cult practice and possibly deriving from pre-Israelite patterns, has been held to be meaningful in a fresh way in the situation of exile, or in the distresses of religious persecution in the time of Antiochus Epiphanes;[38] yet our portraits of its users will be shadowy.

Yet in this recognition of the twofold aspect of the Old Testament material, we may rediscover its meaning for ourselves, and its place within the organic tradition to which we belong; for it derives from a combination of the living word of God with the response of a real community of men. We know only a few members of that community; our picture of the Old Testament people is therefore limited to a description, or attempted description, of the great personalities. Yet with them, alongside them all the time, is the people to which they belonged; anonymous but not to be regarded as consisting of mere nonentities; aroused to faith no doubt by the deeper insights of a Moses or an Elijah, an Isaiah or a Jeremiah, but not just blind followers. They form the rich heritage into which we enter.

When we approach the Old Testament, we may wonder not only at the immense amount of scholarship which is devoted to the study and elucidation of so small a body of material, but also at the power which the Old Testament has always possessed, in spite of all its obscurities, of speaking to men of faith. In academic discussions we may sometimes lose sight of this effective process, from faith to faith. Yet it is a perpetual challenge to us to realize that our understanding of the Old Testament will in fact only grow as we can enter into its experience. In appreciating the reality of the situations in which its message was used and re-used, and the reality of the people to whom and through whom it spoke a living word of hope, we may ourselves discover the secret of its vitality and hear the message which it has to speak to ourselves.

V

An an earlier point I interrupted the main argument to criticize the unduly harsh treatment of editors and glossators which has sometimes crept into the discussion of Old Testament material. I hope that this more positive appraisal of the processes of interpretation may serve to rehabilitate somewhat the humble circles of followers, the pious priests and scribes and teachers of post-exilic Judaism who laboured with much devotion and insight to preserve the word of God whose vitality they felt so intensely. A fuller and better appreciation of this later period is an essential part of our understanding of the text of the Old Testament which it is our concern to interpret.

I hope too that this positive view of the Old Testament tradition and of its vitality may serve to counteract that other deadening tendency, the approach to the Old Testament which has an ulterior motive. It would, of course, be possible to go on from this point to treat of the creative handling of the tradition which marks the New Testament rediscovery of the faith, and its expression in the values of Christian theology. Yet to do so might well obscure the vitality of the Old Testament faith in its own right, and so to reduce the Old Testament – as it is so often reduced in Christian practice – to a collection of tales for illustration, or of morals unnaturally applied, or even to a museum of antiquarian beliefs and practices.

That the Old Testament word of God points beyond itself is true, but what it points to is not some particular series of events as such, but the reality of God, the God whose nature and purpose are revealed in the whole *Heilsgeschichte* and not just in its final act. If it has not infrequently been found healthy for the Christian Church to re-examine its New Testament foundations, it may not be inadvisable for us to be continually reminded that the foundation events of the Christian faith are themselves rooted in a tradition which claims to be no mere dead record of what is over and past, but a living contact between God and man, established and attested within the pages of human history. To interpret the Old Testament tradition without being aware of this will inevitably mean that we miss the vitality of its utterances and the real nature of the processes by which it was shaped.

II

ASPECTS OF THE PROPHETIC
TRADITION

6

Isaiah 1–12: Presentation of a Prophet

The completion in 1972 of the first part of Hans Wildberger's commentary on Isaiah, extending to nearly 500 pages for the first twelve chapters of the book,[1] would suggest a measure of impertinence on my part in proposing in this relatively short discussion to deal with the same group of chapters. On a *pro rata* basis, it might be thought more judicious for me to devote the whole of my time to the consideration of one half verse! But the task which I have set myself is not that of commentary. It involves some wider considerations regarding the nature and function of Isaiah 1–12. It also involves questions which go beyond not only 1–12 but also 1–39, and which indeed raise doubts about the propriety of a method which makes the assumption, as so many commentaries and works of introduction do, that it is possible to consider Isaiah 1–39 as a book separate from the whole in which it is now contained. Such an assumption is so commonly made that it is well to examine once again its propriety and justification.

I

James Barr in his book *Fundamentalism*, in the context of considering how what he terms 'residual fundamentalism' survives, points to the belief in such circles that 'the whole book of Isaiah is still somehow linked to the prophet of that name'.[2] Elsewhere he discusses what he terms 'maximal conservatism', that process by which, if it is forced upon the conservative scholar that, for example, Moses really cannot be responsible for the book of Deuteronomy as it stands, then that view of its origin is to be preferred which takes it back nearest to his authorship (pp. 85–9).

So too what he says about the view of the book of Isaiah as 'somehow linked to the prophet' may be seen as an example of the way in which traditional authorship and hence traditional authority may be regarded as upheld, even where the findings of ctitical scholarship inevitably force the recognition that the book of Isaiah is really not all of one piece.

The problem arises when we begin to attempt a definition of that phrase 'somehow linked'. So much of critical scholarship is still geared to the classic formulations that it is sometimes felt to be hardly necessary to concern ourselves with such apparently outmoded lines of thought. I propose to raise some of these questions because I consider them important; I do not for one moment fear that anyone will suppose that I am thereby disclosing myself as a biblical fundamentalist, though I may have to accept the dubious distinction of being misquoted as having abandoned one of the key points of critical scholarship.[3]

The division of the book of Isaiah into two major sections, 1–39 and 40–66, has withstood the test of time; the further subdivision of the latter into 40–55 and 56–66 less well, and the problem of interrelationship between those two sections remains unresolved.[4] The points of linkage between chapters (34) 35 and 40–55 or 40–66 raise important questions;[5] much of the more recent work on 1–39 has pointed to very considerable difficulties in the way of the oversimple subdividing of that part of the book.[6]

So far as the formation of the whole book is concerned, it is impossible to be satisfied with what we may term the 'accident' theory. It is mere supposition to suggest that, assuming a normal lower and upper limit for the length of a scroll, there were four prophetic scrolls containing respectively Isaiah 1–39, Jeremiah, Ezekiel, and the Twelve, and that of these texts the first, being so much shorter in compass, resulted in a large empty space, and that this was filled, arbitrarily, by the insertion of another collection of prophecy, eventually to be known as chapters 40–66.[7] A more careful expression of this by O. Eissfeldt runs as follows: '. . . our book of Isaiah, in addition to the sections which are at least in the main concerned with the prophet of the second half of the eighth century BC who bears this name (or are regarded as concerned with him), namely 1–39, contains also the two complexes 40–55 and 56–66. These belong to a substantially later date, and . . . were only secondarily added to 1–39 and so came to be ascribed to the eighth-century prophet.'[8] There is some question-begging here. It is, of course, true that the two complexes 40–55 and 56–66 are of 'a substantially later date' than the prophet Isaiah whose activity belongs to roughly 740 to 700 BC. But study of 1–39 has shown how complex a structure this is, and even if extremes of late dating are dismissed – partly now because of the Qumran scrolls – it can hardly be supposed that its compilation really antedates the compilation of the one or two further complexes in 40–66. This could be shown by a consideration of a whole range of recent literature, but it will be convenient to point to the study of H. Barth[9] which attempts to trace aspects of the process by which 1–35 (39) reached its present form. His main concern is with an 'Assyrian' redaction which he associates with the period of Josiah's successes and the collapse of Assyria, 621–614 or 616 BC. But in the process, he suggests (and illustrates diagrammatically) stages in the evolution of 1–35 down to the post-exilic period. The whole discussion works from the assumption that such a division of the book is a primary datum for its examination. At the very end of his study, he expresses the 'accident' theory in a new manner, in the form of a question to which further research is invited. 'The redaction-history of the book of Isaiah was not indeed at an end with the formation of the complex 1–35. Along with the historical appendix of 36–39 there were added 40–66, and it is a difficult question to decide on what grounds this last extension was undertaken. Is it possible – and this final point is put forward with the utmost caution as one for discussion – that we here have an attempt at structuring the book of Isaiah in the familiar three parts known already from Ezekiel and Jeremiah (LXX): 1 (2)–12 doom for his own people; 13–35 (39) themes concerning foreign nations; salvation for his own people?' (p. 232 – my translation). This represents an attempt at giving some sort of rationale for the accident theory; but that is what it remains. The motivation for the addition of 40–66 is external to the book, based here, very tentatively, on the analogy of the book of Ezekiel and one form (LXX) of the book of Jeremiah. But is the analogy valid? Granted that the LXX form of the book of Jeremiah places the foreign nation oracles in the middle, it is very difficult to maintain that the division of the book really corresponds to such a schema as is often proposed for such a tripartite form. Indeed one may wonder whether the two forms of the book of Jeremiah, whichever may be

held to have priority, do not indicate rather the existence of two
basic Jeremianic collections, totally different in kind, to which the
foreign nation oracles have been added in two different manners:
(1) Jeremiah 1–25 which is in character much more like other
prophetic books, and which reaches its climax in the pronouncement of judgment on Babylon and on the nations (25) – the LXX
form provides in part a substitute for this last point and in part a
very elaborate extension of it; and (2) Jeremiah 26–45, which
consists of a collection of narratives illuminating the disaster
(26–36) plus an appendix which is a variant form of the end of II
Kings (37–44)[10] plus a colophon in 45 which is closely linked to
36. The MT form of the book apparently has no regard for the
supposed tripartite division. Why does the MT ignore the pattern,
if indeed such a pattern exists?

The book of Ezekiel comes nearest to the pattern, but it must be
noted that even here 1–24 is not totally doom and 33–39 is certainly
not totally salvation; and the appendix in 40–48 does not come
satisfactorily within that term. An analogy for the supposed
tripartite arrangement may be sought in the book of Zephaniah
where we may divide 1.2–2.3 as doom to Judah; 2.4–3.10 as doom
for the nations; 3. 11–20 as salvation for Judah: but this too is less
than certain.[11] Amos has the foreign nation oracles at the beginning;
Nahum, if it may be included, has its one such complex at the end;
Obadiah has a pattern of doom on Edom followed by restoration
for Judah. Is there really adequate evidence for such a supposed
pattern at all? And certainly in the book of Isaiah, while it is true
that there is a collection in 13–23 (27) which is primarily concerned
with foreign nations, it is not in fact so limited, having, uniquely
among such collections, two passages – 20 and 22. 15–25 (and
possibly we should add also 22. 8b-11 and the curious and
problematical 14. 28) [12] – which introduce the direct activity of the
prophet (not actually mentioned in 22 but implied because of the
reference to the contemporaries Shebna and Eliakim);[13] nor can it
be properly said that 1–12 is really entirely doom on Judah, nor
that 13–35 (39) is concerned only with the nations, and even 40–66
has elements of doom, particularly in 56–66. These generalizations
do little that is satisfactory in the categorizing of prophetic material.
The whole tripartite pattern appears to be a modern invention.

There is a further supposition which needs a question. It is the
commonly affirmed belief that, to quote Eissfeldt again, '. . . The

presence of 36–39 . . . shows that at one time the book of Isaiah must have ended with 35. The narratives have been appended at the end of a book' (p. 408; ET p. 304). There is a one analogy and one only for this: the presence of Jeremiah 52 as a historical appendix at the end of the book of Jeremiah. But this differs in a marked respect from Isaiah 36–39. Jeremiah 52 contains no reference to the prophet; it is an extract from the last part of the books of Kings, in a recension slightly different from that which we have there.[14] It does not show that remarkable intertwining of the activity of the prophet with the course of events which is so important a part of Isaiah 36–39. This equally is an extract from a particular recension of the books of Kings; equally it shows important differences.[15] But here the figure of the prophet has already come to occupy a primary place, and the passage is much closer in form and style to Jeremiah 37–44 which may itself be regarded as such an extract, but from a fuller and more elaborate recension of Kings than that which we know directly (see n. 10). The analogies we have for the insertion of prophetic narrative material, in prophetic books, suggest their placing at significant points, designed to illuminate the context into which they are put. The function of Isaiah 36–39 must be discussed separately;[16] I have elsewhere examined some aspects of the function of Amos 7.9–17.[17] Some further comments will be made below on Isaiah 6. 2–9. 6. A consideration of the Isaiah narrative material in chs. 20 and 22 could throw light on why those passages stand where they do and what function they may be held to perform. There is a possible connection here between the structuring of the prophetic books and the function of prophetic narratives in the Deuteronomic history.[18]

II

These considerations are preliminary to the asking of a fundamental question: Why is there so substantial a book associated with the prophet Isaiah? The accident hypothesis is in reality ruled out partly by the various critical considerations just raised, but also by the fact that the interrelationship between the various elements in the book is such as to point to some degree of affinity or influence or connection of thought and language.[19] It is not in any way to concede the fundamentalist position if we recognize that the arguments for the unity of Isaiah, inadequate as they are,

are not mere figments of conservative imagination. There are linkages between all parts of the book.[20] I do not propose to pursue the matter here, but simply cite as examples two points: (1) the often noted use of the expression *qᵉdôš yisrā'ēl*. If we follow Wildberger's analysis (p. 23), we may observe four occurrences in 1–12 (two 'genuine', two doubtful or later), one in 13–27 (doubtful), five in 28–35 (four 'genuine', one doubtful – all in fact in 29–31), one in 36–39 (also in II Kings); eleven in 40–55; two in 56–66. This expression occurs otherwise only in Jeremiah 50.29 and 51.5 in the Babylon oracles, virtually certainly later than Jeremiah and perhaps to be associated in some degree with the Deutero-Isaianic circle,[21] and in three psalms – 71.22, 78.41 and 89. 19. We may agree with the view that the expression belongs to the Jerusalem cultus, but its marked use in Deutero-Isaiah points strongly to a degree of affinity between that part of the book and Proto-Isaiah. (2) The relationship between 27. 2–5 and 5. 1–7, and that between 11. 6–9 and 65. 25 demand a recognition of the interrelatedness of otherwise quite widely disparate sections. If such alternative uses of the same themes are deemed to be unrelated we may still, as a very minimum, argue for the propriety with which later material – whether in the so-called apocalypse of 24–27, or in the collection in 56–66, or in the glossing, if such it is, of 11. 1–5 with 11.6–9 – has been associated with already existing material whether Isaianic in the sense of 'genuine' prophetic oracles or in the sense of already belonging to an Isaianic tradition. I shall consider a third type of link later.

But the problem still remains: Why, alone among the eighth-century prophets, has Isaiah acquired so enormous a prophetic collection now associated with his name and 'somehow' linked to him? It is begging this question to say, as G. Fohrer does; '. . . in the later period, Isaiah was often considered the prophet par excellence'.[22] That he was so considered is likely itself to derive in part from the very attribution to him of so large a collection; and the fact that traditionally the book of Isaiah heads the 'latter prophets' may be held to contribute to this or to follow from it. We need some evidence to suggest why he came to be so regarded and why this attribution of material to him actually came about. It is towards the answering of this question that I propose now to devote some attention, first in general terms and second in relation to 1–12.

It is of course arguable that Isaiah was the most significant of that astounding group of four men – Amos, Hosea, Micah and Isaiah. But on what basis can such an assertion be made, except by a circular argument from the book itself? The Isaianic corpus itself suggests his greater status, the other collections are modest in extent. But a consideration of the material which may with reason be treated as 'genuine' – a very precarious method, but still a fashionable one – does not immediately mark him out as more remarkable than his near contemporaries. A sober assessment would neither exaggerate nor depreciate his status in that period. But there are some further factors to take into account.

We may perhaps give weight to the fact that Amos and Hosea belong by their message to the now defeated northern kingdom. Yet this disaster to the north could be seen to confirm the validity of their message and this may provide one clue to the process by which that message came to be handed down in a more tangible form than those of their predecessors in the preceding century. Why can we see some indications of continuing influence – Hosea on Jeremiah and Ezekiel, Amos possibly on Isaiah[23] and Zephaniah, but only a modest extension of the collections of oracles associated with them? Micah, associated with a place outside Jerusalem, is often depicted as a prophet of the countryside, set in contrast to the capital. Isaiah is said to be close to the court and the temple, though the evidence for both has been questioned. Did this give him a status, independent of whatever might be his official position, if any, which assisted both the preservation of his message and its amplification? Yet in making this comparison we must take account of the claim made by the tradition preserved in Jeremiah 26. 17–19.[24] Here appeal is made by 'certain of the elders of the land', clearly men of status, to the effect that it was when Micah of Moresheth prophesied in the reign of Hezekiah of Judah, pronouncing doom on Jerusalem and its shrine, that the king, so far from putting him to death, in fact feared Yahweh and propitiated him, so that Yahweh repented of the calamity which he had pronounced against them. Since we have elsewhere a tradition of reform by Hezekiah, simply stated in II Kings 18.4–5 and greatly elaborated in II Chronicles 29–31, but in neither case in any way associated with Isaiah, we might tentatively draw the conclusion that in the tradition utilized by Jeremiah 26, that reform was associated with the activity of Micah. Equally we might postulate some other situation in the reign of Hezekiah, entirely unknown to us, and associate that with Micah's words. But in either case it is evident that for this tradition the status of Micah is extraordinarily high, that is, when we compare it with the status which is suggested by the quite small collection of prophecies associated with his name. Other traces of a broader Micah tradition have been lost, except perhaps for the curious association of his message with a stylized judgment:

> and one kept the statutes of Omri,
>> even all the deeds of the house of Ahab,
>> and you walked in their counsels (6. 16)

a judgment which looks suspiciously like an alternative form to that which becomes the stereotype for Deuteronomic judgment of the northern kingdom.[25] By contrast, the status of Isaiah, while unaltered by the Micah tradition, since the reform is not associated with Isaiah anywhere, is put into a clearer perspective. It was to Micah, not to Isaiah, that later tradition was to attribute a major alleviation of threatened disaster for Jerusalem and its temple.

Now this is a very remarkable fact. It suggests that, whatever the ultimate assessment of these two prophets was to be, there was a moment when it could have been Micah who acquired the greater reputation rather than Isaiah. To redress the balance, we must set over against this the important fact that alone among the prophets, with the sole exception of Jonah ben Amittai in II Kings 14. 25 – an exception which by its equivocal character serves to prove the rule – Isaiah appears in a narrative series in II Kings 18–20 which has a variant form in Isaiah 36–39. I would myself qualify this statement by reiterating that in fact Jeremiah 37–44 provides us with another such integrated narrative, in which the prophet appears bound up with the account and interpretation of the events of Judah's downfall (see n. 10), and more tentatively I would point also to Amos 7. 9–17 for yet a further clue.[26] But neither of these alters the fact that in the form of the Kings text which has come down to us it is the prophet Isaiah who is given a commanding position in relation to crucial events in the reign of Hezekiah: a significant part in the sequence which traces the threats and withdrawal of the Assyrians, and a yet further importance as the prophet of life and death and of ultimate disaster in the exile (see n. 15). We can see in II Kings 18–20 = Isaiah 36–39 the growth of a significant Isaiah tradition, generally recognized as providing us with little information of substance about the actual figure of the prophet, but undoubtedly a vital link in the growth of the concept of his status as prophet. That growth we may associate with his place in relation to the Davidic house and the Jerusalem temple; we may understand it in relation to the evidently historical fact that, in spite of siege and the imminent threat of total disaster, Jerusalem did not actually suffer the fate of Lachish. The Isaiah tradition of these chapters in fact conflicts rather sharply with the doom-laden oracles of what are generally held to be genuine Isaianic material, such as the relentless judgment of ch. 6, the impression created by 1. 4–8 with its possibly appended alleviation in 1. 9, though even that is dire enough, the dark message of 29. 1–8 with Jerusalem brought low, speaking from the earth. Its growth may be in part associated with that aspect of the modification of the Isaianic message which Barth attributes to the Assyrian reaction; the downfall of Assyria, seen in actuality in the latter part of the seventh century, is here projected into the moment of Isaiah's triumphant message to Hezekiah and his taunt-song over the king of Assyria. It provides at the same time a link between that and the moment of judgment in the Babylonian conquest, thus providing for an undergirding both of the prophet's message of doom – it was not to be at the hands of Assyria but at those of Babylon – and pointing beyond to a moment of new life in the use of the illness and recovery, death and life theme, given fuller point in the Isaiah text by the inclusion of the psalm which emphasizes just these themes.[27]

III

Here then we have an important factor in the understanding of how Isaiah acquired status. It is, I believe, of further importance in relation to 40–66, but that I shall not now explore (see n. 16). Before moving on to the next main point that I want to make, I would like to comment briefly on two other lines of thought which may be used to account for the Isaianic corpus and the enhanced status of the prophet.

(1) In a number of recent studies, R. P. Carroll has judiciously examined the value which dissonance theory may have for the interpretation of the prophetic literature.[28] The failure of the prophetic message, the non-fulfilment of pronouncements of doom

or promise, invite the response of transposition of these to a new level, the reinterpretation of particular sayings with reference to situations further into the future. Carroll makes particular use of the book of Isaiah in examining the usefulness of this approach, drawing attention to the totality of judgment in 6. 9–13, contrasting this with the salvation oracles attributed to Isaiah and also to the call to turn from evil in 1.16f.[29] He understands 6 as providing mature reflection on the nature of the prophet's call, suggesting that the failure of his proclamation has been resolved by the affirmation that it was indeed his mission to produce precisely this effect. He further observes that 'this general failure of preaching eventually led Isaiah to retire from active proclamation and to seal up his teaching among his disciples' (8. 16–18).[30] Carroll here contributes to the discussion of the nature of reinterpretation, whether this is undertaken by the creator of the oracles himself or by later editors. He suggests how we may see that the recognition of failure, the non-fulfilment of the message, may itself be a criterion of later success, of confirmation of the validity of the message. Yet it is evident that there must be more to the matter than this. There must be some underlying acknowledgement of the status of the prophet – a status which is not undermined by failure, but which can lead to reinterpretation so that ultimately a pronouncement will be seen to be fulfilled. In other words, the original status of the prophet is a necessary element in the continuing reinterpretation of his words; at the same time that continuing reinterpretation itself contributes to the enhancement of his status by providing confirmation in eventual fulfilment of the validity of what he said. Such an approach contributes to our understanding of the processes of thought by which both the prophet himself and his later editors may be motivated in their handling of material which is problematic; by reinterpretation the prophetic word is given new impetus and the prophet's status is raised. For Isaiah, it would be important to show that the prophet had a recognized status, from which vantage point it became desirable for him and for his successors to offer such an enhancing reinterpretation. To some extent we may recognize the presence of the same problems in the other prophets of the period, particularly in Micah. The approach does not therefore deal fully with the question of why Isaiah is so much enhanced and not Micah.

(2) Allusion is made also by Carroll to a point which has much

engaged other interpreters of Isaiah, namely the committal of his words to disciples in 8. 16–18. For Carroll, this is a good example of withdrawal on the part of one whose message has been found to be unfulfilled, 'of recourse to social support among a group of sympathetic followers whose agreement with the prophet could stimulate him and detract from his failure'.[31] I would not wish to quarrel with the contention that support from others is a necessary element in dealing with the problem of religious isolation. We may see it in the narratives of Elijah, where the claim to total loneliness in his allegiance to God is countered by the evidently symbolic reference to seven thousand faithful (I Kings 19. 14, 18). We may see it in the indications of the tension between isolation and support in the Jeremiah tradition: certain aspects of that tradition stress the dereliction of the prophet, other elements show the degree to which there were those who were on his side – Uriah a like-minded prophet, Baruch a scribe turned associate, the politically powerful family of Shaphan, and even at times the vacillating king Zedekiah. In the case of Isaiah, the evidence is less than clear. Of associates we know of Uriah the priest and Zechariah ben Jeberechiah, 'reliable witnesses' (8. 2) but perhaps 'associates' is too strong a word for these. We know of the '*yᵉlādîm* whom Yahweh has given me' (8. 18), but not whether *yᵉlādîm* actually means 'children' – such as Shear-jashub and Mahershalal-hashbaz – or 'associates, followers, disciples'. The reference in 8. 16 to 'bind the testimony,[32] seal the instruction *bᵉlimmūdāy*' is also obscure. It does not for our purpose matter whether the actions are real or symbolic.[33] The similar expression in 29. 11–12 does not clarify the matter, and in any case looks suspiciously like a reinterpretation of the former. The use of *limmūd* in 50. 4 and 54. 13 point to the meaning 'instructed', as does also Jeremiah 13. 23. The negative interpretation of LXX (*tou mē mathein*) does not help resolve the problem of why the preposition is *bᵉ*, and its negative sense 'so that they are not taught' looks suspiciously like an interpretation in line with 6. 9f.

We are confronted here with two elements of interpretation. There is the commonly held notion that Isaiah withdrew from public ministry. But this is not warranted by the evidence of the text. The fact that we have no historical references in the Isaianic material for the period between the Syro-Ephraimite war in the reign of Ahaz (so 7 and 8) and the threat to Ashdod in 713–711 (so 20) is no basis for the supposition that Isaiah did not speak publicly during that period. We have little basis for allocating prophetic oracles to precise occasions anyway, even if we accept as correct such historical attachments as are provided. There is also here the point of attachment for the often elaborated view that there was a 'school of Isaiah', responsible ultimately for the handing on of his prophetic message, for its elaboration, and in the fullest view of this, providing a context for the activity of his successors in Deutero- and Trito-Isaiah.[34] But such a school is in reality a deduction from the present form of the book.[35] It may find a point of attachment in 8. 16; even if that passage is partly discounted because of uncertainty, we are still in some degree forced both with Isaiah and with other prophets into the view that there must have been those who heard the message and preserved it. There must have been a succession within which the message could be reapplied and reinterpreted. All the discussions of the gradual shaping and reshaping of the Isaianic material, as of other prophetic traditions, points to the existence of such tradents, editors, glossators, and the like. It is to such activity that we owe the prophetic books. But when all that has been said, it is evident that this applies to all the prophetic books, and it still provides no real answer to the problem of why the Isaiah tradition grew to such immense proportions.

I want to suggest that a clue may be found in the actual structure of 1–12, and that this section, separable from what follows, provides a presentation of a prophetic figure and validates his authority in a particular manner.

IV

The structure of the book of Isaiah raises many questions to which answers can be given only very tentatively. The conventional divisions are not entirely satisfactory, with the one clear exception of 36–39, where the fact that these chapters appear in another form in II Kings makes their demarcation obvious. The conventional division after 39 raises difficulties because of the admitted links between the following chapters and 35 at least and probably 34 too.[36] Evidence from structure as distinct from content could prompt a division of 40–66 not as is normally made into 40–55 and 56–66, but into 40–48, 49–57, 58–66, on the grounds that each of these three sections has an identifiable colophon: 48. 22 *'ên šālôm 'āmar yhwh lāršāîm* (there is no well-being for the wicked, says

Yahweh); 57. 21 identically, except for *ʾlôhāy* (my God) for the personal name *yhwh*; and 66. 24, admittedly different, yet making more elaborately the same point that those who rebel against God will know no rest.[37] It is relatively easy to affirm that these colophons are the work of a later editor; less easy to discover what particular purpose was being served by them. It may be more appropriate to ask whether they may not shed light on the structure of the book at one stage of its formation, as markers at the ends of sections.

Division within 1–33 (35) is again clear at certain points only. Titles at 1. 1, 2. 1 and 13. 1 have been seen as indicating the beginnings of sections. I shall consider the first two of these in a moment. The title at 13. 1 coincides with a very marked break in content, introducing the well-defined section which begins here and which is characterized by the repeated use of the technical term *maśśāʾ* (oracle).[38] But where this section ends is open to debate. Conventionally it has been thought that 13–23 offers the foreign nation oracles collection, followed by an 'apocalyptic' section in 24–27. This is then followed by another collection 28–33 (35), built around an Isaianic nucleus.[39] But it must be admitted that there are no very clear lines of demarcation. The so-called foreign nation section includes a number of odd elements: 14. 28 (if the text is correct) introduces a *maśśāʾ* associated with the moment of the death of king Ahaz; 17 (especially vv.4–11) contains elements of judgment on Israel and Judah and an attack on irreligious practices akin to 1. 29–31, and in vv. 12–14 a theme suggestive of the onslaught and overthrow of the nations not unlike both psalm passages which deal with this (e.g. Psalm 46) and the narrative of the overthrow of Assyria in 37; 18. 4 introduces an oracle described as delivered to the prophet presented in the first person: 'Thus Yahweh said to me'; 20 describes a symbolic action performed and interpreted; 22 is a very complex section in which any specific reference is absent in the opening verses, and which then moves over to reflection on Jerusalem's lack of trust in God and reliance on preparations for siege; in 22. 15–25 there are two sections concerned with particular individuals, Shebna and Eliakim. While it is true that 24–27 lack any specific reference, so that various suggestions have been made for identifying particular elements, it can hardly be maintained that this is necessarily more 'apocalyptic' than some of what precedes. And a division between these chapters and 28–33 (35) is again not entirely satisfactory (cf. Kaiser – see n. 38). While we here return to the more specific, in judgments on the north, on Judah and Jerusalem, and in words of promise, we find another of the *maśśā'*-type passages in 30. 6–11, perhaps deliberately transposed to this point. It is difficult not to feel that some passages, particularly in 30–33, are again as much like apocalyptic as are parts 24–27.

By contrast, 1–12 or 1 + 2–12 stand out as clearly marked off. But here there is a further problem. This is the occurrence of titles both at 1.1 and 2.1. The often propounded view that ch. 1 is introductory to the prophecies of Isaiah[40] has certain attractions; yet it may be wondered whether it really is such an introduction, or whether it may not be better understood as a coherent collection of sayings, built of various small units into a structure which can stand alongside other such structures discernible within 1–12.[41] The title at 1. 1 may be designed to cover the whole book – we have seen the uncertainty attaching to the supposition that there was an earlier complete book ending at 35; or it may cover simply the first section, ending at 12.[42]

The title at 2. 1 complicates the issue. Its presence allows the supposition that ch. 1 is a preface added later; it may then be regarded as the title to a small collection, though opinions differ as to how far this collection extends – to some point in 3, 4, 5 or even later.[43] The argument of this discussion would not in fact be fundamentally affected if we were to treat the unit as 2–12 rather than 1–12, but I should like nevertheless to look a little more closely at the occurrence of this title at 2.1 since I believe it may serve to underline the point which I wish to make.

I have argued elsewhere, and still believe rightly, that the title in 2. 1 is instrusive, breaking the more natural link between the oracle of 2. 2–4(5) and the groups of sayings which form ch. 1.[44] So far as I am aware, only Wildberger has devoted some space to refuting this contention (p. 77), but I do not think his arguments are convincing. He makes three points: (1) I suggested that the title is in reality a marginal note, the affirmation of what I described as 'one of the first literary critics', that this oracle, occurring also in Micah 4, is really Isaiah's. Wildberger thinks that 'such a "literary critic" would have made his meaning clear'. It is not evident to me how, lacking the modern practice of footnoting and cross-reference, he could have done this more clearly. The annotator would simply be providing an introduction to the oracle that it is 'the word (*dābār*) which Isaiah ben Amoz spoke concerning Judah and Jerusalem'. It uses *dābār* which makes a good reference to a single oracle[45] rather than *ḥāzōn* (vision; 1. 1) which clearly here designates a whole prophetic corpus or message. (2) Wildberger considers that such an annotator 'would hardly have mentioned Isaiah yet again with his father's name'. But we may note that such apparent superfluity of reference is to be found in II Chronicles 32. 20, 32; 26. 22, as also in Isaiah. 13. 1; 20. 2, and in the parallel texts of II Kings 19. 2, 20; 20. 1 = Isaiah. 37. 2, 21; 38. 1. It would appear that it was more natural to refer to Isaiah with the patronymic than without. The name Isaiah alone, without patronymic, appears in narratives which continue from a mention of the name with patronymic (so II Kings 19. 5, 6 = Isaiah 37. 5, 6; II Kings 20. 4, 7 = Isaiah 38. 4, 21; II Kings 20. 11; 20. 14 (+ *hannābî'* [the prophet]) = Isaiah 39. 3; II Kings 20. 16, 19 = Isaiah 39. 5, 8). The only exception is Isaiah 7. 3, but this too stands in the middle of a narrative, though it is one in which the prophet has not so far been mentioned.[46] On the evidence, it would have been more surprising if the father's name had not been mentioned. (3) Wildberger contends that 'the links of subject-matter between 2. 2–4 and ch. 1 prove nothing, since the theme "Zion" is so very frequent in Isaiah'. This latter statement is true enough, and I did in fact myself point to the not altogether dissimilar structure in 3–4 where a more complex passage dealing with Jerusalem leads up to the promise in 4. 2–6 of what Zion is eventually to be. This does not, however, affect the point that the passage 2. 2–4(5) stands adjacent to ch. 1 where the Jerusalem theme is used, and that this theme does not reappear in the remainder of 2. The question may, in fact, be put another way round by asking why this particular oracle was placed here. It does not properly serve to introduce the rest of 2,[47] but it may be seen to perform a function here in the book of Isaiah not unlike that which it performs in the book of Micah. In Micah the oracle provides a counter to the doom oracle on Jerusalem which reaches its climax at the end of Micah 3; the same oracle in Isaiah 2 provides both a counter to the doom sayings of 1 and a climax to the promises of a new and faithful Jerusalem which appear there in vv. 26–28.

It still seems to me to be more natural to suppose that a later scribe, aware of the double occurrence of the oracle, claimed it for

Isaiah by the simple device of attaching to it a heading almost identical to that in 1. 1, without the chronological information and using *dābār* rather than *ḥāzôn*. But I would wish now to take this further and to qualify my own suggestion somewhat. This insertion may be seen not so much in terms of the activity of a 'first literary critic', but – since I am less than sure that such questions arise except in relation to concerns with authority – rather as part of a process of claiming a particular kind of status for the prophet and a particular kind of authority for this collection as a whole. It is, I believe, geared to the presentation of the prophet as authoritative spokesman.[48]

V

The collection in Isaiah 1–12 is circumscribed by both its beginning and its end. The title in 1. 1 makes this clear, using *ḥăzôn* in a way characteristic of the later handling of the prophetic material. Here the relevance of the same phrase in II Chronicles 32. 32 is clear: the remaining deeds of Hezekiah are recorded in the *ḥāzôn* of Isaiah, within the book of the kings of Judah and Israel. This is the understanding of the whole message and activity of the prophet in one term.[49]

The end of the collection is marked by the appearance in ch. 12 of psalm material. An examination of this suggests some points of interest and relevance. Whatever may need to be said about the earlier stages in the formation of the Isaianic material – and here I have in mind those many studies which have attempted to describe more precisely redactional or interpretative activity and to explore the contexts in which such activity took place[50] – the placing of this psalm material at this point and the clearly indicated new start in 13. 1 invite us to look back over what precedes as a whole. It is also clear that we need to take account of other aspects of the structure of 1–12 in considering this, for if, as seems likely, we may trace within those chapters a number of smaller groupings, even if some are now dislocated, we may need to recognize 12 as having originally formed the climax to such a smaller unit rather than to the whole of 1–12. Such small units may be detected in 1. 2 – 2. 4(5), as just suggested; in 2. 6–22 where the final obscure verse invites contemplation on the frailty and ephemeral quality of human life, contrasted with the immediately preceding recognition of the sole exaltation of Yahweh, using one of the refrain or echo elements of the probably complex structure of this passage;[51] 3. 1–4. 6 forms another such unit, though it is also possible to divide at 3. 15, where 3. 13–15, with their partial reminiscence of Psalm 82, provides a picture of Yahweh as the exalted judge. The structure of the following chapters is more involved,[52] though it has most often seemed proper to see a central unit, 6. 1 – 8. 18 or better 6. 1 – 9. 6, which breaks an already interwoven 'woe' complex (5. 8–24 + 10. 1–4) and a doom poem 5. 25–30 + 9. 7–20), introduced by 5. 1–7 and concluded in 10. 4*b* by the refrain of the doom poem. A convenient link is provided in the 'woe' opening of 10. 5 for a section which extends to 11. 16: judgement on Assyria issues in the theme of new Davidic monarchy, of the gathering of the dispersed, and a second exodus comparable with the first (11. 16); it is to this last that it is possible to see 12 as original colophon, and the exodus echoes make the particular passage appropriate, but we may see a further appropriateness in the passage as linked to the whole presentation of the message of Isaiah in 1–12.[53]

It is commonly held that 12 consists of two short psalms or sections of psalms: 12. 1*b*–3 and 4–6. This division is based largely on the opening of v. 4 which appears to introduce the second extract just as v. 1*a* introduces the first. We may note, however, that these introductory phrases, if that is what they are, differ: 1*a* has the singular verb *we'āmartā* (you will say), 4*b* the plural *wa'ªmartem*.[54] We might have expected two such introductory phrases in the same section to have the same form. The plural of 4*a* might be by attraction to the plural verb of v. 3 (*ûšª'abtem*, you will draw), but then we may wonder whether an alternative division could not be made: 1*b*–2 as one unit in the first person singular, 3–5 a unit in the second person plural. But this leaves us with an isolated v. 6 which uses the second person feminine singular (referring to Zion). Such attempts at analysis strongly suggest that we should better treat the whole passage as a unit, introduced only by the summons of 1*a*. As so often in the psalms, there is a progressive shift in the thought: it moves from the first person spokesman of 1*b*–2, however he may be designated, to the summons to the peoples in 3–5, and from this again to the summons to Zion in 6. Such a progression occasions no real surprise and no awkwardness when the poetic structure and thought are appreciated.[55]

We may then ask whether there is any particular significance in the choice of this psalm passage to stand here, now as colophon[56] to 1–11. We may observe that the passage taken as a whole has some marked similarities to other psalms,[57] notably in vv.2 and 5 to that in Exodus 15[58] and that v.3 could continue the exodus theme of v. 2 by alluding to that of water from the rock,[59] though it may be proper to see here also a reference to the water rituals of Tabernacles.[60] Verses 4–5 utilize the common psalm themes of the exaltation of God and his glorification among the nations; what he has done for Israel is to be of significance for the whole earth. The climax in verse 6 of the rejoicing of Zion uses yet another familiar theme, emphasizing the presence in Zion of the 'holy one of Israel'. A consideration of these themes in relation to the preceding chapters shows some points of interest.[61] The exodus theme is not an Isaianic one, though it is to be found in the clearly later material in 11. 16.[62] We may observe, however, that the final passage in 11. 11–16, which speaks of the gathering of the scattered remnant, provides an echo to the indications of judgment at the hands of both Assyria and Egypt in the preceding material – Assyria most prominently, either directly or by implication, Egypt clearly in 7. 18–19.

The Zion theme of 12. 6 is a clearly Isaianic one, and such a climax to the section is very fitting. The themes of the sole exaltation of Yahweh and of acknowledgement of him and his deeds by the nations, are again used directly or indirectly in 1–11 – the former clearly in 2.6–22 and elsewhere, the latter in 2. 2–4(5) and in 11. 10 and 11.11–16. If, observing the usage of the psalms, we see in the first person singular forms of 12. 1*b*–2 the figure of the king, acknowledging the moment of divine anger which is now past and the restoration which is thus implicit, there is a link to 9. 1–6 and 11. 1–9, as well as to the whole structure of the section 6. 1 – 9. 6.

But quite apart from these rather generalized points, there are two which are more specific. (1) The one is the divine title *qᵉdôš yiśrā'ēl* (holy one of Israel). We have already noted the significance of this title, traceable to Isaianic material and providing a link to the later elements in the book, particularly to 40–55. Here, to be placed alongside the three psalms in the Psalter which use the expression, is another psalm which further exemplifies the context of its use. (2) The other point is the threefold occurrence in vv. 2–3 of the noun *yᵉšû' āh* (salvation), with its clear link to the name of the prophet *yᵉšaʿyāh*, *yᵉšaʿyāhu*.[63] The statistics of the use of the root *yšʿ* show a considerable preponderance of use in the Psalter and in the book of Isaiah, with Judges, Samuel and Jeremiah as the other books in which there is substantial use.[64] Bald statistics are misleading. The frequent occurrence of the root in Judges and Samuel is clearly geared to the presence in those books of numerous narratives which stress how God delivered his people.[65] Usage in the book of Isaiah needs to be described more exactly: the root *yšʿ* is entirely absent from 1–12 apart from 12. 2–3 and the prophet's name. The noun *yᵉšûʿāh* occurs in 25, 26 and 33, none of which can be considered to be genuine Isaiah; it then occurs in 40–66. The hiphʿil of the root occurs in Isaiah 19, 25, 33 (37–38), 35 + 40–66. Only the niphʿal occurs in Proto-Isaiah (30. 15). The noun *yešaʿ* occurs in 17.10 (hardly Isaianic) and in 40–66. Two points may be made about this distribution and its significance. First, it must be observed that the root *yšʿ* is very much a word belonging to psalm-language, and its appearance in Isaiah 12, probably also in 25, 33, 38, and fairly clearly in 35 + 40–66 may be seen as derivable from the psalms which are so clear an influence in these texts. Second, we may ask legitimately whether the large-scale use of the root in the book of Isaiah, outside the genuine Isaianic material (other than the single example of 30. 15 where the word is used in fact in a secular sense 'be safe' rather than with any reference to the idea of divine salvation) may not owe something at least to the actual name of the prophet. How far may we associate one aspect of the development of the Isaiah tradition with the consideration of the significance of that name just as the tradition already contains interpretation and/or reinterpretation of the names Shear-jashub, Immanuel and Mahershalal-hashbaz?[66] We have no means of knowing how the prophet himself viewed his name; the negative evidence of his non-use of the words associated with it implies that it did not enter his thought patterns. But for certain stages of the Isaiah tradition, may we not see here an element in the process by which this one prophet of the eighth century acquired a status which owed something to theological reflection, and thus contributed, alongside other elements, to the eventual primacy of position which he occupied?[67]

If there is validity in these contentions, there is strong inference that ch. 12 provides an interpretative comment on what precedes, drawing out in a final poetic statement the broadest significance of the prophet's person and message. Title and colophon together make a claim for his status, and the inserted note at 2. 1 then stands as an additional underlining of the appeal back from the present structure to the prophet who stands as a shadowy figure of authority in the background.

VI

It must be observed that the information provided by these chapters about the prophet himself is minimal. A typical opening to a commentary[68] on a prophetic book is to attempt an outline of the prophet's life and activity. But certainly in the case of Isaiah, and in fact this is true even of Jeremiah where much more information appears to be available, there is too little tangible evidence, and any presentation of the figure of the prophet is only possible as the one who stands behind the present structure. The information provided by 36–39 cannot be satisfactorily co-ordinated with what else is known, and it is this in part which provides problems for the interpretation of the prophet's person-ality and status. Outside those chapters, only the barest infor-mation is available in 20, and even less in 22. No other direct indication is given of the prophet, who is not mentioned by name after 22 (except for 36–39). In 1–12, apart from the titles, the only section which provides some tangible points of contact with the context of his activity is 6. 1 – 9. 6. This provides an authenticating statement of his divine commission in 6;[69] a brief account of controversy with Ahaz in 7, where we may probably detect two separate elements in vv. 3–9 and 10–17; a symbolic action witnessed, performed and interpreted in 8. 1–4; and an allusive passage in 8. 11–18 which indicates at the outset a moment at which Yahweh 'spoke to me at the taking of the hand', which most naturally suggests a moment of commissioning, and which subsequently, as we have seen, deals with the preservation of the message of the prophet and the status of himself and the *yᵉlādîm* as signs and portents in Israel.

We may observe that this central section provides some historical attachment: it is in the year that king Uzziah died (6. 1);[70] it is in the days of Ahaz, at the time of the Syro-Ephraimite coalition's threat (7. 1–2), a situation also envisaged in the interpretation of the symbolic action in 8. 1–4. While the first of these provides only the barest chronological note – and its precise significance in relation to the material which follows in 6 remains a matter of debate[71] – the reference to the period of Ahaz in 7. 1–2 is of a different kind, being a shorter and variant form of the account of Ahaz' reign which appears in II Kings 16. 1–5. We may note a number of points in this section 6. 1 – 9. 6: (1) the complex nature of the material in 6, with its probable reflection on the interpretation of the prophetic activity of Isaiah;[72] the structure of 7. 1 – 8. 10 in which there is a twofold theme of encounter between Ahaz and Isaiah and a twofold statement of speedy judgment on Aram and Israel in that double material on the one hand and the opening of 8 on the other; (2) the further reflection on the nature of the prophetic commission and message in 8. 11–18, followed by the very obscure passage in 8. 19–23; (3) the final element in this section in 9. 1–6 which may well have been placed thus because it was thought to provide a comment on the status of Hezekiah, already perhaps in this passage beginning to acquire the exalted character which appears more fully in 36–39 and still more clearly in II Chronicles 29–31 and especially in 32.[73] All these suggest that this section of the complex 1–12 is already a highly stylized structure, directed towards establishing the relationship between the prophet Isaiah and successive rulers of the Davidic house. Relationships may be suggested to the themes of the Davidic dynasty as these are set out in II Samuel 7 and 23. 1–7.[74]

VII

It falls beyond the scope of this discussion to attempt more than a brief characterization of the other main sections of Isaiah 1–12, and any such sketch will inevitably do less than justice to the content and function of such smaller units. Nor is it possible here to consider in greater detail indications of the ways in which the units are built up, the separable elements within them, and the problems which arise immediately any attempt is made at judging what parts of the material may be associated more rather than less directly with the prophet of the eighth century. We may observe something of the main elements, treating of larger rather than smaller units for this purpose.

The opening section, which I delineate as 1. 2 – 2. 5,[75] stands now as an appeal and a promise: Jerusalem the unfaithful and judged city of God, over which the lament of 1. 21ff. is pronounced, is to be the true and faithful city, the centre of the religious life of the world. The incorporation in this section of judgment oracles on Jerusalem and Judah, of radical questions regarding the nature and status of the worship of the temple, of attacks on idolatrous practice, makes it appear much more than the often supposed introduction to the book (cf. nn. 40 and 41). Without attempting to resolve the questions which would be raised by pointing to the inclusive structure of the whole book of Isaiah, I would point to the number of points of resemblance between this opening chapter with its appeal and 66, the closing chapter to the whole book, in which comparable radical questions are asked about the temple, about worship: in which judgment is pronounced and a summons issued to the nations to gather to see the divine glory and to acknowledge Yahweh. The final compilers of the book appear to have been sensitive to the import of this opening section and to have echoed it in their conclusion.[76]

The overarching theme of the second section, 2. 6 – 4. 6, is that of judgment upon human pretensions, both in general terms – so especially in 2. 6–22 – and in specific reference to the leadership of Jerusalem and of the supremacy of Yahweh in judgment and his presence in glory in a future purified Zion. The section is punctuated at 2. 22 in a moralizing comment on man, at 3. 13–15 in a judgment scene like Psalm 82 but directed specifically to the rulers of his people for their despoiling of the vineyard which is that people (cf. 5. 1–7), and in 4. 2–6 which provides a counterpart to the themes of 2. 2–5, here expressed not as appeal but as confident statement of the divine will.

As the material now stands, the next elements in the book are broken into two, as has already been noted. The generalized indictment of 5. 1–7 is exemplified in the woes of 5. 8–23 where specific evils are identified and judged, and this is resumed in a general and totally black judgment statement in 5. 24–30, where the opening two verses show the clear links with the remainder of the poem in 9.[77] What follows in 6. 1 – 9. 6 traces both the consistent theme of failure on the part of the royal house and hence of the people, of their disregard of the prophetic message (so in 6. 9–10, 7. 10–17, 8. 5–10, and perhaps also in 8. 19–23*a*). Such royal failure and lack of response is answered in 9. 1–6 in the presentation of a promise of the overthrow of the enemy in a climactic event, and the establishment of a final ruler of the Davidic line. Here is the core of the whole section, in which the question of the status of the prophet and hence the validity of his message is set out; and to this I shall return.

The judgment themes of 5 are resumed at 9. 7 in a combining of stanzas of a long poem of judgment (9. 7–20), with a final woe on the leadership (10.1–4). This in its turn is followed by the interweaving of the theme of divine judgment by the agency of Assyria, and divine judgment upon Assyria. The passage incorporates elements of material picturing the divinely ordered advance of the Assyrians on Jerusalem (so 10. 6–7, (27*d*) 28–32), other elements linked to the depicting of the Assyrians' boastful claims (10. 8–11, 13–14; cf. 36 and 37 for comparable material), now incorporated[78] in a woe-theme on Assyria (10. 5), reflection on its hybris (10. 7, 15), and judgment on it (10. 12, 16–19, 24–26). With these too is incorporated the theme of the restoration of the survivors of the people of God, with their trust now to be absolutely in God himself rather than in the alien power (10. 20–23, and also in vv. 24–26). The section reaches its climax in the contrasting of the overthrow of the most exalted trees (10. 33–34; cf. 2. 13) and the establishment of the Davidic shoot (*ḥōṭer* and *nēṣer*, 11. 1), in a new age of peace and well-being (11. 2–9); this in its turn leads to the summoning of the nations (11. 10), interpreted in terms of the gathering of the dispersed of Israel (11. 11–16) in a new exodus from Assyria. If we look at the whole section, now divided by the inclusion of 6. 1 – 9. 6, we may see that the picture of the vineyard of God's planting which has failed to produce true fruits is answered at the end in themes of total restoration of the people.

To the whole there then comes the colophon of the psalm in 12 which has already been considered.

VIII

The overall impression created by Isaiah 1–12 is of a great wealth of very varied material. There are points at which a good case can be made out for genuine Isaianic sayings; but it is everywhere clear that the words of the prophet have been ordered and amplified to bring them into relationship with subsequent situations. It is not my intention to try to sort out either the genuine from the non-genuine, or the possible situations – reign of Manasseh, period of Josiah's supremacy, moment of Jerusalem's overthrow, loss of the Davidic monarchy as a present political reality, experience of defeat and dispersion, prospect of restoration with the overthrow of the alien power – to which this or that passage may belong, or in which reapplication has been made. I am concerned rather to observe how, in these twelve chapters as they now stand, there is a presentation of the prophet, initiated by the claim of the heading in 1. 1 of the whole message which was delivered, the *ḥāzôn*, which 'Isaiah ben Amoz saw concerning Judah and Jersualem' tied to the period of four kings, Uzziah, Jotham, Ahaz and Hezekiah. That the formula as here presented is late has been clearly demonstrated.[79] Its effect is to direct the reader back from the situation in which he is confronted with the present collection to the moment of the prophet's activity. It is the Isaiah of that historic period who stands behind the message. The presence in these chapters of much that is dark, directed to the theme of judgment and depicting the prophet as himself directly involved in the description of his people as made unable to respond, provides a verifying basis most clear to us in our recognition of the enormous impact on the life and thought of the community of the disaster of the sixth century BC. But in 2. 1, stressing the Isaianic authority of the message of promise of 2. 2–5, and in the colophon, with its emphasis on the salvation of God, echoing the prophet's name, and linked to the variety of hopeful words which intersperse the chapters, there is drawn out most clearly the significance of this prophet, the messenger of doom, now fulfilled, as he is also presented as messenger of salvation. Again, the question whether Isaiah himself was solely a prophet of doom or whether in the context of the involvement which we may detect in him with the themes of Zion and Davidic kingship there was confidence in a nearer or a more distant salvation, remains open to debate. There can be no simple *a priori* judgment of the matter. But as the prophet is presented in these chapters, there is clear evidence of the chiaroscuro by which the prospect of the future is set out against the background of a recognition of failure and doom. Whether the prophet himself or his exegetes were responsible, the prophet appears to us as a man of judgment and salvation.

In the central section of this collection, as we have seen, the prophet is presented as authenticated by his commissioning directly from God, with a message geared to disaster. The obscure word of promise at the end of 6. 13 now provides a pointer forward to the hopeful statements of 9. 1–6.[80] Similarly we are left with an ambivalent impression from the obscurity of the Immanuel sign, which contains both gloomy and hopeful overtones, the former being particularly drawn out in the group of sayings now attached to that sign in 7. 18–25. The emphasis on prophetic commission is again made clear in the allusive wording of 8. 11, and implicit in the preservation of the message envisaged in 8. 16. The prophet and his associates or children become signs to Israel (8. 18).

The question posed earlier in this discussion – Why did so great a tradition come to be attached to this particular prophet? – may in part at least be answered. He has been given that status by the presentation in 1–12. Both the confirmation of his message of doom and the affirmation of the salvation theme associated with his name, provided for the period of exile and its aftermath, with the continuing experience of deferred hope, a clear picture of the reality of the divine word associated with this particular figure.

IX

In a paper in the volume *Beiträge zur Alttestamentlichen Theologie* presented to Professor Zimmerli in celebration of this year 1977, Brevard Childs has offered some reflections on the merely historical tendency of endeavouring to recover 'the *original* meaning of the text as it emerged in its pristine situation'.[81] It is not simply the uncertainties of reconstructing the original situation, the form and impact of the original utterance, which make for the weakness of such a historifying approach, though the difficulties are all too apparent. It is the presence of an underlying assumption about the authority of the divine word which cuts through the problems of discussing how such a divine word can be known to be mediated by assuming the authoritative quality of what is believed to be original. When the ultimate compiler of Isaiah 1–12 invites his readers or hearers to look back to the prophet, it is not with the aim of providing them with some kind of picture of the prophet's activity – for which indeed only minimal information is to be found here – but to show the basis for the acceptance of the present application of what is associated with the prophet to lie in a view of his authoritative status, tied on the one hand to the record of a particular commissioning and on the other hand to the authenticating of the prophet's word in the sequel – that is, in the fulfilment of his word in events, in the continued vitality of that word in new situations. It is in such a perspective that authority for the prophetic word can be claimed; it is, of course, not without its uncertainties, but in that it may be compared with the original situation of the prophet whose claims to speak the word of God do not validate themselves. Indeed the original moment of the prophetic utterance is open to question because of the inevitably unverifiable nature of the prophet's claims.[82] Authentication rests then neither in the reconstruction of the original moment nor in the claim for the particular validity of a subsequent moment of reinterpretation. It rests rather in the continuing process by which prophetic word and receptive hearing interact.

It is clear that there must be a relationship between what is claimed about the prophet and his status here in 1–12 and what may be seen or detected in other literary constructions – in chapters 13–33 with their attachment only very briefly to moments of the prophet's activity or, much more precisely, in the interweaving of narrative and prophetic activity depicted in 36–39. The full impact of that will not be found by harmonization, but by the recognition that the impact of the prophet is to be assessed ultimately through the differing, even contradictory, presentations which are made. Beyond this there will be the whole book now associated with his name, some aspects of which have been briefly touched on in this discussion. It is clear here that questions about the ultimate canonical status of the finished product cannot be satisfactorily resolved without a regard for the stages through which that status was brought about, the appeal in a whole variety of situations, more clearly detectable or only dimly discerned, in which the words of the prophet have been seen to be immediately meaningful. There can be no limiting of the discussion to either end of the process, however much we are forced to recognize the degree to which our discussion is limited by the final form or forms of the text through which alone we have access to the earlier stages. In this, I find myself sympathetic to the re-emphasis in recent years on concern for the status of the canon, but also the attempts at uncovering some of the stages in the process which have marked a good deal of recent writing on the Old Testament.[83] Canon-criticism, as a distinct area of discussion, involves a sensitive appraisal of both the final stages of the according of authority to the biblical writings, and the awareness of the different levels at which this has operated in the eventual determining of the texts handed down to us, stamped with the hallmark of experiential testing in the life of the community to which they belonged.

7

Isaiah 36–39: Structure and Function[1]

It would, I believe, be not inappropriate to give this study the alternative title of 'Isaiah: Prophet of the Exile'. Such a title would readily relate to the earliest attested *external* exposition of the prophecies of Isaiah. I am distinguishing this from our primary *internal* evidence, within the book itself, evidence which is, as is well-known, very difficult to interpret with precision. This earliest external witness is Jesus ben Sira (Ecclus. 48. 17–25). It is, significantly for our discussion of Isaiah 36–39, bound up with a primary consideration of Hezekiah who, with Josiah and David, is listed as a faithful king (cf. 49.4). The passage notes the following elements of Isaiah's activity: it was by his hand that God delivered Judah from the Assyrians (48. 20); Hezekiah stood firm in the ways of David 'as Isaiah the prophet commanded him, the great and faithful prophet, in his vision' (48. 22); 'by his (Isaiah's) hand the sun stood' (48. 23);[2] 'he added to the life of the king' (48. 23); and finally

> 'With a spirit of power he saw the future
>   and he comforted the mourners of Zion,
> To the end of time he shewed things to be,
>   and hidden things before their coming' (48. 24–25).

It is clear that the selection of allusions here is geared to the figure of Hezekiah; we cannot deduce from it any lack of knowledge on Ben Sira's part of other elements in the book of Isaiah. But what is significant is that while he draws his understanding from that presentation of Hezekiah which is to be found both in II Kings and in Isaiah, he reads the story of Hezekiah not primarily in the context of II Kings but in the context of the message of Isaiah, the prophet of consolation and of the future.

I *The Position of Isaiah 36–39*

R. F. Melugin, in his study *The Formation of Isaiah 40–55*[3] sets out some points concerning the relationship between those chapters and what precedes. 40–55 were 'never meant to stand alone'. He argues that 'The closest thing to a setting for chs. 40ff. is the prophecy of Isaiah to Hezekiah in ch. 39 concerning the exile to Babylon'[4], and he cites in support an unpublished lecture by Brevard S. Childs and my own study of II Kings 20/Isaiah 38–39.[5] Melugin believes – though of this I am very doubtful – that there has been a *deliberate* removal of all traces of a historical setting from chs. 40ff.[6] In fact, as he concedes, this is not entirely true: there are two references to Cyrus, and there is enough reference to the fall of Babylon in prospect, to the gods of Babylon and to the general situation, for it to be clear that the historical background is what it has for long now been recognized to be. We may, however, observe that very large tracts of prophetic material lack historical reference. Such references, other than of a very imprecise kind, are very sparse in the whole book of Isaiah (apart from 6. 1 – 9.6 and 36–39), as also, for example, in Jeremiah 1–20. Should we suppose that there has been a general 'deliberate removal' of historical reference? or should we not rather suppose that this is a side-effect of the processes of prophetic exposition underlying the formation of our prophetic books? Precision may have given place to reapplication.

But the main point that Melugin makes is important. By placing chs. 40ff. and 36–39 adjacent to one another, the compiler has enhanced the significance of 36–39 in a quite new direction – and this is not a direction immediately discernible in II Kings – and the context of 40–55 (or 40–66) is given as that of the message of Isaiah, in the dire threat and in the victory over the Assyrians in 36–37, in the threat and promise of 38, with the alleviation of death in life underscored by the psalm incorporated in that form of the text, and in the consequences of Hezekiah's actions in 39 which, as it were, guarantee the exile, and thereby provide an appropriate occasion for 40 ff.

Melugin goes further in another part of his study, though

alluding to the point in his conclusion.[7] He stresses the clear relationship between 40. 1–8 and the material of ch. 6.[8] He recognizes the degree to which both are concerned with actions taking place in the heavenly council[9], seeing in the plural verbs of the opening of 40 a reference to its members.[10] He comments that 'the "I" who is commanded to "cry" (v. 6) is not unambiguously the prophet'.[11] He might have added to this the verbal coincidence of 40.3 in its reference to the *qôl qôrē'* (the voice calling) and 6.4 which refers to the earthquake effect of *qôl haqqôrē'* (the sound of one calling).

We may, I believe, suggest that this reference in 6.4 to *qôl haqqôrē'* is to the deity rather than to the seraphim of 6.3. Such a suggestion can only be tentative and qualified by the recognition that not infrequently in biblical material no sharp distinction is made between the deity and his messenger or his attendant beings.[12] The description in 6.4 is clearly enough of the accompaniments of a theophany: it is when God speaks, at the sound of his thunder (cf. also Ezekiel 1), that there is a shattering effect.[13]

Isaiah's reaction of unacceptability is appropriate to his realization of the presence of the deity and the effect which this produces. The Hebrew would then anticipate in v. 4 what becomes explicit as a description of auditory experience in v. 8. God speaks, the earth moves, man is convicted of impurity; when purification has taken place, he hears again the words of God this time articulated into the demand for response to an already designated office.[14] If the *qôl haqqôrē'* of 6.4 is in reality that of the deity, then the correspondence of this to ch. 40 makes good sense of the latter too. There the opening verses convey the message of comfort (vv. 1–2), and this is continued after the phrase *qôl haqqôrē'*; vv. 3–5 are a further declaration of what is to be done, and the plural subjects of the imperatives would appear to be the same in both cases – members of the heavenly court. Both the almost parenthetic *qôl qôrē'*[15] and the final 'for the mouth of Yahweh has spoken' underline the point that it is the divine word which we are hearing. With great skill the opening of v. 6 plays on the phrase: *qôl 'ômēr* (a voice speaking) – surely the same voice that speaks – with its command *qᵉrā'* which echoes the *qôl qôrē'*. The rhetorical question: 'What should one say?' ushers in not a reply, but a reflection on the contrast between the ephemeral quality of life and the solely enduring quality of the word of God (vv. 6–8), and this in its turn brings out the word of hope in the succeeding verses.[16]

This suggested relationship between ch. 40 and ch. 6 is one pointer towards the understanding of the position of 36–39. With ch. 40 we are thereby presented with what we could call a renewal of the Isaianic commission. But clearly the matter is more complex than this. In a study of Isaiah 1–12,[17] I have pointed out, in considering general questions about the structure of the whole book of Isaiah, that there is no adequate basis for the common supposition that these chapters were added to an already completed first book of Isaiah. Such a book is generally described as being 1–35, though this may well be qualified by the recognition that some parts of those chapters are evidently late – this is particularly claimed for 24–27. It is then assumed that the section 36–39 was extracted from II Kings and placed at the end of the current form of 1–35. This, as generally presented, does less than justice to the complex structure of 1–35, and takes too little account of the degree of interrelationship of language, thought and structure between the various parts of the whole book of Isaiah. It also often takes as analogy the appearance of Jeremiah 52 as a concluding appendix to the book of Jeremiah, without noting the degree of difference between Isaiah 36–39 and that chapter; namely that Jeremiah 52 is virtually a straight variant of the last part of II Kings, whereas Isaiah 36–39, while clearly closely related to II Kings 18–20,[18] shares with that passage and with Jeremiah 37–44 the interweaving of the activity of the prophet with the narrative of the events.[19] Analogy for the placing of these narrative chapters at this point in the book of Isaiah must be sought in the consideration generally of why narratives are placed in prophetic material, what function they perform. This is a general matter which cannot be undertaken here. It must also for each example be done with a due examination of the nature of the material, its particular structure, the function it performs in the context in which it is placed.[20]

If the simple explanation – 36–39 added to 1–35, 40 ff. added conveniently after 36–39 – will not do justice to all the evidence, we must consider other aspects of the positioning of this section. Various attempts have been made at re-opening the question of Deutero-Isaiah.[21] The orthodox view that treats 40–55 + 55–66 as two additional bodies of prophetic material, added to the book of Isaiah, though not without recognition of elements of relatedness, does not resolve all the problems. Most often there has been the recognition that 34–35 have affinities with 40 ff. A recent detailed discussion of Isaiah 35.8–10[22] argues for an updating at this point directed towards the hope of a return from exile, superimposed on a text concerned with 'an eschatological renewal of (Palestine)', but not with return and therefore pre-exilic in date. The suggestion is made that it is the position of this particular passage which has led to its being so reinterpreted to provide 'a pronouncement which would lead excellently into the prophecy of Deutero-Isaiah'.[23] More broadly, we may recognize the wealth of material in 28–33 not unrelated to 40–55;[24] much in 28–33 is concerned with the fate of Jerusalem, and clearly goes well beyond the situation of Isaiah,[25] culminating in 33, a passage, which, however described, clearly brings out the theme of the glorification of Zion.[26] The placing of 36–39 underscores this prospect of a restored Jerusalem. That hope is expressed also in a variety of comments in prophetic collections associated with words of Isaiah both in the opening chapters of the book and in 28–32; it is drawn out more fully in 33, 34–35. And 36–39 gives to it the firm basis of a complex prophetic narrative in which the message of Isaiah is held in a historic context and geared to the personage of Hezekiah. That it is then followed in 40 ff. by the confirmation of that message of hope in immediate assurance, shows the link between what are presented as aspirations and what appear now as immediate realities. There is further sequel to this in the warning notes which echo through 40–55 but come especially to be heard in 56–66.

II   *The Structure of Isaiah 36–39*

The placing of 36–39 may be seen to be most opportune for creating a context in which 40 ff. offer a response and show the use in fuller form of themes which are present in passages in the preceding chapters. We may then ask whether the structure of 36–39 contributes to this function. It is immediately apparent that there is no satisfactory chronological sequence in these chapters, and only a minimum of precise information. All the incidents are associated with the reign of Hezekiah, but beyond that no clear picture emerges of the order of events. Discussion of the complex problems of 36 and 37 is not here necessary. The literature on this theme is immense; and I refer simply to Brevard Childs' *Isaiah and the*

Assyrian Crisis[27] for his discussion of the problems of the divergent material and their relationship both to the events that may be discerned in them and in the Assyrian records and to the shaping and functioning of the material.

A. K. Jenkins has attempted to get behind the present association of the narratives with Sennacherib and the year 701, to raise questions about a possible different origin for the material.[28] Whether or not this particular attempt can be regarded as proved, it underlines the importance of recognizing the degree to which the material in these chapters has been modified to reach its present form. Jenkins takes seriously the date at 36.1, the 'fourteenth year' of Hezekiah, assuming the correctness of the synchronic dating of Hezekiah's accession in the third year of Hoshea (II Kings 18.1); the text thus provides a chronological scheme, though not necessarily a correct one. The materials of 36 and 37 would on this basis be associated with that fourteenth year – i.e. about 714 BC – and originally linked to a deliverance of Jerusalem under Sargon II; the illness theme of 38, which guarantees Hezekiah fifteen further years of rule, would – on the basis of twenty-nine years of his reign – belong to that same moment or shortly after (38.6 indeed associates it with deliverance from the power of Assyria and protection of Jerusalem); and while 39 could belong somewhat later, the precise relation to the activities of Merodach-baladan being difficult to determine, it would be possible to take more precisely the 'at that time' of 39.1 as meaning that all three component parts of this section could belong to almost the same moment. Jenkins accepts such a chronology, and his major concern is to suggest the plausibility of associating the material primarily with the period of Sargon II and to indicate how, in an ongoing reinterpretation, the major narratives came to be associated with the period of Sennacherib. There is difficulty here. It is not easy to see why, on this assumption, such a supposed deliverance under Sargon did not hold its place, especially since it is so evident that Judah suffered very heavily under Sennacherib. Why transpose a deliverance theme from the earlier to the later moment? Is it sufficient to point to the capture of Lachish and to see the non-capture of Jerusalem as a point of such reassurance as to invite the updating of the older materials to this? Jenkins has strong evidence for suggesting that the literary history of this section is even more complex than has often been supposed; I am less sure that he has resolved the problems of chronology.[29]

If we look at the material as it stands, we observe the difficulties of supposing a chronological order. We may see the rough chronological notes: *bayyāmîm hāhēm* (in those days) (38.1), *bā'ēt hahî'* (at that time) (39.1), as comparable to other link phrases in the book of Kings.[30] They are not to be treated as precise evidence, but rather as devices by which the compiler draws together what he believes to be significantly related material. We recognize that the fourteenth year of 36.1 and the fifteen years of 38.5 tie the narratives with the tradition of a rule of twenty-nine years by Hezekiah. This could mean that the illness preceded the attack by Sennacherib in 36–37. Similarly, if we suppose that Merodach-baladan's ambassadors were in Judah, not really to inquire after the king's health or to offer congratulation, but to gain support for alliance against Assyria, then this would appear likely to belong to the early years of Sennacherib's reign, when Merodach-baladan was active, rather than to a period after the Sennacherib campaign had in effect brought about the subjection of Judah. If this is so, then the order of the materials as now presented is lacking in true chronology, and we may ask whether the order is not dictated by interests other than chronological or historical.

The twofold narrative of 36–37 – and I leave on one side the analysis and interrelationship of what are clearly two parallel forms – is concentrated on two themes. The one is the theme of divine victory over the claims of the Assyrians; the other is that of the piety of Hezekiah and his response to the emergency. There is overlap and we may recognize that in the combining of the two strands, there has been some conflation. The first narrative presents the *hybris* of the Assyrian king: in the highly stylized wording of 36. 4–10 there is a clear pattern. Where do you trust? Is it in military power? Is it in Egypt? Is it in Yahweh whose shrines Hezekiah has abolished (vv. 4–7)? The last three are then repeated in divergent form: You have no military power. Egypt is unable to help. It is Yahweh who has sent the Assyrian (vv. 8–10). After an interlude (vv. 11–12), the second speech of the Rabshakeh elaborates the theme of the uselessness of trust in Yahweh, developing it first in terms of an offer of a new promised land (vv. 16–17) in which the Assyrian speaks the language of Deuteronomy, and second in terms of the failure of the gods to deliver any land from Assyrian power (vv. 18–20). Significantly in v. 21 the officials give no answer, with the comment 'for it was a royal command: Do not answer'. I believe the significance of this lies not in any supposition that Hezekiah was trying to gain time, or that he did not trust his officers to make wise replies: but that there is no answer from men to a blasphemer: the answer comes from God. This would suggest that this motif is here used for a specific theological purpose; and the same may be said of the preceding material too. The remainder of this part of the material portrays the appropriate ritual of approach to the deity, through the prophet Isaiah, and the pronouncement of reassurance and deliverance by the prophet (36. 22–37. 7). The Assyrian has claimed divine warrant for his actions, and has – somewhat inconsistently – claimed the impotence of Yahweh to deliver: he is answered simply by direct divine word.

The second part of the material is introduced by what appears now as an interlude in 37. 8–9, in which we may detect the joining of the two narratives. This second part begins with the same theme of the powerlessness of the gods, Yahweh included (vv. 10–13). The central part of this narrative, introduced by vv. 14–15, is the prayer of Hezekiah (vv. 16–20): it is on the theme of the creative power of Yahweh, the recognition that the Assyrian Sennacherib has indeed been able to overthrow the gods of the nations, but they are non-gods. It is Yahweh who can respond to the prayer by delivering Judah from Assyrian power so that all the nations may know that he is Yahweh alone. The prayer is markedly related to psalm passages and to Deutero-Isaiah. The answer comes in a message from the prophet Isaiah (vv. 21–22*a*) to which the real sequel appears only at v. 33 in the assurance that the city will not be taken, the Assyrian will withdraw (vv. 33–35). The final verses (vv. 36–38) describe disasters to the Assyrian army and to its king. These verses may represent the true ending of the first narrative; but I think it more important to observe here, as elsewhere within this section, the skill with which divergent elements have been drawn together.

This is also apparent in the inclusion within ch. 37 of two further elements. The first is the poem of 37. 22*b*–29, clearly also at certain points closely related to Deutero-Isaiah and providing a broader comment on the *hybris* of the Assyrian ruler. It employs ironically the self-glorifying style of the royal inscriptions. The second is the element of reassurance and hope in vv. 30–32, underlined by the final words *qin'at yhwh ṣᵉbā'ôt taᶜᵃśeh zō't* (the zeal of Yahweh of hosts will perform this. Cf. 9.6 and see below). This promises miraculous restoration, and is described as being a sign (*'ôt*, v. 30). These two elements are not fully integrated, they represent an extension of the narrative material. The latter of them is related to 4. 2–6 and more closely still to 10. 20–23 (24–26).

What we may remark as of considerable interest in this whole section is the degree to which, while the material is at some points linked with Isaiah, who appears as the spokesman of Yahweh, there are contacts with the wider Isaianic tradition, and beyond that with Deuteronomy and the Psalms.[31]

I have treated the themes of 38 and 39 already in my 1974 study of those chapters, calling them 'an interpretation of the Babylonian exile'.[32] The theme of 38, the illness and recovery of Hezekiah, is verbally linked with the preceding section, in the use of *gnn* of the protection of Jerusalem in 37. 35 and 38. 6, alongside the difference of usage of *yšᶜ* and *nṣl* in the same verses. 37. 35 and 38. 5 are also linked by their Davidic reference. The illness narrative incorporates the theme of deliverance from Assyria alongside that of deliverance from death, and it is this latter theme that is more fully elaborated in the psalm, where images of death, of the pit of Sheol, are employed to contrast with the restoration to life and well-being.

Significant in the Isaiah 38 treatment of this theme is the absence of the medical procedures adopted by the prophet in II Kings 20. 7; 38. 21 is clearly an addition designed to recall this element. Of further importance is the absence from this form of the material of any element of choice or deliberation on the part of Hezekiah. The prophet declares – using exactly the same words as are found in 37. 30 – 'this is the sign (*'ôt*) to you'. The piety of Hezekiah is expressed, as in 37, in the offering of a prayer, the style of which is much simpler, emphasizing the loyalty and right life of the petitioner. It is noteworthy that the whole of the narrative is compressed so that the divine answer comes as an immediate response to the prayer.

By contrast, Isaiah 39 presents the story of the ambassadors virtually exactly as it appears in II Kings. Its theme is of submission to Babylon, the inevitability of exile, the downfall of the Davidic monarchy. The comment of Hezekiah, as I have argued else-

where,[33] represents the acceptance of the rightness of divine
judgment. The pious king is thus portrayed as the one to whom
the future judgment is disclosed through what may be described
as the inadvertence of his conduct. As the material stands, no
blame is attached to Hezekiah. We may legitimately suspect that,
underlying the present form of the material, there is an older
narrative in which Hezekiah comes under divine judgment through
Isaiah because of his involvement with a foreign power – a theme
more fully developed in regard to Egypt in Isaiah 30–31; but this
is now unstated. The king discloses exactly what he has done and
accepts as right what the prophet has pronounced. The final phrase
may be seen as a pious comment: doom cannot come in the time
of righteous Hezekiah. The absence of this in LXX[B] in II Kings
20. 19 may indicate it as a later addition,[34] but it serves that
purpose just the same, and may represent one further indication
of the growth of the Hezekiah legend.

Set alongside 36 and 37, these two chapters present a further
theme. The assurance of deliverance from Assyria of the first two
chapters, continued by overlap into 38, is to be seen as a contrast
to the handing over of all Judah and its royal house into the power
of Babylon. But the one is not to be read without the other. The
overwriting of the Assyrian narratives with the assurance of divine
power, of the overthrow of the *hybris* of an alien ruler, indeed of the
impropriety with which he has offered a new promised land to
God's people, make it clear that there are pointers forward to
the promise of restoration which in the book of Isaiah follows
immediately. It is a point at which we may again ask how far in
handling the form of the material in II Kings we must consider
the relationship to the Isaiah presentation. It remains a problem
to know why there is so little cross-reference to the prophetic
material in the Deuteronomic History, though no lack of reference
to prophecy.[35] We may perhaps consider whether sufficient of
cross-linkage is to be found in these chapters to the book of Isaiah
for the reader to be, as it were, invited to consider the narratives
in the light of their other context. Is he perhaps already being
invited to read the story of Hezekiah as it is to be found read in
Ben Sira, with a full consciousness of the disclosure of hidden
things before they come about?[36]

III   *The Function of Isaiah 36–39*

Structure and function overlap, and in the previous part of this discussion a number of pointers to function have been suggested. A somewhat fuller statement may now be attempted of the function of this whole section 36–39 within the book of Isaiah.

We cannot, of course, forget that this passage appears in another, closely similar, form in II Kings 18–20; but, however important for textual questions and indeed for points of interpretation the comparison of such duplicate texts may be, we must not be led away from consideration of the question: What function does this text perform in this particular context? It is the failure to deal with this which often mars commentaries where the commentator elects to omit altogether or to handle only sketchily a text which appears elsewhere. When writing the commentary on Isaiah for the *Interpreter's One-Volume Commentary*,[37] I found myself put under restraint in writing on Isaiah 36–39, because, in the common view, these chapters belong in II Kings, and it is there that they will be fully handled.[38] I was limited virtually entirely to points of difference, which meant little more than commenting on the psalm in 38. But this is to ignore what these chapters do to the book of Isaiah, how they function within it. How they affect the book in which they stand is a legitimate subject of study.

On the common view that 36–39 have simply been extracted from II Kings and added to an already complete book of Isaiah (1–35), we might at the very least say that they provide some supplementation to our knowledge of Isaiah and of his utterances; delicate problems will arise as to how far we may extract elements of the original message from this material. The discussion of that question is not my intention. But even that simple purposeful level of the insertion of the material raises further questions about the effect produced in the book, and the more clearly we detect cross-linkages with other parts of the book, the more evident it is that there is a much more significant function being performed here.

My discussion of Isaiah 1–12[39] was directed towards attempting some elucidation of the question why so large a body of prophetic material has come to be associated with Isaiah, and answering this partly by consideration of the particular presentation to be found in 1–12 which, alone with 36–39, is a clearly demarked collection in the book. In some respects the title given to that study:

'Presentation of a Prophet' could be applied to 36–39: it is in part concerned with portraying the nature and function of Isaiah in relation to a particular series of narratives. We might equally observe the converse: it presents a series of narratives, linked in part by the illumination of their meaning in the presentation within them of the prophet. In that respect there is a valuable parallel to be drawn with the material of II Kings 16 and its analogous material in Isaiah 7–8.[40] The former presents the reign of Ahaz with no mention of Isaiah; the latter utilizes some elements of the same material but uses them to provide a lead in to the activity of the prophet. A perfectly legitimate deduction from this – and one that may be seen to be confirmed in the detailed examination of the material – is that a form of 36–39/ II Kings 18–20 can be postulated in which the events are recounted without any mention of the prophet. A full discussion would involve fuller consideration of that hypothetical *Urtext*. It is a hypothesis which raises questions also about the reason for there being in II Kings this one lengthy section involving Isaiah, but no such presentation of him in relation to Ahaz.[41] The clue, I suspect, lies in the figure of Hezekiah, and this is a point to which I want to devote further attention.

While I have suggested that 36–39 may be held to resemble 1–12 as a presentation of the prophet, it can be more closely argued that it resembles one section within 1–12, namely 6. 1–9. 6. This has been generally agreed to be a unit, though not a unity. It is marked off by the occurrence before and after of material of the same kind – the poem with refrain of 5. 25–30 and 9. 7–20,[42] itself contained within the woes of 5. 8–24 and 10. 1–4.[43] It resembles 36–39 in that it offers the only substantial section of the Isaiah compilation in which direct connection with narrative material is provided. Indeed the only other sections which contain elements of narrative are to be found in 20 and in 22. 15–25; and the only other date, apart from the evidently prefatory 1. 1, is in the curious 14. 28 on which a further comment will be in order later.

More significant are points of relationship between 6. 1–9. 6 and 36–39 which may be briefly noted:

1. The historical note, with its chronological indication, in the opening of 6. 1 and 7. 1 and again in 36. 1. Of these the latter two are related to II Kings 16. 5 and 18. 13. Apart from 1. 1 and 14.

28, these are the only precise chronological notes in the book of Isaiah.

2. Both events, in 7. 3ff. and 36. 2ff. are located at the same place, by the water conduit. In neither case does this play any further part in the narrative; arguably it is connected with the siege situation in both instances. It provides an incidental point of cross-reference.

3. The use of the sign (*'ôt*) in 7.11, 14 is very similar to that in 38.7 (22), and further to that already mentioned in 37.30. In fact, the wording of the offer of a sign in 7.11 – 'go deep' (*ha'mēq*) and 'on high' (*l'mā'lāh*) – could well be compared to the use of the roots *'lh* (go up) and *yrd* (go down) in 38.8, which also incorporates repeated use of the word *ma'alôt* (steps) (five times).[44] Furthermore, we may observe that the offer of a sign in 38 – and here the Isaiah text differs from that of II Kings – resembles the offer to Ahaz in ch. 7. A contrast may be seen between Ahaz' refusal of the sign and Isaiah's insistence on it in ch. 7, and the willing acceptance of the sign by Hezekiah with no hint in the narrative of a request. Did the compiler responsible for the Isaiah form of this text modify the story to remove elements from its already familiar (? II Kings) form which he felt to be unsuited to its function in the book of Isaiah, to draw out this contrast between Ahaz and Hezekiah?

This use of the sign theme is picked out by Melugin as a link between various elements in the book of Isaiah. He extends the point more broadly, noting 8. 18, which is of interest as falling within the same section as 7. 11, 14. He also comments on the further examples in 19. 20; 20. 3; 37.30, and the way in which this is taken a stage further in 44.25; 55.13 and 66.19. Of these, 8.18, with the theme of *y'lādîm* as signs (using both *'ôt* and *môpēt*), provides an extension of 7.14. 37.30, within the section 36–39, helps to bind together the two sections 36–37 and 38. The other occurrences are less close. The sign of 19.20, with reference to the divine deliverance of the Egyptians who turn to Yahweh, may be seen to be echoed in 66.19 which similarly deals with the gathering of the nations (though neither appears to be related to the use in either 6.1–9.6 or 36–39). 20.3 is also less close, though like 8.18 it uses the two terms *'ôt* and *môpēt*. 44.25 is disconnected, being concerned with false signs. 55.13 forms a colophon to the chapter, perhaps to the larger unit also; it is possible, though less clear, that it is intended to echo the Davidic theme of 6.1–9.6. Melugin's comment goes rather further than the evidence: 'The place of Deutero-Isaiah in the collection may well be related to the redactor's theology of the place of signs in the prophetic word.'[45] But though there is too little ground for such a sweeping statement, there is evidence of relationship between the sign theme in chs. 7 and 8 and 37 and 38.

4. The climax of 9.6 and that of 37.32, already noted, are uniquely in the phrase *qin'at yhwh ṣᵉbā'ôt taʿᵃseh zō't* (the zeal of Yahweh of hosts shall perform this). It occurs only in these two passages (and the II Kings parallel). The use in both shows its ambivalent quality, to be found in other examples of the use of *qin'āh*: Yahweh shows his concern both in his wrath at Israel and at the nations, and in his mercy and salvation. (The theme is aptly summed up in Joel 2.18: *wayᵉqannē' yhwh l'arṣô wayyaḥmōl ʿal-ʿammô*, Yahweh became jealous for his land and took pity on his people.) Both these narrative or partly narrative sections, which alone in the book provide a full contextual setting for the activity and message of Isaiah, are evidently concerned with themes of judgment and of deliverance. The former plays its part in the presentation of Isaiah in 1–12; the latter has a comparable function in relation to the chapters which precede and follow it.

5. The reference to *maʿᵃlôt 'āḥāz* (38.8) – whatever it denotes – provides another link.[46] If, as has been argued,[47] the phrase is a gloss in II Kings 20.11, the Ahaz reference appears only in the Isaiah form of the text. Is there yet again here a small modification in the Isaiah form of the material designed to draw out the contrast between Ahaz and Hezekiah? The point would be clearer if we had a better idea of the precise meaning of the allusion, but if, as is often supposed, it refers to a supposedly idolatrous shrine erected by Ahaz, the reference could carry with it the further implication of the contrast between pious Hezekiah and impious Ahaz.

6. To this last, we may add other indications of the contrasting of Hezekiah and Ahaz. Modifications in the text in Isaiah 7 as against that of II Kings 16 make the point that the threatening forces of Israel and Aram are in fact powerless, and the fears of Ahaz and his court are groundless. Isaiah 7.2 and 4 bring out this theme of unnecessary panic. By contrast, the text of Isaiah 36 preserves the theme of Assyria's power, omitting II Kings 18.14–16 in which Assyria is bought off by Hezekiah. The effect is thus to stress the propriety of the conduct of Hezekiah, whose response to

the Assyrian threat is a ritual of penitence, and an appeal to the deity; at no point is fear directly associated with Hezekiah or his officers; only the reply of Isaiah, in markedly liturgical terms, tells the king *'al tîrā'* ('fear not', 37.6). The contrasting picture of these two kings is already discernible within the II Kings material; it is taken a stage further by the presentation of the one without reference to Isaiah in II Kings 16 and of the other with full-scale reference in II Kings 18–20. Yet other developments are detectable in Isaiah 7 and 36–39. The later stage still is to be seen in the Chronicler, where the contrast is of the most extreme kind.[48] We may also note here that Isaiah 14.28 as it stands refers to the death of Ahaz. It may be right to emend the text, but the MT contains a possible further hint. The death of Ahaz marks the accession of Hezekiah, and who better than such an ideal king to bring overthrow to Philistia and the establishment of Zion in security (14.20–32)?[49]

In my study of II Kings 20, I drew attention to some aspects of this growth of the figure of Hezekiah, both within the biblical material and beyond. We may now add a little more to this in the recognition that the message of hope for the future, which in Ben Sira is linked to the Hezekiah references, as we saw at the outset, is already, by the placing of 36–39 where it stands in the book of Isaiah, used to provide a contextual basis for the prophecies of chs. 40ff. The basis for those prophecies is shown to rest in the relationship between Hezekiah and Isaiah, idealized king and prophet of judgment and salvation. And to this we may add the further consideration that 6.1–9.6 is ordered around the theme of the Davidic monarchy, its failure (and hence the failure of the people – so in 6, 7 and 8) and its future prospect, expressed in the concluding oracle in 9.1–6.[50] We cannot in this resolve the question of the child in 7.14; but if he is a royal child, or was interpreted as such a one, has he come to be associated with Hezekiah in the process of reinterpretation? And what more fitting than to conclude the section in 9.1–6 with a royal oracle designating a new and ideal Davidic king, and to suppose that here too the operative factor in interpretation has been the growth of the idealization of Hezekiah. The link then from 6.1–9.6 to 36–39 would be even stronger. Hope for the future, to be expressed in Davidic terms only once in the later chapters (55.3), is nevertheless associated with Davidic promise. Have we here one element in the process by which

Davidic hope, in royal terms, comes to be transformed, as appears to be the case in the Chronicler, into a theologized concept?[51]

Much of this exposition is of necessity tentative. It is an attempt at exploring more fully the possible links of 36–39 with the book as a whole, to give more ground for Melugin's claim than is, I believe, to be found in his brief discussion of the point. The basis for the words of hope and salvation is here declared to rest in the realities of a historic situation – no longer to be unravelled fully – in which deliverance is portrayed, new life out of death is granted, the Babylonian exile is foretold. It is another aspect of that process by which the acceptance of the disaster provides a basis for a new hope, a stage towards the further reassessments of that disaster and hope which are to be found in early and later post-exilic writings.

8

Historians and Prophets[1]

The relationship between an event and the accounts which are given of it has long been known to be very difficult to define precisely. The problem was given classic expression in the experiment carried out by a professor of psychology who arranged for a gang of hooligans to interrupt one of his classes and afterwards invited each member of the class to write an accurate account of what had happened. The witnesses to an occurrence, no matter how observant they may believe themselves to be, and no matter how much they attempt to record, as they believe, with impartiality what they have experienced, inevitably introduce some element of personal choice and experience into what they record. Even the camera, which, we are told, 'cannot lie', is in the hands of an operator; his use of it and his selection of what falls within the range of its lens may well produce a one-sided account of the events which it is recording.

If this is true of even the most trivial of everyday occurrences, it is more obviously the case with events which have deep significance for those who are involved in them and for those who subsequently attempt to record what happened and why. The result is that no single account of a momentous event is likely to be sufficient to do justice to it. If we had only one Gospel in the New Testament (leaving aside the rather more difficult question of whether the Gospels can really be regarded as intended to supply 'accounts' rather than to present a case) our problems of interpretation might seem to be considerably simplified. In reality we should be in a much worse position for understanding the events which lie behind the narrative, since we should have a single-dimensional account rather than the multi-dimensional which is offered by the four Gospels taken together. That the events of Israel's early history are presented in several narratives and traditions rather than in one may sometimes be a source of despair to those who try to unravel their complexities; but when we find ourselves confronted with only one narrative about a particular incident, we realize how little we have on which to base satisfying conclusions about its nature and meaning.[2]

The approach to such pluriformity of narrative and interpretative material is, however, no easy matter. And the apparently easiest approach, that of harmonization and reconciliation, is both inadequate and insidious. Again, if we consider the example of the Gospels, we may be profoundly thankful that we were not left with the Diatessaron of Tatian or with some other Gospel Harmony, ancient or more modern, instead of with the diversity of the Gospels as they stand. As many who have attempted to write a life of Jesus have discovered, it is only by a process of oversimplification and of suppression of the problems that an apparently coherent order can be set out. The overall presentation of the early history of Israel suffers under the same disadvantages. And here the insidiousness of the harmonizing process appears. For we may very easily be led, by reason of the desirability of having some sort of framework within which to work, to superimpose upon the complexity of the traditional material a schema which has in reality been derived from harmonization. It would be unjust to characterize the *History of Israel* by John Bright[3] as an example of such a procedure; yet it is the case that the reader may in some measure be lulled into a false security by what does sometimes appear to amount to an acceptance of a traditional and conventional understanding of the course of events, into which the whole has been fitted. By contrast, the often apparently negative approach of Martin Noth in his *Geschichte Israels*[4] may very well arrive at wrong answers; but it has the merit of being much more prepared to question the harmonizing outline and to leave open questions of order and interpretation to which the answers are very difficult to achieve.[5]

The basic weakness of the harmonizing procedure derives from what seems to be its securest point, that of the givenness of historical events. An event must have happened; a historical figure must be real. There must have been a certain order of occurrences making up the event; they must have taken place on particular days and at precise times. The person must have been a certain kind of man, born and brought up in particular places and at particular times. Either there is no historical reality at all, and we are dealing entirely with fiction; or there is absolute precision of time and place. It may or may not be possible for us at the present moment to know or by any means discover the precise details, but they must be there. Of course, this is true; but it is minimal. In other words, what might be known on this basis is so meagre and so lacking in significance, relatively speaking, that the knowledge of it contributes very little to real understanding.[6]

Events have their order and persons their reality; the delusion, however, from which we are apt to suffer is, that, provided we can get the available information in our texts into the right order, show the precise interrelationship of this facet and that, demonstrate the way in which the one presentation expresses a particular *Tendenz* and the other the propagandist aims of a certain school, then we shall be able to reconstruct something – an event or a person – which lies beyond the uncertainties of interpretation. This is a delusion. The recall of events is not unmediated. Even their apprehension by the persons involved is influenced by the processes of minds which select and order observed phenomena; the recounting of what happened, even a few moments later, inevitably introduces simplifications, selections, interpretations. Accounts of the same occurrence by more than one person, whether directly involved or offering an account based on the available evidence, produce yet further differences of presentation. Nor is it the case – and here again we encounter a common delusion – that the eye-witness is able to offer a more correct or more coherent account than someone who attempts a reconstruction on the basis of varieties of evidence. A court of law, faced with a multiplicity of often conflicting statements about what happened in a given criminal case, must come to a decision about what is the truth of the matter; our whole apparatus of justice depends upon the belief that such judgments, though not provable in the sense that they cannot be regarded as unassailable, are nevertheless reliable. So too the historian who writes at some distance from the events may be in a better position to give a true appraisal than one who is so involved as to see only a part of what makes up the whole.

This has a consequence which is not always sufficiently faced in biblical study. It is the recognition that the attempt to get back to the original form of a narrative, or to get back to the *ipsissima verba* of a prophet, or the original sequence of events as seen and understood by those involved – even supposing that such an attempt can meet with success – does not automatically supply us with a more authentic or more intelligible or more correct assessment of what the events were or what the words meant.

We have to resist a double temptation. On the one hand, we have to guard against the insidious dangers of harmonization and simplification. On the other hand, we have to recognize that the more ancient is not necessarily the more true. The truth about an event or about a person is discoverable only as a result of a much more complex process of investigation of the materials available to us. It involves a careful examination of what they are, and a judicious assessment of what they mean. The event or the person we are seeking to elucidate stands behind the materials which we have; we may hope to illuminate facets of the events or aspects of the influence of the person. It may not necessarily be to our advantage to co-ordinate them neatly into a systematic presentation.

In a number of cases, the Old Testament offers alternative presentations of a particular situation. The study of many of the traditions concerning the earlier period of history involves us in the consideration of differing accounts of the same event, or differing estimates of the same person. But in a limited number of cases, there is a difference which is of particular importance to the discussion of the event and its significance. These are cases where the same situation is delineated on the one hand with the inclusion as an active participant of a prophetic figure, on the other hand without any mention of such a person. In view of the many questions which arise in regard to the prophetic interpretation of history, and the relationship between the prophet and political events, this is a point of great interest. And the attempt is made here to elucidate some of the questions which arise out of an examination of the alternative statements. Two examples are examined in what follows: the case of Isaiah and Ahaz in the period of the Syro-Ephraimite crisis, and that of Jeremiah in the period of the fall of Jerusalem.

I. *Isaiah and Ahaz*

The relationship between Isaiah and Ahaz, like that between Isaiah and Hezekiah in the time of the Assyrian crisis, is one which has evoked many comments. But insufficient attention has been given to the study of the alternative sources separately, without the assumption being made, explicitly or implicitly, that we know before we begin what kind of relationship is to be affirmed. In fact, for stricter accuracy we ought to speak of the problem of interpreting the position of Ahaz in the period of the Syro-Ephraimite crisis on the one hand, and the problem of interpreting that same position with the added complication of the presence of Isaiah on the other. Our two major sources of information, Isaiah 7 and II Kings 16, offer just such different appraisals of the situation. But we must also add our third source, II Chronicles 28; this we should do partly because it has come to be recognized in recent years that the Chronicler's history does contain a considerable amount of material, not in the books of Samuel and Kings, which rests upon sound and older sources and which must be evaluated in its own right.[7] But a more important claim for its consideration rests in the fact that here, in about the middle of the fourth century BC, we have an author, historian and theologian, who takes the pieces of the tradition as they are known to him and creates a new pattern out of them. His construction is of interest in itself; like the others it may shed light on the way in which the tradition has evolved, and like them it may shed light both on the origins of that tradition and on the particular approach to it which was dictated by the theological and other presuppositions of the authors. It would be inappropriate to add to these three a consideration of other oracular material in the book of Isaiah which might belong to this particular moment; for that would be to introduce an uncertain element before an approach has been made to the problems. Only subsequently, in the light of the discussion, might there be an examination of the oracles to see if there are other passages which are relevant.[8]

We may therefore proceed to examine each of these three sources in turn, discussing only those aspects of them which are relevant to the matter under consideration. Many other questions which arise are necessarily left untouched or only mentioned.[9]

II Kings 16

The text of II Kings 16 begins (vv. 1–4) with the stereotyped formula for the kings of Judah. The judgment passed is entirely negative, and in particular a specific reference is introduced to a practice mentioned elsewhere for the period of Manasseh (21.6; 23.10) and for the northern kingdom (17.17), namely that of 'causing his son to pass through fire'. It has been contended that this was an emergency ritual conducted in the time of national crisis when the invasion of Syria and Israel threatened, a comparison being made with the action of Mesha of Moab (3.27). This latter is described as an *'ōlāh* (sacrifice); and the same may be implied for the rite attributed to Ahaz by the similar statement of Jeremiah 19.5. But the linking of the sacrifice with this particular crisis is hypothetical. It is not impossible that a more general condemnation of religious practice has been made specific to Ahaz, and not too much weight should be laid on the point.

Verse 5, loosely linked by the temporal *'āz* (then), an indeterminate conjunction, notes the advance of Rezin and Pekah against Jerusalem in war, their besieging of Ahaz, but their inability to fight (*wᵉlō' yākᵉlū lᵉhillāḥēm*). The meaning of this expression is not clear, but it is not impossible that the plural verb is here used pregnantly to suggest 'carry through the campaign'.[10]

Verse 6 records another event of the same period. It appears likely that the reference to Rezin and Aram is erroneous, due to the influence of the preceding verse, and that we should here find only a reference to the recovery of Elath by the Edomites. The collocation of this setback for Judah with what precedes amplifies the impression of crisis; Ahaz was involved in a threat to his capital and also a threat to an important trading and mineral centre. Economic problems accompanied the political. It is reasonable to see here the compiler linking together different elements of the material to heighten the picture of emergency.

Verses 7–9 describe the sending of ambassadors to the Assyrian ruler, indicating submission and appealing for help against Aram and Israel; the appeal was supported by a bribe made up of silver and gold from temple and palace. A response was forthcoming; Damascus was besieged and taken, its people exiled and Rezin put to death.

Verses 10–18 relate how Ahaz himself went to meet the Assyrian king at Damascus, and how he arranged for an altar which he saw there to be copied in Jersualem. The narrative details various further 'reforms' carried out in the temple by Ahaz' command. The details need close examination if they are to be adequately assessed. As they are here presented, they are explained as being carried out *mippᵉnē melek 'aššūr* – 'because of the king of Assyria'; this may mean either 'at the instigation of the king of Assyria' or 'as an act of respect, ingratiation'.

There is no doubt in the writer's mind about the nature of these changes in the temple. We may note, however, that they fall into two groups. Verses 10–16 are concerned with various changes in the use of the altars. The new altar is used by Ahaz, and the bronze altar before Yahweh is moved over to the north side. Ahaz instructs that the great altar is to be used for all the general sacrificial practice, the bronze altar for his own inquiring of Yahweh. The details are not entirely clear. Verses 17–18 introduce two new elements; the removal of a good deal of bronze – was this because of shortage of metal? – and of the 'barrier of the sabbath' (or following LXX the 'base of the tribunal') and of the 'entrance for the king'. It may be that these objects were specially connected with the royal prerogative, and that their removal was dictated by the Assyrians; it is equally possible that these alterations, and perhaps some of the others, were really part of that gradual modification of temple fittings to which various allusions are made. They may have been interpreted entirely in a negative sense because of the verdict on Ahaz, and by themselves they provide little clear evidence of his relationship to Assyria.

Verses 19–20 provide a normal concluding formula for the reign of Ahaz.

This account of the period of Ahaz in II Kings 16 contains, within the framework of the opening and concluding formulae, elements concerning the attack on Jerusalem, the loss of Elath, the appeal to Assyria, the alterations made in the temple. The relationship between these elements is provided by the compiler; it is open to question how far he has given a historical arrangement. Two of them are precisely linked together – the attack on Jerusalem and the appeal to Assyria. The visit of Ahaz to the Assyrian king could be chronologically subsequent to this; or it could be an alternative version of the appeal, representing a different account of how Ahaz made his submission. The interpretation of the alterations in the temple could derive from an attempt at correlating Ahaz' policy there with his submission to Assyria. The integrating of the Elath incident into the sequence shows one aspect of the compiler's method; he heightens the impression of Ahaz' distress by this means, but since no time note is given other than the vague 'at that time', we have no means of knowing whether his interpretation of the relationship is sound.

The narrative impresses by its coherence, the elements being built together into a whole which confirms the view of Ahaz as a religiously bad king as depicted in the introduction. No mention is made of Isaiah or of any part played by him in the events. In this the narrative contrasts sharply with that for the reign of Hezekiah as described in II Kings 18–20, where virtually the whole of the main section, with the exception of 18.13–16, involves the part played by Isaiah in the events. We may note, however, that the account of Hezekiah's reform in 18.4–6 is paralleled in some degree by another account found in Jeremiah 26.16–19 in which the prophetic role is played by Micah.[11]

Isaiah 7–8

The relevant section in the book of Isaiah is more difficult to delimit. Where it begins is clear, for the opening of Isaiah 7 overlaps with II Kings 16. It is clear that the various passages which make up vv. 1–17 all belong to the period of Ahaz, less certain that vv. 18–25 do. The opening of Isaiah 8 is also closely linked with the same crisis; but how much of what follows belongs there? This is very difficult to determine. As so often in the prophetic books, the way in which the material is divided up affects exegesis, and although a new beginning appears to be marked by Isaiah 9, even this is not absolutely certain. All we can with certainty recognize are the exegetical procedures by which other prophetic material has been built into passages which can with good reason be assigned to particular moments. We cannot necessarily use this material for illuminating the way Isaiah himself saw the crisis in the time of Ahaz; we can use it only to consider the way in which that crisis was seen to have a deeper significance by those who handed on the prophetic tradition.

If we begin with the more securely established opening of Isaiah 7, we note various clearly defined elements.

Verse 1 has a date formula to introduce a passage almost

identical with II Kings 16. The latter simply introduces with *'āz* (then), but this is natural since the preceding verses there provide the chronological setting. Is one text dependent on the other, or are they independent transmissions of a historical statement? It has been rightly noted that the effect of this verse is to draw a parallel to the opening of ch. 6. We may also observe that the following verse provides a different introduction to the material which follows and that it is not quite consonant with v. 1. This could suggest that v. 1 was added to provide the link with the preceding chapter and to clarify the chronology which is not specified in what follows. At the moment, however, we are considering the meaning of the text as it is now structured. Does the last clause of the verse mean 'he could not fight (successfully) for it',[12] or should we read the plural and translate 'they could not carry through the campaign against it'? If the former sense is right, then the absence in Isaiah of the phrase 'they pressed Ahaz hard' (*wayyāṣūrū 'al- 'āḥāz*) is strange; if the latter,[13] then right at the start we have a significantly different statement, and the absence of the preceding phrase is intelligible. The compiler of this passage avoids any suggestion that Ahaz was really in danger; he stresses right at the start that the allies could not succeed in their campaign. By this procedure, he paves the way for the contrast between the fears of Ahaz and the royal house and the confidence of Isaiah.

Verse 2 provides an alternative introduction. No date is given, but the situation is made quite plain, and an explicit statement is made of the formation of an alliance between the two northern countries. Unlike the preceding verse, this one refers not to Ahaz but to the royal house, and it stresses the state of panic induced in both the royal house and the people. The panic is vividly sketched in a phrase.

Verses 3–9 offer a narrative not paralleled elsewhere, introducing a prophetic oracle. It is a tantalizing narrative, because it raises questions to which we have no answers. Who was the child named Shear-jashub? No explanation is given of the name, though the assumption has readily been made that this son had been named on an earlier occasion and his appearance at his moment with Isaiah served as a reminder to Ahaz of the message then given. The child plays no part in the narrative; no further allusion is made to him, so that we have no means of knowing what was involved. The most we can say is that the existence of another piece of oracular material in 10.21–22 in which this phrase is used together with others reminiscent of the oracles in the chapters which precede, in a passage unlikely to be earlier than the exile, appears to indicate that the originally negative intention of the child's name has subsequently been overlaid with more positive interpretation. Whatever may be said about the name, it is difficult in the context of Ahaz' situation to see it as anything other than a gloomy warning, a warning that the people will be reduced to a remnant – whether a remnant which will return from exile or a remnant which will return to God; only later could this term 'remnant' take on a more positive sense with a reference to those miraculously saved from the overwhelming disaster of 587 BC.

It is a reasonable assumption, though no more than that, that the encounter between Isaiah and Ahaz was timed to coincide with the king's inspection of the city's water supply in the period either before the siege began or during the siege. No further reference is made to the location, though a subsequent link might conceivably be found in the oracle on the waters in 8.6ff. If so, this is a further reason for seeing the whole structure of this passage as suggesting an interwoven 'sermon' on a theme.

The whole passage in 7.3–9 is formed as an address of instruction by God to the prophet; whereas in some such accounts we find a note of the prophet carrying out the divine instruction, no such indication is given here.

The word of God to this situation is contained in two different elements:

Verses 4–6 contain a somewhat overloaded and hence rather prosaic injunction to Ahaz not to fear the activity of the two northern kings. Its prosaic character is in large measure due to the elaboration of the wording to make clear to what particular situation the references are made. The last phrase of v. 4, the latter half of v. 5, and perhaps also the final words of v. 6, may all be so regarded. But attempting to arrive at an original poetic utterance is hazardous; the most we can do is observe that there is a strongly rhythmic flavour to certain of the lines here. The injunction to Ahaz is not to fear the insignificant actions of the two kings – the derogatory phrases of v. 4 emphasize this. Verses 5–6 clarify the intentions of the two kings; they plan *rā'āh* (calamity); they plan conquest so as to bring Judah under their control, appointing their own nominee as king. The name of this ruler, with patronymic only, is given at the end. Whether this name is an original part of the pronouncement or an explanatory note,[14] it provides an important piece of information, of which the significance was no doubt known to the readers. The person referred to was presumably a notability of some kind, since otherwise he would not be a suitable choice.[15] The delicacy of Ahaz' position is evident.

Verses 7–9 contain an evidently poetic oracle, also probably subsequently elaborated in 8*b*. The precise meaning of the phrases used in these verses, turning around the word *rōʾš* (head) is not clear; the most probable view is that they depend on a proverbial use. The culminating words of v. 9 provide the fullest contrast to the attitude of fear which is brought out both in the introductory v. 2 and in the injunction of v. 4. The passage has been extended with a reference to some later situation; but the precise reference of the 65 years of 8*b* remains uncertain.

With vv. 10–17[16] we move over into a new and quite independent section, linked without any chronological note to what precedes and described as a further address by God to Ahaz. The problems of this passage are so considerable and the difficulties of interpretation have been so much discussed that to enter into even a fraction of the questions and the approaches would be out of proportion to the present discussion. We may concentrate on two or three central points. The pronouncement of v. 16 is the most crucial for our relating of this passage to the same crisis as the preceding one. Here the assurance is given that within a brief space of time – its exact term is not clear – 'the territory of whose two kings you are in terror will be forsaken'. It is, on this basis, reasonable to assume that the sign offered by the prophet to Ahaz in v. 11 and refused by the king on grounds which are said to be those of false piety, is a sign to give assurance that the devastation or the withdrawal will take place. The text does not make so direct a relation of the different elements as this, but so it appears natural to interpret the passage. The intervening offer of a sign in spite of Ahaz' refusal is associated with the assurance of withdrawal also. Whatever the precise connotation of the sign of the child – and this has been discussed to and fro – it would appear difficult not to see it as so related as it is now presented. But to this is added the complication of the very difficult words of v. 17. What is meant by the wording here? Does it indicate a further note of promise? Is God offering blessing, namely the blessing of a restored Davidic kingdom, a going back to the moment before the disaster of division? Or does it indicate a disaster commensurate only with that disaster? The latter sense appears to be indicated by the reference to the king of Assyria at the end of v. 17; but if that is a gloss, we must interpret the text on two levels, with and without the specific application.

Without the gloss, the prophetic word, like that of vv. 3–9, appears to be one of answering faith to the royal doubt. Just as in the earlier passage, Ahaz is exhorted not to be afraid, and warned that lack of trust in God will bring disaster; so too here the implication is that there is a centre of faith, expressed in the naming of the child as '*immānū-'ēl* (El is with us), which represents the willingness of God to protect Judah and Jerusalem. With the gloss the whole passage is converted into a message of doom on Judah, the negative aspect of the previous passage being extended into a total rejection of Judah such as is to be found in Isaiah 6. The ambivalence of the prophetic word is at its most explicit.

This negative interpretation is further emphasized by the oracles which follow in vv. 18–25. These all echo the theme of doom, expressing this however in various forms. The judgment at the hands of Egypt and Assyria in vv. 18–19 indicates a much less politically motivated assessment of the situation than the application of v. 20 to 'the king of Assyria'.[17] It is an important indication of the way in which the oracles of the prophets of this period have been read in the light of disasters at the hands of Assyria; the prophets themselves appear, on given occasions, to have made comments which were much less narrowly politically tied. Verses 21–22 take up the theme of the child in v. 15, but it is very difficult to determine whether the basic point is that of judgment – so v. 21 in all probability – or promise to a remnant – so v. 22 possibly though not certainly. Verses 23–25, perhaps to be linked in thought with the judgment oracle of 5.1ff., is again a negative pronouncement.

8.1–4 provide another statement comparable with that of 7.3–9 and 7.10–17, this time in the form of a symbolic action, the birth of a child to Isaiah and his wife, the prophetess; the action is publicly attested, the fulfilment of the symbol is assured, and its message is explicit: before the child can say father or mother – a different time note from that in 7.15–16 – Assyria will have plundered Damascus and Samaria. The judgment at the hands of

Assyria is here quite clearly stated; the implication that Ahaz need have no fear is also plain.

The discussion could be – perhaps should be – further extended with an examination of the verses which follow, in which related themes are developed. But perhaps it may be sufficient to note that the theme of judgment, so apparent in the preceding chapter, is further drawn out; that the theme of lack of trust, and its consequence of disaster, is elaborated. The theme of '*immānū-'ēl* is picked up, though with considerable obscurity, in vv. 8ff. There is here interwoven a series of oracular pronouncements which would suggest that we are dealing with an elaborate presentation of the prophet's message in which the particular occasion to which it is attached – that of the Syro-Ephraimite crisis – is seen as an illustration of a typical attitude, fear, lack of trust in God, unwillingness either to accept the reality of God's protection or to heed the dangers of which the prophet warns.

But if we look at the whole presentation, what are we to say about Isaiah and Ahaz? We may at the very least make certain negative comments. The prophet is not here described as telling Ahaz not to appeal to Assyria; Assyria appears as an instrument of judgment, in the first instance on the other two countries (so explicitly in 8.4), and in the development of the theme on Judah also (so 7.17, 7.18 [with Egypt], 7.20, 8.7). That the prophet is aware of the reality of divine judgment on Judah is clear from chs. 5 and 6, though no dating is given to the former. But in neither case is there any indication of the precise nature of the judgment to be inflicted.

How far do our assessments of the relationship between Isaiah and Ahaz depend upon a tacit reading into this passage of the information provided by the already complex section in II Kings 16? Should we not rather see in Isaiah 7–8 an expression of two elements which belong to the message of the prophet – for which there is attestation elsewhere, namely, his interpretation of the significance of Jerusalem and his belief in the imminence of divine judgment? That these two elements are not immediately reconcilable may perhaps suggest that neither can be taken alone to the exclusion of the other, and that we may have, expressed in a variety of ways within the collection of prophecies, a critical appraisal of a Jerusalem theology which oversimplified the issue in terms of the inevitability of divine protection but which nevertheless had a right understanding of the reality of the presence of Yahweh in his holy city and temple; perhaps we should also see a critical appraisal of a merely negative judgment prophecy which would seem to pronounce nothing but doom and see the only possible future in terms of the total overthrow of Jerusalem.[18]

II Chronicles 28

The third form of the presentation of the period of Ahaz is to be found in the work of the Chronicler. As in the case of II Kings, we are able to judge something of the method of the writer of the work from the way in which he shapes his materials. Comparison may be made between the procedures adopted in one part of the work and in another. Our purpose here is not, however, to engage in general discussion of method and outlook, but to look at the particular shaping of this part of the material.

Verses 1–4 provide an introductory formula, corresponding closely to the text found in Kings, with some slight modifications of detail. The Chronicles text has a plural *bānāw* (his sons) for the singular *bʿnō* (his son), and this generalizes the evil condemned. If it were right to think of a single emergency provoking an extreme sacrifice (so the singular form), the plural is unlikely to suggest either the sacrifice of several sons on one occasion or several occasions on which sons were offered. The plural would more probably indicate the general practising of a rite specially condemned by the historians and prophets.[19]

Verse 5 introduces the Syro-Ephraimite theme. But it does so in a striking manner. First, this theme is directly linked to the evils which have been indicated in the preceding verses; second, the two attacking kingdoms are separated and both indicated as instruments of divine judgment upon Judah. So Aram attacks and defeats Judah and carries away a great number of captives to Damascus; then Israel attacks and inflicts great loss on Judah. This is quite a different understanding of the events from that offered in both the other sources.

Verses 6–7 provide the details of the latter campaign in terms of actual losses. First Pekah of Israel is described as killing a hundred and twenty thousand on one day, all warriors, 'when they forsook Yahweh the God of their fathers'. Then Zichri, a mighty man of Ephraim, is specially mentioned with a reference to his killing one of the king of Judah's sons, and also the household officer and the king's deputy.

Verses 8–15 introduce a remarkable narrative of the taking of captives from Judah to Samaria, and how they were there met by a prophet named Oded. He preaches them a sermon, explaining that the defeat of Judah was the result of divine judgment and reminding them of their own guilty status in the presence of Yahweh. Their action will bring down divine wrath. His words are backed up by leading men of the Ephraimites who forbid them to bring the captives and spoils into the city because they will thereby increase the already great guilt of Israel. So the army abandons its spoils, and the leaders already named see to the captives being clothed and fed and take them to Jericho, leading those who are in a weakened condition on asses.

The story is a highly improbable one, but this does not affect the interest which it arouses. Its placing in the narrative serves to draw out a significant point about the Chronicler's treatment of the north; the utter condemnation of the north is more than once accompanied by appeals of this kind, as also by indications that there were those in the north who were pious and conscious of guilt.[20] Yet it is hardly to be supposed that we have here merely an arbitrary insertion or a piece of gratuitous invention. The hypothesis that some part of the book of Hosea (5.8–7.16) belongs to the period of the Syro-Ephraimite war is unproven; but such an interpretation gives added point to what appears there, and would suggest that there were those in the north as well as in the south who viewed the activities of the northern kingdom as highly dubious. It is possible that stories of atrocities in this period were handed down; it is possible that there were stories of captives restored – we might, very conjecturally, find a reason for this in the pressures of Assyria which came shortly after to be felt. Out of such materials – historical and fictional – a coherent narrative of theological importance has been built.

Verses 16–21 now turn to the theme of the appeal to Assyria.[21] In a sense the emergency is over with the restoration of the captives; but here again the point is to show the overriding faithlessness of Ahaz. Verses 17–19 bring in various other elements by way of explaining the position. The Edomite menace is made more specific; so too is a Philistine attack and occupation of cities in Shephelah and Negeb. And these are explained, with yet another repetition of the point, as due to the judgment of God upon Judah, but this time specifically because of the sins of Ahaz. The final verses introduce another new variant. It is explained (v. 20) that the king of Assyria made things more difficult for Ahaz and did not help him. The despoiling of temple and palace and of the houses of the nobility to bribe Assyria did not avail (v. 21).

In this passage we see how a different complexion is given to the whole meaning of the events. Should we perhaps see here a relationship to the Isaiah material which interprets the coming of Assyria as judgment? If so, we have an example – and there are others – of the Chronicler's use of prophetic material and prophetic interpretation without any mention of the prophet's name.[22]

Verses 22–25 offer another elaboration, this time of the theme of the temple alterations. These are associated with Damascus, not with Assyria.[23] Ahaz worships the gods of Aram because they have defeated him and are thereby proved stronger than Yahweh.[24] He uses the temple vessels and other equipment to make not one altar but many, throughout Jerusalem. He elaborates worship throughout the land, and so provokes Yahweh's wrath.

Verses 26–27 provide a concluding formula.

This whole construction by the Chronicler is a remarkable *tour de force*. Elements of the older tradition as known from II Kings are utilized, but differently combined. Other materials are also introduced. The order is different, the presentation though not entirely coherent nevertheless creates a powerful impression. It uses a prophetic motif without the introduction of a known prophetic figure but only of Oded who acts as a spokesman for the Chronicler's own theology. Its significance rests first in its own impact and the light which it sheds on the Chronicler's theology. But it serves also to remind us that the traditions which we have here and elsewhere are already given shape when we come to handle them; we have no untouched sources, but presentations which are theologically viable and distinct, valid in themselves but not direct portrayals of the particular historical situation.

The title of this section is 'Isaiah and Ahaz' and deliberately so. For the focal point to our appraisal of the situation comes down in the end to an attempt at understanding what was the position occupied in these years by the prophet whose significance was in the long run to be so much greater than that of the king to whom he spoke. But our assessment has to be set soberly in the context of all the available material, and this means the recognition that a historian who was also himself no mean theologian could tell the story of Ahaz without either mention of the prophet or allusion to his teaching (so in II Kings), and that another historian who was really much more theologian than historian could do the same with the possible difference that in his reassessment he may have been influenced by the development of the prophet's teaching which is found in the book of Isaiah. Alongside these we have the narrative and oracle complex of Isaiah 7–8, now a highly complicated structure interweaving various pieces of material, showing many cross-linkages and much inner exegetical activity, and itself not mentioning some of the things which we might have expected to be mentioned, but seeing the events in the light of certain underlying theological principles.

If we merely conflate these statements, we impose another construction of our own, a construction which may or may not be true to the historical sequence, now so difficult if not impossible to discover. If we say, as so many commentators and textbooks have said, that Isaiah advised Ahaz not to appeal to Assyria, we may be making a correct deduction from the available evidence; it may be that, though it is not said, it is implied in the prophet's words enjoining trust in God. But the fact remains that the traditions which handed down and interpreted this moment of history and experience did not so describe the situation. In the three forms in which we have them, we are offered more elaborate and more relevant statements about the relation between faith and fear, the relation between human disobedience and divine judgment, the meaning which events can have for those who come after and live in other situations. We must beware lest in merely trying to reconstruct the origin, we overlook this broader significance.[25]

II. *Jeremiah and the Fall of Jerusalem*

A remarkable feature of the Old Testament material as we have it is the fact that it was possible for the compilers of the great Deuteronomic History to cover the period of the monarchy with only a single real reference to the great prophets to whom in our modern study we rightly devote so much attention.[26] This lack of correlation between the 'histories' and the prophetic books has often been commented on, and various solutions have been proposed to explain the curiosity, but none is very satisfying. It remains a fact that the particular form of the historical narrative that has come down to us in I and II Kings – and I emphasize the point that it is this 'particular form' – does not make any such reference as we might expect.

What is remarkable for the prophets of the eighth century is even more strange for the prophets of the seventh and early sixth – Jeremiah and Ezekiel. For the latter we might offer the explanation that his concern was much more with the Babylonian situation. But for the case of Jeremiah who was in Jerusalem all the time and of whom a number of narratives are preserved which place him in the thick of the political manoeuvres of the period, the omission is very difficult to understand.

The alternative form of the last part of II Kings found in Jeremiah 52 also contains no mention of the prophet. But this leads us on naturally to consider yet another alternative form, found also in the book of Jeremiah, in ch. 37–44, in which the prophet appears substantially. This section raises a number of points which I wish to consider for the purpose of illuminating both the problem of the accounts of the fall of Jerusalem and the position and attitude of the prophet Jeremiah in relation to the events.

It would be inappropriate here to enter into discussion of the structure and formation of the book of Jeremiah, but it will be convenient if I indicate briefly what appears to me to be the most useful approach to these questions. The consideration of the problems of the Isaiah material makes it appear necessary, as has now been worked out much more fully by B. S. Childs,[27] to take account of quite separate tradition elements presenting divergent impressions of the prophet and his message. It has seemed to me for some time that a similar approach is necessary to the Jeremiah material. There may be usefulness in the source-analysis so commonly practised and largely deriving from the work of Mowinckel, but it amounts to very little more than putting together in each source material of similar kind. For the purposes of discussion this may well be valuable, and we may note the usefulness in a similar direction of the suggestion of John Bright that a type which he terms the 'prophetic reminiscence' may also be distinguished.[28] But this further group overlaps proposed source divisions and this suggests that these are not separate sources but only kinds of material. We may therefore more usefully look at the present structure of the book and see that it consists of two major divisions, together with a collection of foreign nation oracles and an appendix in ch. 52. Such a 'block' approach has recently been usefully put forward again – it is not in fact a totally new idea – by C. Rietzschel in his study *Das Problem der Urrolle*.[29] There is much in this study which is open to criticism, but his approach has assisted in crystallizing out my own understanding of the book.

We may distinguish chs. 1–25, a collection of prophetic oracles with some narrative, closely comparable with other prophetic collections, and 26–45 which is largely made up of narrative material with some isolated and grouped oracles. But within this second section, we should, I believe, distinguish 26–36 and 45 from 37–44; the former, ending with the special word to Baruch, forms a rounded whole, a unified structure of interlinked narratives into which is built as an integral part the oracular collection in 30–31. It is centred upon a series of narratives concerning Jeremiah, and concerned with the whole problem of the doom of the state and the hope of restoration. 37–44 is of a different nature. It opens in the annalistic style of the books of Kings. It includes at 39.1–10 a section concerning the capture of Jerusalem by Nebuchadrezzar which corresponds very closely to 52.4–16 and II Kings 25.1–12. Furthermore, in 40.7 – 41.18 there is a long section which offers a much longer account of the governorship and assassination of Gedaliah than the very brief narrative of II Kings 25.22–26, a section not present in the Jeremiah 52 form of the narrative. In both the narrative of the fall of Jerusalem and that of the governorship of Gedaliah, Jeremiah does not appear at all. In other words, Jeremiah 37–44 offer us a series of narrative sections, all concerned with the period from the time of Zedekiah to the years shortly after 587, in some of which Jeremiah appears as an active participant, in others of which he is not mentioned. The structure and content of this section thus provide interesting parallels to the Kings and Jeremiah 52 forms; but all three need to be considered separately as well as together. The form of the material offered by the Chronicler offers yet another construction of the events. Such an investigation provides an essential introduction to any discussion of the position and attitude of the prophet in the moment of the city's collapse.

There are several ways in which variant forms of a text may be studied. An obvious method is to set out the different texts in columns and make a detailed comparison, and clearly for the minutiae of textual criticism and interpretation this is a necessary procedure. It is not, however, entirely satisfactory for the study of the particular presentations, since it concentrates our attention on points of similarity and difference rather than directing our minds to the question of what the particular author or compiler was setting out to do. Just as the study of the Chronicler's work may be vitiated by continual cross-reference to the books of Samuel and Kings, for we may then not really see what the Chronicler is doing, so here, while we must make reference to other forms of the text, we must also see each of the forms for itself. With four presentations of the fall of Jerusalem, even though in some parts the differences are minimal, we have insight into four ways in which the material could be handled. Ideally therefore we should examine each of these presentations in detail, and consider both what is included and how, and why the particular emphases are made. This cannot be done fully here, but in order to give a proper picture of what is done in Jeremiah 37–44, it is desirable first to have a brief look at the two presentations in II Kings and Jeremiah 52, and subsequently to make a reference to the Chronicler's presentation too.

II Kings

The narrative of Zedekiah begins at II Kings 24.18 with the normal historians' introductory formula (vv. 18–20*a*); this differs from the normal in one important respect, namely that v. 20*a* introduces the one clear statement of the meaning of the events which are recorded in the following chapter. It was 'on account of the anger of Yahweh that it came upon Jerusalem and Judah until he had removed them from his presence' (cf. 24.3).

24.20*b*–25.21 records the events: (1) the rebellion of the king, the siege of the city and its fall, the capture and fate of Zedekiah (24.20*b*–25.7); (2) the general policy of the Babylonians in regard to the city and temple, and the people (vv. 8–12); (3) the temple vessels and furniture (vv. 13–17); (4, which appears to continue 2), the fate of the leaders and the final judgment comment of v. 21*b* 'Judah was exiled from its land' (vv. 18–21).[30]

It is not uncommon to say that this marks the original end to the book; certainly it has a finality about it which makes the sequels a little unexpected. But for the moment we are concerned not with indications of earlier stages in the formation of the book, but with the material as we now have it. In the presentation offered to us in II Kings, there are two further elements: (1) the governorship and assassination of Gedaliah (vv. 22–26); (2) the release of Jehoiachin (vv. 27–30).

The overall structure of this section of the work thus shows a preliminary comment on the inevitable outcome in terms of exile and this fulfilled in the statement of the exile actually taking place; but the events are given a wider meaning. This is done first in relation to the loss of Gedaliah – and if any hope rested in Judah, where the *dallat hā'āreṣ* (the poor of the land) alone are said to have been present (so 25.12), this hope is now brought to an end; second in relation to the release of Jehoiachin. I have argued elsewhere[31] that it is unrealistic to view this last note as a gloomy comment on the absolute loss of hope, and that it is to be seen as a sign that with the exiles there is some indication of the already active power of divine grace. The Kings' presentation thus issues in a token of promise, not in Judah but in Babylon. That Jehoiachin may soon have died is not immediately relevant, for it is not the life of the king as such that counts, but the restoration of the people's representative; in him the people of the future is embodied, and one line of hope clusters around the members of that line.[32]

Jeremiah 52

Whereas the last part of II Kings when considered separately is clearly not to be fully understood without reference to what precedes, the existence of Jeremiah 52 as a section independent of any other shows a handling of the tradition which is clearly closely related but also has a certain freedom. It provides a finale to the whole book and may be seen therefore as designed to offer a comment on the meaning of the events in the light of the activity of Jeremiah.[33] It can thus be regarded as providing a middle term between II Kings and Jeremiah 37 – 44, for although as in II Kings, Jeremiah does not appear, yet the fact that this section is used by way of comment on the Jeremiah material shows an awareness of the relationship between the prophet and the events and their meaning.

There are many small points of difference between the two texts. Particularly in the section on the temple vessels and furniture, the

Jeremiah 52 text is considerably fuller.[34] But the most substantial difference lies in the absence in Jeremiah 52 of any reference to Gedaliah; instead, vv. 28–30 offer a short summarizing statement of the extent of the exiling of the community, providing more modest figures than II Kings but adding a third deportation not mentioned in the other forms of the material. It could be argued that the Gedaliah section is omitted because the book of Jeremiah provides a much more substantial form of this particular tradition. But one might equally argue that the whole of this chapter is really virtually redundant in the light of the content of Jeremiah 37–44 and other material in the book. It is more natural to suppose that this form of the material, originally quite independent of the book of Jeremiah, takes up an even more negative attitude than does II Kings towards the situation in Judah. The implication of v. 27 with its reference to the captivity of Judah (so in II Kings) is made explicit by the detailing of the numbers deported in each stage of the events. Thus nothing was left to Judah which could have any real significance for the future. The completion of the narrative with the release of Jehoiachin then serves the same purpose as in II Kings; the king is released and this is a token of the working of divine grace.

We have thus two forms of the same material, and in points of detail they confirm one another or provide variant textual evidence which is of considerable importance. More still, they represent two stages of the same tendency: the process by which it came to be increasingly felt that the future lay with the exiles and not in Judah. Both offer the same modest degree of hope; the one provides the climax to that great historical work which passes judgment upon the whole life of the people from the conquest to the exile; the other provides a comment on the book of Jeremiah. In effect, it is saying, this is the meaning of the message of the prophet. His words of doom on Judah and Jerusalem find here their fulfiment, and their confirmation; there is no future except in that act of promise which is declared as the final note. This is how Jeremiah appeared to this particular editor of his book.

Jeremiah 37–44

It will be evident that in the confines of this discussion the many problems of this part of the book of Jeremiah can only be very lightly touched. The purpose here is rather to look at the general structure of the section, to see what elements it contains and to see how they are built together into a larger whole.

We begin (37.1) with the chronological note concerning the reign of Zedekiah as in II Kings 24.18. But this is followed by a general judgment on the king, his servants and the population in general (so here surely *'am hā'āres*, people of the land) for their failure to attend to the words of Yahweh mediated by Jeremiah. This paves the way for the Jeremiah material which follows. Thus whereas the theme of judgment in II Kings is offered in quite general terms as the result of the wrath of Yahweh, here the explicit comment is made which ties in disobedience with the prophetic word. The compiler of this section is leaving no doubt about where the standard of judgment is to be found.

This theme, disobedience to the word of Jeremiah, is then elaborated in a series of interwoven narrative sections.

(1). 37.3–38.28*a*. From 37.3 to the end of 38, where the annalistic material resumes, we have various elements which do not apparently form an original unit, but which together give a powerful impression of the prophetic word and its impact. The separate units may be briefly described:

37.3–10 is set at that moment during the siege when the advance of the Egyptian army caused a Babylonian withdrawal from Jerusalem. (The incident is not alluded to in II Kings, which pictures the siege as relentless and quite unrelieved.) First we have a formal deputation sent to Jeremiah asking his intercession;[35] there is a link here to the wider Jeremiah tradition (cf. e.g. 14.11) which recognizes the function of the prophet as intercessor but points to the negation of this function in view of the state of the people. Thus the theme of disobedience is implicit in the request for intercession; and this is made plain by the explicit words of the reply in which the theme of repudiation of false trust in Egypt (again a motif of the Isaiah tradition) is made the occasion for a word on the absoluteness of judgment at the hands of the Babylonians who are thought of as being miraculously strengthened for their task of destruction (v. 10).

37.11–21 follows, a narrative which is set in the same general situation, the period of Babylonian withdrawal which made egress from the city possible. On a charge of desertion, Jeremiah is arrested and imprisoned; from prison he is summoned secretly by Zedekiah so that the latter may hear the divine word. It is a message of nothing but doom. The story records the king's protection for Jeremiah. He is kept in prison, but with a daily allocation of food until all the food was gone. The implication of the final phrases is that this continued until the fall of the city. The significance of the story appears to rest in its affirmation of the validity of the divine word of judgment; even Zedekiah, unwilling to obey the divine word to him by Jeremiah, is nevertheless shown as acknowledging its rightness.

Chapter 38 continues and repeats the same themes. No chronological relationship is indicated with the preceding, but it is clear that the two offer variants of the same underlying tradition.[36] There is a rich prophetic tradition associated with the period leading up to the fall of the city. Here we find Jeremiah openly speaking to the people (cf. 37.4), the words of his message being given at second hand. With royal permission, the leading men put Jeremiah in a pit. From this he is rescued at the king's command – the narrative element of Ebed-melech gives a picturesque turn to the story. Again the motif of secrecy, and the promise of royal protection; the message of doom, amplified in terms of submission to Babylon as the only way of escape, and a firmer stress laid upon the demand for obedience. The motif of secrecy is filled out in the last verses, and the story ends with Jeremiah still in the guard-room until the city's fall.

These two alternative narratives have been set together, and as in the case of other such pairs, their position has been in some measure accommodated. The end of ch. 37 simply leaves Jeremiah in the guard-room, though the implication is that this is until the city fell; 38.9, by mentioning that there is no food left in the city, provides an apparent chronological link to the end of 37. In reality there is no room for both. But the result is an added stress on the point which is being made. Obedience can still save king and people; but it was disobedience which brought disaster. The tone having been set at the beginning, nothing is spared either to show the truth of this affirmation or the possibility, at any moment, of recovery; and the outcome being clear, the emphasis rests upon the weakness of the king, and the opposition of his associates. There is no way out but judgment.[37]

The two sections together thus illustrate the necessity of the judgment that follows, and the effect is to provide a narrative of the fall of Jerusalem which is theologically much more coherent, though also more diffuse, than that provided by II Kings (and Jeremiah 52). The effectiveness of the II Kings narrative lies very largely in its lack of moralizing, its very slight reference to the reasons for the disaster; almost without comment, the final disaster is described as taking its course. This narrative in Jeremiah 37–38 makes clear the point which is inferred in the II Kings material; and it brings out the prophetic judgment which is present in II Kings. Here the prophetic judgment is attributed to the central figure of the moment, just as the prophetic role of Isaiah is drawn out in the narrative of the Assyrian crisis. What is true of the events leading up to the disaster, is then shown to be equally true in what follows.[38]

(2). 38.28*b*–40.6. The narrative of the fall of the city (38.28*b*) 39.1–10 picks up the chronology from the beginning of ch. 37. It records the capture of the city, the escape and capture and fate of Zedekiah; the systematic destruction (though without mention of the temple),[39] the exile, and the installing of the poorer members of the community.

This is followed by 39.11–40.6 which consists of various elements, rounding off the narrative of the fall of the city and providing a link to the next main section, that dealing with Gedaliah. It is clear that there is duplication of material here too, for the opening verses, 39.11–14, tell of the special protection for Jeremiah at the hands of the Babylonians; without any detail it relates that he was entrusted to Gedaliah. The point is reached at which the Gedaliah narrative may begin. But before this, we have another narrative element, providing a link back with 38, the protection offered to Ebed-melech (vv. 15–18); the doom of king and city is thrown into sharper relief by the recording of obedience and piety and their reward. That the Babylonian commander is revealed as an instrument of the divine will is more fully brought out in 40.1–6 where in a more elaborate form the idea of protection for Jeremiah, the mediator of the divine word of judgment which has now been fulfilled, is set out.[40] Again the narrative leads up to the position of Gedaliah, and the way is open for the next part of the material.

Thus again, in comment upon the more purely historical narrative, with its relatively bald statements, we have Jeremiah traditions woven together to stress the meaning of events. Even in the disaster there is a word of hope; it is centred upon pious men, even upon an enemy who obeys the divine will, though unwittingly; the prophet of doom is himself the object of special protection.[41]

(3). 40.7–41.18 offers a long and important narrative concerning the period of Gedaliah's office and his assassination and its consequences. This corresponds to the very brief account given in II Kings 25.22–26. The appointment of Gedaliah is noted in the preceding verses in the Jeremiah text, but the gathering of the various leaders to Gedaliah appears in both here, with additions and variations in the Jeremiah text. The oath sworn by Gedaliah to the assembled leaders is also in both. Thus II Kings 25.22–24 is covered fairly closely by the text in Jeremiah 40.7–10. But the Kings text then has nothing but a brief statement of Ishmael's visit and the assassination (v. 25), and a brief statement of the fear of those who were left and of their journey to Egypt (v. 26). The Jeremiah text offers first a considerable account of the situation in Judah, and reveals the steps towards the re-establishment of agricultural life (vv. 10–12); it provides an explanation of the action of Ishmael, showing his association with the Ammonite king and indicating how a warning was given to Gedaliah which he refused to accept (vv. 13–16). The assasssination is described, localized at a meal held for Ishmael and his associates with Gedaliah at Mizpah (41.1–3). This is followed by a curious incident which is very difficult to understand fully, that of the visit of pilgrims from the central part of the land, and the murder of most of them, with a little piece of topographical information concerning the cistern into which the bodies were put (vv. 4–9). The narrative of Ishmael continues with a note of the captives he took, and of the pursuit by the associates of Gedaliah and of Ishmael's escape when the captives were rescued (vv. 10–18). These last verses then provide a link to the renewed appearance of Jeremiah in their comment on the intention to go to Egypt.

(4). Chapters 42–44 are made up of several sections, but the point of immediate importance is the reappearance of Jeremiah in the sequence. It records the inquiry addressed to the prophet, seeking advice as to what should be done by 'all this remnant' (*šᵉ'ērīt*). To the promise made by Jeremiah that he will give them a true answer, they affirm that they will obey the word which comes (42.1–6). The reiterated statement of obedience and the calling of God himself as witness lends weight to the people's words; the theme is linked back with that of 37, for obedience gives life and disobedience means disaster.[42] Thus as soon as the message is given, promising protection, proclaiming the reversal of divine intention towards his people, and forbidding the projected journey to Egypt, with appropriate indications of the utter disaster which will befall those who disobey, it is clear that there is no way out in this direction. The text of 42.7–22 is rich in hortatory phrases and warnings; and the gloomy outcome is already anticipated in the latter part of the address, contrasting sharply with the words of promise which mark the first part. There is a strong sense of the inevitability of disobedience and doom.[43]

43.1–7 reintroduce the theme of disobedience, combined with a denial of the authority of the prophet's word. This serves to emphasize that the people view the prophet's advice as treasonable, comparable to that which he offered during the siege of the city, a complete abandonment of the community to the enemy, whereas in reality it is the way of trust and submission to the divine will which offers life.

So 43.8–13, judgment is upon Egypt. The theme of these verses is quite different, yet it fits into the pattern of the interpretation of Babylon as the instrument of the divine will, and therefore as the power within whose orbit there is the way of life for Judah.

The hope engendered in the establishment of Gedaliah was lost in part by assassination; yet not entirely, for to those who remained there was still a way of life in submission. Now that they have chosen the road to Egypt there is virtually no way out. Chapter 44 again stresses the consequences and indeed the inevitability of disobedience; for such is the community which has gone into Egypt that none can escape. It seems probable that the original sense of this chapter is that there is no hope here; as it now stands both v. 14 and v. 28 recognize the meagre prospect of the return of a few fugitives, a few who escape the sword, as the judgment upon them is expressed, not explicitly but tacitly in the judgment which is brought upon Egypt. The theme of judgment upon Egypt in 43 is picked up at the very end, and the parallel drawn between this judgment on Egypt at the hands of Babylon and that upon Zedekiah. The same principle is at work.

It will be appropriate to return in a moment to the working out of the themes of these chapters. But before this, we may just very briefly look at the Chronicler's picture of this situation.

II Chronicles 36.14–21

The Chronicler's interpretation of this moment begins in the conventional fashion with chronological data and theological verdict upon Zedekiah. But at once we are into an area of interpretation in which the significance of the proclamation of Jeremiah is drawn out. It was unwillingness to submit to the divine judgment spoken by Jeremiah which brought disaster. Rebellion against Babylon is noted as proximate cause, and indeed the *wᵉgam* emphatic of v. 13[44] draws attention to the fact that the disobedience expressed itself precisely here. These are not two separate causes, disobedience and rebellion, but one, disobedience, that is rebellion, as indeed the latter part of the same verse makes clear. The theme is developed in vv. 14–16, with a homiletical note, stressing the continued disobedience as well as the persistent warning. The mercy of God was great, but in the end it was a case of '*ēn marpē*' – no remedy, none to assuage. So judgment – Babylonian conquests, total handing over of the people without sparing and, the vessels and treasures taken to Babylon, temple and city destroyed, and all who survived taken into exile. The land is left to enjoy its sabbaths.[45]

No word here of any left in the land, not even the poorest; no mention of Gedaliah, nor of fugitives to Egypt; not even of the release of Jehoiachin; only an interpretation of the exile in terms of prophecy, in terms of a carrying through of the sabbath law which had been ignored, so that now the land could be restored by the keeping of sabbath, and eventually the people restored through a new and also prophesied act of grace in the figure of Cyrus.

The logic of the presentation is complete. Without the disaster of exile, which was divine judgment, and without the exile as a breathing space, a sabbath rest, there could be no new people of God.[46]

It is not possible here to draw out in full detail the significance of these various presentations. The title of this section is 'Jeremiah and the Fall of Jerusalem', and it will be appreciated that only one aspect of that subject is really here under consideration. There are other points to be extracted from Jeremiah 1–25 about the conception of the inevitability of disaster brought upon an unfaithful people; there is more to be learnt and considered in its own context from Jeremiah 26–36 about the reasons for the disaster and the meaning which is placed upon it. What appears in Jeremiah 37–44, set side by side with the three other presentations which we have briefly considered, is an estimate of the place of the prophet within the events.

The historian who attempts a study of a period is inevitably a selector of the information and interpretation to be offered. It stands out – to us at least – as a remarkable fact that one such could write the story of the final downfall of the kingdom of Judah without any mention of the prophet who, as we read the Old Testament, is so closely involved in the events. This presentation exists in the Old Testament in two forms: II Kings and Jeremiah 52; and, as we have seen, both lay the same essential stress on the meaning of the disaster in terms of the loss of Judah and Jerusalem and the hope which rests alone – and that very modestly – in the community in exile and its restored captive king. The presentation offered in Jeremiah 37–44 is another version of this narrative. So long as strict rules of copying do not apply, any copy of an ancient work is inevitably in some measure a new work ('new edition' one might say, but this is too modernistic a term). Jeremiah 37–44 offers a new presentation of the period; it does so by interweaving traditions in which Jeremiah appears with others in which he does not. There is the same kind of skilful literary artistry here which we can discern so often in Old Testament writings. There are anticipations of what comes later; there are cross linkages of thought and language; there is balance of structure; there are parallels to be drawn, and double narratives to be detected. This must be treated for itself, as what it is, and this, in my view, firmly disposes of any suggestion that we have here – or indeed anywhere else – a Jeremiah *Leidensgeschichte* – a passion story of Jeremiah, as if he were somehow thought to be the centre of the story. He is not. There are incidents here which have to be taken into account in a total attempt at assessing the personality of the prophet. But he is here as the expression of the divine word. And how right the Chronicler is when in his new presentation, generations later, he picks out as the crucial moment not this or that incident of the career of Jeremiah, but the fact that he at this moment of time typified the whole prophetic movement, expressed the absoluteness of the divine judgment upon the finally collapsing Judah.

Jeremiah 37–44 offers an overall presentation. It is like the other forms in that it too rules out the possibility of any future apart from the disaster to Judah. The Chronicler, from his later perspective, looks at the total situation and sees that – as he reads the events – only the exiles in Babylon count. The fuller narrative of Jeremiah 37–44 makes the reasons for this plain and shows the kind of thinking from which the Chronicler derives his understanding.

Such an interpretation of the period was not accidental; it arose out of the progressive judgments of God. Zedekiah refused the one hope offered, and the city must therefore fall. Gedaliah provided a new focus of hope, but he was to lose his life – the point is merely stated, but the warning to Gedaliah provides the indication that this need not have been.[47] The remnant after Gedaliah had the opportunity of obeying the prophetic word, but it failed to do so, and hence in Egypt it came under the final word of judgment. What is left, as the narrative now stands, is the most meagre hope – though this is now underlined by the presence after ch. 44 of the promise to Baruch in ch. 45; and if, as I believe, that really belongs with 36, it nevertheless has been meaningfully placed as a comment on the final doom of the Egyptian refugees. Baruch, the prophet's disciple, is there a type of the one on whom promise rests.

But that is not really part of the presentation; it is a later clarification of meaning in the light of other material. For this historian or theologian, the working out of divine judgment in the person of Jeremiah is complete; the lines of hope peter out. The judgment upon Judah rests.

There is, however, one last point tbe made. It concerns the method by which we handle the Jeremiah tradition, and brings us back to the consideration of the structure of the book which was mentioned earlier. If it is right – as I believe follows from the nature and structure of this section – to treat Jeremiah 37–44 as an alternative form of the narrative of the fall of Jerusalem and its aftermath, which includes a placing of Jeremiah in the events as interpreter, as presenter of divine judgment, then we have here a source of information of value at two levels. First, it reveals to us how one particular compiler could see the meaning of events in relation to the prophet; in other words it shows us one particular aspect of the Jeremiah tradition. Whatever may elsewhere have been preserved about Jeremiah, whatever other estimates may have been given, here is one; a curtain is lifted on one moment in the handing down of what was to be said about the prophet's function. Second, but inevitably indirectly because mediated only in this particular form, we have a source – one of several – from which we may very tentatively work back towards the prophet. This can only be done if we limit our attention for the moment to what this presentation provides, and this is part of the justification for this present discussion. If we wish to know what Jeremiah said and thought in the situation leading up to 587 and after that catastrophe, then we can affirm that the impact of his personality was such that the compiler of these chapters could present him like this. This does not mean that the information provided is somehow unreliable; it means that what Jeremiah was could be so described. It is an incomplete picture, it is selective, it is utilized in a particular kind of presentation.[48]

Our task therefore is not to pick out what we consider to be reliable, historical elements, and add these to similar information extracted from elsewhere. It is to see here one way in which Jeremiah could be viewed. Thus his relationships with Zedekiah, with the leaders of the Jerusalem community, with the Babylonian conquerors, with Gedaliah, with Johanan and his associates, are all points at which we meet with the prophet and out of which we can attempt an assessment of him. The advantage of such an approach is that it opens up a broader measure of understanding, even though it may in the end confront us with elements of tradition which are in some ways irreconcilable. The prophet, standing as he does at this critical juncture of his people's history and faith, deserves more than a simple judgment. He needs not a flat photograph, but three-dimensional sculpture. He is a key figure into the depiction of whose personality there has been projected much of the rich texture of thinking at this time and in the years that followed.

9

An Interpretation of the Babylonian Exile: A Study of II Kings 20 and Isaiah 38–39

There is a certain 'Looking glass' quality to the title of this study
– by which I mean that Lewis Carroll's White Knight, whose
analysis of the relationship between names and titles is the classic
one, might well have insisted that this is only what it is called,
whereas in fact it is about an interpretation (namely my own) of
an interpretation (namely that of the writer of II Kings 20 and
that of the writer of the parallel but not quite identical material
of Isaiah 38–39), which is there offered not apparently of the
Babylonian Exile but of certain incidents of importance in the
reign of King Hezekiah of Judah around the end of the eighth
century BC. The introduction of the Babylonian Exile into this is
not my own, since it is already inherent in one moment in the two
narratives; but the understanding of the section in terms of
interpretation of the Exile is something which needs to be discussed.
It is here that I believe we may see the distinctive character of the
narratives in their present forms.

Brevard Childs in his monograph *Isaiah and the Assyrian Crisis*[1]
has analysed and discussed the material of II Kings 18–19 and
their parallel in Isaiah 36–37 very fully. He has shown the problems
of reconstructing history from this material; he has shown the
variety of interpretations which the interwoven sections reveal.
And he has gone further in considering the particular nature of the
Chronicler's narrative in II Chronicles 32.1–23 which he describes
in terms of *midrash*,[2] interpretation and elucidation of already
existing written narratives, designed in part to alleviate difficulties
which the reader may discover in the narratives, in part to direct

his attention to the significance for the reader of the narratives which he reads or with which he is assumed to be familiar. This understanding of the Chronicler's method and purpose is a valuable one, for we may often see how, even when he does not include narratives found in the earlier Deuteronomic History, he assumes knowledge of them and invites his readers to see their significance in the new presentation which he offers.[3] The understanding of the Chronicler's work as *midrash*, or its understanding in homiletic terms, avoids some at least of the misconceptions concerning his intentions which have often led to an underestimating of the value of what he was doing.

Childs' study is devoted solely to that part of the Isaiah/Hezekiah material which is concerned with what he designates 'the Assyrian crisis', and does not include any consideration of the two further narratives which are to be found in the next section as this is presented in its twofold form in II Kings and in the book of Isaiah. Clearly he had enough to handle in that very complex and difficult passage. But there is some disadvantage in not looking at the next stage as well, since we may legitimately ask what effect the inclusion of the two narratives of II Kings 20 has upon our understanding of the preceding group of narratives and upon our interpretation of this particular historical moment. And we shall have occasion also to observe how the Chronicler handles these two items and the way in which he understands their relationship to the main narrative.

Whatever our judgment of the precise historical relationship between the account of Hezekiah's illness and the visit of the ambassadors from Merodach-baladan of Babylon and the preceding (as they now stand) accounts of Sennacherib's invasion and withdrawal, we must take account of the fact that in the text a close chronological relationship is indicated by the use of convenient though vague phraseology in the case of the first – *bayyāmîm hāhēm* 'in those days', a typical link expression – and by the similar wording *bā'ēt hahî'*, 'at that time', and by the precise reference to the illness of Hezekiah, in the case of the second incident.[4] Such link phrases must be taken with some seriousness. They are a cause of irritation to the historian since they tell him not what he might want to know but only that the compiler saw, in his interpretation, a chronological link, or perhaps more properly some link of meaning. They may, like the archival *'āz*, 'now, then', be merely introductory words. But it would seem more probable that we should see in them a belief on the part of the compiler that the incidents so introduced have some relationship with what precedes, and perhaps we should even see the deliberate offering of an interpretation of what precedes by the inclusion at this precise point of two further separate narratives.

Problems of history and chronology are, of course, important in the full study of such incidents as are here related. The assessment of the proper dating of the illness of Hezekiah must depend upon discussion of the very vexed problems of the whole chronology of his reign, the only precise point of vantage here being the belief of the narrator that the moment of illness lay fifteen years before the end of that reign – though how much reliance is to be placed on this is a point which would equally need to be discussed since it has to be correlated with the compiler's belief about the chronology of the second incident. The activities of Merodach-baladan of Babylon are sufficiently attested in the Assyrian records for us to be able to form some picture of the position of this quite notable character. The periods of his rule in Babylon 721–710 and 703, the date of his ousting of Marduk-zakir-šumi from the throne there,[5] allow some latitude in the fixing of possible moments for the sending of ambassadors, but it is more likely that it belongs in the second period of his activity and coincides with the movements against Assyria in which Hezekiah was involved early in Sennacherib's reign.[6] The precise answer is not material to this discussion, however, since exact chronological relationship between the narratives is not the point at issue. We may simply observe that, though there is no independent confirmation of the sending of ambassadors to Jerusalem, such a move makes good sense in the general context of upheaval in which Merodach-baladan appears as a prime mover and Hezekiah as a not unimportant figure in the western aspect of this endeavour, as we may judge from the Assyrian record of his involvement over the deposed Padi of Ekron.

Nor do we need here to prejudge the questions regarding the dating of the Assyrian attack or attacks on Judah, though it would appear that the events presupposed by the preceding chapters, II Kings 18–19 and Isaiah 36–37, are more likely to have followed the sending of these ambassadors than to have preceded it. This does raise a different question, however. For while it may be that the present order is due to a lack of precise chronological information on the part of the compiler, and the arrangement of the material in its present order has no special significance, it would appear more likely that the arrangement, whether or not chronological information was available, has some deliberate purpose. We are accustomed to expecting the Chronicler to arrange events theologically rather than chronologically. The earlier compilers of the Deuteronomic History also had presuppositions or theological axes to grind which made them able, even if we may believe they knew better chronologically, to put materials in a significant rather than a merely chronological order. The point is one which must be borne in mind as we examine the nature and purpose of the narratives concerning Hezekiah's illness and the visit of the ambassadors.

II

It will be convenient to begin by examining the nature and intention of the narrative of the ambassadors in II Kings 20.12–19/ Isaiah 39. (The concluding formula for the reign of Hezekiah in II Kings 20.20–21 is not relevant to this discussion in view of its relationship to other such formulae and also in view of its absence from the form of the text found in the book of Isaiah.)[7] We are not here concerned, as has already been indicated, with endeavouring to establish exactly what happened, with attempting to discover the exact nature of the message which was sent to Hezekiah or the exact terms of the discussion which ensued. We are concerned simply with asking questions about the material here provided, in an endeavour to detect what interpretation is being placed upon this by the narrator and/or compiler of this section or of the whole work. To some extent we shall here have to leave open certain questions, though it might be possible on the basis of our understanding of the present intention of this passage to consider some aspects of the relationship between the various stages which may reasonably be postulated in the development of the whole Deuteronomic History.[8]

The accounts tells us nothing directly about the purpose of the ambassadors' visit. It opens simply with a statement that Merodach-baladan sent 'letters' – or perhaps 'emissaries'[9] – and a gift, an expression of the proper exchange of courtesies between rulers. The occasion of the visit is indicated solely in terms of Hezekiah's illness, the previous narrative being thus closely interwoven with this one. It is a reminder that, whatever the true chronology, we are being asked to read the two together. We are informed that 'Hezekiah was glad to see them,'[10] and 'he showed them the whole of his treasury,[11] silver and gold and spices and fragrant oil, and the whole of his armoury,[12] even everything that was found in his stores; there was not a single item which Hezekiah did not show them, either in his palace or in his kingdom'. The small differences between the two texts do not affect the sense; the vital point is brought out in the concluding words which pick up what preceded. Here it is underlined that he showed them *everything*.

With this short introduction we are brought at once to the centre of the narrative as it is now presented, in the sudden, and we may feel, inevitable, appearance of the prophet Isaiah. As is so often the case in prophetic interviews, the conversation opens with what we can see to be a rhetorical question: 'What did these men say, and from whence did they come to you?' We need not be so literal-minded as to ask how it comes about that Isaiah is ignorant of what is going on, since it is so very evident from this and other such narratives that the real significance of the questions is to lead the king to commit himself in his reply in such a way that prophetic comment upon his actions follows as a direct sequel to his own involvement. If we were being literal-minded and supposing that the story as narrated contains the actual course of a conversation, then we might be tempted to ask why Hezekiah, to whom the prophet Isaiah was, after all, well known, and who might be supposed also to have some idea of the kind of techniques which prophets are so often reported to have used, did not make either an evasive reply or at least a cautious one. Instead, we find that he involves himself totally with what seem at first sight to be extravagantly unnecessary words. The second question is answered first: 'They have come to me from a far country, from Babylon'; the other question is left unanswered, but is immediately picked up and clarified in a further prophetic question: 'What did they see in your palace?' The real point is reached, and the reply represents a total commitment of the king: 'Everything which is in my palace they saw (the inverted order of words places the emphasis where the Hebrew places it); there was not a single item which they did not see in my stores.' The conversation has effected two things. It has underlined the place from which the ambassadors have come – a far country, Babylon; it has also repeated the theme of 'everything' – 'not a single thing' has been left unviewed by these visitors.

We may properly, when we read a narrative which is told with evident literary skill, see significance in the repetitions and emphases which are employed. The mention of Babylon as the place of origin in the opening has been picked up and underlined, not simply by the repetition of the name but by its definition as 'a far country'. The description of the showing of everything to the ambassadors is reiterated in the account given by Hezekiah; *everything* was shown, *nothing* was left unseen. We may with some propriety already suspect that it is these two elements which are significant to the narrator.

And so it proves to be the case. For the sequel, so inevitable when prophets ask questions and those who are addressed find themselves awkwardly involved as a result of question and answer, is in the pronouncing of a prophetic word of judgment, based precisely upon these two elements. 'Hear the word of the LORD. The time is coming when everything which is in your palace and everything which your predecessors have stored up, right down to the present time, will be carried off to Babylon; not a single item will be left, says the LORD.' The emphasis on totality, already twice set out, is picked up again, with the same balance of expressions – everything, not a single item; and the theme of Babylon is related to it. The latter point is given a further twist in a word of judgment upon the whole royal house: 'And some of your descendants, those of your actual line [this is a paraphrase designed to bring out the effect of the text's double statement][13] will be taken and will become officers [or perhaps eunuchs, though the word is not necessarily so narrowly defined] in the palace of the king of Babylon.'

The response of Hezekiah to this prophetic pronouncement is somewhat puzzling. The first part of it is clear enough; 'Good is the word of the LORD which you have pronounced.' Since it is evident that such a pronouncement of doom, even if placed in an uncertain future, can hardly be regarded as 'good' in the simple sense of that word, we may recognize that what Hezekiah is here made to do is acknowledge the rightness of the pronouncement. It is a word of acceptance: 'I accept the truth of the divine word.' The second part is much more difficult to interpret. Literally the text may be rendered 'And he said: Is it not if well-being and security shall be in my lifetime?' (so II Kings) or 'For there shall be well-being and security in my life-time' (so Isaiah).

There are I think three ways in which we may understand this second comment.

1. The first is that which is found in many of the translations and commentaries: it is to understand Hezekiah's remark as a smug comment. Thus the New English Bible, paraphrasing slightly, has 'thinking to himself that peace and security would last out his lifetime'.[14] 'It does not matter what happens to my descendants; all that matters is that this disaster now foretold is for a future date, and who cares what happens then?' I find this really very unlikely. Not that I do not think that – again if we were supposing that this narrative gave us an exact transcript of the conversation – Hezekiah, like anyone else, might not be somewhat relieved to know that the holocaust would come at a later date: Après moi le déluge. But in the context of a significant conversation, such smugness seems totally out of place.

2. The second possibility is a much more real one; it is that Hezekiah's words are a kind of auspicious pronouncement designed to avert disaster. We may compare the narrative in which David waits for the news of the battle against Absalom. The watchman spies a messenger coming and reports to the king, and the king says: 'If he is alone, then he brings good news.' Then as the messenger comes nearer, the watchman sees another man running, and this too is reported to the king, who says: 'He too brings good news.' Finally the watchman reports that he recognizes the running of the first man as being like that of Ahimaaz ben Zadok, and the king comments: 'That is a good man; and he comes for good tidings.' There is clearly in these comments a desire to avert bad news; the repeated emphasis on good news makes it clear that the king is, as it were, making a prophetic statement, foretelling the result of the battle as in his favour. In the whole section there is, of course, a deep irony in that the good news which David desires is of the life of his son Absalom, whereas the good news which is coming is that of the overthrow of his rebel son and the ensuring of the continued reign of David (II Samuel 18.24–27). If this approach is adopted in the Hezekiah narrative, then the sense would be: 'May there not be well-being and security in my lifetime', i.e. 'Please God that I may be spared from seeing such doom.'

3. The third possibility is that we should see here the direct counterpart to the first statement: the divine pronouncement is to be accepted, but there will be well-being and prosperity in Hezekiah's lifetime. The Isaiah form of the text is introduced by emphatic *kī*, 'There certainly will be well-being and security in my lifetime.' The same effect is produced by the different formula in II Kings, *hᵃlō 'īm*, 'Is it not the case that . . .' or 'Surely there will be . . .'[15] The obscurity of this is removed if we ignore the order of narratives found in the biblical text and correlate this brief allusion with the theme found in II Kings 18.4 and enormously elaborated in II Chronicles 29–31, namely that of Hezekiah the great reformer. It is quite evident that the reference in II Kings 18 is unrelated chronologically to what follows, though now it offers both an exemplification of Hezekiah's right conduct mentioned in 18.3 and prefaces the military successes and the withdrawal of the Assyrians which provide the themes of what follows. We may observe the existence of an alternative tradition for the reform of Hezekiah which is found in a unique reference in Jeremiah 26.17–19 which tells us, quite surprisingly, that it was at the judgment oracle of Micah (no mention of Isaiah!) that Hezekiah and all Judah not only did not kill the prophet for uttering such words (as some were threatening to kill Jeremiah in a comparable situation), but 'they feared the LORD and they appeased him' and so the word of judgment was withdrawn. Here we have a tradition of repentance and reformation which differs from that of the Isaiah material; but it provides us with an analogy on which we may base the suggestion that in this all too concise wording put into the mouth of Hezekiah there is a reminder of his loyalty and reform. We may observe that this interpretation is in some measure confirmed by the Chronicler's handling of this incident (II Chronicles 32.31). He assumes his readers' knowledge of the whole story and does not relate it himself, but simply comments on this as being an occasion when the divine protection and blessing attended Hezekiah: 'So too it was in the incident of the emisaries of Babylon who were sent to him to find out about the sign which had occurred in the land, when God forsook him, testing him so as to know his true disposition.' For the Chronicler, this was a moment in which the nature of Hezekiah's obedience was disclosed, and though tested he was found to be loyal. We may observe that this interpretation of the passage has a counterpart

in the Josiah narrative when the doom in Judah is pronounced as coming after Josiah's death (II Kings 22.15–20).

But we may go two stages further in the understanding of this passage, for there are in the narrative two points, already noted, which need further comment. We noted that the two themes of the opening material are 'Babylon' and 'everything'. The first of these has an obvious significance when we read the whole work in which this narrative is now embedded. It was indeed to Babylon that exiles from Judah, including King Jehoiachin and his entourage, were to be taken, little more than a century later. For the reader of the whole, the reference could not but have a particular meaning. It is not the Babylon of Merodach-baladan but the Babylon of Nebuchadrezzar; but the two belong together. As this section of material stands in the book of Isaiah, it appears as a preface to the whole section, from ch. 40 onwards, which is devoted to the message of the unnamed prophet of the exile, the so-called Second Isaiah. However we may explain the literary history of that structure, we may see that there was here a clear awareness that the true meaning of this narrative was to be sought in its relation to the exile. But there is a further detail to be added to this. When Hezekiah replies to the prophet's question: 'Whence did they come?', he does not say, as we might expect, simply 'From Babylon', but 'From a far country, from Babylon.' The point is a nice one, and we must beware of building too much on a single word; but it is significant that this expression 'a far country' and other similar wordings are particularly used with reference to the remote places to which men may be exiled, or to places from which the exiled members of the community will return. Salvation comes from afar, from a land of exile (Jeremiah 46.27); those who are far off, the exiles, will come and rebuild the temple (Zechariah 6.15); the exiles are 'my sons afar off' (so Isaiah 43.6 and cf. also 60.9; 60.4; probably also 49.12; Zechariah 10.9 and perhaps Jeremiah 31.10); the exiles will remember Jerusalem from afar in a context which clearly indicates Babylon (Jeremiah 51.50). While there is no complete uniformity of usage, many passages which use this word or others closely related clearly refer to the exile in Babylon. The use of the words 'far country' here would be likely to carry with them the overtone of 'land of exile'.[16]

The second point is more important; it concerns the repeated emphasis on 'everything, not a single item to be left', and with this goes the repeated use of the verb *rā'āh* 'to see', five times in these verses. We have noted that the point about 'everything' is made three times in this passage; first in the description of what Hezekiah showed the ambassadors; second in his reply to the prophet; third in the prophet's word of judgment. It is extremely improbable that such repetition is without particular meaning. To understand it we must go a little further afield. The emphasis here is upon what Hezekiah *showed*, upon what the ambassadors *saw*. Seeing is to be recognized as having a fuller significance here than mere observation.

There are two possible lines of approach to this matter. The first line is to see here an example of the significance of 'seeing' in quite general terms. Of this numerous indications appear in the Old Testament; for example, to 'see' one's enemies (*rā'āh b* – to look *on*, as older renderings have it) is to be powerful over them. To see objects, whether in prophetic vision or in actuality, may involve a particular kind of relationship to them and their meaning. To 'see the land', as in Deuteronomy 34.1–4. may involve a confidence of possession, a foretaste of occupation.[17]

The second line is to consider the relevance here of a suggestion made by Professor David Daube in his *Studies in Biblical Law*.[18] He illustrates here certain features of the biblical material with reference to a particular aspect of Roman law which he believes sheds light on practices which may be detected elsewhere. The principle involved is that of a procedure termed *traditio* as applied to the taking over of something which cannot be physically handed over to the new owner. In a normal day-to-day purchase, no problem arises since the exchange can be effected at the same time as the payment is made. But for the purchase of a house or a piece of land – and we may observe that this is still a matter for proper procedure – a more complex situation exists. Roman law provides for this by a deliberate viewing of the house or land in question, a formal moment at which the exchange is deemed to have taken place. A somewhat analogous procedure appears to have existed at Nuzi in which transfer of property in the case of dowry is associated with shoes as a legal symbol. Reflection of some comparable practice may perhaps be detected in the rather obscure references to shoes in Deuteronomy 25.9 and Ruth 4.7.[19] Without overpressing the analogy, Daube suggests that certain allusions in the Old and New Testaments may be understood in this way. He stresses that such a viewing must be accompanied by the owner's intention to hand over the property.[20] Thus the viewing of the land by Moses from Mount Nebo before his death in Deuteronomy 34.1–4 is not to be regarded as simply a matter of allowing the old leader, forbidden entry, to have a last wistful look at the land which he will never really see. As has been suggested, it may involve more significant seeing: Daube believes that it is to be understood as a formal legal act of taking possession. Similar examples may be seen in Genesis 13.14ff. where Abraham is in fact made to anticipate the Mosaic act of taking possession of the land; in Deuteronomy 3.27f. where Moses sees the land from Pisgah; in Matthew 4.8f in the story of Jesus' temptations, when the devil shows him all the kingdoms of the world; in the parable of the guests who made excuses when invited to the feast, one of whom had bought a piece of land and must go to see it (cf. Luke 14.18), not to be seen therefore as a trivial excuse, but as a formal legal act without which the purchase would be void.[21] The Hezekiah narrative may be seen to belong here, and thereby its significance is made clear. The king shows the ambassadors from Babylon everything in palace and kingdom; the prophetic judgment explicates this by saying that everything in effect now belongs to Babylon. It is true that there is absent from this the feature of 'owner's intention to sell' noted by Daube, but here we may legitimately trace the further interpretation of the analogy. It is in fact God who has decreed the handing over of the land – it is his, after all – and Hezekiah has become his unwitting agent in bringing about the loss of the land. By letting these ambassadors see everything, Hezekiah has handed over the possession of everything in Judah to the enemy and has anticipated the exile. Though the disaster itself belongs to the future – the time is coming – the essential legal take-over has already ensured that exile will take place.

It will be evident that the interpretation of this element in the narrative does not depend on either of these suggestions; the repetitiousness and hence the emphasis of the language would in itself be enough. But either or both of these would make possible a greater degree of precision in interpretation.

Thus we have in this narrative an anticipation of exile which serves to make two points. In the first place, the experience of exile when it comes may be understood to have been foretold in prophetic judgment; and not merely that, its reality and its legality are established by royal action and prophetic interpretation. The point is then in part that of other prophecy-fulfilment patterns to be found in the Deuteronomic History; it is also an assurance that the disaster of the exile is to be attributed not to some accident, but to the divine will operating through the prophetic word, itself linked to the behaviour of a particular ruler. In the second place, we may observe here a theme which is not fully worked out in the Deuteronomic History but which is carried to its logical conclusion by the Chronicler. The implication of the last part of II Kings is clearly that nothing of any significance was left in Judah, though there is other evidence, notably in Jeremiah, to indicate that this is not a wholly correct description of the historical situation. The emphasis of this passage is a carrying further of that point: everything, every single item, is to be carried to Babylon. The Chronicler, in II Chronicles 36, makes this explicit in his description of a totally empty land, able now at last to 'enjoy its sabbaths' (v. 21), its rest from an evil population.

We may also note that the Chronicler, who uses this theme of the ambassadors in a different way, has in fact made use of the Babylon theme. In II Chronicles 32 he makes no reference to Babylon, and none to the prophetic judgment. When in II Chronicles 36 he comments on the final judgment, it is in terms of the prophecies of Jeremiah, or in more general terms with reference to the prophets sent repeatedly (so vv. 12, 15f.). But he appears to have offered in II Chronicles 33 a *midrash* of this passage in II Kings by making it applicable not in general terms to Hezekiah's descendants, but precisely to his son and successor Manasseh. This ruler, described, as in II Kings 21, as totally evil in his ways, falls under judgment and is described as carried away captive to Babylon. The judgment, it is implied, falls here; and at the same time the Chronicler provides an anticipation, a type, of the exile of the succeeding century, and with it also a type of restoration; for the wickedest of the rulers of Judah (as he is in the older narrative) is now shown to repent and when restored to become an ardent religious reformer. We are not here concerned with the improbabilities of this narrative, though it is evident that it will not do as history. What we observe is the way in which a motif is used, and elaborated, and the theme of exile and restoration is demonstrated in the portrayal of this Manasseh as himself undergoing both, a clear pointer to the meaning for the whole community of both judgment and repentance and restoration.[22]

III

We may move to the other narrative in II Kings 20.1–11/Isaiah 38, that of the illness and recovery of Hezekiah. It is a narrative which contains many points of interest, not least in its illumination of an aspect of prophetic activity – the medical aspect – which is otherwise little touched on in prophetic material in the Old Testament.[23] Here is a prophet who does not simply pronounce death and life; he prescribes the medical treatment appropriate to the restoration to health.[24]

It is not my purpose here to discuss the many and difficult questions which arise in this narrative. We may detect clearly enough that there are two separate elements which have been brought together. There is the theme of illness and recovery which is in fact complete in 20.1–7/38.1–6, at which point the Hebrew text pronounces the recovery of the king and no further explanation is really needed.[25] This has now been combined with a quite separate motif which in the Isaiah text becomes the primary one, that of the sign by which the recovery of the king is to be assured. The precise nature of this sign, and its miraculous quality, present a number of detailed questions of interpretation, since the text and meaning, particularly of 20.11/38.8, are by no means entirely clear.[26] For our purpose it is sufficient to note that the adding of this miraculous motif serves to underline the significance of Hezekiah's recovery; this is no unimportant moment, it is one to which the reader's attention is being especially directed. He is invited to read a fuller meaning here. It does, in fact, mark one stage in the evolution of the figure of Hezekiah towards both the larger conception of him found in II Chronicles and the even higher estimates which may be found in later Jewish writings.[27]

The effect which is produced by this now complex narrative is to underline the major significance of the illness and recovery of the king. The narrative is, we may properly assume, based upon a genuine tradition concerning illness and recovery; it may, with its fifteen years of extra life, have been geared into the archival information about the reign of Hezekiah. But its importance is not limited to that historical aspect; it is linked rather to the understanding of the period of Hezekiah as crucial for the understanding of Judah's fortunes as a whole. It is here too that a major point of difference between the II Kings and Isaiah forms becomes relevant. In the Isaiah text, there is added to the narrative of the illness and recovery a psalm appropriate to the situation (38.9–20). Such inclusion of psalm passages in narrative contexts may be paralleled at several points in the Deuteronomic History: in Deuteronomy 32, the Song of Moses (not 33 which is of a different kind): in I Samuel 2, the song of Hannah: in II Samuel 22–23, two psalms associated with David. The relative rarity of such insertions suggests that we should not suppose that they are the result of the desire of a scribe to brighten up the narrative by quoting a piece of poetry or even to preserve ancient poetic passages which might otherwise be lost, but rather of an endeavour to draw out the significance of the narrative by the use of poems which point to important elements which it is desired to underline. Thus Deuteronomy 32 at the very least draws out the whole significance of the themes of the land and its possession and of the disobedience and response of Israel to the acts of God. I Samuel 2 not only provides a comment on the birth of Samuel, but points to the theme of monarchy and to the power of God to bring down and to raise up; II Samuel 22 and 23.1–7 provide comments on the significance of the Davidic house, interrelating the themes of divine judgment and restoration. The psalm is Isaiah 38 is not simply an appropriately worded psalm of thanksgiving for deliverance in time of distress, here seen as apposite to the recovery of the king. It is a comment on the larger significance of that recovery in the context of the whole work. For its concentration is on that experience expressed in terms of restoration to life, being brought back from the pit, using a series of metaphors which we may find, for example, in the poems of Lamentations and in certain passages in Jeremiah, employed in relation to the experience of exile.[28] Its climax is reached in a point which may be paralleled in other such psalms,[29] the act of praise and worship in which the individual is joined by the community. Such a climax here provides a pointer to that longed-for restoration of the temple and its worship which is seen as the sequel to disaster in the fuller working out of the theme in the writings of the Chronicler. The illness of Hezekiah and the death sentence upon him thus become a type of judgment and exile, and in that measure they run parallel to the theme of judgment which is found in the ambassador story which follows;

but the theme of restored life and continuing rule which follows upon Hezekiah's strong appeal to the deity, is a pointer to the possibility of such a restoration for the community. We may observe that the Deuteronomic History is very cautious in its hopes for the future; but it is prepared here to offer the hint, a hint much more fully developed in longer sermonic passages in Deuteronomy itself (e.g. Deuteronomy 28, 29, 30), that the future well-being of the people belongs in a new entry to the land and a total commitment to obedience, an obedience of the kind to which Hezekiah makes appeal as he asks for a respite from the sentence of death.

IV

This line of interpretation, if it is acceptable, provides some clue to the reason for these two narratives standing together at the end of the Hezekiah section. We might be tempted to argue that the compiler has placed them here because he regarded them as less important than the much longer narratives which precede, those which introduce so fully the themes of the Assyrian threat and its withdrawal. We might suppose them to be merely in the nature of an appendix to the main material. But it is more satisfactory to see their inclusion as providing comment on and illumination of what precedes, and it is in the light of this that we may for a moment look back at those preceding chapters and ask ourselves what difference to their interpretation this conclusion makes.

Before we do this, we may note that something of the same kind of 'reading as a whole' is desirable also in the case of the very different alternative presentation in II Chronicles 29–32. If we are right in seeing the Chronicler as providing a new interpretation of already familiar themes, then we may see that the effect is produced by a similar device. The enormous concentration on the detail of reform in chs. 29–31 now provides an introduction to the very short account of the Assyrian invasion and withdrawal, and the even shorter allusions to the illness and ambassador themes, which are handled in a way similar to that in which the Chronicler often uses older themes, pointing to the consequences of faith – as in the Assyrian campaign – and to the consequences of pride and ingratitude – as in the illness theme – and of the testing of faith in the ambassador theme. What might easily have been total disaster – Hezekiah's ingratitude for the recovery of his health is said to have been the occasion for divine wrath against Judah and

Jerusalem – was averted by the submission of king and people and the withdrawal of judgment. The visit of the ambassadors too was an occasion of testing in which Hezekiah the reformer is shown to have stood the test in spite of being forsaken by God. We are in fact here invited to read both backwards and forwards: Hezekiah the reformer is the king to whom these things proved in the event to be occasions for divine blessing and accepted reproof; a king to whom such experiences could come and in which he could be found to withstand danger is one whose life must be read in the light of that loyal and reforming activity.

So we may ask, in regard to II Kings 18–20/Isaiah 36–39, what effect upon the whole is produced by our awareness of what is to follow the Assyrian section of II Kings 18–19/Isaiah 36–37. I would like to point simply to two elements which, as it seems to me, invite an integrated reading of the section. The first is in the much misunderstood speech of the Rabshakeh in II Kings 18.28–35; the second in the poetic oracle in 19.21–28.

1. The interpretation of the speech of the Rabshakeh in the light of Assyrian information about policy in regard to rebellious cities and lands is of interest.[30] It does not, in fact, need an Assyrian parallel to explain the verisimilitude of an appeal to a besieged city to submit and accept favourable terms, for this is a common device in warfare (cf. I Samuel 11). It has the advantage to the attacker that persuasion to submit will spare him the necessity of a prolonged campaign, the costliness in time and manpower of carrying through a successful siege and capture of the city, the risks and uncertainties which must always attend such a campaign; on his side there is some degree of bluff, since he is endeavouring to persuade the besieged that his victory is certain. For the besieged the attraction of accepting terms offered before the final onslaught is evident; the eventual terms, if the city is captured, will inevitably be worse, much life will be lost, the consequences will in all probability be disastrous; on their side the degree of bluff in the negotiations depends upon their estimate of the strength of the besiegers and the strength of the city, and their possible hopes of relief from their allies. But what is significant in this instance is not this general negotiating procedure; nor is it appropriate to attempt to discover in the terms offered by the Assyrians some precise detail of what attractions they were holding out to the inhabitants. It is the kind of claims which are being made. The

presence of Deuteronomic as well as prophetic language in the Rabshakeh's speech has often been noted.[31] What has not been clearly observed is that the main point in the speech is in effect a parody of the divine promise of the land to Israel. Instead of the propriety of stating: 'Hear the word of the LORD: thus says the LORD' – expressions proper to prophetic judgment and promise, we have 'Hear the word of the supreme king, the king of Assyria; thus says the king.' Instead of an exhortation not to trust in other gods or powers, we have a reversal of this. Instead of a ridiculing of foreign gods which are powerless to deliver, contrasted with the theme of the God of Israel as alone able, we have that theme used to suggest the impotence of Israel's God. And most central of all, instead of the granting of the land to Israel as the act of a God whose promise it is, we have the arrogant claim of the Assyrian that he will take them into a land of promise, and that there they will live and not die. It is the most blatant parody of the assurances of Deuteronomy that God gives his people the land – much of the effect of Deuteronomy is produced by the sonorous repetition of that promise – and with it the assurance of life and not death if only Israel will accept the way of obedience and not that of disobedience (e.g. Deuteronomy 30). We need to remember that when the work in which this stands was brought into its final form, the land had been lost; the promises of Deuteronomy are set against the background of that loss. The hope of the future lies in belief in the reality of those promises and confidence that they are being renewed. The hope rests there, not in any spurious hopes which might be based on political calculation; it is the expression of a confidence which the narratives of II Kings 20 underline in their exposition of exile and restoration.

2. The poem in II Kings 19.21–28 is not an easy one to interpret. It appears to contain elements which are linked to the oracles of Isaiah of Jerusalem, and phrases which point to a link with those of the Second Isaiah. But essentially it makes the same point as is being made in the previous section, the point that supreme power and control rests with Israel's God. The Assyrian ruler who claims his power in terms which at one point suggest a parallel with the Exodus – 'I dried up with the soles of my feet all the rivers of Egypt' (accepting that this is probably what is meant by a phrase which refers as it stands to 'the rivers of the besieged place') – is in fact under divine judgment, and is to be led captive just as he led others

captive. (This too is a point taken further by the Chronicler in his handling of the theme in II Chronicles 32.2–6.)[32] Again we may see this as being read in the exilic context and see how a much fuller meaning is imparted to it against that background, and appreciate how, in the final form of this material, within the context of the whole work in which it belongs, there is an understanding that the present condition of the community is both to be seen as the proper result of divine judgment and to be understood in the light of the promises and power of God. We may see too that this element in the Sennacherib narrative, together with the illness and ambassador themes, particularly with the former in its extended form in Isaiah 38, make the placing of the whole section in its position in the book of Isaiah more intelligible as explicating the relationship, however it is precisely to be described, between Isaiah of Jerusalem and that unnamed successor whose words have been bound in with his in the present form of the book.

V

I have entitled this study 'An Interpretation of the Babylonian Exile', and have for this purpose isolated one section of a work which must be read as a whole. In doing this there are clearly certain disadvantages, for it is not fair to an author's purpose to extract one element of what he has set out. Yet the understanding of that purpose is made possible not only by the total impression which it makes, having regard to the whole sweep of his pen, but also by the detection in his handling of the material at his disposal, and no doubt, if we could but know it more precisely, in his selection from that material, the lines of his thinking and the depth of his appeal to his contemporaries to understand their situation aright.[33]

We may, though only tentatively, trace a possible line of development in the traditions concerning Hezekiah. Behind the present series, there are discernible, on the basis of comparable material, narratives dealing with the major moments of Hezekiah's reign – a Hezekiah-Sennacherib tradition, a Hezekiah-illness tradition, and a Hezekiah-Merodach-baladan tradition. As we now have them, each of these, in its different ways, shows the integrating of the figure of Isaiah into them; but each or all of them may in fact depend on alternatives in which the action of the prophet was not mentioned. The significant position given to

Isaiah in them is indicative of the already enhanced position of Hezekiah, over against the figure of his predecessor Ahaz where actually existing prophetic (Isaianic) material does not appear in the most coherently presented form of the narrative in II Kings 16.[34] If we ask why Hezekiah is given this treatment, we may no doubt properly detect part of the reason in the actual historical situation, and in particular the tradition of Assyrian withdrawal in 701; perhaps we should see a reason also in the collapse of the Northern kingdom and the consequent inevitable focusing of hope in Judah. The upsurge of nationalism, expressing itself in religious reform, may be seen as a counterpart to this. This king comes to be associated with prophetic influence in a more positive manner, though not without its clear indications of judgment, as in Micah 3.12; cf. Jeremiah 26.17–19. The other major collocation of prophecy with royal narratives is to be found in that whole series concerning Elijah and Elisha and their association with the condemned dynasty of Omri and Ahab.

The prophetic association with Hezekiah provides the occasion both for deliverance themes – particularly as these are worked out in the Sennacherib sections of II Kings 18–19/Isaiah 36–37, and further in the illness motif – and also for the declaration of coming and inevitable judgment in the Merodach-baladan theme, though the disaster is to lie beyond Hezekiah's reign. There is here already a pointer to the subsequent development of the Hezekiah motif. It will be seen more fully elaborated in the Chronicler's narratives (II Chronicles 29–32) where the special place of Hezekiah is drawn out both in reform and in success in a situation of military danger and in the testing moments of illness and Babylonian embassy – though each of these instances has its aspects of uncertainty. An interim stage in the development may be seen in the Isaiah 36–39 form of the material. This does not include any equivalent for II Kings 18.14–16 (though it does have a verse corresponding to 18.13), the account of Hezekiah's submission to Assyria and payment of tribute; it adds to the divine action in the healing of Hezekiah by stressing the miraculous sign (a theme taken further in II Chronicles 32.31) and by adding the psalm of thanksgiving. Hezekiah is on the way to becoming the ideal king, but his ideal position is not reached without some warnings of the risk of disobedience and pride. Beyond this again lie the later elaborations of the Hezekiah theme. It is set out in Ben Sirach 48.17–25, associated especially with Isaiah; it is to be found in later much more elaborated messianic speculations and hopes concerning Hezekiah. In rabbinic writings, the theme of his messiahship is worked out, associated with a specially designated birth in Isaiah 7 (on the view that the child to be born was the king's son),[35] raised virtually from the dead in his illness, and so himself the receptacle for a great range of hopes for the future, already adumbrated in points in the older narratives.[36] It is perhaps therefore not too much to claim that we have here in him a degree of foreshadowing not only of exile and disaster but also of restoration and hope.

10

The Death of Hezekiah: A Pointer to the Future?

The death of Hezekiah is described in two passages in the Old Testament: II Kings 20.21 and II Chronicles 32.33. It is not mentioned in the parallel text to II Kings found in Isaiah 36–39, nor is it included in the list of items concerning the king in Sirach 48.17–25. This latter is not easy to assess. It belongs in the context of a section which gives prominence only to certain kings, and among these David, Hezekiah and Josiah are singled out as the only faithful rulers (49.4). The only other kings mentioned by name are Solomon and his foolish son Rehoboam. Of the latter only his folly and the rebellion of Jeroboam is recounted. Solomon's falling under the control of alien women leads on into condemnation, and to a statement of his death. The death of David is implicit in the text (47.12); that of Josiah is not mentioned. The point may be worth fuller discussion, but in any case we may observe that the account of Hezekiah, which here concerns us, is very closely built not primarily on the presentation offered in II Kings 18–20, but on that found in Isaiah 36–39.[1]

I   *Hezekiah in the Book of Isaiah*

The presentation of Hezekiah in Isaiah 36–39 has been my concern in two earlier studies. In the former of these,[2] the attempt was made at drawing out the particular significance of the two narratives in Isaiah 38 and 39 (II Kings 20). They are shown to provide pointers to the understanding of the exile and to the hope of restoration; their position in the book of Isaiah raises questions about the structure of that book; the presentation of Hezekiah both here and in the Chronicler (especially II Chronicles 32) looks forward to later rabbinic material in which Hezekiah appears as a messianic figure[3]. In the second study,[4] the fuller consequences in relation to the placing of the material in the book of Isaiah are examined, and it is suggested that we are here provided with a counterpart to Isaiah 6.1-9.6 – with a series of points of correspondence and contrast – a counterpart which serves to present the activity of Isaiah in the period of Hezekiah as the historic occasion for the giving of words of consolation which follow in Isaiah 40ff.

In the course of these studies, a number of points related to the differences in the texts of II Kings 18–20 and Isaiah 36–39 are considered. In particular it may be noted that the account of the Assyrian attack in Isaiah 36 lacks any reference to the material contained in II Kings 18.14–16: the text begins in 36.1 with a verse exactly corresponding to II Kings 18.13, but proceeds directly to the Assyrian threats of 18.17ff. (36.2ff.). The effect is immediately to modify the picture of Hezekiah from a rebel and a political contriver – implicit in the II Kings text – to that of a king of absolute faith and trust when confronted by the Assyrian onslaught. This provides a marked contrast with the portrayal of Ahaz in Isaiah 7 which, in fact, presents Ahaz as a king who lacks faith, a picture markedly darker than that provided in the corresponding II Kings 16.[5] Ahaz has already moved down the scale, approaching the low point reached in the vivid picture of II Chronicles 28;[6] Hezekiah has moved up the scale towards the idealization to be found in II Chronicles 29–32, in Sirach 48 and beyond.

The Isaiah 36–39 text also differs from that of II Kings 18–20 in that it includes no mention of the death of Hezekiah. The concluding summary of the reign in II Kings 20.20 and the brief mention of his death in 20.21 do not appear. We observe that also missing from the Isaiah text is the statement about Hezekiah's accession to the throne, the positive comments on his reign and on his reform, on his rebellion and his conquest of Philistia (II Kings 18.1–8; the following verses 9–12 are not relevant, since they offer only a brief alternative to the account of the fall of the Northern kingdom, already given in 17.1–6). The absence of both the beginning and the end of the narrative suggests strongly that, whoever was responsible for placing this material in the book of

Isaiah, was concerned only to include those parts of the story immediately germane to its function there. But while this may be admitted, we may feel some surprise that there is no mention of the favourable features of Hezekiah's policy, and in particular of his reform. By comparison, the omission of II Kings 18.13–16 is easy to understand.

One difficulty in any speculation regarding the reasons for the omission of the opening and concluding verses, is the lack of precise analogy. The section in II Kings 18–20 is unique in that its major sections are concerned with the only one of the so-called writing prophets who appears in the narrative books (the mention of Jonah ben Amittai in II Kings 14.25 is not a real exception). The only near analogy is to be found in Jeremiah 37–44,[7] but in this instance we have no parallel text, only the shorter presentation in II Kings 24.18 – 25.30 in which Jeremiah is not mentioned. To postulate a form of the Kings text containing the longer presentation is pure hypothesis, though I believe such a hypothesis to be a reasonable one. There is also the case of Jeremiah 52: this chapter, as a parallel to II Kings 24.18 – 25.21 and 25.27–30, while it is clearly of considerable importance, is precisely related to the Kings text; it covers the same section as is covered in Jeremiah 37–44, lacking only the account of Gedaliah (II Kings 25.22–26) and including at that point a further statement of deportation (Jeremiah 52.28–30). There is no question here of the omission of beginning and end of the text utilized; the omission of the Gedaliah episode and the addition of details of the third deportation are clearly important features of the alternative text, but do not help with the particular question at issue here.

Two suggestions may be made. First we may note that, although there is no previous allusion to Hezekiah in the book of Isaiah, except in the formula of 1.1, clearly an editorial element, there are two points at which his presence may be detected in the interpretation of the text.

1. The critical view of the Davidic monarchy, explicit in Isaiah 7 and implicit in Isaiah 6, finds its counterpart in the oracle on the Davidic child hailed in Isaiah 8.23 – 9.6. As this oracle is placed, following the negative material dealing with Ahaz, it occasions no surprise to find that later interpreters saw here the figure of Hezekiah.[8] We may legitimately ask whether this was not already

the intention of the compiler(s) of Isaiah 6.1 – 9.6.

2. Isaiah 14.28 refers to the death of Ahaz. That the text is frequently emended to eliminate any reference to Ahaz may result in the significance of the statement being overlooked. If we take the MT seriously, the moment of the death of Ahaz is that of the accession of Hezekiah.[9] The oracle which follows in 14.29–31 – probably not a single unit – is clearly concerned with a threat from Assyria (or a later imperial power) attacking from the north. Its relation here to a further saying in 14.32 concerning the firm establishment of Zion, a markedly psalmic saying, provides links with comparable material in numerous sections of the book (e.g. 12.1–6; 32; 33; as well as 36–39 itself). The theme of the overthrow of Philistia might be connected with the note of Hezekiah's conquest of that area in II Kings 18.8. This is not mentioned in II Chronicles, but the text there (32.22f.) extends Hezekiah's achievements by referring to God's deliverance of him and of Jerusalem from the power of 'Sennacherib king of Assyria and from the power of all his enemies', and recounts the bringing of offerings from 'many' and the honouring of Hezekiah by 'all the nations'. The theme of the establishment of Zion is very precisely associated with Hezekiah in Isaiah 36–37 and again in Isaiah 38.

Both these passages suggest that for the compiler the preparation has already been made for the introduction of Hezekiah in 36.1 without any need for further explanation of his position as king. Indeed, we may go further and see, in a number of passages preceding Isaiah 36–39, other elements of preparation, particularly in the royal oracle in 32.1ff. Material which might originally have involved a negative appraisal of Hezekiah's policy – so ch. 20 and 22.8*b*–13 and perhaps also the very problematic 22.15–25 – contains no direct reference to him. A picture emerges which appears to be very different from that which we may trace from the Assyrian records of the period.[10]

When Hezekiah appears in 36.1 with apparent abruptness, we may thus see an ongoing feature of the book: the critique of the Davidic dynasty, so sharply presented in ch. 7, has been followed by indications of a coming new king in whom the promises to David are to be realized. The mysterious child of 7.14; the oracles of 8.23–9.6 and 11.1–10, and the other passages in the succeeding chapters, already mentioned, provide repeated indications of this hope, with implicit or slightly more direct pointers to Hezekiah (only 14.28 is really precise[11]). The Hezekiah presented in 36–39 is just such a king, and his significance is shown both in his response to the Assyrian threat and in his new life out of death granted in response to his prayerful appeal in ch. 38. He then becomes the one through whom exile is decreed in ch. 39, a narrative remarkable for its skilful reversal of a negative view of Hezekiah (which must underlie the present form of the material) into one which shows his effective symbolic action.[12]

If we then ask why there is no summary of his reign and no account of his death such as appear in II Kings 20.20–21, the answer may be given that, in the view of the compiler of the book of Isaiah, the significance of Hezekiah was not yet complete. It is in the context of his involvement in the certainty of exile that there is the occasion for the giving of the oracles of hope and restoration that follow.[13] We may indeed ask whether the confident chapter division between 39 and 40 and the consequent separating of 40–55 or 40–66 precisely from what precedes, however much it may have brought gain in a proper appreciation of the prophecies of Isaiah of Jerusalem,[14] may not have served to obscure the nature of the purposeful arrangement of the material of the book. Is there perhaps a case for seeing the opening verses of chapter 40 as in reality the concluding and hopeful answer to the decree of exile in ch. 39? The degree of parallel structure between 6.1–9.6 and 36–39 would be even more strongly seen if 40.1–11 as a counterpart to 6.1–13 provided both a rounding off for the preceding narratives and an introduction to what follows.[15]

II   *The Death of Hezekiah in II Chronicles 32*

If the non-mention of the death of Hezekiah in Isaiah 39 is thus intelligible, we may turn to another aspect of the question, that raised by the description of that death in II Chronicles 32.33. Whereas the conclusion to the reign of Hezekiah in II Kings 20.21 uses the simple formula: 'Hezekiah slept (lay down = *škb*) with his fathers',[16] the Chronicler has a much longer statement: 'Hezekiah slept (*škb*) with his fathers and he was buried (literally: 'they buried him', the impersonal construction) in the uppermost (*maʿᵃleh*) of the graves of the sons of David and all Judah and the inhabitants of Jerusalem did him honour at his death (*kābôd ʿāśû-lô bᵉmôtô*)'.

In view of the Chronicler's substantial expansion of the Hezekiah material, concentrating on his reforming activities in three whole chapters of the text (29–31), while handling much more briefly and often allusively the themes of the Assyrian withdrawal, of his illness and the affair with the Babylonian ambassadors, it is not surprising to find amplification also of the theme of his death. It is in line also with the way in which, in a number of points of detail, the achievements of Hezekiah are expanded, even universalized, in the final chapter of the account (II Chronicles 32).[17]

The first element in the account of the death of Hezekiah here concerns the place of burial. The particular word used to indicate the grave (*ma'aleh*), elsewhere has the meaning of 'ascent, a way up, hence a stairway'.[18] It seems very probable that in this context it should be held to indicate 'the uppermost of the graves'.[19] This in itself, if the interpretation is correct, could point to the honouring of Hezekiah above his predecessors: it is another element in the idealization of the king.

The second element is the strange expression which speaks, allusively, of some honour (*kābôd*) done to Hezekiah by 'all Judah and the inhabitants of Jerusalem'. What precise sense may this expression be held to have? The combination of the verb '*āsāh* with the noun *kābôd* is also found in Genesis 31.1, but the expression there quite clearly refers to wealth: 'he (Jacob) has acquired all this wealth' (*kābôd* = wealth, as, for example, in I Kings 3.13 where *kābôd* is paralleled by '*ôšer*). No analogy exists for the particular expression found in II Chronicles 32.33. In default of any other evidence, we may most naturally suppose that the phrase, perhaps in reality a quite common one, though occurring in this way in the biblical text only once, means exactly what it says: 'they did him honour', an oblique way of saying 'they honoured him' which might otherwise be expressed by the *pi'el* of the root commonly so used. It could presumably also mean: 'they acquired wealth for him', in the sense that they gathered together valuable gifts which were in some way to be associated with his burial, possibly treasures to be buried with the king; but the interpretation as 'wealth' seems less likely.

The Septuagint rendering corresponds very closely to the Hebrew text, adding to it only in that it renders *kābôd* by the double expression *doxan kai timēn*; the word pair has virtually the effect of a superlative, 'the greatest possible honour' (cf. also Peshitta).

The Targum has a literal rendering. The Vulgate, however, has a more precise interpretation: 'et celebravit eius exequias universus Iuda et omnes habitatores Hierusalem' (all Judah and the inhabitants of Jerusalem celebrated his burial). This rendering is of particular interest in the light of two other passages in II Chronicles. In II Chronicles 16.14 it is said of the death of king Asa that 'they burnt for him a very great burning' (*wayyiśrĕpû-lô śĕrēpāh gĕdôlāh 'ad-limĕ'ôd*). By contrast, II Chronicles 21.19 states of the condemned king Joram that 'his people did not make for him a burning like the burning of his fathers' (*wĕlō'-'aśû lô 'ammô śĕrēpāh kiśĕrēpat 'ăbôtâw*)[20].

It is evident from this latter statement that it was regarded as normal practice to 'make a great burning' at a king's death, and this is confirmed by Jeremiah 34.5. Here Jeremiah says to Zedekiah: 'In peace (well-being) you shall die, and with burnings (like those) of your fathers, the kings who preceded you, so they shall burn for you' (instead of *śĕrēpāh*, the Jeremiah text uses the cognate word *miśrĕpôt*).

There are two other apparent references to burning in connection with death. These are in I Samuel 31.12f. and Amos 6.10.[21] Both passages raise difficulties because they seem to assume the cremation of the dead, a custom which is not attested otherwise for ancient Israel.[22] G. R. Driver[23] has argued that *śārap* in these passages is not to be understood in its common meaning of 'burn', but is to be assigned to another root meaning 'anoint', and hence that there is a reference to the use of spices in connection with burial. This is in fact specifically stated in II Chronicles 16.14, but the placing of spices in the grave or on the funeral bier – the sense of *miškāb* here is not clear, though the former, with perhaps particular reference to the actual niche for the body, seems more probable – is clearly distinguished from the making of a fire. Driver's explanation appears possible, but it does not in fact help in clarifying the expression used in the Hezekiah passage. Nor does it appear clear why, if *śārap* really does denote anointing in I Samuel 31.12 and Amos 6.10 (NEB adopts Driver's interpretation in both passages), the same should not be said of the passages noted above where it has been assumed that there is reference to a fire (II Chronicles 16.14; 21.19; Jeremiah 34.5; NEB follows the common interpretation here). Could these passages also refer to the use of spices as normal in royal burials, and their omission as abnormal and therefore indicative of divine displeasure? The stumbling block of a double allusion would remain in II Chronicles 16.14, where the use of spices is quite explicit – using unambiguous vocabulary – and appears to be totally distinct from the use of *śārap*. Or does this text in fact mean: 'they filled it (the niche or bier) with spices . . .: they carried out for him an exceedingly great spicing'?

We are thus left with an uncertainty about the precise nature of the celebratory custom alluded to in these other passages. There does not appear to be a reference to embalming, since II Chronicles 16.14 is explicit in stating that the spices were placed in a particular position, not that they were used for the body. And Genesis 50.2,26 use the technical term *ḥnṭ* for embalming in the case of both Jacob and Joseph; though it must be admitted that the context is Egyptian rather than Palestinian, and the term is not used elsewhere in the biblical text in this sense.

This discussion can only very partially be held to illuminate the Hezekiah passage. At first sight the analogies with passages referring to *śᵉrēpāh* suggest that the *kābôd* mentioned in II Chronicles 32.33 might also be such. But if this is so, we may still ask why the Chronicler did not use the same explicit term as had been used in the two other passages. Did he wish to convey something more by the use of *kābôd*?

The pointers here are imprecise. The fact that it is the whole people who make a *kābôd* for Hezekiah suggests the analogy with the making of a *śᵉrēpāh* elsewhere: it is an act of honour, and the use of *kābôd* serves then to underline the position which Hezekiah has reached in the tradition. The matter does not, however, stop there. Later Jewish speculation about the position of Hezekiah as Messiah raises the question whether the use of this particular term may not in some measure have contributed to that further development. In a study of later Hebrew usage concerning the resurrection of the dead, J. F. A. Sawyer mentions *kābôd* as a significant word, with a particular reference to Psalm 73.24.[24] Here *kābôd* is associated with *lāqaḥ* ('to take', mentioned but not discussed by Sawyer), a term associated with the translation from life to the presence of the deity both in the case of Enoch (Genesis 5.24: *wᵉʾēnennû kî-lāqaḥ ʾōtô ʾᵉlōhîm*, he was not, for God had taken him) and in that of Elijah (II Kings 2.5). Was the Chronicler, by using here the word *kābôd* for the celebration of Hezekiah's death, deliberately adding to the Hezekiah legend, or perhaps reflecting yet another aspect of an already growing body of tradition concerning him? He was not in any way suggesting a resurrection for Hezekiah, but he may have assisted in the further development of the Hezekiah tradition by using a word which could later be held to suggest something of that kind. Hezekiah is not yet a messianic figure in the later, technical, sense; but he is certainly already being idealized out of all recognition, and clearly in large measure out of relationship with the much more sober view of him which might be extracted from contemporary non-biblical material and from a critical appraisal of the biblical material itself. But this last is another theme in itself.

11

The Biblical Interpretation of the Reigns of Ahaz and Hezekiah

1. *The Available Biblical Material*

Narrative and archival information concerning Ahaz occupies the whole of II Kings 16; some small part of this appears also in Isaiah 7, where v. 1 is close to II Kings 16.5; Ahaz is mentioned also in vv. 3, 10 and 12 in material not paralleled in II Kings. The death of Ahaz is recorded in Isaiah 14.28 though arguments have been adduced for removing his name by emending the text.[1] A very markedly divergent account of Ahaz appears in II Chronicles 28, and 29.19 refers to Hezekiah's reversal of Ahaz's action in respect of sacred vessels. In addition, note may be taken of the reference in Isaiah 38.8 to the *ma'ªlôt 'āhāz* (the stairs(?) of Ahaz) paralleled in II Kings 20.11 where it is, however, lacking in LXX*,[2] which may suggest that it is intrusive there in the MT. II Kings 23.12 refers to the *'ªlîyyat 'āhāz* (? upper room), clearly in reference to an idolatrous practice. In Isaiah 38.8, 1QIsª has *bm'lwt 'lwt 'hz 't hšmš*. These last allusions, their meaning and interrelationship, are problematic.[3]

Narrative and archival material concerning Hezekiah appears in II Kings 18–20, the main part of which is found also, in a partially deviant text, in Isaiah 36–39. II Chronicles 29–32 has a sharply divergent account of Hezekiah, in which only ch. 32 covers, in substantially abbreviated form, the material found in the Kings and Isaiah texts.

The following discussion does not attempt to deal with all the many problems of content and structure, of viewpoint and shift, revealed by these texts. Nor will many of the details be considered except where they appear relevant to the main issues of interpretation with which this study is concerned. The intention here is simply to look critically at the interpretations offered by the biblical narrators and commentators with a view to some elucidation of the material.

II.   *The Assessments*

Ahaz in II Kings is given a negative comment, similar to that passed on numerous kings of Judah: 'he did not do that which was right in the sight of Yahweh his God as David his father had done' (16.2). The account which follows exemplifies certain aspects of his conduct. In the Chronicles account there has been a noticeable shift so that in effect he has become the worst king of Judah, thus taking the place of Manasseh in the Kings presentation, since Manasseh in Chronicles has become an evil king repentant and hence a reformer. The assessment of Ahaz in Isaiah 7 is also negative, in part directly, though largely by implication. In particular the negative shift in this material in comparison with II Kings 16 may be noted. This is especially clear in Isaiah 7.2, 4 which so presents the attitude of king and royal house as to suggest a state of totally unnecessary panic.[4]

Hezekiah in the narrative in Kings is approved, and indeed the style of the approval finds its counterpart only in the Josiah narrative (see II Kings 22.2). In fact, the Hezekiah statement goes further. In addition to the generally favourable mention of 18.3, comparing Hezekiah to David, we are further told in 18.5 that 'after him there was none like him among all the kings of Judah', together with a rather loosely added final phrase 'and who were before him', often regarded as a gloss.[5] While this may be a correct view of the final phrase, it is nevertheless itself a further indication of a process by which the stature of Hezekiah has reached ever higher levels.[6] The two approving statements in 18.3 and 5 enclose a note on the so-called 'reform of Hezekiah' in 18.4, which not only records the more conventional removal of high places, pillars and asherah, but specifically the destruction of the 'bronze snake which Moses had made'. The second approving statement in 18.5 is part of a larger unit which records Hezekiah's trust in Yahweh (5*a*), his total adherence to Yahweh (6*a*) and his obedience to the commands given to Moses (6*b*). Hence Yahweh was with him, so that he was successful in all that he undertook: he rebelled against the king of Assyria and did not serve him (7); and he conquered the Philistines and their territory (8). Apart from this last item, we may perhaps best see these statements as a kind of anticipatory summary of what follows in the succeeding chapters. These contain a rich assemblage of material, which in effect serves to show the deliverance of Hezekiah from the Assyrians (chs. 18–19) and from death (20.1–11); and prophetically reveals the coming Babylonian conquest and exile (20.12–19).[7] The final summary of 20.20 adds a reference to his action in regard to the water supply for Jerusalem, an item which is not in any way directly integrated into the assessment of Hezekiah. The recording of this may be neutral, a piece of archival information. It very naturally suggests the action of a good ruler who provides for the needs of his capital by bringing the water supply into the city (*hāʿîrāh*). We may perhaps suppose it to have military significance, because we may readily link it with the siege of the city by the Assyrians; but that is not stated in the text, and it is equally possible to regard it as expressing a general rather than a specific benevolent intention. In the context of the whole presentation of Hezekiah, it provides one further element suggestive of the approval of him as ruler.

The contrast between Ahaz in Kings and in Chronicles is matched by the converse for Hezekiah. What in II Kings 18.4 is a minimal reference to a 'reform' has as its counterpart the very substantial reform narrative which extends through II Chronicles 29–31. The idealization of Hezekiah is continued in the presentation in II Chronicles 32 of various elements of the Hezekiah story, at some points so abbreviated that it is clear that it is assumed that the Kings narrative or something like it is familiar to the reader. It underlines divine protection, has a slight warning note in 32.25, but ends with overwhelming approval of the king.[8] It is in various ways clear that already in II Kings, and still more clearly in II Chronicles, we are moving towards that glorification of Hezekiah as 'Messiah' which appears in Jewish writings.[9]

III.   *The Historical Context*

II Kings 16.7–9 provides a not entirely lucid statement of the political situation in the reign of Ahaz. It records that he sent messengers to Assyria, using a formula of subservience 'your servant and your son' (*'abd^{e}kā ûbin^{e}kā*).[10] The appeal was for deliverance from Aram and Israel. Ahaz sent silver and gold from the temple and from the royal treasury as a present to Assyria.[11] Assyria captured Damascus and 'exiled it to Qir',[12] and Rezin, king of Aram, was put to death. However, the status of Ahaz remains unclear in this narrative. Does his submission formula imply that he was already a vassal of the Assyrians, in the position of a subordinate ruler as 'servant and son'? Or should we suppose that this was his initial act of subservience and that rule by Assyria over Judah existed from this date?[13]

Some clarity on these questions may be provided by examining the rebellion of Hezekiah which is noted in II Kings 18.7 and reiterated by implication in 18.13–16. It is significant that 18.14 uses the verb *ḥṭ'* (do wrong) to indicate infringement of the vassal status. Furthermore, an indemnity is required by Sennacherib and set at three hundred talents of silver and thirty talents of gold. Finally, 18.15f. shows Hezekiah obtaining part or all of this indemnity by using materials from the temple and royal treasury. We may note that the same phrases are used of Ahaz in II Kings 16.8.

The background to this information is often filled in so as to offer a full and coherent picture, but the reconstruction is inevitably uncertain. II Kings 16 contains no comment on Ahaz's appeal to Assyria; any negative view of it depends rather on the broader context in which Ahaz is condemned. Equally, and more significantly, no comment is made on this issue in Isaiah 7. What we find here is an oracle against fear and a message of doom to Aram and Israel (7.4–9). No reference is made to Assyria in this passage. What is evident is that the opening of Isaiah 7 and the following oracle imply rather clearly that the panic of the Davidic house was unwarranted. It is often stated, as if it were self-evident, that Isaiah warned Ahaz against appealing to Assyria for help, but this is not in the text. If it is proper to regard it as a logical position for the prophet to hold – comparison may be made with the warnings of reliance on Egypt in Isaiah 29 and 31 and such a position would place him in the succession of Hosea with his warnings against political intrigue (e.g. Hos. 7.11) – we must still ask why the text does not make the point explicit. In the passages which follow (the end of Isaiah 7 and on into ch. 8), the 'king of Assyria' glosses in 7.17, 20 and the fuller Assyrian references in 8.4 and 7 draw out the theme of doom for Judah at the hands of Assyria. The implication of wrongful trust is present in 8.6 and 7, but again the text as it stands appears rather to emphasize that because of divine protection Ahaz and his court had no need to fear Aram and Israel. It also emphasizes that a king who lacks faith in Yahweh must expect doom at the hands of Assyria. But the two elements are left in suspense. Assessment is made problematic by the very evident glossing of the text and the difficulty of deciding to what context that glossing belongs.

The overall picture of Ahaz suggests that a particular politico-religious view, namely that appeal for help to an alien power was to be regarded as bad theologically, has contributed to the negative assessment of that particular king in the context of the more evidently religious condemnations which are offered of him. To those we must return.

On the other hand, the portrayal of Hezekiah in II Kings 18–20 shows him as desirably, by implication, rebelling against Assyria (18.7), submitting to Assyria and paying an indemnity (18.14–16). The relationship between these and other elements in the narrative has been an area of long debate.[14] A markedly contrasting narrative, or more probably double narrative, in 18.13, 18.17–19.37, shows the total inability of the Assyrians to bring about the capture of Jerusalem, and the total defeat of the army and the death of Sennacherib. The various elements of this complex section all contribute to the overall picture of disaster for Assyria and deliverance for Judah. In the context of information from Assyrian sources, it is clear that the overrunning of Judah which Sennacherib claimed, and which is implied in 18.13, did not include the capture of Jerusalem itself. It is clear that there was a major political and military crisis for Judah. It is clear also that if the Assyrians had captured Jerusalem, the narratives could not have been so conceived. The effect is to produce a political judgment which is also a religious judgment. Jerusalem was not captured by the Assyrians, and Hezekiah was the agent of that deliverance, which is clearly described as effected by direct divine intervention against all the political and military odds. Therefore, Hezekiah delivered Judah from the Assyrian yoke, and the implication is that his rebellion against Assyria was linked to this deliverance. This perspective is further underlined in the course of the illness narrative of 20.1–11 (especially v. 6).

Thus we may see that the narratives offer a political assessment in which Ahaz is adjudged to be a bad king and Hezekiah a good king. For good measure II Kings 16.6 adds the loss of Eilat, so placed as to indicate an additional item of judgment to the Aram and Israel reference of 16.5.[15] Again this theme is extended in the Chronicler's presentation.[16]

IV.   *Religious Assessment*

The treatment of Ahaz begins in II Kings 16.2*b* with a general and conventional condemnation. This is followed in 16.3–4 by three elements: a reference to his conforming to the practices of the kings of Israel (cf. II Kings 8.18, 27); a statement that he passed his son through the fire in accordance with the abominations of the dispossessed nations of Canaan; and a reference to worship on the *bāmôt* (high places) and *gᵉbā'ôt* (hills) and 'under every green tree' (cf., e.g., I Kings 14.23). Of these, only the second is distinctive, but even so the condemnation is generalized and not entirely exceptional.[17] The theme of religious impropriety is by implication continued in 16.8 which refers to his taking silver and gold from the temple and the palace treasury for the payment of the *šōḥad* (bribe).[18] If, in context, this may be intended to suggest religious impropriety, this is not explicitly stated. As already noted, a similar point is made about Hezekiah (II Kings 18.14–16).[19]

Much more specific detail appears in 16.10–18.[20] Here Ahaz is presented as travelling to appear before Tiglath-Pileser in Damascus, and as seeing there an altar of which he sent full details to Uriah the priest.[21] While it has often been assumed that this altar was of Assyrian design, and it is associated therefore with the political relationship between Judah and Assyria, it would appear much more probable that it was in fact Aramaean and belonged to the Damascus temple.[22] The sequel tells of the construction of the altar by Uriah according to the plan sent; the emphasis on the precise following out of the instructions suggests an ironic use of a formula frequently to be found in the descriptions of the tabernacle and other matters in the Pentateuch (cf. e.g. Exod. 39.32). This formal connection would appear to be an important element in the derogatory treatment of Ahaz; though at another level it could be read as indicating the degree to which exact divine instructions, as they might be understood, were executed. In 16.12f. Ahaz returns to Jerusalem, and sees the altar – a phrase which implies his approval and acceptance of it;[23] and he offers sacrifice on it, of which the details are supplied. A resulting rearrangement of cult furniture is described in 16.14f., showing that the bronze altar before Yahweh was moved, brought from in front of the temple, that is, between the altar (it is not clear which) and the temple, and placed to the north side of the altar (again it is not clear which). The text is by no means clear and is possibly overloaded. But the nub of the matter appears when it is stated that the new altar is to be for all major and royal and national sacrifices, while the bronze altar, in its new position, is for the king's own inquiries (*bqr*) of the deity. The section concludes with a repetition of the obedience formula (as in v. 11, see above), again suggestively ironic, but also potentially indicating the carrying through of instructions which are purportedly divinely given.

16.17–18 list some further alterations in the shrine. Ahaz 'cuts off' (*qṣṣ*), a term evidently intended to be derogatory. The details are not entirely clear, for the terms are uncertain, but a reference appears to the bronze oxen under the sea and their replacement by a stone support. The text clearly implies the removal of the bronze, perhaps also its cutting up. Is this robbing the temple for a bribe (cf. 16.7)? Is it taking the bronze for some other purpose? Or is it a replacement of worn, damaged, broken temple equipment by new? Can we assume that replacement of bronze by stone, which would be much stronger for holding what may have been a weighty object, was necessarily a nefarious procedure? We are also told of the removal of *mûsak* (Q) or *mîsak* (K) (?cover) of *haššabbāt* (?sabbath).[24] The text continues: 'which had been built in the temple and the outer entrance for the king he turned round the temple of Yahweh'. The meaning is very unclear.

At the end of v. 18, there is a statement which appears to refer back to everything that precedes. It was done *mippᵉnê melek 'aššûr* ('before the king of Assyria'), which appears to imply that all the alterations depicted were due to Assyrian requirements or to meet the Assyrian ruler's demands.

Some further indications of Ahaz's improper religious activity are implied in the reference to the *ma⁽ᵃlôt'āḥāz* in Isaiah 38.8 (cf. II Kings 20.11, though the text there is less sure), and to the *⁽ᵃlîyyat 'āḥāz* in II Kings 23.12, where altars are built on the roof of the *⁽ᵃlîyyat*. Uncertainties about what is referred to make it difficult to know just what is meant, but it is a fair assumption that these were viewed as undesirable objects or constructions.

II Chronicles 28.16–21 provides a fuller portrayal of disaster, beginning with an appeal to the 'kings' (plural) of Assyria. Reference is made to what appears to be the tribute Ahaz paid from temple and palace, with the sardonic comment that it did him no good (20–21); Ahaz engaged in idolatrous practice, worshipping the gods of Aram (22–23), which might be an interpretation of the altar theme of II Kings; he engaged in wrong cultic acts and such evils as the destruction of holy vessels and the shutting of the temple doors (24*a*); and he built a multiplicity of altars in Jerusalem (24*b*–25). The description provides a further though in some respects more generalized statement of Ahaz's irreligion, paving the way for a direct reversal of his actions by Hezekiah in II Chronicles 29.19.

It is clear that Ahaz is depicted as an evil king from the religious point of view, and this is pressed even further in the Chronicles material than in Kings. But is this the only possible interpretation of what we may detect in the Kings narrative? We may note that the items are capable of being viewed rather differently if we start from a neutral view of Ahaz.

1. The tribute/bribe theme, as we have seen, has its counterpart in the Hezekiah material in II Kings 18.14–16; in that context it does not carry any obvious overtones. Hezekiah used the temple treasures; he removed gold with which he had adorned the temple. It is, however, significant that this element of the Hezekiah material is absent in the more idealized presentation in Isaiah 36–39.[25]

2. The building of a new altar and the revision of religious practice does not in fact at any point directly imply idolatrous practice in the Kings narrative. In fact there is stress on the carrying out of all the normal rites, and no suggestion in the Kings text that Ahaz was worshipping any other deity.[26] How far should we regard the building of a new-style altar as alien in intent? Or should we view it as an updating and improvement of the facilities for worship in the Jerusalem shrine? After all, the fact that the

pattern of the Solomonic temple belongs in the general Near Eastern context and was built by Phoenician craftsmen according to familiar patterns is normally accepted as no indication in itself of alien practice. We may observe that a number of the cult installations of that shrine can be regarded as having parallels to cult objects elsewhere, and some of them, for example the two pillars Jachin and Boaz, are of doubtful interpretation, suggesting survivals of older ritual practice. The further note that the existing bronze altar was now to be used for the king's own inquiring of the deity could be held to imply a more specific piety, though more probably it provides an elusive clue to some aspect of royal worship.[27]

3. The statement that these actions were performed 'before the king of Assyria' mipp*enê melek 'aššûr) has been thought to indicate religious subservience to the Assyrians. As the text stands there is a strong implication of this in that the appeal to Assyria opens the section at 16.7 and the reference to Assyria concludes it at v. 18; thus the whole passage is implicitly related to the one theme. But it appears to be very clear that the Assyrians did not require religious conformity from vassal states; practices such as those of Manasseh's reign, often regarded as due to the Assyrian demands, are only doubtfully if at all associated with Assyrian religion.[28] The text could just as well suggest that it was because of Assyrian tribute demands that certain political actions were taken, but without any necessary religious implications.

4. The problems of detail in the text leave many uncertainties, especially in 16.18. The MT *šabbāt* does not seem to make sense and is more probably a deliberate change from *šebet* to imply that Ahaz disregarded or repudiated some sabbath object or rite. If the *šebet* refers to a throne of the king in the shrine, perhaps in some way linked to the royal cult,[29] then could not Ahaz just as well be removing a cult object which, by its particular religious associations, could be regarded as improper in the eyes of a reformer? If, as seems possible, the text also alludes to some special entrance for the king – though the wording is obscure – could it originally have suggested that he removed from the house of Yahweh (*hēsîr mibbēt yhwh*; MT *hēsēb bêt*) some privileged entrance for the king thought, again by a reformer, to be improper?

Of course, such comments as these can be no more than tentative, but what they might suggest is that if we start from an unprejudiced position with no prior assumption that Ahaz was a bad king religiously, these actions could be seen as acts of religious reform. Had he been viewed favourably, would they have been acceptable? Is he a bad king religiously because he is regarded as a failed king politically? A similar comment may be made on some aspects at least of the Saul tradition.

On the other hand, Hezekiah is a religious reformer and viewed favourably. A general statement of approval in 18.3 is followed by the conventional removal of *bāmôt*, breaking of *maṣṣēbôt*, cutting down of *ʾašērāh* in 18.4*a*. In 18.4*b* he is credited with the smashing of the *nᵉḥas hannᵉḥōšet* made by Moses, with the comment that the Israelites had been sacrificing to it and that it was called *nᵉḥuštān*. In II Chronicles 29–31 the reform theme is expanded to enormous proportions, but the detail does not here concern us; it is one element in the progressive idealization of Hezekiah.[30] What comment should be made on Hezekiah's actions?

1. II Kings 18.22 records a comment attributed to the Rabshakeh: Hezekiah has removed high places and altars and has commanded that worship should be offered in Jerusalem alone. While too much weight should not be given to the imaginative construction of the Rabshakeh's speech in which we may find a number of examples of Deuteronomic theology turned upside down (especially 18.29–32), such a statement could represent a reflection of actual adverse comment on Hezekiah's actions made by opponents. It is more probably a reflection of later attitudes, for centralization of worship is not alluded to in the reform statement of 18.3–4; hence it looks more like a reading back from Josiah and related to the Chronicler's elaboration. We may perhaps better see in this passage an ironic comment, not unrelated to the Ahaz material: Ahaz and his priest ironically carry out all that is ordered, simply compounding disaster; Hezekiah is ironically described as the king who has offended God by misplaced religious changes, though clearly, in the view of the narrator, the very opposite is true.

2. A much clearer point is to be seen in the removal of a cult object traditionally associated with Moses, and the explanation of this with a palpably contrived comment on its being treated as an idol.[31] Here we may legitimately ask whether, had Hezekiah been politically adjudged to be a bad king, this piece of religious 'reform' might have been seen as a sacrilegious action and hence disastrous?

V.   *Hypothesis*

The degree of hypothetical suggestion in what precedes will be apparent, but since we have progressed so far along such a line, may we not build a final construction, an overall hypothesis of a different possible view of these two rulers?

1. Could we not argue that Ahaz by submission to Assyria assured Judah of surviving the disaster which overtook the northern kingdom at that very period? Since we have no completely clear notion of where Isaiah stood, and the text does not tell us that he counselled against appeal and hence submission to Assyria, we cannot be sure whether he preferred a quietist policy, nor whether, had such a policy been adopted, the Assyrians would have been satisfied with an absence of clear indication of allegiance. What we do know is that in a very delicate political situation, and a real threat to his throne, since the nominee ben Tabeal[32] of Isaiah 7.6 must have been a viable candidate to take his place, Ahaz managed, contrived perhaps, to keep his throne and his kingdom intact. To survive may have been more important than to make futile gestures of independence.

2. Could we argue – and see here the evidence of Isaiah 20 and the Assyrian material which points to Hezekiah's involvement in rebellion in 713–711[33] – that Hezekiah by rebelling, more than once, seriously risked total disaster to Judah? If the Assyrians had not withdrawn from the siege of Jerusalem, which they were perfectly capable of capturing as they captured Lachish, and Judah had fallen totally in 701, not losing just the forty-six cities claimed by Sennacherib, what would have been the verdict on Hezekiah? We know that Judah remained in fact subservient to Assyria for the next three-quarters of a century. The text, both in Isaiah and in II Kings, clearly implies a quite opposite and historically inaccurate view, namely that Judah was totally delivered from Assyrian power. Hezekiah seems to have had a better press than he deserved.[34]

3. One wider consideration could be a further factor. We may ask whether it is right to detect in the royal narratives of the last century and a half of Judah's history an artificial alternating pattern which has imposed itself on the rulers. A later and more complex interwoven structure is to be found in II Chronicles; Ezekiel 18, with its alternating figures, provides another example

of a pattern. Ahaz bad, Hezekiah good, Manasseh bad, Josiah good, Jehoiakim bad (omitting the insigificant Amon and Shallum): it is a pattern which makes for good preaching, but is it not just a little too good to be true?

VI. *Conclusion*

This study is not written with a view to reaching firm historical conclusions. It is an attempt at looking beneath the surface of existing narratives and assessments to see how valid they are in the way in which they are designed to be read; to ask whether, if we stand at another angle to them, they may not look rather different. It would be just as unsatisfactory merely to reverse the conventional assessments. Kings, as politicians, are likely to be a mixture of good and bad; their religious policy, if we may judge by analogy, may combine genuine religious concern with political judgment. What does not seem entirely realistic is the over-simple black and white assessment. And the fact that the Chronicler could take the Kings' judgments a stage further in the case of Ahaz and Hezekiah, while effecting a substantial reversal in the case of Manasseh and Josiah, suggests that the motives of the presentation could be more important to consider before we accept the portrayals as given.

Gösta Ahlström in his writings has more than once shown himself to be a skilful iconoclast. This particular piece of turning upside down is offered as a tribute to that independence of judgment and critical acumen which mark his scholarship and which put all of us in his debt.

III

TOWARDS THE CANON

A Judgment Narrative between Kings and Chronicles? An Approach to Amos 7.9–17

In the present form of the book of Amos, 7.9–17 is set within the group of four visions gathered in 7.1–8; 8.1–2(3). The section is clearly marked off from what precedes and follows. The vision sequence is clearly interrupted by this, the only narrative passage in the book.

Apart from the strikingly different book of Jeremiah, the prophetic books of the Old Testament contain few actual narratives. The Jeremiah case is so different and the relationship of the narratives to the Deuteronomic 'school' of writing raises such complex questions, that it is clear that it must be treated as in many ways a quite distinct problem.[1] Prophetic narratives are not uncommon in the books of Samuel and Kings. Of these, one series, II Kings 18.13–20.19, reappears with some significant differences in Isaiah 36–39.[2] Some others of them, together with new ones, appear in the books of Chronicles. The difference between this type of prophetic material and that which is found in the prophetic books may be roughly stated: the former present stories about prophets in which their utterances are incorporated, usually briefly; the latter provide primarily collections of oracular and other such material, attached at some few points to brief narrative or annalistic (chronological) statements.[3]

Apart from these narratives in Jeremiah and Isaiah, there are only four passages in the prophets which can properly be described as narratives. (I would exclude here, because of their different character, the accounts of call experiences or of visions [e.g., Isaiah 6; Jeremiah 1.4–10], in which such narrative as is present is limited to the sphere of relationship between prophet and deity, and involves no other human participant.) One of the four is the book of Jonah, clearly *sui generis*; the second is Ezekiel 11.1–13, a remarkable and in many respects unique passage, in which, however, the narrative element is really only in vv. 1 and 13, the theme of Pelatiah's death being thus subordinated to the oracular material.[4] The third appears in Haggai 1.12–14 where the narrative describes the response to the prophetic word; it forms part of the framework to the oracles, and the structure of this book is again, with Zechariah 1–8, *sui generis*.[5] The fourth is the Amos passage with which we are concerned.

I. *Structure and Main Features*

G. M. Tucker has presented a form-critical study of vv. 10–17[6] and a number of the points which he makes, in relation to form and purpose, will need further comment. He does not discuss whether the passage really begins at v. 10 or whether v. 9 ought to be included with it, but for the most part assumes, although the point is made explicit once,[7] that v. 9 is either a comment on the preceding vision or visions[8] or a link verse designed to connect the narrative passage with the preceding visions.[9]

We may observe that, while this fragment could have been added to the third vision to clarify its meaning, it is certainly not part of the vision series, nor is it at all clear that it does really provide a clarification of v. 8. The four visions of Amos 7–8 form a perfectly balanced and structured unit: visions 1 and 2 (7.1–3, 4–6) form a matched pair, and so do visions 3 and 4 (7.7–8; 8.1–2). It is true that 8.3 is an addition standing outside the series,[10] and this might suggest that 7.9 is comparable, but against this may be set the close relationship between v. 9 and vv. 11 and 16. Verse 9 may in some measure be seen as the 'text' upon which that which follows is a narrative 'exegesis' (see below). A near parallel is to be found in Jeremiah 26.18–19, where the citation of Micah 3.12 provides the introduction to the interpretative narrative comment.[11] We may observe that Jeremiah 26.18 introduces the prophetic citation with a statement of the name of the prophet Micah and the occasion of his utterance; the relevance of this to the Amos passage will be suggested below.

Verses 10–17 contain, briefly outlined, the report to Jeroboam

(10–11), the command to Amos (12–13), and the prophetic response (14–17). Tucker, after a full discussion of alternatives, stresses the element of 'authentication' in the narrative. Near parallels may be seen in what we may term 'prophetic conflict' material, such as Jeremiah 28, where the element of authentication may be held to be significant, perhaps even primary. But to this we shall return.

We may also observe the degree to which word play enters into the passage. One element of such word play turns on the use of *gālāh* (go into exile); this appears first in v. 11 in an oracular utterance which partly overlaps v. 9, but introduces the new motif of the exile. This may be seen as a first stage in the exposition of v. 9, for the phrase *weqamtî ʿal-bêt yorobeʿām beḥāreb* (I will rise against the dynasty of Jeroboam with war) becomes *baḥereb yāmût yorobeʿam* (in war Jeroboam will die), and is then elaborated with *weyiśrāʾēl gālōh yigleh mēʿal ʾadmātô* (Israel will go into exile from upon its own land). This theme is picked up further in v. 17, where the judgment by the sword is applied to the priest's sons and daughters, the theme of *ʾadāmāh* (ground) is developed in terms of disinheritance (*teḥullāq*, be distant), of exile (*ʾadāmāh ṭemēʾāh*, unclean land), of death (*tāmût*, shall die), applied to Amaziah. The passage is rounded off by the repetition of the exile clause of v. 11. We may further ask whether there is intended to be a play upon the exile theme in that Amaziah may be held to be attempting to 'exile' Amos from the Northern kingdom, and this is countered by Amos' pronouncement of exile for Amaziah and Israel; but this is more remote and there is no verbal link.

II.   *Language and Thought*

The examination of the language of 7.9–17 reveals a small number of suggestive points:

1. The proper name *yiśḥāq* (Isaac, vv. 9, 16) occurs only here and in Jeremiah 33.26 and Psalm 105.9; elsewhere it is always written *yiṣḥāq*. In the Jeremiah passage it appears in a formulaic reference to the patriarchs of a kind which is probably a late feature both in the Deuteronomic writings and in Jeremiah;[12] dating a psalm is notoriously uncertain, but it is unlikely that Psalm 105 is early. No other reference to Isaac appears in Amos; such references are limited in the Old Testament to the narratives in Genesis, to

the patriarchal threefold formula (in Exodus to Numbers), to
the corresponding formula which appears as a probably late
amplification in the Deuteronomic writings,[13] and six times in the
Chronicles, of which three are in lists, one is in the citation of
Psalm 105 (*yiṣḥāq*), and two are in prayers using the formulaic
threefold phrase. The general lack of patriarchal references in the
prophetic writings makes any conclusions unsatisfactory, but we
may note that a reference to Isaac stands out as unexpected in
Amos, and that the spelling variant may be late.[14]

2. Whereas in the oracles cited in vv. 9 and 11 Jeroboam is
referred to simply by name, in v. 10 he is described as *melek yiśrā'ēl*
(king of Israel). Such a specification is natural in a narrative
context, and particularly appropriate in narratives in which both
kingdoms are mentioned; in this context, within the book of Amos,
it is odd.[15] The name occurs otherwise only in the heading in 1.1.

3. The verb and noun from the root *qšr* occur frequently in the
books of Samuel, Kings, and Chronicles.[16] It is also found in
Jeremiah 11.9 and in Isaiah 8.12, although its precise sense in
the latter is problematic; indeed, the context in Isaiah presents
difficulties of both text and interpretation.[17] In the sense of
'conspiracy,' which is appropriate to both the Amos and the
Jeremiah passages, it finds its clear parallel in a variety of narratives, especially in Kings.[18]

4. *kûl* (hiph. contain) in v. 10 occurs otherwise in Kings,
Jeremiah, Ezekiel, Joel, Chronicles.[19]

5. *nāṭap* (hiph.) in v. 16 appears literally of the flowing of liquid
in the late 9.13.[20] Of prophetic speech, as here, it is found in Ezek.
21.2, 7, parallel with *nibbā'* (prophesy), and in the difficult passages
Micah 2.6, 11.

6. The usage of *ḥōzeh* (seer, v. 12) is most frequent in the
Chronicler,[21] although there are occurrences also in II Samuel
24.11; in Isaiah 29.10 (probably a gloss); 30.10; 28.15 (probably
a textual error); in Micah 3.7, parallel to *qōsᵉmîm* (enchanters).
The verb appears in Amos 1.1, but is not otherwise used in the
book; in the visions the verb is always *rā'āh* (see).

7. To these we may add a number of smaller points. The use of
bāmôt for 'sanctuaries' in v. 9 is discussed below; the only other
occurrence in 4.13 is quite distinct. *bôqēr* (? cattle-man, v. 14) is a
hapax legomenon; the often proposed emendation to *nôqēd*, to conform
with 1.1 and to fit more properly with *ṣō'n* (flock), can hardly be

regarded as necessary, but would still leave us with a word not used in the oracles. *bôlēs* (? prick, squeeze, v. 14) is also a *hapax legomenon*, and *šiqmîm* (sycomore figs, v. 14) is unique here in Amos; their technical use, like that of *bôqēr*, sets them somewhat on one side as evidence. More significant may be the occurrence only in this passage in Amos of *znh* (play the harlot, v. 17); *ṭāmē'* (unclean, v. 17), the nearest parallel to 'unclean land,' here, is in Josh. 22.19 (*'ereṣ*) of the land beyond Jordan remote from the tabernacle, probably a late passage; *miqdāš* (sanctuary, vv. 9, 13); *ḥlq* (divide, v. 17), only here of the division of land. But the usage of these words elsewhere is very wide, and their absence from the remainder of Amos may or may not be important. Less significant too, because of their very common use, are *brḥ* (flee, v. 12), *ḥebel* (rope, v. 17), *yākôl* (be able, v. 10), *'ānāh* (answer, v. 14).

In addition we may note that *šlḥ* (send, qal) occurs only in v. 10, elsewhere in Amos in pi. (7) and hiph. (1); *ysp* (add) occurs in v. 13 with *l* and inf.; elsewhere with inf. alone.

8. We must also note that other vocabulary in this passage is found, with greater or less frequency, in other parts of the book of Amos. It may be doubted if there is any other sufficiently clear difference of usage to warrant a distinction being made.[22] Similarly, it may be noted that some words which occur quite frequently elsewhere in Amos are not found in 7.9–17: thus *'ādônāy* (my lord, 25), *'elōhîm* (God, 15), *hinnēh* (behold, 14), *yôm* (day, widely used, especially of the day of Yahweh), *ya'ăqôb* (Jacob, 6), *ṣĕbā'ôt* (hosts, 9), *šûb* (return, 13).

It is clear that such linguistic evidence is insufficient to suggest any conclusions in other than tentative terms; the most that it may allow is that, if there are other indicators, the narrative is less close to Amos than it is to narratives in the historical books, and it might be designated as later than Amos.

So far as the content of the message is concerned, as it is here ascribed to the prophet, we may observe that the theme of judgment on the royal house is not found elsewhere in Amos; the theme of the exile (vv. 11, 17) occurs in a number of other passages (with *gālāh* – 5.5, 5.27, with specific reference to 'beyond Damascus'; 6.7; 9.4 has *šĕbî* (captivity); cf. also the picture of driven cattle in 4.2–3). Doubt has been expressed about the genuineness of some of these passages, in particular those that use *gālāh*. It may be noted that other judgment themes in Amos are in terms of destruction rather than of exile. The point may be left open, with the recognition that there is a possible linkage here of both thought and language. The theme of destruction of sanctuaries is also to be found elsewhere in Amos: so 5.5 with its word play *gālāh*/Gilgal, where there is also the implied transformation of Bethel to Beth-awen (more characteristic of Hosea; cf. 4.15; 5.5; 10.5); and 9.1 with its theme of judgment on the temple buildings. Such themes in Amos are, however, more related to doom for the worshippers (e.g., 8.14) than specifically to downfall of the shrines.

We may summarize this very limited evidence by saying that the words attributed to Amos in 7.9–17 are not unrelated to what we may observe more generally in the Amos tradition, but that on balance they are not quite what we should expect. If we were looking for 'genuine' sayings, it is more probable that we should find them elsewhere. This might suggest that what we have here is nearer to what a narrator might tell *about* the message of Amos, rather than oracles directly attributable to him. It is more or less what we might regard as a summary of his message, but less clear that it is really couched in words that he would have used.

III.   *A Conjectural Reconstruction*

The theme of conspiracy (*qšr*) already noted is particularly characteristic of the narratives of the books of Kings, and it appears in certain blocks of material.[23] Of these blocks, the most distinctive is that which appears in relation to the Northern kingdom from Jehu (II Kings 9) to Hoshea (II Kings 15.30). But we may observe that the theme is also used of Judean events; and further extended in II Chronicles 24–25.

What is noteworthy in the narratives of II Kings 9–15, insofar as they concern the Northern kingdom, is that they show the origins of the dynasty of Jehu/Jeroboam II in a prophetic narrative which utilizes the *qšr* motif, together with a precise promise of four generations (10.30), and that this is echoed in 15.12 in the sequel to the *qšr* of Shallum which marks the end of that dynasty (15.10). The *qšr* theme is then taken two stages further in the Pekah and Hoshea material in 15.25, 30. Remarkably, we have a positive prophecy, attributed to Jonah ben Amittai, for the reign of Jeroboam II (14.25), and the narrator offers a theological appraisal of this in 14.26–27.[24] The absence of a prophetic judgment on the dynasty of Jeroboam at this point is noteworthy. It is, of course, exactly comparable with what we observe in II Kings 24–25 where we should expect at least an allusion to Jeremiah. We may, however, see in Jeremiah 37–44 a form of the narrative which incorporates Jeremiah material and relates his message explicitly to the fall of Jerusalem.[25] Is it possible, in view of the use of the *qšr* motif in Amos 7.10, that 7.9–17 is a relic of such a judgment narrative? This would argue for the existence of two forms of the Kings material: the one (as we know it) not including any reference to Amos,[26] the other (as here postulated) presenting Amos as the prophet of judgment on the dynasty of Jehu/Jeroboam.[27]

It would go considerably beyond the scope of this study to examine fully the vexed problems of I Kings 13,[28] but its possible relationship to the Amos narrative must be considered. The views in which a link is entertained cover a wide range.[29] That there is some relationship appears inherently probable. It is clear that the oracle put in the mouth of the unnamed prophet in I Kings 13 is a prophecy *ex eventu*, designed to be specifically linked to the Josiah narrative. Does it perhaps replace a different judgment oracle?[30] The theme of judgment on the altar is reminiscent of Amos 9.1, although the wording is different. There are two verbal links with Amos 7 – the phrase *'ākal leḥem* (eat bread, food, I Kings 13.8–9 [16, 19]; Amos 7.12), a crucial theme in I Kings 13, subordinate but not unimportant in Amos 7; and the use of *bāmôt* (I Kings 13.2; Amos 7.9), a term not otherwise found in Amos in this sense (see above).

Is it possible that there were in existence two forms of the story, associated either with Amos or with an unnamed prophet? The one, in which there is conflict between prophet and king (Jeroboam), was utilized in I Kings 13,[31] and attached to a complex of other prophetic legends, in particular to a prophetic grave tradition (I Kings 13.30–31; cf. II Kings 23.17–18),[32] a tradition comparable in some degree to that associated with Elisha (II Kings 13.21). We may note that the shift of this narrative, in which judgment is pronounced upon Jeroboam and his dynasty, from Jeroboam II to Jeroboam I would be not simply the result of a confusion between two rulers of the same name, but rather an expression of the desire of the eventual compiler of Kings to correlate his view of the apostasy of the North, especially as associated with Bethel, with his view of Josiah as the instrument of divine judgment upon it.[33] It is thus an expression of the overall pattern in which the kings of the North are throughout condemned for their adherence to the apostasy of Jeroboam ben Nebat. The other form of the story, in which there is conflict between prophet and priest (Amaziah), although behind the priest stands the king (Jeroboam), has come to us inserted into the vision material of Amos, interrupting the sequence but providing an authentication of Amos' status in that it incorporates elements suggestive of the call motif.[34] What has already been said about the linkages and non-linkages of thought and language with Amos would suggest that we leave open the question whether the narrative was originally associated with Amos or not. Clearly it was believed to be so when it was inserted in Amos 7. On the other hand, it is easier to see an anonymous narrative coming to be attached to a known prophet (cf. I Samuel 9), than to suppose that an Amos narrative lost its identity.

A further line of investigation emerges when we consider II Chronicles 25.14–16. As a preliminary we may recall that this too is in a context which utilizes the *qšr* motif.[35] For Athaliah (II Chronicles 23), Joash (II Chronicles 24), and in relation to the latter, Zechariah the son of Jehoiada the priest (24.21), and again for Amaziah (25.27), this motif is either taken over from the Kings narratives, or is added by the Chronicler. It is within this context that we are told of an act of apostasy by Amaziah, king of Judah. A prophet, unnamed, is sent to him by God to accuse him: 'Why have you directed inquiry to the gods of a people when they could not deliver their own people from your power?' Amaziah's reply runs: 'Have you been appointed King's counsellor? Hold your tongue (*ḥdl*)! Why should you be put to death?' Significantly, the sequel runs: 'So the prophet did hold his tongue, but he said: "I know that God (thus) counselled to destroy you, because you have done this thing and have not heeded my counsel".'[36] It is noteworthy that there is a word play on the root *yʿṣ* (take counsel), picked up also at the beginning of v. 17 in the next section of narrative. More significant is the content and character of these verses.

There is no parallel to II Chronicles 25.14–16 in the Kings material. Should we suppose pure invention, or can we deduce whence the Chronicler derived it? The former is not likely in view of the Amos/Amaziah narrative and also that of I Kings 13. We may observe three forms of comparable material: a narrative of prophet (unnamed) and king (Jeroboam) in I Kings 13, which concerns apostasy; a narrative of prophet (Amos) and priest (Amaziah) who reports to the king (Jeroboam), in which the primary theme is judgment for religious failure (explicitly in Amos 7.9); and a narrative of prophet (unnamed) and king (Amaziah) in II Chronicles 25, which concerns apostasy. We may note further that in each case there is an attempt at silencing the prophet which fails. In particular there is a degree of correspondence between II Chronicles 25.16 'the prophet ceased (*ḥdl*)' but nevertheless is shown to have had the last word, and the Amos narrative in which the prophet is commanded to stop prophesying (*lōʾ tôsîp ʿôd lᵉhinnābēʾ*) in the North, but goes on to make a dire pronouncement against the one who dares to infringe the divine prerogative of commanding the prophet to speak. The natural inference is that the Chronicler was making use of a form of the same tradition which we have in the other two passages; this tradition preserved the name of Amaziah, and so the Chronicler attached it in a suitable position to his account of the king of that name. It provides a good example of the Chronicler's exegetical method.

IV. *Some Possible Consequences*

That Amos 7.9–17 may be a tradition about the prophet (or about a prophet) independent of the other material in the book appears clear enough.[37] That it is part of a larger unit would also seem quite possible.[38] Its function is not biographical,[39] nor does it set out to relate how Amos' work in the North came to an end.[40] May it not simply be that the basic purpose of this narrative is to pronounce doom on the one who, like Jeroboam in I Kings 13, Jehoiakim in Jeremiah 36, and Amaziah in II Chronicles 25, endeavours to deflect the true will of the deity and the mediation of his word?

If it is proper to regard the passage as a fragment, extracted from a narrative source, then can we suggest a reconstruction of at least its opening? It is clear that it would not open with a bald oracle of doom. There are various possibilities. We may follow the wording of Jeremiah 26.18 and suggest: 'Amos of Tekoa prophesied at that time (or in the days of Jeroboam king of Israel) and said: Thus says Yahweh of hosts. . . .' Another possibility would be to

follow I Kings 13: 'And behold a man of God (Amos) came from
Judah at the behest of Yahweh to Bethel and said. . . .' A third
would be to follow II Chronicles 25.14: 'So Yahweh sent a prophet
(Amos of Tekoa) to him. . . .' Comparison might also be made
with such forms as occur in I Kings 14.7–11 and 16.1–4.

Within the judgment narrative, the purpose of the appeal to
prophetic authority in vv. 14–15 may be seen as undergirding the
prophetic word with a claim to divine commission. This is of
particular interest if we associate the narrative in the overall
pattern with II Kings 9. The dynasty of Jehu was divinely
appointed by Elisha, and the stress on divine authority is underlined in the account in 9.1–10. The designation of Jeroboam in II
Kings 14.27 as saviour of Israel makes his position appear secure.
By what right then can a prophet from Judah pronounce doom on
this royal figure and royal house? The credentials of the prophet
must be challenged. The narrative of I Kings 13 has the king
endeavour to have the prophet arrested. Amos 7 presents the
attempt at frustrating the divine will by having Amaziah order
the prophet out of the country.[41] The response in each case is
catastrophic. In I Kings 13.4, the king's outstretched arm is
withered so that he cannot withdraw it. In Amos 7, the priest's
attempt is countered by the appeal to a divine commission which
is ineluctable, and the priest who dares to counter that commission
himself falls under judgment (vv. 16–17). The attack on a true
prophet is an attack on God himself. The same point is implicitly
made in II Chronicles 25.14–16 and also in Jeremiah 28.

Insofar as the prophetic word in Amos 7.9–17 can be seen to
counter that of Elisha in II Kings 9 and also the more immediate
word of blessing on Jeroboam in II Kings 14.27, there is implicit
a contribution to the wider theme of the validity of the prophetic
word. A valid word of prophetic promise may be seen to be
overtaken by a further word of doom. Similarly (as for example in
Jeremiah 33.10–11 and other passages in Jeremiah 32 and 33) a
word of doom may be overtaken by a further word of blessing. If
we may postulate that this Amos passage stood in a larger narrative
context, we may see it as saying, for example to the exilic or post-
exilic community, that prophetic messages may be updated, their
terms modified, their full significance understood only when they
are seen in a larger context.

The question: 'Was Amos a prophet?' has bedevilled a great

deal of the discussion of 7.14–15. From one point of view, the question may be simply answered. The claim to a commissioning from God in v. 15 underlines the authority of the prophet's word which follows in vv. 16–17, countering the attempted prohibition of his activity in Bethel. We may observe also the use here of a familiar form, found particularly clearly paralleled in II Samuel 7.8: *ʾᵃnî lᵉqaḥtîkā min-hannāweh mēʾaḥar haṣṣōʾn* (I took you from the field, from behind the flock),[42] stressing both the legitimation of one who is exalted to high office and a convention of lowly origin. By that very emphasis on origin, and by implication on the lack of qualification for office, the motif underlines the divine prerogative, just as this is done in other call material by stressing unwillingness (so Moses, Jeremiah) or unfitness (so Isaiah, Ezekiel).

Some of the wider problems of interpreting the response of Amos in v. 14 need not here detain us. The present writer's preference is for the interpretation of the negatives as interrogative: 'Am I not a prophet?'[43] Alternatively we may suppose emphatic *l/lû/lā*.[44] The meanings of *nābî'* (prophet) and *ben-nābî'* (son of a prophet) may then most naturally be understood as parallel.[45] If the latter is held to denote 'member of a prophetic guild,' then we must see Amos as claiming such guild membership, too.[46] This a much more natural interpretation than to suppose that the statements of v. 14 are in contrast with those of v. 15: the latter explicates the basis of the prophetic status, and more specifically the basis of the commission to the North which has been called in question.

Two further possible consequences may be briefly adduced.

(1) The recognition of the nature of this narrative passage and of its possible original place outside the book of Amos makes it particularly important that we should not conflate evidence from it with evidence from the oracular material, without very careful prior consideration of the kind of information which may be legitimately extracted from each. This is a basic principle of biblical (and other) interpretation, too often honoured in theory and ignored in practice.

(2) If this is an Amos tradition, can we deduce what became of the prophet? Did Amos, like the unnamed prophet in II Chronicles 25.16, 'hold his tongue,' though not without having the last word?[47] Can we infer anything further from that passage? The king threatens death to the unacceptable prophet: are we to suppose that he overlooked the final relentless word and let the prophet go

unharmed? That prophets could be put to death, even extradited for that purpose, is clear from Jeremiah 26.20–23. We are not even told that Amos accepted the orders of Amaziah, although it may be proper here, as with the absence of any reply from Jeroboam, to draw no deductions from the silence of the narrative, which has presumably no concern with this point. But we cannot simply draw the conclusion that Amos went back to Judah and wrote down his prophecies. The arguments for that depend solely on suppositions regarding the making of the book of Amos; it does not follow, because we see Amos only alone and only confronted by an opponent, that there were none in the Northern kingdom to hear and heed his words and none associated with him to preserve the tradition of what he said.

From this discussion, we may perhaps add a slender piece of evidence for an alternative view of what became of Amos. If we see a possible relation to the other prophetic narrative of I Kings 13 (II Kings 23), that of the grave tradition, then we may ask: Was there a tradition of a grave of Amos at Bethel?[48] Admittedly, it is more proper to treat the two main themes of I Kings 13 as originally separate, but perhaps there is here a clue, if not to historic truth, at least to a possible source of origin for the much later tradition that Amos had died a martyr's death, a tradition which may be said to have at least as much basis, if not more, than the supposed 'martyrdom of Isaiah' under Manasseh.[49]

The tentative result of this inquiry is to look behind the present position of Amos 7.9–17 to consider its original nature and function. The passage may then be considered at two levels rather than one.

In its present position, set in the context of Amos' visions, it serves, like other call narratives and other conflict narratives,[50] to indicate to those who gathered and to those who heard the prophetic words, the authority of the prophetic message. An appeal is made to the reality of his commission by God, and the validity of that commission is undergirded by the prophetic word of doom to Amaziah and his family and of exile for Israel. The fulfilment, and therefore the validation, of that word belongs to history. The whole message of the prophet is thereby validated and its continuing function as the Word of God assured for a later generation.

Its position, as postulated by this discussion, was originally as part of a narrative concerned with judgment on the Northern kingdom, and as such stood in a form of the Kings material which, like Jeremiah 37–44, elaborates the function of the prophets in the period of the monarchy, thus underlining still further the theme of prophecy and fulfilment already present in the familiar form of the text. It serves more particularly to authenticate the judgment on the Northern kingdom in the period of Jeroboam II, delivered by a prophet in the face of opposition, with the opposing functionary himself caught up in the doom he seeks to evade. As a further element within this, we may see that the exiling of Amaziah to an 'unclean land' is correlated with the exiling of Israel, and the figure of the priest becomes, as it were, a type of the subsequent fortunes of the people – the more significant reference of the passage being then beyond the doom of the North to the eventual doom of Judah in 587.[51]

The existence of such alternative forms of the text is already demonstrated by the presentation of Samuel-Kings in the books of Chronicles, which offer a highly homiletic version of the earlier material.[52] Other clues may be seen in the LXX form of the Kings text. The recognition of such alternatives, deducible often only from fragmentary information, does not of itself actually increase our direct knowledge of the wider range of literature available in ancient Israel, but it does enable us to get a fuller picture of the complex processes of the evolution of that literature toward what eventually comes to be fixed in a canonical form. It is a pointer to the degree to which canonical fixation of particular texts is the result of what must be regarded as chance factors, although we may always endeavour to discover reasons for the choice of one particular text-form rather than another. The inclusion of the Isaiah material in the familiar form of II Kings (chs. 18–20), with the possibility that behind that too lies a 'non-Isaiah' form of the Hezekiah narrative,[53] is a further reminder of that chance element, here illuminated by the fact that Isaiah 36–39 offers yet another alternative text. These points are important in the consideration of the canon and a warning against too narrow a view of canonicity and canonical authority, for the texts that have come down to us, when considered in all their various forms and presentations, do not in fact provide a basis for a simplistic view of biblical authority.[54] They demand a careful consideration of the significance of all the forms in which materials appear, and an endeavour to discover, within those forms, clues to the circumstances and beliefs of the communities in which the literature was brought into being. It is out of such a richness of tradition that the subsequent interpretations of both Judaism and Christianity can grow.[55]

13

The Open Canon

I. *Psalters and Liturgical Collections*

It is convenient to begin this discussion with 11QPs^a – the so-called Psalter from Cave 11 at Qumran, edited by J. A. Sanders.[1] This consists of some small fragments and a long continuous section, though the damage to the scroll breaks the continuity of the text. Nevertheless, identification of particular psalms is clear enough to enable us to see that it contains a part of a 'psalter', that the order is different from that in the canonical psalter, and that it includes a variety of other psalm passages, some already known in Syriac and as Psalm 151 in the LXX, others not so known; as well as a comment about the number and nature of the compositions of David. (With this last we may compare I Kings 5.9–14 (EVV 4.29–34) and the colophon to Psalm 72.)

But is it a Psalter? The assumption made by Sanders in editing, which he would maintain in the face of criticism by referring to the existence of other Qumran Psalters among the Cave 4 material, to be published by P. W. Skehan – also with deviant order – has been challenged y M. H. Goshen-Gottstein in an article in *Textus* 5, and in his challenge he is supported by Talmon in a footnote to his own article in the same volume.[2] Goshen-Gottstein's often obscure argument leads to the point that this is not a 'psalter', but a liturgical collection; and he therefore ranks it with later works of the latter kind rather than making so close an association with the canonical psalter as Sanders has done.[3]

We may recognize that a line is to be drawn somewhere. Later liturgical collections, whether Jewish or Christian, are not psalters, even if they contain a majority of psalms. But the problem is not as simple as this. For the question immediately arises as to whether the canonical psalter itself is not really to be defined as a 'liturgical collection'. We know that it does not contain all available psalms – witness the existence within the Old Testament of many which might have been included, and particularly that of Habakkuk 3 which bears all the marks – title and colophon included – of a psalm belonging to a psalter (or liturgical collection). At some point a collection of psalms for liturgical purposes was made, and if those scholars are right who see a connection between the number 150 and the triennial reading of the Law, then there may here be a clue to the situation in which this particular collection was formulated. The evidence is not conclusive; there is much that points in this direction, though some unsolved difficulties remain. If such a view is right, then we may legitimately ask whether the LXX Psalter is a deviant version of this, its different divisions of the psalms and its addition of an extra psalm indicating a difference of liturgical 'use', perhaps an attempt at better correspondence to the triennial practice. This at least is more probable than that Psalm 151 was added because it was noted that no psalm in the psalter fitted the occasion of David's contest with Goliath. In this case too, does the colophon to Psalm 72 indicate a different and earlier liturgical collection, as has often been supposed? And do the Qumran 'psalters' simply provide us with further alternatives, designed to correspond with the particular usage of the community at different stages of its development or even to different 'uses' within the community?

The psalters have been chosen as a first example of the kind of problem with which we are confronted. At some point, historically, a line is drawn between the 'canonical psalter' and 'liturgical collections' no longer enjoying the same status because a particular psalter has been recognized as canonical and fixed. But how far are we limited to a particular 'canonical liturgical collection' because this, for various historical and other reasons, came to be fixed, presumably in the first century AD? The LXX, which largely confirms the MT, points to an earlier existence for what was eventually canonized, but even this does not enable us to say with certainty that this was the only psalter in use in the first century AD.

But from the point of view of use in the Christian church, certain questions arise. What limits do we impose on the use of other psalm material, alongside the canonical psalter? Here we may point to the common use of various 'Canticles', some of which are Old Testament psalms from elsewhere, others of which, such as the Benedicite, may be regarded as extended versions of such psalms, in this case of Psalm 148. How far beyond this may we legitimately go, in the use of psalms such as are known to us now from Qumran, some of which – as for example those earlier known in Syriac – might easily have stood in the Psalter and do indeed so appear in some manuscripts? How far is there evidence that the early Christian community had a knowledge of a wider range of psalmody than we have? It may be that Paul in Rom. 3.10–18 was using not a catena of Old Testament quotations, but a fragment of a deviant form of Psalm 14=53; does this perhaps point to a deviant psalter? What questions do these points raise for doctrine? For example, are there any doctrinal consequences to be drawn from the new psalm discovered in 11QPs[a], identified by Sanders as part of Psalm 118, but as I have shown elsewhere,[4] not really Psalm 118 at all but a new psalm which in some measure overlaps that psalm, a point which has now been completely confirmed by the publication by Y. Yadin[5] in *Textus* 5 of a hitherto concealed new fragment of 11QPs[a] which actually contains enough of Psalm 118 to show that this psalm appeared elsewhere in this psalter? The text of Psalm 91 found in 11QPsAp lacks four hemistichs at the end; the omission could be accidental or deliberate, but it could also indicate a deviant text form.[6]

II. *Textual Deviations*

Psalm 145.13*b* is not in the MT; it is properly supplied in the RSV from one Hebrew ms. (Qumran), LXX, Syr. The psalm is an alphabetic acrostic with this the *nun*-verse. It is doctrinally innocuous: 'The Lord is faithful in all his words, and gracious in all his deeds.'

This particular psalm appears in 11QPs[a] with a refrain between each verse, just as Psalm 136 has it in the canonical psalter. From this we may deduce that antiphonal use was at some point not uncommon, and that the RSV may be correct when it so translates the words of Ezra 3.11 as 'and they sang responsively', though the Hebrew could also mean 'they began to sing and to praise'. We have here an indication of liturgical use, though this again is what we may term 'doctrinally innocuous'.[7]

But while what has been noted so far does not appear to present any very serious problems, the same is hardly true as we begin to extend the point further. The Old Testament itself offers a variety of duplicate texts, and while in a number of cases the differences are such as to make it clear that on a balance of probability we may be able to explain the one form as more original than the other, it is more often true that we find ourselves confronted simply with variant texts, of both of which we must record that they are valid in the sense of representing good tradition, and that the discovery of an original is not possible, and indeed may not even be particularly important: Psalm 18 = II Samuel 22; Isaiah 2.2–4 = Micah 4.1–4. Obadiah is duplicated in Jeremiah, etc. In each case we may be able to determine what we might term the more primitive text; but from the point of view of our understanding of the religious tradition, each has its validity. Or we may go a stage further and compare Jeremiah 7 and Jeremiah 26, which are not duplicate texts but offer alternative presentations of, in part, the same material: each such presentation is valid in itself; it presents us with important material concerning both the prophet and his activity and the way in which such information has been variously handled in the tradition. We cannot really prefer one to the other. And the same is clearly true, when we are considering theological significance, when we take side by side the parallel traditions denoted by J, E and P, or by Samuel-Kings and Chronicles.[8]

So far these examples are all within the biblical canon, and do not immediately present a major theological problem except in so far as we have to interpret the diversity of tradition in theological terms. But we may also cite the most obvious examples which involve non-canonical material. The text of Samuel is now, in part, available to us in four different forms, though they are interrelated in a complex manner – MT, LXX, Chronicles, Qumran. The latter three may not inappropriately be grouped over against MT, but they are not to be taken as identical. For some passages at least we can show at least three clearly divergent forms of the text, as for example in I Samuel 1. For Jeremiah too, the problem is complex. We have for long known that MT and LXX diverge sharply in length, and that although many differences may be explained as due to an expansiveness in MT or a conciseness in LXX, there are major differences in certain respects both in order and content. Now Qumran offers us texts which have affinities with both of these, and yet not identity, so that we have a yet wider range of textual variation.

While it is true that in many cases such deviant texts are simply of interest in that they help in the correction of minor errors, they nevertheless also offer deviant readings which cannot be viewed entirely as matters of indifference. And indeed where do we draw the line between the textual variant which is of no real significance and the one which, apparently equally small, may affect the exegesis of the whole passage – and if so, is of significance for any doctrinal statement which may be in some way linked with the passage?

The questions raised by these preliminary considerations may be simply formulated. How far can we recover a 'true' text, except on the basis in many cases of good probability? If that implication is sound, how far does it matter, on the grounds that two forms of a text may represent two equally good theological statements or religious traditions? Where do we draw the line and say that such uncertainties are not a matter of importance for doctrine, as it is commonly said that the variants in the New Testament manuscript tradition are not such as to affect the main doctrinal tenets? How true is such a claim, and indeed how far can doctrinal tenets be held to be related to a text which is itself multiform and of which the exegesis is therefore richer than it would be if the text were absolutely certain at every point?

This raises a further general question of doctrinal interest, namely, is truth simply one, or is it, at least in its biblical formulation, much more complex?

This in its turn raises certain questions about biblical theology which are not without their relevance to the wider doctrinal field. How far, in biblical theology, have we been dominated by the urge to unify, or, if that is not possible, to select what we consider central and to regard the rest as peripheral? For the Old Testament this has often meant *Heilsgeschichte*, with a consequent neglect of Wisdom, or 'cult and tradition' with a consequent neglect of persons. For the New Testament it sometimes seems, particularly in German scholarship, that so great a stress is laid upon one part of the New Testament that the rest is automatically put out of focus, and Paul or John or Hebrews is given a priority which is questionable unless or until we know more about the intricacies of early Christian life and thought.[9]

III.   *The Question of the Canon*

The canon of the Old Testament as we know it is the result of a partly deliberate, partly unconscious process of selection of those writings which are regarded as being in some sense authoritative. (The existence of the canon does not in itself define the nature of its authority). The process was clearly a gradual one, involving both decision and acceptance; clearly it was not possible to foist a book upon a community which did not acknowledge it. More possible would be the withdrawal of a book felt to be for some reason unsuitable, which might then, after a period of disuse in public worship, come to be largely or entirely ignored. (One might instance the Shepherd of Hermas in relation to the New Testament canon; perhaps I Maccabees and Ben Sirach provide appropriate Old Testament examples.)

Different religious groups within the broad definition of 'Judaism' took different lines in regard to the canon. The Samaritan community accepted the Torah as canonical; it is not really clear whether they never went beyond this, or whether at some point a deliberate exclusion of the prophetic writings was made because they were regarded as distorting the true picture of the religious development; this true picture, from the Samaritan viewpoint, was supplied by other literary material which never acquired anything like canonical status. The Samaritans had their own understanding and interpretation of the succeeding periods.

The narrower Jewish community's position is much less easily described, at least so far as the period before AD 70 is concerned. Much of the evidence suggests that it is hazardous to speak in terms of a Jewish orthodoxy before that date; the variety indicated in the New Testament and in the Qumran material, as well as the pointers to this in post-biblical literature, suggests that no hard and fast lines can be drawn, and that various groups, sharing some views and not others, co-existed in this period. What is true more generally appears also to be true of the canon. That all groups shared a special veneration for the Torah is clear. Ample evidence of this appears in New Testament controversy; it appears equally or more clearly in the writings of Philo where quotations from the Torah enormously outweigh those from other Old Testament books. It is clear too that the prophets – and the evidence of Ben Sirach, both in prologue and in the historical survey of chapters 44ff., indicates that this means both Former and Latter – were accepted alongside the Torah. This is less clear in Philo, but not necessarily in doubt; it is clear from New Testament references to 'Moses and the Prophets' (Luke 16.29; 24.27); it is clear from the definiteness of reference to this section of the canon in contrast to the less well-defined naming of the third section. If the counting of manuscripts is any guide, it may well be that the evidence of Qumran will also confirm this,[10] though the element of chance needs to be taken into account and also the very evident prevalence of manuscripts of books not in the canon, e.g. Enoch. New Testament quotation also points in this direction, though it is much less clear that it points to a tripartite canon and still less to an order of books as known to us in the Hebrew canon as now presented. (Luke 24.44 – Law, Prophets, Psalms – might indicate the three sections, but more probably indicates liturgical practice; Luke 11.51; Matthew 23.35 – Abel to Zechariah – is very doubtful. The Zechariah may be the one mentioned in II Chronicles 24.21, but there are other possibilities; and the presupposition that Chronicles stood last in the canon depends upon the very dubious view that the order of books was already fixed and supposes codex form. Except in so far as order is dictated by content, it is difficult to suppose that order is at this stage a relevant consideration.)

Behind this recognition of Law and Prophets there may be some decision, not known to us; it is conceivable, though unproven, that Ezra had something to do with the former. It is possible, and indeed not unlikely, that the pressures of the Antiochene persecution in the second century BC led to the question: Which books are really holy and therefore worth dying for? a question which was raised again for the Christian church in the period of Diocletian, though at that time a much greater degree of acceptance of an already definable canon seems to be demonstrable.

But while general agreement, certainly for the Torah and generally also for the Prophets, may be presupposed for the early first century AD, it is clear – and this has been brought out by A. C. Sundberg in his *The Old Testament of the Early Church*[11] – that there was no such agreement regarding the canonicity of other books. The broader range of such books reflected in the LXX and often associated with Alexandria is in fact to be found equally in Palestine, as witness particularly the evidence of the New Testament and of Qumran. Alongside books which were eventually to be regarded as canonical, other works are cited in a similar manner, or alluded to in a way which presupposes that they are sufficiently well-known. The manuscript evidence from Qumran indicates the high regard in which some of these works were held. (There does not seem to be evidence, however, for wider use and knowledge of what may be termed the more purely sectarian works from Qumran, and this suggests that the Qumran community is to be regarded as one which had its own special forms and institutions, as did other groups of which the Christian community was one, but that the wider range of literature such as Enoch and Jubilees is not to be regarded merely as a sectarian product but as shared by various groups.)

That a new situation was created by the disasters of AD 66–74, and particularly by the destruction of the temple, is clear. It is difficult not to see considerable reflections of this in the New Testament, perhaps especially in Hebrews. For the Christian community, however much it may have withdrawn itself from the more extreme Jewish nationalist groups, the political situation was very delicate. Whereas it might have been advantageous earlier to claim Jewish adherence and so the privileges accorded by Roman practice to the Jewish community, such a situation was now hardly so simple. Suspicion of Jewish activity may be supposed to have led the church into various lines of thought – whether repudiation of Jewishness to avoid association with a now suppressed nationalist movement, or a claim to true Jewishness to show that nationalism had been a mistake. Reflections of such attitudes and perhaps of others may be detected in the New Testament. For the Jewish community the position was acute, but the political pressures were not isolated from other movements of a different kind, particularly in relation to the problems of text and exegesis and authority, arising out of the various viewpoints adopted towards the accepted Scriptures. The problem of interpretation of the Law which had for long developed with considerable tensions within the community by way of oral law, designed to elucidate the application to contemporary situations, demanded a certain re-thinking of the position and nature of the Scriptures. The combination of these elements may be found in the apologetic writings of Josephus, who presents in his *Antiquities* a picture of what Judaism really is, in his *Against Apion* a more deliberate apologetic, including a statement about the Scriptures and their authority, and in his *War* a nearer apologetic for both his own position and that of the survivors to explain how they came to be in their predicament. The so-called Synod of Jamnia is perhaps simply a systematizing of what went on in discussion, by way of definining what was meant by Judaism, what its Scriptures were, what text was accepted, what principles of exegesis were to govern it, and all by way of defining in somewhat conservative terms the present position, and thereby also excluding the wilder fringe groups, such as Christians and apocalyptists.

What Jamnia did was to make precise the limits of the canon of the Old Testament for Judaism by drawing the line between certain accepted – already known and loved – books, and others which were too much in the hands of the *minim*, the heretics. They appear to have considered how far certain books or passages were suitable for use in public worship – e.g., Ezekiel 1, Proverbs, Song of Songs, Ecclesiastes – because of various difficulties that they raised; it is doubtful whether they were really discussing the possibility of excluding such works. It is not unlikely that they were assisted in their delimiting of the books by what would appear to us to be rather arbitrary considerations – that the number should be 22 or 24, that they should belong to a defined, prophetic period, Moses to Artaxerxes. But no one consideration seems to have dominated, certainly not that of language, since it now appears reasonable to suppose that Tobit and Judith could both have been included on linguistic grounds as well as being regarded as belonging to the canonical period. The decisions did not bring to an end the use of a wider range of literature; I Maccabees and Ben Sirach continued to be known – the latter survived in Hebrew at a much later date – and it is clear that Josephus and the Midrash and Talmud know much more than is in the canon.[12] Indeed a great deal of the determining of the interpretation of the canonical material derives from this broader tradition, and passed thence into the mediaeval Christian commentaries and so into more modern use. Of this the traditional views on authorship and composition of Old Testament books form the most obvious element.

The Christian views of the canon of the Old Testament still

remain diverse. The development may be placed alongside that of the text, in the struggle which is epitomized in Jerome's eventual championship of the Hebrew, against those who claimed that the LXX, itself having undergone considerable modification in relation to the Hebrew (cf. Origen), was purer and the Hebrew corrupted by Jewish ideas. The battle was largely won for the MT, but today we may wonder at times just how sound the victory was. That the MT represents an ancient tradition is clear; but it does not represent the only ancient tradition, and LXX and Qumran together provide an important counterweight. Similarly, the acceptance of the Jewish canon of the Old Testament – traced by Sundberg through the Fathers – represents in some ways a rather hollow victory. A compromise position – that of Jerome – and an attempt at solving the issue – that of Trent – are what remain. For the conflict over the position of the apocrypha still remains unresolved; for some Christian groups it is still anathema, belonging to the as yet unforgotten prejudices against the Scarlet Woman; for most others it is largely ignored or unknown. Even if it appears from time to time in the lectionary it is often with an alternative so that the ears of the congregation need not be offended with such out of the way matter. (The Church of England has some I Maccabees, Wisdom and Ben Sirach, but alternatives are offered on Sundays. I do not think Judith ever appears; it would no doubt raise the sort of protests which are produced whenever we get Judges.)

The position of the books beyond the apocrypha – which is itself a rather odd collection – remains even less clear. These too have not been rejected altogether, but have tended to remain in remote Christian communities such as that of Ethiopia. They are not without their claims to a canonical position, in view of their New Testament use. This is a double-edged argument, for it has been held that the New Testament books which use them – e.g. Jude – are not really worthy of a place in the canon because they quote non-canonical works; or the reverse has been held, e.g. by Tertullian. It would be interesting to know whether the possession of such a wide range of books has led such Christian churches into 'heresy', or whether it is heretical opinions which have made these books acceptable.

The problem of the canon is raised afresh by these considerations and it is raised in three forms: what canon do we accept? what canon should we accept? how useful, historically and theologically, is the concept of canon?

These questions are raised by the whole range of textual and literary and historical points just indicated. A minimal textual deviation may raise no point of theological import; but the interpretation of a passage may well in the end depend on a number of such minor points. The alternative versions of some passages invite the question: what do we mean by canonical authority? Extra passages in some texts and not in others raise the question of the extent of the canon – do we read only Old Testament Daniel or Daniel with its apocryphal additions? is the Hebrew form of Esther necessarily superior to the Greek? is the longer MT text of Jeremiah more valid than the shorter LXX? Comparable questions in the New Testament are raised by the pericope of the woman taken in adultery and the alternative endings of Mark. And having gone so far, at what point do we draw a canonical line – to include or exclude the apocrypha, the pseudepigrapha (and if so what list?), the other writings now becoming known? What criteria are there for canonical definition?

IV. *Doctrine and Canon*

Sola scriptura remains the emphasis for many Christian communities; ultimately at least that is where they feel they stand. But what scripture, and how?

The Thirty-nine Articles of the Church of England state the matter in Article VI:
'Holy Scripture containeth all things necessary to salvation . . .
In the name of the Holy Scripture we do understand those Canonical Books of the Old and New Testament, of whose authority was never any doubt in the Church.' (Never? but what of some of the New Testament books, and of Esther?)

'And the other Books (as Hierome saith) the Church doth read for example of life and instruction of manners; but yet doth it not apply them to establish any doctrine.' (How far is this a proper understanding both of the delimitation and of the function of the canonical books and the apocrypha? It reveals a curiously moralizing attitude to the apocrypha.)

A number of other statements might be cited which say similar or essentially similar things. We may ask what is the meaning of such statements, and how far we should want now to re-state them in the light of a different understanding of the nature of the biblical material.

G. A. F. Knight, in his *A Christian Theology of the Old Testament*,[13] an odd book and one which is very limiting in its curious conception of a theology circumscribed by five moments appearing in both Old Testament and New Testament, states a position which both perpetuates the traditional view of many Protestant churches and attempts an explanation of its legitimacy. He writes:

'Therefore, any doctrine which we may discover in the Apocrypha, that is nowhere paralleled by a similar doctrine of the full 'five moment' period in the story of Christ as it is revealed in the New Testament, is not likely to be an authentic element in the total biblical revelation.'

('Not likely' – a curious way of expressing the point, but it has the merit of allowing the Holy Spirit a very thin end of a wedge.)

'On the contrary, the intertestamental literature as a whole, inclusive of the Apocrypha, can mislead us as we look for the fulfilment of the Old Testament in the New Testament. The Apocalyptic literature characteristic of the intertestamental period (sc. the book of Enoch) tends to lose faith in God's purpose and ability to use Israel as his instrument of redemption, and to lose sight of the prophetic conception of the fundamental significance and relevance of this earth in God's scheme and plan' (p. 213).

So much for those who believe that in order to understand the New Testament aright we must see it in its historical context and recognize that while its categories are often those of the Old Testament, they are Old Testament categories updated in the usage of the intertestamental period. It may be doubted whether Knight gives a sound estimate of the intertestamental literature; it is certain that, like not a few biblical theologians, he finds it convenient to suppose that we can pass straight from Old to New Testament, with a nice simple 'prophecy-fulfilment' or typological pattern, without taking account of the extremely complex cultural situation in which the New Testament came into being.

Vatican II, widely hailed in many Roman and not a few Protestant circles as marking a real recovery of the proper status of Scripture, hardly really touches on the problem. It emphasizes[14] that the canon belongs within the church – an oversimplification of the process by which the canon was formed – and that interpretation too belongs within the church. The teaching office is 'not above the word of God, but serving it, teaching only what has been handed on, listening to it devoutly, guarding it scrupulously, and explaining it by divine commission and with the help of the Holy Spirit; it draws from this one deposit of faith everything which it presents for belief as divinely revealed'. From this it goes on to stress the unity of Scripture, tradition and church, and while it subsequently admits the presence of human elements in Scripture, it denies the possibility of error and bypasses any discussion of the problems of interpretation.

Here at any rate, the issue of Scripture and doctrine is hardly faced, since it is presupped that doctrine can always be found in Scripture, though the precise nature of that finding is by no means clear. It ignores any contribution which might be made to the understanding of Scripture in non-Christian circles, though for many of us the Jewish approach has often been revealing, and indeed much of what passes for Christian interpretation is really Jewish interpretation channelled through mediaeval comment-aries. The real problem of the relation of doctrine to biblical material is not raised, and there would seem to be the risk that in so far as Roman Catholic laymen (and probably priests too) have welcomed the statement of the return to Scripture, they are too little aware of how easily such a definition tends to become nothing other than the fundamentalism which afflicts the Protestant chur-ches in spite of the battle over biblical scholarship, a battle supposedly won but in fact still marking the sharpest division within the churches, much sharper than any ecclesiological division we face.

Again we must ask: What do we mean by Scripture as foun-dation? How do we check doctrinal statement by it? How far are those of us who are on the biblical side shirking our responsibility by retiring into a cosy biblicism, and those who are on the doctrinal side tending to ask of us a neat and firm statement of what the biblical material means so that the check can be made?

In much recent discussion, particularly during the years of the biblical theology revival, there has tended to grow up a type of theological thinking which supposes that a theological statement in biblical terms is more likely to be true than one that is not; and a consequent opinion that a good biblical sermon is likely to be theologically sound. As a reaction to this is a certain tendency to develop a form of theology in which every biblical term is automatically suspect. Is there somewhere a right relationship to be established?

The question is raised here only in relation to the problem of the canon, because there it seems to be central.

V.   *The Open Canon*

We may distinguish three ways of looking at the canon:

1. *The historic canon.* It is possible, within certain limits, to describe the canon, and say, up to a point, why it came to be what it is. Differences of opinion exist as to its limits on this basis, but in general it is possible to give a reasonable picture. But the more precise the picture, the more evident it is that, like other matters which involve theological questions, it is tied into certain historical situations and determined by certain historical patterns. How far are we in our situation bound by decisions which stemmed from such situations in the past? We may term the canon normative, in the sense that it provides us with certain basic information without which we would have no knowledge of what we mean by Christian as distinct from general theistic truth; *but how far does normative mean definitive?* What is very evident and important is that the canonical Scriptures, however precisely defined, have exerted an influence on the community which has revered them, and that the books of the canon are what they are to the contemporary church because they have been interpreted within that community.

2. *The canon within the canon.* From the point of view of use virtually no one uses the whole canon indiscriminately. The practice of reading chapter by chapter in order is virtually gone; and even that practice was in fact also open to the recognition that there are some passages which may be regarded as key passages. Liturgical and lectionary practice provides a limited canon; it may be proper sometimes to judge a liturgy or a lectionary by whether it is very narrow – as may often be the case where the practice depends upon the decision of the individual minister – or whether it is rightly broad without becoming unintelligible to the many. Such use is always in some degree at the mercy of ecclesiastical or subjective pressures – the placing of a biblical passage, or its choice, may be determined by a particular view of its meaning, or its selection in the lectionary may be the result of a particular

pressure of individual or committee. An argument here for the historic canon is that it provides a salutary check to the subjectivism of individual or church; there may be times when it is good to be reminded that historically Esther, Ecclesiastes, Song of Songs and even the Epistle of James (*pace* Luther), are all within the canon. From the point of view of interpretation, the canon within the canon is always held in balance by the whole canon; we do not read I Chronicles 1–9 in worship, but we cannot understand the theological contribution of the Chronicler if we forget that those chapters are there.

3. *The open canon.* If we are to be ecumenically minded, then the canon is already in some degree open by reason of the differences of practice within the churches. Unless we obtain an artificial uniformity, this is one of those matters in which we may expect and perhaps wish there to be a continuing diversity and consequent enrichment. The edges of the canon are already somewhat indistinct. For the Old Testament scholar this is evident in that he cannot discuss Old Testament literature without an awareness of the context in which it came into being; he is conscious that a narrative or a psalm or a proverb may have no beginning in the simple sense; the creation myths in the Old Testament cannot be understood in isolation, and the origins of the psalms must certainly be traced back beyond Israel. Not that this extraneous material is in any sense canonical; but it cannot just be shut off as irrelevant. Equally for the historian of doctrine and of interpretation it is clear that the way in which Scripture has been understood and used has depended upon the particular viewpoints of an age, and that while no church has made the writings of its fathers canonical, it has done the next best thing by tending to read Scripture in their light, whether it be Augustine or Aquinas, Luther or Calvin, Hooker or Wesley.[15] Historically the canon was closed; can it be said to be closed theologically?

If it is common to an argument to lead up to a conclusion after all alternatives have been set on one side, it might seem that this is a plea for an abandonment of the historic canon. Yet history is just one of the things we cannot abandon, and confusion is only created by pretending that we can. If there is a plea, it is that through this question we may raise afresh an issue in which every discipline of Christian theology is involved,[16] and we cannot retire each into our own particular refuge. G. E. Wright, in his Harvard

Convocation address of 1962, pointed to the well-known tendency of Old Testament scholars to hob-nob with the orientalists, and church historians to want to be thought respectable by the secular historians. I would add to this the desire of philosophers of religion to stand well with pure philosophers, and that leaves only the New Testament scholars and the dogmaticians with nowhere to go. Yet it is seriously true that our specializing and departmentalizing constitute a weakness – and one which we expect students to resolve for themselves – with the result that when we confront such a question of importance as the nature of biblical authority and the meaning of the canon in relation to the statement of Christian truth, we are not always sufficiently in a position to handle it together so as to provide answers which will help forward the thinking of the church. And all too easily we fall back into our own area, the biblical scholars regarding this as an issue which must be solved in dogmatics – forgetting that our whole *raison d'être* depends on its solution – and the systematicians complaining that 'you can never get a straight answer to any question which you put to a biblical scholar'.

14

Original Text and Canonical Text

In a volume entitled *Canon and Authority: Essays in Old Testament Religion and Theology*, I have offered some comments on the nature and possible background to Amos 7.9–17.[1] It appears possible to see that passage as a narrative belonging primarily to a sequence such as is to be found in II Kings 14, providing the judgment pronouncement on the northern kingdom and its ruler Jeroboam II. In this manner it would be like the Isaiah narratives of II Kings 18–20, which exist in a closely similar but not identical form in Isaiah 36–39, and also to the prophetic narratives of Jeremiah 37–44 which offer an extended version of the last section of II Kings.[2]

In the concluding paragraph of the study of Amos 7, I ventured to point to some of the questions which arise from such a view for the understanding of the nature of the literature and of its authority. It is with one aspect of those questions that I wish to deal briefly in the present discussion. In this particular instance, the hypothesis proposed is that the text in Amos 7 may be read at two different levels. The first level is that of the actual text with which we are familiar, as a narrative providing comment on the activity of Amos, perhaps providing what we may term a contextualizing of his message and of the authority of that message, comparable with other prophetic passages (e.g., Jeremiah 11.21–23 and Jeremiah 26) in which a personal confrontation defines the status of the prophet and hence of his message. The second level is hypothetical. Whether or not that hypothesis is accepted is for the moment of lesser importance, since there are other cases where the double occurrence of the same text offers a comparable situation. The second level proposed posits that we may read the text detached from its present context and set in another context, the narratives of the reign of Jeroboam II in II Kings 14, in which a different understanding of its function may be discerned. The two levels thus described are not unrelated,, but the impact of the former within the vision series of Amos 7.1–8 and 8.1–3 is not identical with the impact of the latter, taken alongside narrative elements in II Kings 14.23–29 which speak of Jeroboam's military successes, and perhaps offering an alternative interpretation of that king's reign to be considered in relation to that unexpectedly positive appraisal which vv. 25–27 provide.[3] We may indeed go somewhat further and suggest that behind both the actual and posited use of this narrative there are tradition elements which provide some clues to its formation and also to its subsequent use.[4] For our purpose the questions posed are: What kind of 'authority' pertains to such alternative forms of a text and to such alternative points of use? Can we separate 'authority' from 'function' or 'effect'? Can 'authority' be in any satisfactory manner detached from questions of context and use?[5]

I. *'Canonical' and 'Inspired' Writings*

The questions thus raised find important and stimulating comments in the comprehensive study of the canonical problem of S. Z. Leiman. Of particular importance is the careful investigation of the distinction to be drawn between the concepts of 'canonical' writings and 'inspired' writings.[6] The recognition that these terms, or more strictly, these concepts, since they may be described in a variety of ways, need not coincide, is one of the bases on which Leiman demonstrates the unsatisfactory nature of much of the handling of the biblical, extra-biblical, Talmudic and Midrashic evidence in the discussion of the nature and evolution of the Hebrew canon.

It would appear, however, that more needs to be said than Leiman has done, to elucidate the evolution of such concepts and of the various meanings which may be associated with them. There is a tendency in his discussions, in the first and last parts of his book, for the concepts of 'canonical' and 'inspired' to be treated almost as if they were at all stages of the development equally understood, and it may be doubted if a satisfactory overall understanding can be achieved unless closer definition is attempted.

In Leiman's understanding 'a canonical book is a book accepted by Jews as authoritative for religious practice and/or doctrine, and whose authority is binding upon the Jewish people for all generations' (p. 14) As an ultimate definition this is intelligible and its application to the Old Testament as understood in the Christian community is also relevant, with certain qualifications which would need to be entered. It may be doubted, however, whether such a far-reaching definition is really satisfactory when the earlier stages of the process of canonization are examined. Leiman, in support of his definition and of its relevance to earlier stages than those of final canonization, cites four passages from the Torah, one each from P, J, H and D (Exod. 12.14 and 12.24; Lev. 24.3; Deut. 23.7), where in each case stress is laid upon the 'binding and enduring character of specific laws'. (pp. 24f.). The expressions used are clear: *lᵉdōrōēkem ḥuqqat ʿôlām* (for your lifetime an eternal statute); *ʿad ʿôlām* (forever); *kol-yāmêkā lᵉʿôlām* (all your lifetime for ever). But we may question whether in their context they already have the meaning which is ultimately attached to them when the writings with which they are associated are fully acknowledged as canonical. A comparable position exists with regard to the injunctions that particular legal collections are to be preserved intact, with imprecations against anyone who ventures to add to or subtract from them.[7] The claims to unalterability and to perpetual authority are no doubt intended as absolutes; but they do not prevent modification of laws in the course of time, as both the Old Testament laws and those of the Ancient Near East generally clearly show. What is established in perpetuity is clearly understood to be authoritative; the reality of its replacement or modification or reinterpretation is to be seen not as negation of it – though a deliberate repeal may occur but rather as its continued application to new circumstances. Its authority is not in fact to be seen as narrowly defined in terms of absolute unalterability; it is in its acceptance as a basis upon which subsequent claims, equally to permanence, may be based. The whole structure of the biblical canon rests upon the assumption that earlier stages of authoritative writing can be discerned, and that these continue to operate in the eventually modified text-forms which are given a final and fixed shape. In fact, though this moves over into another area of discussion which is not my concern here directly, the final fixed text-form which is accorded full canonical status is clearly itself subject to the modifications which are implied by reinterpretation. In Jewish and Christian communities the way in which biblical authority operates is clearly interlinked with the ongoing exegesis of the texts by which their contemporary authority is affirmed and applied. Canon and tradition both have their place.

II.   *The Nature of Authority*

The nature of the authority claimed for particular legal enactments is that they are divinely sanctioned, whether this is expressed in terms of the actual writing of the words of the law by the deity himself (so e.g., Deut. 5.22) or indirectly (as e.g., with Moses or in the Code of Hammurabi) by the divine authorization of the ruler or other personage by whose means the laws are decreed or upheld. To a greater or lesser extent this implies or states that the laws are divinely inspired. This may be by a process in which each individual law is described as directly transmitted by the deity to the leader (so in much of the Mosaic law) or more generally is considered to have such a basis because the leader himself is divinely inspired, as a charismatic figure, on whom the spirit of the deity rests (so e.g., of the Davidic ruler in Isa. 11.2). The wider range of authoritative writings may then be defined in terms of their having been composed by particular individuals whose divine inspiration is otherwise claimed or attested, and hence the movement, already within the biblical material but taken to its logical conclusion in subsequent comments upon the biblical books, to associate all writings regarded as authoritative with appropriate personages: Baba Bathra 14b–15a provides the clearest statement of this.[8] The same process is, of course, observable in the apostolic authorship claimed for New Testament writings. Such a view ultimately depends upon a combination of two factors: the recognition, within biblical narratives and certain consequences drawn from them, that these particular named individuals were inspired, a claim which may be expressed in the form of call-narratives or other commissioning material, or in terms of the directness of the communication to them by God of specific revelations; and the eventual clarifying of this in terms of a period of inspiration to which these personages belong, the period from Moses to Artaxerxes for the Old Testament, the apostolic age for the New. Such a concept of a period of inspiration is clearly imposed subsequently. It may derive in part from the desire to clarify what books are authoritative and what is the status of other writings not so regarded. It may also be the result of a need to define the nature of belief or practice in terms of a recognizable standard, enshrined in writings accepted on other grounds as authoritative but needing definition over against other claims that may be made. Neither in the Jewish community nor in the Christian can it be said that these bases resolve all the problems; the variations in canonical lists in different Christian communities and the different status accorded to particular writings indicate this.[9]

The underlying claim to authority rests in the statements made about the actual delivery of a message from God to his chosen agent, expressed in various forms: it may be in some such expression as 'Thus YHWH showed me . . .' (e.g., Amos 7.1) or 'God said to him . . .' (e.g., Hos. 1.4); it may be put in the form of 'Thus says YHWH' (e.g., Isa. 50.1); or it may take the form of an inserted 'Thus says YHWH' or 'Oracle of YHWH' in a prophetic collection, often marking the end of an oracle, though sometimes, as apparently in Haggai and Zechariah 1–8, used for added emphasis. Yet other forms appear in narratives in which the deity is described as speaking directly, or in a dream, or through some mechanical device utilized for the discovery of the divine will. The range of the evidence for this and the variety of the forms is very great indeed, and it does not need to be surveyed here, since the point at issue is simply the way in which such authority is claimed. Particularly significant are cases where the authoritiative word of God is set over against a non-authoritative pronouncement. This appears in various prophetic conflict narratives (notably Jeremiah 28 and II Kings 22); but it may also appear in the form of a modification of a previously claimed divine word (so e.g., in Jeremiah 32.36).[10]

This again pinpoints an aspect of the question. The word of judgment on Judah, Jerusalem handed over to Babylonian power, is claimed to be a divine and hence authoritative word, but also shown to be superseded by a subsequent and equally authoritative word. Yet it is observable that, in the eventual compilation of the book of Jeremiah, the former is preserved alongside the latter. Unless the superficial view is taken that the later oracle is merely the work of a 'lunkhead' editor,[11] validity is given both to the propriety of the judgment oracle in its historical context and to its continuing significance as an expression of a proper understanding of an aspect of the divine nature, and also to the oracle of promise which sets this judgment oracle aside, viewed as the expression (whether by Jeremiah or by some later interpreter) of a conviction of the reality of God's power to restore. In the eventual understanding of both sayings in the canonical book of Jeremiah, weight will be given to them in accordance with the particular styles of interpretation characteristic of the circles in which appeal is made to the biblical material.

This example indicates the degree to which there must be seen to be correlation between the original word delivered in a particular situation and accepted as authoritiative by a particular audience, and the subsequent modifications of it, by way of repeal, reinterpretation, shift of understanding, in yet other particular situations in which the new form is accepted as authoritative by other particular audiences. There is clear interlinkage between these, since the original word and its re-presentation both belong within the same tradition; the status of the original form is a presupposition for the status which belongs to its subsequent form. Both the original text and its subsequent modification or reinterpretation may be held to have continuing validity.

III.   *'Original' Text and 'Canonical' Text*

Two movements may be detected here, and they may be seen to be in opposite directions. There is the desire, often expressed explicitly but more often implicit in various lines of biblical study, to obtain the 'original' word of the prophet, if possible with a projection of the actual situation of its original utterance and with a discernment of its original impact on a particular audience; to discover the original form of a narrative or a psalm, and so forth. The explicit or implicit aim here is to recover what is felt to be nearer to the moment of inspiration and therefore to the point of authority. There is the alternative recognition that what eventually came to be regarded as authoritative in the life of the Jewish and Christian communities was the canonical text and in particular either the Masoretic Text (and in particular that form of it as *textus receptus* which eventually came to be enshrined in manuscripts viewed as entirely reliable) or, as for long periods in Christian communities, versions such as the Septuagint and the Vulgate. The latter does not necessarily exclude the former; it may either take the simplistic view that, for example, the book of Amos is entirely the authoritative word of the prophet; or it may, openly or tacitly, set aside as accretions those elements which are regarded as 'non-genuine' and make its appeal in effect to one form of a 'canon within a canon', by which only the 'genuine' is believed to have validity.

The two alternatives presuppose somewhat different views of the nature of biblical authority. Part of what is involved in both cases is a proper desire to recover a reliable text. This may be at the level of endeavouring, on the basis of manuscript evidence and of understanding of the nature of scribal transmission, to establish a true *textus receptus*, freed of errors due to the mischances of the processes by which texts evolve. It may, in the light of the evidence of the versions and of non-Masoretic forms of the text, attempt to get back behind the Masoretic form to a text-form or text-forms which can be established for an earlier stage of transmission, though immediately here a different question is being raised insofar as the evidence points to more than one form and therefore to the problem of deciding which, if any, is the true and authoritative form. The relation of text to community of use is here clearly relevant; but already the question of 'true' text and 'deviant' text is an issue of some difficulty. One may observe that the text-form authoritative for a particular community at a particular moment does not necessarily prove acceptable to another community either at that moment or subsequently. Part of the complex relationship between Jews and Samaritans or between Jews and Christians is to be seen in regard to the degree to which the acceptance of different texts provides a basis for differing views; the effecting of compromise, an agreed text for the purposes of debate, may be seen to be as vital to the conversations between Jews and Christians in the second century AD as in discussions between different Christian groups in the twentieth century.[12] Beyond this lies the long process of tracing back the evolution of a particular text to what is discerned as its point of origin – the prophetic utterance or the event believed to underlie a narrative, to take the two easiest examples. Ideally, on this line of approach, this leads to the recovery of the *ipsissima verba* of the prophet and to the exact description of the event or even beyond that, since all description is both interpretative and selective, to the event itself. Both of these are at the level of claiming authority, and the authority claimed is in fact at the same essential point, that of history. The prophet spoke the divine word in these terms on this occasion: here, it is felt, is the directness of authority without intermediary. But this begs all the questions which must be asked about the nature of divine-human communication, and assumes an understanding of revelation which can hardly be justified on adequate philosophical grounds.[13] Equally, the supposition that the recovery of an event as historically verifiable carries with it the authentication of a theological statement made about that event, is the transparent error of much popular thought about the meaning of the Old Testament. That Jerusalem is known to have been captured by the Babylonians in March 597 BC neither validates nor invalidates the affirmation of Jeremiah that 'this city is delivered by YHWH into the power of the Babylonians.' The prophetic affirmation too demands examination at a philosophical level, while at the same time it needs to be considered in the particular social and political and religious context in which it was spoken.

A different aspect of the problem emerges from a consideration of the psalms, though it is not restricted to that area of the literature. This appears in the existence of deviant forms of the same psalm within the Psalter, as for example Psalms 14 and 53, where difference of function and consequently different appraisals of the authority accorded to the same psalm must be considered with no context other than what may very tentatively be constructed from either a consideration of point of use in worship or possible relationships with what precedes and follows. It appears more markedly where psalms exist not only in deviant forms but also clearly in part have a different exposition for the same material presented in two such markedly different ways. Psalm 29 provides an even more complex example. This psalm has its alternative contexts, the one in a partial reappearance in Psalm 96 (29.1–2 and 96.7–9), where the differences are of considerable exegetical importance; the second in the further appearance of the latter in I Chronicles 16 (96.1–13 and 16.23–33), and here the differences in the text and the relationship of these verses to the other psalm material (related to Psalm 105) which precedes them in I Chronicles 16, raise yet other exegetical questions. But behind this is the persistently argued view, with differing claims and explanations, that Psalm 29 is somehow nearly allied to a non-Israelite proto-type.[14] This raises a more fundamental question about authority, for if it is right, whether fully demonstrable or not in this particular instance, to argue that Israel 'took over' Canaanite psalmody along with other of the appurtenances of the Canaanite cult in shrines which were assimilated to Yahwism, then this argues also first for the recognition that such material already had its own authoritative place in the Canaanite religious tradition, and second for the acknowledgement by Israel of that authority as real. At the same time, the re-use in a new context imposes on the material a new claim to authority which itself provides the basis for further reinterpretation.

IV. *The Levels of 'Canonicity'*

There is a link here with the awareness, so important for the appreciation of the narrative traditions, that the re-telling of a story,[15] implies a certain view of it. A piece of rich bawdy (taking here Wharton's own example of Judg. 16.1–3) may have its place at a secular level in whatever was ancient Israel's equivalent of the after-dinner speech; but the narrators of the different levels of Judges 13–16 have invested it with an authoritative status which shows it as a vehicle of theological perception. Much such material in the Old Testament canon may invite the impatience of a modern reader, especially if he hears it in the snippety use of a lectionary geared to the supposed inability of any congregation to listen to more than a few verses read consecutively. As part of a larger whole, as part of the canon as such, it may be making a claim which is not to be ignored.

The levels of 'canonicity', that is of acceptance as speaking authoritatively and in a binding manner, are not to be limited. The authority of the biblical word is neither a matter of finding an 'original' text which is accepted as coming direct from God; that search is often unproductive, but it may also take us back in a sense too far. Nor is it a matter of acceptance only at the finally agreed 'canonical' form. It is in this, as in so much else, in the end of a matter of balancing alternative claims, recognizing the degree of circumscription by time and circumstance which belongs to any stage in the evolution of the biblical text, 'original' or 'canonical', and acknowledging that authority rests in the interaction between text and reader, text and expositor, in the creative moment which such an interaction provides. The validity of that experience of authority is itself a matter of adjudication, where questions of the religious tradition, of the adequacy of doctrinal formulation, and of the philosophical propriety of what is experienced must all play their part.

It is a matter of regret to me to discover, too late, that this article was written without knowledge of the study by James A. Sanders, 'Adaptable for Life: The Nature and Function of Canon'.[16] The points of similarity are numerous, and it is satisfying to find so much support for the lines sketched out here. It is a pleasure both to acknowledge this and to extend good wishes to Dr Sanders on his move to Claremont!

EPILOGUE

The Old Testament Religious Tradition: Unity and Change

For a large proportion of those who claim to stand within the Christian religious tradition, the celebration of the Eucharist or Holy Communion or the Mass is an important or indeed a central element both in worship and in faith. It is true that there are groups within the tradition who do not give any place at all to that particular element. Some would assert that such groups thereby show themselves not in reality to belong to the tradition, though it must be doubted whether, if the theological stance of such groups is properly assessed, such a rigid and exclusivistic attitude is appropriate. But while a large measure of unanimity is observable, it must also be recognized that there is no uniformity of practice and no uniformity of interpretation of what it is that is being done and what is meant by it theologically. Yet it is not surprising for it to be felt by those who consider the Christian tradition from the outside that there is here one element which, for all the qualifications which may need to be entered, shows a degree of coherence and indeed of unity for that tradition.

I use this particular illustration because of a discussiom with an expert in Iranian studies and in Zoroastrianism (Professor Mary Boyce of the University of London) who used it – also as an illustration – in the presentation of arguments about the continuity of Zoroastrian tradition, arguments concerned with the approach to a particular and delicate problem, that of estimating just what kind of religious position was occupied by Cyrus, founder and first imperial ruler of the Persian empire, or, more strictly, of the Achaemenian empire. (The use of the term Persian would too easily imply that there is a readily traceable continuity from that period in the sixth century BC at which the empire began right through to much later, even to modern times: the celebration of its 2,500th anniversary under the late Shah may be seen as an expression of belief in such continuity. The belief in continuity may also be seen, perhaps with greater realism, as part of a propaganda exercise of a high order of effectiveness: the myth of 2,500 years of rule by an empire especially noted for tolerance in the conventional view is belied both by its more recent reputation under the Shah and after and also by a nearer understanding of its most ancient history.) The claim for religious continuity in Zoroastrianism – and such a belief is natural enough within that tradition – was made with an appeal for support from those within the Christian tradition for whom the continuity of the Eucharist would, it was thought, be recognized as making clear that what is now done under that name is what has been done since the establishment of the rite at the Last Supper.

Now since I am neither an ecclesiastical historian nor a liturgist, I do not propose to analyse the possible ways in which Christians might wish to speak of such a continuity or unity. It is evident enough that very different comments can be made on the matter. It is clearly enough the case that a recognizably related religious celebration can be traced back through the centuries; and that there is a closeness of relationship between Pauline statements about the institution (especially I Corinthians 11) and the evidence of the Gospels. I would hesitate to comment on how far that evidence in the New Testament goes towards establishing the authority of the claim to dominical institution. There are too many problems in the evidence for the answer to be simple. It constitutes one area of the wider discussion of the relationship between developed practice, the history of which we can trace with some degree of coherence from the date of the New Testament writings down to the present day, and what lies behind the evidence of the earliest sources. It is at this point that we are aware that the concept of continuity meets with difficulties. It is also the case that, while a claim for almost universal observance of a practice gives a strong impression of unity, an examination of the detail of later development and interpretation shows not merely sharp divergence but at numerous points – and continuing down to the present situation – such sharpness of conflict as to have in the past occasioned religious persecution and murder in the name of religion, as well as claims and denials of validity which, however charitably stated, constitute a strong barrier to the often vaunted moves towards unity which have been in vogue over the last few generations.

This illustration contains the problematic elements which also confront us in attempting to assess the nature of the Old Testament religious tradition. It is evident that there is an element of coherence which makes it appropriate to speak of that tradition as stretching out over the centuries covered by the Old Testament period. The more precise definition of the beginning is a delicate matter; the end is in one respect definable approximately by the completion of the biblical writings and of their textual forms. But the tradition itself is not so limited and calls to be considered within the two major contexts into which it has evolved, the Jewish and the Christian (with a recognition that the Samaritan tradition offers another alternative, and that in some measure Islamic tradition, however different its stance, yet another). Both Jewish and Christian thought have taken over the older tradition, with the difference that the former would see the relationship more plainly in terms of a continuum, where the latter, while normally retaining a strong sense of regarding the Old Testament tradition as part of its own, lays primary stress on what is often stated in terms of a radical new moment.

But how is the coherence of the religious tradition to be described or defined? In some degree the problem runs parallel to that of writing an adequate history of the Old Testament period. This involves the handling of the biblical material which must be the primary evidence: the assessing of the relevance of the non-biblical, which includes both ancient and long-familiar texts and ancient but newly-discovered texts: the interpreting of non-verbal artefacts which shed light, even if the light is at times a flickering one, casting perplexing shadows; and the placing of this evidence in a context, the provision of appropriate models for understanding. The holding together of all this, and the recognition of its inadequacy, its incompleteness, make the task a delicate one. And central to that awareness of delicacy is the fact that complete detachment in the handling of it is hardly attainable. The lack of detachment may be the inevitable result of our standing within the tradition ourselves in one way or another: this may bring with it the advantage of a natural sympathy for what we are handling, but it involves our needing to be aware, as it is often difficult to be aware, of the degree to which our involvement influences our particular choices in interpretation. It can also, of course, be the result of quite different factors affecting our judgment. The supposition that someone who does not in any way share in the tradition is for that reason unbiased is an illusion: detachment and total lack of prejudice are impossible. In a more extreme position, the assumption that the tradition is invalid, that it represents a way of interpreting human experience that is based on a misapprehension, is just as capable of producing one-sided interpretation as are the attitudes of professed believers.

II

The analogy with the problems of writing a history of Israel is clear enough. A survey and a critique of the issues is offered by Whitelam.[1] In particular he draws attention to the degree to which much, though not all, such history writing tends to use the biblical text too simply, in effect often giving what is little more than a paraphrase of that text for certain areas and periods.[2] Whitelam was writing before the publication of the history of Hayes and Miller,[3] which, in an effective manner, provides at each stage an outline of what the biblical text itself offers for the particular period, and examines why it cannot be used straight, and what possibilities of interpretation are possible in the light of the available evidence. For most students of the Old Testament, the insuperable difficulties of a real reconstruction of the earliest periods are apparent. If, with Soggin and others, we are inclined to suppose that a real and coherent history only becomes possible with the Davidic monarchy, in fact the lacunae for the monarchical period are such that coherent accounts are not really possible there, even if we recognize a reasonable chronological frame. I would myself go further and suggest that for the whole period of the monarchy, including the antecedent Samuel and Saul period, and in particular for that of David and Solomon, our evidence in the biblical text is little more than anecdotal: it is story rather than history.[4] Laments at the meagre amount of information available for the understanding of the history of the Achaemenian period – a 'period without history' as it has been termed – provoke a certain amusement at the assumption that we really know any more about the periods which precede it.

The reason for the problems lies largely in the nature of the texts we are compelled to handle, even if we accept Whitelam's criticisms and also accept his appeal for a much more fully contextual and comparative study which can make possible a more adequate understanding both of texts and artefacts. Just before the publication of Soggin's history, I heard him read as a paper some parts of his methodological statement.[5] It seemed appropriate then to comment that what he was presenting as a bold innovation in maintaining that we can only begin a real historical procedure when our evidence becomes clear in the monarchical period, was in fact rather conservative. It must be taken to a much more radical position, that of recognizing that the present form of our texts is post-exilic – however much it may be argued for their being virtually complete at an earlier date, a point on which views differ sharply. They belong to a period quite other than that which they describe. What we recognize as the problems of utilizing the books of Chronicles applies equally to the supposedly earlier texts. At every point we must ask why the narratives and other material are presented as they are: what kind of stylization has been undertaken, what degree both of selectivity and of contextualization has been provided for material which is or may be of earlier origin. The Old Testament tells a story: it is a good story, exciting to read, inspiring to hear, full of deep insights into human nature and into the ways in which human attempts are made at understanding the meaning of the world in religious or other terms. But it is a story.

If we only hear that story, and use it as a framework into which we fit the diverse evidence available to us, what we eventually reach is likely to be simply what the Old Testament intends us to hear. This is rather like the hailing, at the end of the eighteenth century and the beginning of the nineteenth, of the supposed discovery that Josiah's law book *was* Deuteronomy – a view subsequently refined but still essentially maintained: for that is surely exactly what the narrators in the books of Kings intended their readers to recognize. What the Old Testament intends us to hear has its own interest and value; but it constitutes only one level of reality. For its full and proper appreciation, it must itself be subjected to critical examination. The interpretation of history offered by the book of Daniel, like that offered by a modern

millenarian movement, may not provide any historical information
as such: as giving insight into particular styles of thinking, either
may assist in the illumination of the context in which it was formed,
and hence contribute to our knowledge of the past at another level.

III

Religious traditions, like historical traditions, take a particular
view of the past. When the book of Jeremiah looks back:

> I remember the devotion of your youth,
>> your love as a bride,
> how you followed me in the wilderness,
>> in a land not sown.
> Israel was holy to the Lord,
>> the first fruits of his harvest.
> All who ate of it became guilty;
>> disaster came upon them . . . (Jeremiah 2.2f.)

we are invited to see here a description of the early history and
religious life of the people If we had no other information available
to us, we should conclude, taking the text straight, that the
community now addressed in Jerusalem had once lived in a totally
different physical environment. The context, quite apart from the
implication of the recall, suggests that the present state of the
community religiously is quite different from what it once was.
The final clauses imply disasters for others interrupted as due to
their interference with holy things, believed to cause guilt and
calamity. If we were to take this passage in isolation, we could
build up a sketchy but nevertheless valuable picture of how the
community saw itself.

Put into a wider context and related to other biblical material,
we should find some confirmation of that picture. The numerous
narratives of the wilderness period do in part conform to it: there
is stress in them on a closeness between people and deity, expressed
in a variety of ways, and there are narratives which show the defeat
of various opponents, and an interpretation of their defeat picturing
them as facing disaster because of particular religious and moral
attitudes. In addition, the change over from an earlier and different
style of life to the settled and urban context of the Judah of the
seventh to sixth centuries BC is given detailed description.

However, the narratives do not provide only that. They also, and repeatedly, depict a totally different view, and numerous narratives underline that that early period was one of failure and disobedience rather than the harmonious one here suggested. The diversity in historical explanation provided by modern scholarship underlines the problematic nature of the evidence. Furthermore, a broader and comparative look at such an element as this in Jeremiah points to a further possibility. The concept of an ideal past is so prevalent in historical and religious traditions as to make it at least open to doubt whether it can be given precise historical credence. As an interpretation of the development of a religion, it is also open to doubt. That this is so is clear from an examination of any religious tradition, and the recognition that, even if not universal, the idea of a pure and satisfactory start – often centred on a notable and ideal personality – is extremely common. The idealization of the personality or personalities may often be traced. We have only to consider the way in which Philo handles the figure of Moses, himself already an idealized personage in the biblical traditions, to recognize that such descriptions must be assessed both within the context of the evidence for the early stages of the religion and within that of the wider indications of how such religious founder figures are interpreted. So too – and in that same context – the early Christian movement was faced with the need to explain and present the figure of Jesus in ways which were intelligible within a particular intellectual and religious climate of opinion. If they had not done so, they would have been unable to communicate what they felt and believed. In the same way, the mere repetition of descriptive and interpretative statements from that period in the contemporary world does not necessarily – or even probably – convey very much to communities for whom such a linguistic and ideological context is unknown or at best unfamiliar.

The myth of a pure and original religion is a strong element in Old Testament thought. The period of the very beginnings; the period of the patriarchs; the exodus and wilderness traditions; the conquest stories; the idealization of the Davidic-Solomonic period (cf. I Kings 4.24f.; Zech. 3.10) – all these include as an important element the belief that there was a period in the past when the relationship between God and man was close, sometimes to the extent of stressing the actual physical presence of the deity in the human sphere (e.g. Genesis 2; 18; Exodus 33; Judges 13). The narratives also include numerous indications, set against this purity tradition, of human failure. This too is traced back virtually to the beginning. It serves to underline the contrast, and we may see in it an important element in the appeal and warning to contemporary readers of the story that they should not be like their forefathers (e.g. Zech. 1.1–6; and numerous passages in Deuteronomy), who, even when confronted with the reality of the deity's presence, or who heard his voice from the mountain, or received the divine word by the agency of Moses and the prophets, fell away from a known pure standard and thus assisted in the undermining of the ideal life which Israel supposedly once lived. When such a far-reaching claim is made as we see in Jeremiah, there is an intelligible appeal to those addressed to recover the past, a past which is both a past as it is believed to have been and a past as it ought to have been. In either way, the reality of that more acceptable or totally acceptable state is affirmed.

The clearest and most significant point in such a presentation is in the picture provided by the biblical texts showing Israel's religion as a desirable survival from the pre-conquest period: the religion of a non-settled community, variously defined, then corrupted by the alien forms of belief and practice which belonged to Canaan and indeed to everyone else. Doubts cast on the historicity of the conquest concept as an adequate way of understanding the political development of the community at least provide a context for raising similar doubts about the long-established procedure by which Israel's own theologians, most readily illustrated in the Deuteronomic writings, interpreted in terms of such corruption everything which did not conform to their understanding of what the religion should be.

The biblical text itself raises doubts about such a simplistic view. A good example is to be found in that passage in Hosea which, anticipating what may be a concept of the exile of the north (or of part of the community there) or of the Babylonian conquest and the sixth century exile of part of Judah, stresses that

Israel shall dwell many days without king or prince, without sacrifice or pillar, without ephod or teraphim (Hos. 3.4).

Whatever precisely is to be made of that curious list, we may recognize that the immediate sequel in the promise of a recovery of Davidic kingship suggests that that institution has its positive, divinely ordained, place. Of the four religious objects or practices mentioned, sacrifice at least normally is positively assessed, though there are qualifiers; the ephod as religious object or garment or whatever is also most often viewed at least neutrally; the remaining two, pillar and teraphim, are eventually seen in negative terms. This indicates that what at one period is deemed acceptable may in another be rejected. So too the term *ba'al* is in some contexts acceptable but in others repudiated; *'ādōn*, in spite of alien religious connections, remains respectable. These are examples both of the changing evaluation of religious ideas and terminology and of the inconsistency with which a developing religious tradition operates.

In the light of the biblical hints at the presence of male and female deity symbols – either carefully covered or provided with negative comment – and in the light of the archaeological evidence, substantially added to in recent years, for the presence of a female consort of Yahweh,[6] we are increasingly forced to recognize that, whatever the Old Testament eventually asks us to believe about the religion of ancient Israel, it was much less distinct, much closer to its religious context, than that later idealization and critique suggests.[7] It is of interest to observe how often in attempts at interpreting the earlier stages of religious belief – for example that of the patriarchs – analogies from contemporary practice or, in some instances, from much remoter supposed parallels, have been adduced to explain the particular style of belief which, it is thought, may be detected within and behind the present form of the material. Yet in general, in spite of the pressures of the evidence to the contrary, a really serious appraisal of the realities of religion in the monarchical period has been made more difficult by the often still prevalent assumption that the ideal past was a reality; that the religion of the wilderness was of a kind so different from that of Canaan that a syncretism of the two could only be viewed with hostility, or its acceptance regarded as an unsatisfactory and uneasy compromise. In fact, much of our evidence, particularly in regard to the royal elements in the development of the religion, points either to the large-scale acceptance of other forms of belief, or, as it would seem more natural to assume, to a recognition that there never was such a simple distinction between one style of religion and another.[8]

IV

Part of our problem lies in the repeated attempts made to define the uniqueness of Hebrew religion. Tied up with this is the felt need to define precisely what constitutes an Old Testament theology. Only if we can somehow resolve these questions – it seems to be implied – can we explain the religion which eventually survived, in Judaism and in Christianity, to provide a context for our own thinking. Yet in reality that uniqueness – which we do not need to doubt, though we must give it a context in recognizing the uniqueness of every form of religious tradition and not just that of the Judaeo-Christian line – must lie in the whole process of change and flux which we may detect within the biblical record itself. It is to be found through statement and counter-statement; by repeated and varied attempts at re-expressing and remodelling ideas and practices handed down; in the expression of belief in poetry, in liturgical forms; in the critique of contemporary life by which religious beliefs are both applied and hence tested and also restated in more contemporary terms. It is a continual process of change, and one which does not end with the final shaping of the texts through the later years of religious communities in which the texts themselves provide both the anchor for faith and a source and support for modifications of belief and presentation. Indeed, as has now been shown more systematically by Michael Fishbane,[9] this interaction between text and life is itself part of the process by which the texts as we have them have been shaped. They are a central element both in witnessing to the flux and in enabling it to take place, and hence in enabling the texts to continue to have life within a changed and still changing community. I am not competent to speak about other religious traditions, and, in those which have such texts, the relationship between religious life and written texts is not identical to what we observe either in Judaism or in Christianity[10]. Yet it is difficult not to suppose some kind of analogous action and reaction taking place in all living religions. What a community believes itself to be is at least in large part determined by what its tradition, written or unwritten, holds, and by the ways in which it keeps interacting with its own past.

V

The modernization of theology is a topic which often produces more heat than light. For those who are suspicious of or hostile to change, it is always easy to contrast the stability of the past – in particular that ideal age in which the Christian creeds were formed or whatever precise parallel or analogy may be adduced in Judaism – with what is thought to be a reprehensible willingness, indeed eagerness, to change the faith by adjusting to contemporary styles of thought. Such an issue as the ordination of women to the priesthood is by its opponents seen, at least in part, as pandering to the changes in social conditions and customs and as disregarding the universal view and practice of the ancient church with which the contemporary church must remain not merely in continuity but in conformity. The assumption that change is a response to modernity is, of course, in some degree justified; but all too easily that assumption includes the hidden view that what is new must be in some way inferior to what is old. And this is another part of that view of the past which sees it in terms of ideal beginnings and gradual corruption. (Of course, we have to beware of those who believe that only the newest can be true.)

But it is clear that an examination of the past shows the erroneousness of such assumptions, or at least their very limited and partial validity. Both for Jews and Christians the religious tradition claims that at a certain point in time – in the case of Moses and in the case of Jesus – a radical change took place. We may see it epitomized in the statement that God made himself known to the patriarchs as El Shaddai, 'but by my name Yahweh I did not make myself known to them' (Exod. 6.3): a new name implies a new nature. And comparably in the New Testament we have the contrast drawn between the 'many and various ways' in which God spoke in the past and the speaking 'in these last days . . . by a son' (Heb. 1.1f.). In both cases, we need to set such a claim to newness in the context of the more complex evaluation of the old and the new which is to be found in the traditions. But there is in these claims a degree of rejection of the past which is part of the process of change. It is valued both positively and negatively: the new experience provides a context for the fuller explanation and understanding of the old. Thus at the crucial moments of both religious systems there is an element which demands the acceptance of the new as now determining the nature of the faith.

What may thus be presented in a specific moment is in fact exemplified at every moment that we can in any way describe. An illustration from the post-exilic period of Old Testament history and thought may clarify the point. We can see this very clearly in that moment of change, which is also a moment of continuity, the experience of the years of Babylonian rule and its sequel in Achaemenian takeover. The use for this period of the two terms 'exile' and 'restoration' is convenient but misleading:[11] for a variety of reasons, neither term is accurate, the first because, however little we know of the Palestine of the Babylonian period, we cannot assume a vacuum, and 'exile' produces a tendentious emphasis; the second because equally it makes assumptions – which are closely based on a dangerously simple reading of the biblical texts – about the nature of the political change-over from Babylonian to Achaemenian authority. At the same time, those two terms epitomize something of the way in which the biblical description is offered: a concept of a break with the past which represents a moment of judgment and of rejection of a false position reached in the years, particularly the later years, of the monarchy; and a concept of a new start which is expressed not in terms of newness but in terms of revival of the true past. Wherever we look in those biblical texts which in some measure reflect this moment – and that extends far beyond the narratives and prophecies directly associated with it – we see that there is concern for continuity with the past, of recovery of the past, of a new life which is genuinely what the past stood for and what must now be re-established. That this understanding is not all of one piece will be obvious. Detailed examination of the material constantly reveals aspects of the variety of thought. It is too simple to describe this in terms of conflicting parties, though there is little doubt that there were real conflicts: a religious system which showed no controversy would be dead indeed. But it turns around different emphases, appeals to different elements in the tradition, and in particular – and here again Michael Fishbane – the diversity with which the material, both in writing and in the tradition of practice, is reinterpreted.[12]

What again might really occasion our surprise – and here we are back again at our initial question – is that with all the variety of interpretation there remains nevertheless a strong sense of belonging together. Not entirely, however. For just as at an earlier and crucial moment, we may see a political division between north and south which takes on religious significance – or perhaps had it already –, so in the later biblical period we may see that, while the bonds of unity were strong, they were not so strong as to prevent such sharp divisions as those which created the Samaritan community, and Qumran, and Christianity. There come points at which a religious community finds itself confronted with such radical discontent that division is inevitable, however much it will be bewailed by those who think that unity is all. We may regret the bitternesses with which such divisions are often attended, and we may also recognize that divisions will often persist long after their original causes have ceased to be operative. But we may also recognize that division and difference has often itself been part of a process of rethinking, of reform, of discovery of truth, without which the eventual outcome would be poorer.

VI

Such an understanding of the richness of a religious tradition applies very properly to the Old Testament. It is, I suspect, not without its relevance to some of our contemporary problems, both in regard to Old Testament interpretation and in regard to reformulations of ancient belief in a modern context. For in both areas there is a false attraction to the supposition that there is a unity which has always existed and which therefore must not be broken; whereas in reality unity has always been a measure of compromise in holding together different and sometimes mutually exclusive views. Whenever the lines are drawn sharply, there is deeper conflict produced. Where there is at least some degree of listening and appreciation, there is the possibility of enrichment of thought. For the most part, the matter lies across the borders of the two: there are those for whom the drawing of sharp lines appears to be of the essence of preserving their faith intact, and those for whom such a rigid approach (as it is seen) constitutes a denial of the living nature of a religion which, it is claimed, knows no boundaries of time or space. For those who believe they must claim to allow no change, adjustments in theological statement and language often appear to be changes for the sake of a contemporary fashion of thought. There are others for whom adherence to the past looks more like a matter of old-fashioned conservatism which loses contact with the real world.

Truth and its maintenance needs something of both: a firm hold on the past and a full consciousness of the present. Fortunately for contemporary faith, the adjustment of past to present has gone on in spite of us. However much we may sometimes hope or believe that we are maintaining the past, even recovering the primitive, we are in fact making the adjustments without which faith ceases to be real.

NOTES

The place of publication of books cited in the notes is London unless otherwise stated.

1. Continuity: a Contribution to the Study of the Old Testament Religious Tradition

(Inaugural Lecture in the Samuel Davidson Chair of Old Testament Studies delivered at King's College London on 10 October 1961; published by Blackwell, Oxford 1962.)

1. There is great literary skill and religious sensitivity in the way in which the compiler of the narratives – whether this was at the oral or written stage of the transmission – has interwoven the Samuel motif with that of the sons of Eli: 2.11 – Samuel, 2.12–17 – sons of Eli, 2.18–21 – Samuel, 2.22–25 – sons of Eli, 2.26 – Samuel, followed by the duplicate judgment stories in 2.27–36 and 3.1–18 which both introduce the further motif of the substitution of a true priesthood for that of Eli. Cf. also below.

2. On this, cf. the article of Jan Dus, 'Der Brauch der Ladewanderung im alten Israel', *TZ* 17, 1961, 1–16.

3. Cf. M. Noth in *Festschrift A. Bertholet*, ed. W. Baumgartner et al., Mohr, Tübingen 1950, 404ff.; *History of Israel*, A. and C. Black 1960; reprinted SCM Press 1983, p. 101.

4. Cf. also I Samuel 8.1–5 on Samuel's sons. The motif 'good father, bad son(s)' is a recurrent one, cf. also Gideon-Abimelech, David and his sons in II Samuel, Solomon-Rehoboam, the recurrent pattern in the kingship of the northern kingdom (e.g. I Kings 15.25–27) where a continuing protest is to be found against the hereditary as distinct from the charismatic principle (cf. A. Alt, 'Das Königtum in Israel und Juda', *VT* 1, 1951, 2–22, esp. 7ff.). It may be seen also in Ezekiel's use of the idea (Ezekiel 18). [Cf. below, p. 258, n.8.]

5. Cf. I Sam.2.35 (echoed also in the other narrative in I Sam. 3.13, where v. 12 appears to be a linking verse to the previous chapter), I Kings 2.35.

6. Cf. for example the duplicates already noted (n. 1) in I Samuel 2 and 3, but also the divergent judgment on Hophni and Phineas. In I Samuel 4 the narrative of the deaths of the sons of Eli at the capture of the Ark is told as an unmitigated tragedy with no comment on their evil behaviour. No blame is attached to them for the loss of the Ark. It is possible that there is an underlying blame attaching to all Israel for presuming to bring the Ark into the battle (I

Sam.4.3–4), but if so it is nowhere made explicit. (Cf. II Sam.11.11 where the presence of the Ark is mentioned as normal.) No comment in the narrative suggests that the capture of the Ark by the Philistines is to be seen as a judgment upon Israel at all. In fact the loss of the Ark is part of the larger purpose of God as appears in the sequel, for thereby he discomfits the Philistines. (Cf. A. Bentzen, 'The Cultic Use of the Story of Ark in Samuel', *JBL* 67, 1948, 37–53.) The wife of Phineas also appears as a woman of deep piety, whose last moments are clouded by the realization that Israel has lost the Ark. Glory has departed. God has withdrawn himself (I Sam.4.21f.).

7. Cf. above n. 1.

8. This aspect of the problem of continuity is discussed by N. W. Porteous in a paper entitled 'The Prophets and the Problem of Continuity' read to the Society for Old Testament Study in Oxford in July 1960 and published in *Israel's Prophetic Heritage: Esssys in honor of James Muilenburg*, ed. B. W. Anderson and W. Harrelson, SCM Press and Harper, New York 1962, 11–25. It is to this paper, which touches on some of the points covered in this lecture but follows rather different lines, and to the discussion which followed its reading, that I owe the stimulus to choose the subject of Continuity as that of my inaugural lecture. Professor Porteous kindly lent me a copy of his typescript since the printed version was not yet available.

9. Porteous in 'The Prophets and the Problem of Continuity' very properly lays much stress on the essential contribution of the 'quiet in the land'. Cf. also my 'Crisis and Evolution in the Old Testament', *EvQu* 25, 1953, 69–82, esp.p. 80; and my 'The Vitality of the Word of God in the Old Testament' (Essay 5, pp. 61–75).

10. Cf. Genesis 19, 34, and more especially 35.1–4.

11. There is mention only of Isaiah in what seems to be in some respects a rather fanciful narrative (II Kings 18–20, Isaiah 36–39), though none of Amos and Hosea in spite of the common elements of condemnation of the north. [See also Essays 6–11].

12. Cf. Jeremiah 39, 40, 41, and other sections. [See Essay 8, pp. 121–51].

13. And, we might add, about Ezekiel, for the non-mention of Ezekiel cannot be explained merely by saying that he was in Babylon and certainly not used as an argument in favour of the traditional view that he was already there.

14. As for example by Edward Roberton, *The Old Testament Problem*, Manchester UP 1950, 40f., 137f., 158.

15. We may probably also trace this situation in some measure to geographical conditions. Cf. L. Köhler, *Hebrew Man*, SCM Press 1956, re-issued 1973, 149.

16. Cf. the reactions of later Judaism, as for example in mysticism and the Karaite movement, to the rigidity of the central uniform pattern, and the many examples of reaction to narrow orthodoxy in the history of the church. In the Old Testament we may point to the various attempts at codification and unifying – e.g. in Josiah's Reform – and while recognizing the enormous influence of this, see nevertheless how much richer the tradition of later years really is. Cf. also below on the significance of such movements towards uniformity for the maintenance of continuity.

17. Cf. Ninian Smart, 'The Uncertainty Principle in Religion', *The Listener*, 17 August 1961, 244f.

18. [Cf. O. H. Steck, 'Theological Streams of Tradition', in *Tradition and Theology in the Old Testament*, ed. D. A. Knight, Fortress Press, Philadelphia 1977, 183–214.]

19. Cf. G. E. Wright, *God Who Acts* (SBT 8), 1952, 103.

20. Cf. J. Robinson in a review of *On the Authority of the Bible* by Leonard Hodgson and others (SPCK 1960), in *The Kingsman*, 1960, no. 3, p. 39.

21. *Studies in Deuteronomy* (SBT 9) 1953; *Moses*, Lutterworth 1960; *Genesis* (OTL) 1961. Of *Moses*, G. W. Anderson (Society for Old Testament Study Book List, 1961, 52) writes that it 'is an admirable approach to the understanding of the continuity of Biblical religion'.

22. G. von Rad, *Theologie des Alten Testaments*, 1, Kaiser, Munich² 1958, 2 1960.

23. [Subsequently translated: *Old Testament Theology* 1, 2, Oliver and Boyd, Edinburgh 1962, 1965; reissued SCM Press 1975].

24. Usefully set out by G. W. Anderson, *Critical Introduction to the Old Testament*, Duckworth 1959, 55f.

25. Cf. J. Muilenburg, 'The form and structure of the covenantal formulations', *VT* 9, 1959, 347–65.

26. Cf. e.g. the study by W. Beyerlin, *Die Kulttraditionen Israels in der Verkündigung des Propheten Micha* (FRLANT 72), 1959.

27. Cf. especially Psalms 78, 105, 106, 114, 135, 136. See also A. Lauha, *Die Geschichtsmotive in den alttestamentlichen Psalmen* (AASF, B56, 1) 1945; A. Weiser, 'Psalm 77. Ein Beitrag zur Frage nach dem Verhältnis von Kult und Heilsgeschichte', *TLZ* 72, 1947, cols. 133ff.; H.-J. Kraus, *Psalmen* (BK 15), 1960, lvi-lxi.

28. On this, see G. von Rad, *Theologie des Alten Testaments* I, ²1958, Part II, B; ET 129–305. I prefer to follow Noth and others in making the division between the Tetrateuch and the Deuteronomic History, while recognizing the interconnections between the material which underlies both of these immense works. Cf. M. Noth, *Uberlieferungsgeschichtliche Studien* I, Niemeyer, Halle 1943 [ET, JSOTS 15 and 50, 1981, 1986]; *Überlieferungsgeschichte des Pentateuch*, Kohlhammer, Stuttgart 1948 [ET, *A History of Pentateuchal Traditions*, Prentice-Hall, Englewood Cliffs, NJ 1972]. See also the discussion, which rejects Noth's view, in O. Eissfeldt, *Einleitung in das Alte Testament*, Mohr, Tübingen ²1956, 289–98, and esp. 296 where the interrelationship between the two approaches is discussed. [ET *The Old Testament: An Introduction* Blackwell, Oxford 1965, from 3rd German edition, 241–48, esp. 246f.]

29. [Cf. relevant essays in *The Hebrew Bible and its Modern Interpreters*, ed. D. A. Knight and G. M. Tucker, Scholars Press, Chico 1985.]

30. Cf. L. Köhler, *Hebrew Man*, SCM Press 1956, 104ff.

31. Cf. for example, Isa. 2.1–4(5), Micah 4.1–4(5); Obad. 1–10; Jer.49.7–22; Joel 3.16 (Heb.4.16); Amos 1.2.

32. Cf. Beyerlin, op.cit., 8 and the literature mentioned in the footnotes there.

33. Cf. Jer.23.32: 'I did not send them or charge them'. Cf. also Ezek.13.7.

34. Cf.below; cf. also Beyerlin, op.cit., 91f., and Essay 5, pp. 61–75.

35. On use of conventional psalm-forms for the expression of piety, cf. Eissfeldt, *Einleitung* (²1956), 571 [ET (see n. 28), 465]. With reference to certain passages in the book of Job, Eissfeldt writes: 'When the Jew utters a lament, he does so in traditional forms, and if a poet wishes to present a sufferer, he puts into his mouth the conventional laments.'

36. Cf. A. Weiser, 'Das Deboralied', *ZAW* 30, 1959, 67–97, where he suggests that the Song of Deborah is a liturgical composition designed to incorporate the victory over Sisera into the pattern of the *Heilsgeschichte*.

37. The psalm, we may assume, was not arbitrarily chosen. Its immediate link with the story of Hannah is slight, consisting simply in the reference to the fertility of the barren in 2.5. Its appropriateness lies rather in the realization of the relationship between the public occasion to which the psalm originally belongs and the personal situation of the worshipper. That a royal psalm (cf. v.10) can be used as a vehicle of personal devotion shows the reapplication of cult-liturgical material and so provides an important piece of evidence to show the interrelatedness of the two aspects of religious practice. There is no clue as to the date at which this reapplication became possible, but the presence in Jeremiah's Confessions of what appear to be cult-liturgical forms utilized for the expression of the inmost feelings of the prophet, suggests that we do not need to look only to a very late date for it. The re-application of royal psalmody would, of course, be demanded by the end of the monarchy, but it is not by any means impossible that such re-use was already familiar at an earlier date. This would be an important factor in enabling the older liturgical material to bridge the gap between the pre-exilic and post-exilic orders. Cf. also n. 35.

38. [Cf. my *Exile and Restoration* (OTL), 1968].

39. References to the literature on this point may be found in H. H. Rowley, 'Ritual and the Hebrew Prophets' in *Myth, Ritual, and Kingship*, ed. by S. H. Hooke, Clarendon Press, Oxford 1958, 236–60, esp. 240ff.; cf. *JSS* 1, 1956, 338–60. See also the discussion in *ExpT* 70, 1959, 297–300, 341–2. The sharp contrast of 'cult' and 'word' (cf. P. Volz, *Prophetengestalten des Alten Testaments*, Calwer, Stuttgart 1938, p. 56, and cf. also his article 'Die radikale Ablehnung der Kultreligion durch die alttestamentlichen Propheten', *ZST* 14, 1937, 63–85) is in some ways a hangover from a too narrow Protestantism. Cf. also S. Mowinckel, *Religion und Kultus*, Vandenhoeck and Ruprecht, Göttingen 1953, 7ff., 136f., and the interchange between Rowley and Snaith, *ExpT* 53, 1946–47, 69–71, 152–3, 305–7.

The prophets' criticisms suggest that if a choice could be made and had to be made, they would prefer a religion without cult to a religion without obedience. But we may question whether the idea of such a choice has any reality in the Old Testament context. At least the contrast is not quite as we might see it, for the later development of thought by which such practices as prayer and almsgiving came to be seen as a substitute for sacrifice (cf. G. F. Moore, *Judaism*, Harvard UP, Cambridge, Mass. 1927–30, I, 505ff., II, 13ff., 171ff., 220ff., etc.) is in a sense a substitution of one external observance for another and by no means guarantees the inner reality. New Testament criticisms confirm this (cf. Matt.6.1ff.), and so do many passages in later Jewish writings. The inner reality may be present or it may not; the forms will still be there. A form-less – i.e. a cult-less – religion is unthinkable (cf. Mowinckel, op.cit., 8; G. F. Moore, op.cit., II, 5).

40. Cf. also Beyerlin, op.cit. and Porteous' paper (see n. 8 above).

41. Cf. Rowley, *The Faith of Israel*, SCM Press 1956, 101.

42. In this respect the much greater immediacy of the prophetic experiences – Amos 3.7f., Hosea 1.2ff., Micah 3.8, Isaiah 6 – is important, though the caution indicated in the next note must be observed.

43. Cf. Mowinckel, op.cit., 10: 'It is certainly true in the world of religion that if two people say the same thing, it is nevertheless not the same.' Where, as in the case of the patriarchs, comparison is made with the expressions found in other ancient documents, these expressions are not necessarily to be immediately interpreted in the sense which seems most obvious to us. On 'personal religion' in the patriarchal narratives, cf. H. Cazelles, 'Patriarches', *Supplément au Dictionnaire de la Bible*, VII, 1961, cols. 142f.

44. Cf. J. Hempel, *Das Ethos des Alten Testaments* (BZAW 67), 1938, 41ff. [See also H. Vorländer, *Mein Gott. Die Vorstellungen vom persönlichen Gott im Alten Orient und im Alten Testament* (AOAT 23), 1975.]

45. This against, e.g., L. Köhler, *Theologie des Alten Testaments*, Mohr, Tübingen ³1953, v–vi and 171–89 (ET, *Old Testament Theology*, Lutterworth Press 1958, 7, 181–98). Köhler had a blind spot with regard to the cult which he described as an alien element – which it is, but it is nevertheless an essential part of Israel's life and experience of God. To describe it as 'Man's expedient for his own redemption' (title of ch. 52) perhaps better to be rendered as 'Man's attempt at saving himself' and to say that 'there is no suggestion anywhere in the Old Testament that sacrifice or any other part of the cult was instituted by God. It knows only the regulation of already existing sacrifice by divine instruction' (171, ET 181) is unduly narrow in approach. It misses, for example, the whole intention of the P work which traces the institution of the sabbath to God's creative act and pictures the people on the threshold of the promised land as a community centred in worship around its God.

46. Cf. R. de Vaux, *Les Institutions de l'Ancien Testament* II, Éditions du Cerf, Paris 1960, 325f. (ET, *Ancient Israel*, Darton, Longman and Todd 1961, 440f.). Such a grafting may be seen in the festival Passover/Unleavened Bread, cf. de Vaux 389ff. (ET 488ff.).

47. Cf. e.g. Eissfeldt, *Einleitung*, 692f. [ET 560ff.].

48. Cf. my 'Criteria for the Maccabean Dating of Old Testament Literature', *VT* 3, 1953, 113–32; see 132, where a comparison is made with the formation of the New Testament under the influence of persecution. What books are so sacred that a man must die rather than give them up? The Qumran literature reveals that different views could be taken on that vital issue.

49. Cf. Eissfeldt, op. cit., 692 [ET 560].

50. Attested in writing at a very early date by such codes as that of Lipit-Ishtar, (*ANET*, 159ff.), Eshnunna (ibid., 16ff.,) and Hammurabi (ibid., 163–80).

51. Porteous in the paper mentioned in n. 8 above stresses the importance of 'books', i.e. written documents, for preservation and hence for continuity.

52. Cf. e.g. E. Nielsen, *Oral Tradition* (SBT 11), 1954, 33, quoting Engnell and Nyberg: 'reduction to writing is linked with a general crisis of confidence.'

53. G. von Rad, *Moses*, Lutterworth Press 1960, 80, traces the history of election, revelation, law and the vision of final purpose to Moses, the central figure within the pattern based on the *credo*.

54. Cf. the relationship of this to the later elaborations of law in Rabbinic thought, a point discussed by Professor J. Weingreen in his presidential address to the Society for Old Testament Study in London in January 1961 on 'The Continuity of Tradition from Old Testament to Early Rabbinic Times'. [This paper was not published, but its line of thought was further developed and may be seen in *From Bible to Mishna*, Manchester UP 1976.]

55. Cf. the extreme Rechabite attitude, which in its complete repudiation of the civilization of Canaan must have viewed some aspects of the main prophetic movement as disquieteningly 'progressive'. In certain respects Hosea represents a holding together of the negative attitude ('back to the wilderness') and the positive ('it is Yahweh who gives corn and wine and oil'). A similar problem is that of assimilation to Hellenistic standards in the Greek period. The issue is no simple one, set out in black and white, being of the nature of the *Quid academiae et ecclesiae?* of later debates. [See also Essay 11, pp. 181–92. The real nature of the Rechabites remains under discussion. For a summary, see F. S. Frick, *IDBS*, 1976, 726–8, with bibliography.]

56. von Rad, *Theologie* I, 340(ET 343), describes the Deuteronomic History as a 'Gerichtsdoxologie' i.e. an act of praise directed to God in acknowledgment of the rightness and justice of his judgment.

57. II Kings 25.27–30; cf. von Rad, *Studies in Deuteronomy* (SBT 9), 1948, 90f., and *Theologie* I, 341 (ET 343). Also L. Köhler, *Theologie des Alten Testaments*, 78f. (ET, 93).

58. Cf. too the evaluation of the events expressed in the various poems of the book of Lamentations. It may be relatively easy to decide that these are not by Jeremiah, but when this decision has been made we are again faced by a twofold (indeed it is even more varied than this) estimate of what the events really meant within the divine purpose.

59. Daniel 9. Cf. my 'Two Old Testament Historical Problems of the Early Persia Period', *JNES* 17, 1958, 13–27; cf. 23–7 on the 'Seventy Year' period. [Cf. also my *Exile and Restoration* (OTL), 1968, 240ff.]

60. *Contra Apionem* I, 8, 38–42. The presence here of the apologetic motive – the Jewish scriptures are shown to the Gentile world as a unified whole – is an important aspect of the concept of canonicity. Cf. R. J. H. Shutt, *Studies in Josephus*, SPCK 1961, 53ff., esp. 57f.

61. The final words of Samuel Davidson's Confession of Faith are: 'The canonical books are normative only to a certain extent. No fixed line can be drawn between them and the non-canonical, which are also normal, but in a less degree' (*The Autobiography and Diary of Samuel Davidson*, T. & T. Clark, Edinburgh 1899, edited by his daughter Miss A. J. Davidson. Cf. also *The Canon of the Bible*, Kegan Paul 1877, ³1880, esp. 262ff.). Miss Davidson's statement appears to need explanation: it sounds a little like 'some are more equal than others'. [For wider aspects of the discussion of canon and recent bibliography see e.g. S. Z. Leiman, *The Canonization of Hebrew Scripture: The*

Talmudic and Midrashic Evidence (Transactions. The Connecticut Academy of Arts and Sciences 47), Archon Books, Hamden, Conn. 1976, and R. Beckwith, *The Old Testament Canon of the New Testament*, SPCK 1985.]

62. E.g. W. Eichrodt, *Theologie des Alten Testaments*, Klotz, Stuttgart, I, [6]1959, II–III, [3]1950; ET, *Theology of the Old Testament* (OTL), I, 1961, II, 1967.

63. Cf. H. Graf von Reventlow, 'Grundfragen der alttestamentlichen Theologie im Lichte der neueren deutschen Forschung', *TLZ* 17, 1961, 81–98.

64. Reventlow, op. cit., 96, compares Noth's article, 'Die Vergegenwärtigung des AT in der Verkündigung', *Evangelische Theologie* 12, 1952–53, 6–17: 'In the great festivals . . . history became contemporary again in worship, not external history, but the saving acts of God, including judgment and promise and demand' (16). This leads on to the idea of the actualization of the Old Testament in worship, and so to the realization of our continuity with it because it comes to us in the church, transmitted to us in the covenant people of God. [Comparable comments need to be made on the continuing Jewish context of use.]

2. *The Theology of Tradition: an Approach to Old Testament Theological Problems*

1. Paper presented at a meeting of the Bangalore Theological Association on 7 October 1970, and published in the *Bangalore Theological Forum* 3.2, 1971, 49–64.

2. *Continuity* (Essay 1, pp. 3–16).

3. In *Israel's Prophetic Heritage: Essays in honor of James Muilenburg*, ed. B. W. Anderson and W. Harrelson SCM Press, and Harper, New York 1962, 11–25.

4. [Cf. also 'The Temple Vessels' (Essay 4, pp. 46–60).)]

5. Cf. the discussion by F. Willesen, 'The Cultic Situation of Psalm 74', *VT* 2, 1952, 289–306. [See also 'Continuity and Discontinuity' (Essay 3, pp. 31–45).)]

6. [Cf. also 'The Biblical Interpretation of the Reigns of Ahaz and Hezekiah' (Essay 11, pp. 181–92.)]

7. Cf. the corrective statements on this in regard to Jeremiah in E. W. Nicholson, *Preaching to the Exiles*, Blackwell, Oxford 1970, esp. 16ff., 34ff., and G. Wanke, *Untersuchungen zur sogenannten Baruchschrift* (BZAW 122), 1971, esp. 155. Also my 'Historians and Prophets' (Essay 8, pp. 121–51, see p. 150).

8. See previous note, and also 'Aspects of the Jeremiah Tradition', *IJT* 20, 1971, 1–12.

9. So Leonard Hodgson, *For Faith and Freedom* (Gifford Lectures), Blackwell, Oxford and Scribners, New York 1956–57, vol. II, 228.

10. [Cf. now M. Fishbane, *Biblical Interpretation in Ancient Israel*, OUP 1985, 48–50 for fuller development of the interpretation of this passage.]

11. E.g. in Ps.104.29c. The bracketing of the Aramaic verse Jer.10.11 is, of course, entirely intelligible, though one might wonder why this should not be a footnote. Such passages, in square brackets, are defined as being 'late additions to the Hebrew text'. But surely Hag.2.5a can be equally so regarded.

Deut.2.10–12; 2.20–23; 3.11 and 3.13*b*–14 are bracketed (in round brackets) for a different reason.

12. James Barr, *Biblical Words for Time*, SCM Press ²1969, 172, cf. 164.

13. John Bowker, *The Targums and Rabbinic Literature. An Introduction to Jewish Interpretations of Scripture*, CUP 1969, see Preface p. xi.

14. [Cf. my 'An Authoritative Version of the Bible?', *ExpT* 85, 1972–73, 374–7.]

15. [See especially James Barr, *The Semantics of Biblical Language*, OUP 1961, and *Comparative Philology and the Text of the Old Testament*, OUP 1968.]

16. [For some of the wider issues, see my 'Goddesses, Women and Jezebel', in *Images of Women in Antiquity*, ed. A. Cameron and A. Kuhrt, Croom Helm, London 1983, 245–59.]

3. *Continuity and Discontinuity: Rehabilitation and Authentication*
(Published in *Tradition and Theology in the Old Testament*, ed. Douglas A. Knight, Fortress Press, Philadelphia and SPCK 1977, 215–34.)

1. O. H. Steck, 'Theological Streams of Tradition', *Tradition and Theology in the Old Testament* (see above), 183–214.

2. J. L. Crenshaw, 'The Human Dilemma and Literature of Dissent', op.cit., 235–58.

3. Cf. my *Continuity* (Essay 1, pp. 3–16), see p. 14.

4. Not leprosy (Hansen's disease); see e.g. E. V. Hulse, 'The Nature of Biblical "Leprosy"', *PEQ* 107, 1975, 87–105. [The precise nature of this 'impurity' is still a matter of debate. It is described as affecting persons, buildings and garments.]

5. Thus 'discontinuity is resolved in the discovery of a continuity within it' (*Continuity*, above p. 15).

6. The Moabite scribe who wrote, 'Chemosh was angry with his land' (Moabite Stone, lines 5–6), may be seen to fit the experience of defeat at Israel's hands into an intelligible pattern. Restoration of relationship brings victory and the re-established contact of people and deity.

7. Cf. II Kings 20.1–11 for the first – a literalist would suppose that death for Hezekiah then becomes certain at the fifteen-year term; I Kings 22 provides a prophesied example of the second; I Kings 1–2 a somewhat sorry picture of the third.

8. The dynasties of Omri and Jehu are sufficiently extensive for it to be clear that the North did not reject the principle (as A. Alt argued: 'Das Königtum in Israel und Juda', *VT* 1, 1951, 2–23 = *Kleine Schriften zur Geschichte des Volkes Israel*, vol. 2, Beck, Munich 1953, 116–34 = 'The Monarchy in Israel and Judah', in *Essays on Old Testament History and Religion*, Blackwell, Oxford 1966, 239–59; for cogent criticism, see T. G. G. Thornton, 'Charismatic Kingship in Israel and Judah', *JTS* 14, 1963, 1–11.) One factor in the greater instability of the North must be the greater power attaching to military leaders, usually the new claimants to the throne (cf. also the interesting reaction of Joab as military commander to his position at the siege of Rabbath-Ammon in II Sam.12.28; another than Joab might well have taken the kingdom, the dynasty, for himself). But such a claimant needs religious

support if he is to establish some continuity with what has preceded, and hence the stress on prophetic revelation of the divine will in the change.

9. F. Willesen, 'The Cultic Situation of Psalm 74', *VT* 2, 1952, 289–306.

10. The same point must be made in regard to the poems of the book of Lamentations. If at certain points there appear to be clear references to 587 BC – and there are admittedly very few that are really clear – there is no adequate ground for supposing that the poems originated then, rather than being examples of a particular form which, like some in the Psalter, have been given great precision. Equally they are seen to be applicable to other situations, both precise and historical (the fall of Jerusalem in AD 70, the crucifixion of Jesus), or less precise and personal, linked to the experiences, inward or outward, of the ordinary worshipper.

11. The relationship of the prose and poetry is, of course, more complex than this. For a particular attempt at handling the problem of the poem in relation to its celebration of the event, cf. A. Weiser, 'Das Deboralied', *ZAW* 71, 1959, 67–97.

12. Cf. my comments in 'Aspects of the Jeremiah Tradition', *IJT* 20, 1971, 1–12, especially pp. 5–6.

13. For renewed discussion of such problems, see P. D. Hanson, *The Dawn of Apocalyptic: The Historical and Sociological Roots of Jewish Apocalyptic Eschatology* Fortress Press, Philadelphia 1975.

[Both this and other works on the post-exilic period tend towards a too rigid division of the community into distinct parties. My own subsequent studies (e.g. 'Archaeology, Politics and Religion: The Persian Period', *Iliff Review* 39, 1982, 5–24, and 'Historical Problems of the the Early Achaemenian Period', *Orient* 20, 1984, 1–15) have suggested a much more varied scene.]

14. On weeping and laughter as ritual forms, cf. F. F. Hvidberg, *Weeping and Laughter in the Old Testament: A Study of Canaanite-Israelite Religion*, Brill, Leiden 1962 (original Danish, *Graad og Latter*, 1938), cf. especially 144f. Hvidberg does not mention this passage.

15. Cf. my 'The Temple Vessels' (Essay 4, pp. 46–60).

16. Cf. R. R. Wilson, 'The Old Testament Genealogies in Recent Research', *JBL* 94, 1975, 169–89, and *Genealogy and History in the Biblical World* (Yale Near Eastern Researches 7), Yale UP, New Haven 1977.

17. Cf. K. Koch, 'Ezra and the Origins of Judaism', *JSS* 19, 1974, 173–97, see 190.

18. Cf. R. J. Coggins, *Samaritans and Jews. The Origins of Samaritanism Reconsidered*, Blackwell, Oxford and John Knox, Atlanta 1975, 143f.

19. Cf. references and discussion in my *Exile and Restoration: A Study of Hebrew Thought of the Sixth Century BC* (OTL), 1958, 124ff; K. Baltzer, 'Das Ende des Staates Juda und die Messias-Frage', in *Studien zur Theologie der alttestamentlichen Überlieferungen, Festschrift G. von Rad*, ed. R. Rendtorff and K. Koch, Neukirchener Verlag, Neukirchen 1961, 33–43.

[Cf. now also my 'Exile and Post-Exile: Continuity and Reformulation of the Davidic Theme', in *Religious Belief in an Age of Turmoil. Festschrift L. G. Geering* Wellington, New Zealand 1986.]

20. U. Kellermann, *Nehemia: Quellen, Überlieferung und Geschichte* (BZAW 102), 1967, see 154–59; W. T. In der Smitten, 'Erwägungen zu Nehemias

Davidizität', *JSJ* 5, 1974, 41–8. For criticism of Kellermann, cf. e.g. S. Herrmann, *A History of Israel*, ET SCM Press and Fortress Press, Philadelphia 1975, 319.

21. Cf. the summarized treatment under *chriō* in *TWNT* 9, 1973, 482ff.; *TDNT* 9, 1974, 493ff.

22. Cf. A. Fitzgerald, 'A Note on Psalm 29', *BASOR* 215, 1974, 61–3, including some bibliography. [See also literature on p. 295, n.14.]

23. See the discussion by A. S. Kapelrud, 'Tradition and Worship: The Role of the Cult in Tradition Formation and Transmission', *in Tradition and Theology in the Old Testament*, 101–24 – another study in the volume in which this essay appeared.

24. A comparison may here be made with some of the points made by B. O. Long, 'The Social Setting for Prophetic Miracle Stories', *Semeia* 3, 1975, 46–63. Stories about the prophetic institution may serve to validate it in a period of stress and uncertainty.

25. We may note the antagonism which is associated with Jeremiah's comparison of the destruction of the Shiloh shrine with that foretold for Jerusalem (Jeremiah 26). Such a reaction is expressive of the horror and fear felt at such a prospect. A similar horror may be seen in the reaction to Paul in Acts 21.27–29.

26. Cf. J. Neusner, 'Emergent Rabbinic Judaism in a Time of Crisis: Four Responses to the Destruction of the Second Temple', *JQR* 21, 1972, 313–27 = *Early Rabbinic Judaism: Historical Studies in Religion, Literature and Art* (SJLA 13), 1975, 34–49.

27. Cf. E. Nielsen, *Oral Tradition: A Modern Problem in Old Testament Introduction* (SBT 11) 1954, p. 33, citing the views of I. Engnell and H. S. Nyberg (see my *Continuity*, Essay 1, pp. 3–16, see p. 14 and p. 256, n. 52).

28. Cf. the discussion in D. A. Knight, *Rediscovering the Traditions of Israel* (rev. ed. SBLDS 9), Missoula 1975, 9f. 390f.

29. Cf. my *Continuity*, loc. cit. (n. 27 above).

30. Clear examples of this may be seen in the earlier materials incorporated in the Priestly Work, where the inconsistencies are resolved partly editorially but more frequently by the simpler device of requiring a given passage (e.g. Genesis 2) to be read in the context of another (Genesis 1) which then superimposes its meaning upon the earlier material.

31. Cf. B. S. Childs, *The Book of Exodus* (OTL), 1974, 553–81 for a very full discussion, which does not, however, sufficiently examine the question of what attitudes may have been taken by Northerners to this theme. Cf. M. L. Newman, *The People of the Covenant: A Study of Israel from Moses to the Monarchy*, Abingdon, New York 1962, 182.

32. Cf. my 'The Theology of Tradition: An Approach to Old Testament Theological Problems' (Essay 2 pp. 17–30, see pp. 17f.).

33. Cf. ibid. pp. 28–30; and also W. McKane, 'Tradition as a Theological Concept', in *God, Secularization and History: Essays in Memory of Ronald Gregor Smith*, ed. E. T. Long, University of South Carolina Press, Columbia 1974, 44–59.

4. *The Temple Vessels: a Continuity Theme*
(Published in *Studies in the Religion of Ancient Israel (VTS* 23), 1972, 166–81.)

1. On this theme, cf. J. Vollmer, *Geschichtliche Rückblicke und Motive in der Prophetie des Amos, Hosea und Jesaja* (BZAW 119), 1971. This study rather overstresses the forward-looking aspect of prophetic thought, but it provides a useful critique of that exaggerated view which sees the prophets too onesidedly in terms of 'the tradition'.

2. *Continuity* (Essay 1, pp. 3–16.)

3. 'The Theology of Tradition – an approach to Old Testament Theological Problems' (Essay 2, pp. 17–30. Also Essay 3, pp. 31–45.)

4. Cf. e.g. the statue of Gudea of Lagash with its building plan, *ANEP*, No. 749.

5. R. E. Clements, *God and Temple*, Blackwell, Oxford 1965.

6. A particular example of this may be seen in Neh.13.4–9.

7. Cf. above p. 18 [Cf. also Essay 3, pp 31–45, for fuller development of the theme.]

8. J. Gray, *I and II Kings* (OTL), ²1970, 760.

9. On this theme, cf.G.von Rad, *Deuteronomium-Studien* (FRLANT 58), 1947, esp. 55ff., ET *Studies in Deuteronomy* (SBT 9), 1953, 78ff., and my 'Vitality of the Word of God in the Old Testament' (Essay 5, pp. 61–75.)

10. So in RSV and NEB. So too J. Gray, op.cit., 767.

11. J. A. Montgomery, *The Books of Kings* (ICC) 1951, 563 offers no comment on the meaning of v. 15; he seems to imply that the gold and silver vessels were kept whole, though, since he offers no translation of the text, it is impossible to be sure. He offers a harmonizing comment that 'these must have been small articles left over from the earlier looting'. But this is an unwarranted assumption. It would be more natural to think that new vessels had been introduced under Zedekiah. It is in the Jeremiah text (see below) that the theme of two stages of removal appears, not in Kings. Montgomery also assumes that v. 13 indicates the breaking up of the larger pieces, and v. 14 the carrying away intact of the smaller ones. This may be so, but the whole context hardly warrants so confident an affirmation.

12. J. Gray, op.cit., 767.

13. We may note that the Ahaz narrative provides an example of the obverse: Ahaz is the disrupter of continuity by his destruction of vessels.

14. Cf. my comments in 'Historians and Prophets' (Essay 8, pp. 121–51, see pp. 141f.) and 'Aspects of the Jeremiah Tradition', *IJT* 20, 1971, 1–12.

15. We may arrange the traditions in a logical (though not necessarily chronological) order. Jeremiah 40–42 has a positive appraisal of Gedaliah and advice to those who set out for Egypt to stay in Judah; II Kings 25.22–26 contains only a brief reference to Gedaliah and his assassination; Jeremiah 52 has no reference to Gedaliah; II Chronicles 36 equally has no reference to Gedaliah, and its attitude to Judah is even more strongly negative.

16. Cf. J. Gray, op.cit., 760f. for 24.13f.; he treats 25.13–17 as an integral part of the narrative. Cf. J. A Montgomery, op.cit., 554ff. on 24.13ff. and 563 on 25.13–17: 'an intruded antiquarian but historical note'.

17. The subject of the parallel text of Jerusalem's fall and its aftermath in Jeremiah 37–44 is discussed in my articles noted in n. 14. This Jeremiah text in ch. 39 provides an important witness to a variant text. We may observe that the whole section provides examples of being both a shorter version than that in II Kings (so the 'temple vessels' theme) and a longer version (so Jeremiah's actions and the Gedaliah narrative). The relationship between the two texts is not to be viewed as a simple one.

18. For this theme, cf. also Hosea 2.

19. The shorter LXX text contains essentially the same material.

20. So e.g. Gray, op.cit., 760 with reference to Jeremiah 27.19f., which makes the same point.

21. Cf. on this the article 'Historians and Prophets' (Essay 8, pp. 121–51.)

22. Again here the LXX is shorter, but the main point is not affected.

23. There are other 'omissions' in the LXX text in this section, but they do not affect the overall interpretation.

24. W. Rudolph, *Jeremia* (HAT 12³), 1968, 177.

25. Cf. the reversals in 32.36ff. and 33.10ff. E. W. Nicholson, *Preaching to the Exiles*, Blackwell, Oxford 1970, 12, criticizes the suggestion, made by J. Bright (*Jeremiah* (Anchor Bible 21), Doubleday, Garden City, New York, 1965, lxxii) 'that . . . there has been some misunderstanding of the prophet's teaching by those responsible for the sermons'. He speaks instead (13) of 'a conscious and deliberate development of the prophet's teaching'. But in a number of cases, such as those here mentioned, there appears in the long run to be a much more radical handling of the material than could be naturally covered by 'development'.

26. For the full discussion of this passage, cf. K. Galling, 'Das Protokoll über die Rückgabe der Tempelgeräte' in *Studien zur Geschichte Israels im persischen Zeitalter*, Mohr, Tübingen 1964, 78–88, updated from its original publication in *ZDPV* 60, 1937, 177–83.

27. The list here, whatever its origin, is clearly designed to stress completeness and also to underline that care for the vessels which is elsewhere a concern of the Chronicler (cf. I Chron. 9.28ff.).

Galling (cf. especially his conclusion, op.cit., 88) argues that the terminology, the numbers, and the comments on the state of the vessels, all point to these verses (Ezra 1.8–11*a*) depending on the original (Aramaic) document of the year 538 BC. This view does not sufficiently deal with the problem of what actually happened to the vessels (cf. below, for a further comment). If the main arguments are accepted, then they point to the use of a document, but it is more probable that, as in other instances, the Chronicler has applied a document belonging to one situation (an inventory of actually existing vessels) to a quite different moment. An immediately adjacent example may be seen in Ezra 2 = Nehemiah 7; but there are many such cases of reapplication in the Chronicler's work.

28. Cf. my *Exile and Restoration* (OTL), 1968, 25ff. and references there.

29. K. Galling, *Die Bücher der Chronik, Esra, Nehemia* (ATD 12), 1954, 200.

30. Cf. Galling, *Studien*, 79.

31. Again we may see a continuing of piety, of care and guardianship, and of emphasis on the total number of the vessels.

32. Cf. my *The Age of the Chronicler*, Supplement to *Colloquium – Australian and New Zealand Theological Review*, 1970, 24–27.

33. Cf. on the levitical orders and their link to the tabernacle I Chron.9.17ff., in which the guardianship of the temple vessels is particularly stressed (so vv. 28f.).

34. We may also note that the Second Isaiah in 52.11 makes use of a similar theme in which the bearers of the sacred vessels are enjoined to make the return to Zion. The suggestion has been made to me by A. Gelston that the theme of the temple vessels could be regarded as an appropriate Old Testament counterpart of the 'restoring of the gods' claimed by the Cyrus Cylinder. Certainly we may see a parallel, since such a restoration is in either case connected with the re-establishing of religious and cultic continuity.

35. Cf. the earlier part of this discussion, where the degree of uncertainty about the interpretation of II Kings 25.13–17 is indicated. But whatever we may say of this passage, it remains clear that II Kings 24.13 is contradicted by Jeremiah 37–38; II Kings 25 still cannot accord with Ezra 1.

5. *The Vitality of the Word of God in the Old Testament: A Contribution to the Study of the Transmission and Exposition of Old Testament Material*

1. This paper, originally delivered as a lecture at the Commemoration at Cheshunt College, Cambridge in May 1957, was read in this revised form at the Swedish Theological Institute, Jerusalem, Israel, in May 1961, and published in its *Annual*, vol. 1, 1962, 7–23.

2. The closing formula occurs only in 14.11.

3. Cf. my discussion of this in relation to the dating of Old Testament material in the Maccabean period: 'Criteria for the Maccabean Dating of Old Testament Literature', *VT* 3, 1953, 113–32.

4. In the 'Instruction of Amen-em-opet' ch. IV, cf. *ANET*, 422; D. Winton Thomas (ed.), *Documents from Old Testament Times*, Nelson 1958, Harper and Row, New York 1961, 178.

5. Cf. also I. Seeligmann, 'Voraussetzungen der Midraschexegese', *VTS* 1, 1953, 150–81, see 168, where he discusses the interrelationship in greater detail.

6. Cf. on this Seeligmann, op.cit., 156, who also compares IV Ezra 8.34–35.

7. R. H. Pfeiffer, *Introduction to the Old Testament*, Harper, New York 1941, corrected reprint 1948.

8. G. von Rad, *Deuteronomium-Studien*, (FRLANT 58, NF 40), 1947, 58; ET, *Studies in Deuteronomy* (SBT 9), 1953, 82.

9. Contrast Pfeiffer, 405f.

10. Von Rad, *loc.cit.*; my translation of the German text, since the printed English translation is here inaccurate.

11. Lewis Carroll, *Alice in Wonderland*. Cf. also Seeligmann, op.cit. esp. 152ff.

12. Compare also the positive judgment on Jeroboam II in II Kings 14.25–27. The Chronicler was later to take up this more positive appraisal with his insistence upon the possibility – always open though seldom heeded – that all who were faithful in the North could join themselves to the true people in Judah. Cf. II Chron. 11.13–17; 30.10–11; 34.33; Ezra 6.21.

13. On this last point, cf. Seeligmann, op.cit., 169. On reinterpretation more generally, cf. H. Wheeler Robinson, *Inspiration and Revelation in the Old Testament*, OUP 1946, 171f. With reference to Isa.7.14 and Micah 5.3 he wrote: 'Subsequent generations read into it another and possibly larger meaning, often with justification. The prophetic oracle in particular lends itself to this treatment, which is legitimate enough if the spiritual continuity with the original meaning is maintained' (172). This statement does not define 'justification': the example given suggests that the messianic application of certain passages is so justified. Nor does it define 'spiritual continuity': Wheeler Robinson continues: 'This rules out much allegorization as purely arbitrary', but does not so vague a term as 'spiritual continuity' admit of almost anything, unless it is carefully discussed? These issues are the concern of the wider consideration of the problems of Old Testament exegesis.

14. L. Köhler, *Der hebräische Mensch*, Mohr, Tübingen 1953, 163f.; ET *Hebrew Man*, SCM Press 1956, reissued 1973, 176f. Köhler wrote this passage originally in 1931.

15. Cf. also G. von Rad, *Theologie des AT*, I, ²1958, 218ff.; ET *Old Testament Theology*, Oliver and Boyd, Edinburgh 1962; reissued SCM Press 1975, 1, 219ff.; E. Janssen, *Juda in der Exilszeit* (FRLANT 69) 1956, 17.

16. *Hebrew Man*, 168; German 164.

17. Cf. D. J. Wiseman, *Chronicles of Chaldaean Kings (626–556 BC) in the British Museum*, British Museum 1956, 28.

18. It is not always sufficiently clearly observed that Jeremiah 25 provides a parallel to 36, just as chs. 7 and 26 are parallels. In 36, there is a full narrative with some indication of oracular material: in 25 only the briefest of chronological data, and otherwise oracular material. 25.3–7 contains a summary of Jeremiah's message of warning and exhortation, 25.8–11, 13 contains a statement of judgment at the hands of Nebuchadrezzar. The meaning is now modified by the exegetical comments of vv. 12 and 14 which have reapplied the oracles against Judah so as to make them relevant to judgment on Babylon. 25.13 is, as it were, the colophon of the scroll of ch. 36.

19. The precise intention of the earlier oracles is immaterial. Reapplication is made whether the older Scythian theory is accepted, or, as is much more probable, the oracles refer primarily to the Assyrians, a revival of whose power might well be anticipated in the years following the death of Ashurbanipal in about 631 BC. That the picture of the 'foe from the north' has certain ideal elements may well also be true.

20. This point may be made whether or not it is maintained that Ezekiel's activity falls into two distinct periods, different both as to period and as to place: before 587 in Jerusalem and Judah, after 587 in Babylonia. In any case, the disaster of 587 demanded a new perspective. Cf. also N. K. Gottwald, *Studies in the Book of Lamentations* (SBT 14), 1954, 84f.; L. Černý, *The Day of Yahweh and Some Relevant Problems*, Filosofická Fakulta University Karlovy, Prague 1948, 20; D. R. Jones, 'The Traditio of the Oracles of Isaiah of Jerusalem', *ZAW* 67, NF 26, 1955, 226–46, see 244.

21. Cf. L. G. Rignell, *Die Nachtgesichte des Sacharja. Eine exegetische Studie*, Gleerups, Lund 1950, see summary on 243f.; K. Galling, 'Die Exilswende in der Sicht des Propheten Sacharja', *VT* 2, 1952, 18–36; P. R. Ackroyd, 'The

Book of Haggai and Zechariah 1–8', *JJS* 3, 1952, 151–6, and also the commentary on Zechariah in the *New Peake Bible Commentary* Nelson 1962, 646–55, see 646–51.

22. Jones, (see n.20).

23. [I am much less certain now that this verse does refer to disciples: the text is clearly problematic. Over recent years, it has been increasingly recognized that the concept of a 'school' preserving the words of Isaiah is too rigid to correspond to reality.]

24. It is difficult to avoid the conclusion that Isaiah too anticipated complete disaster, cf.29.1–4, and that to him the deliverance was an unexpected and unmerited act of divine grace, cf.1.7–9. But a full assessment involves discussion of the relationship between the oracular content of Isaiah 36–37 (II Kings 18.13– 19.37), where it stands in the context of a historical 'legend', and the oracles of the other chapters in the book of Isaiah. To treat these two types of material as if they were identical is clearly not satisfactory. [See also Essay 7, pp. 105–20; and Essay 9, pp. 152–71.]

25. Cf. also Seeligmann, op.cit. (n.5 above); 168, who refers to the reapplication of Amos's and Hosea's prophecies to Judah, and notes the reinterpretation of Amos 5.7 in Acts 7.43.

26. It does not seem necessary here to enter into the question as to whether the prophets themselves – working within a conventional religious pattern – did not derive this exegetical principle from a yet earlier stage, namely from the use and re-use of 'set' oracular pronouncements, particularly in association with the cultic functions of prophecy. The suggestion that Amos 1–2, for example, shows indications of an already elaborated cursing ritual (cf. A. Bentzen, 'The Ritual Background of Amos 1.2–2.16', *OTS* 8, 1950, 85–99), whose form is already well developed, may lead to the inference that older patterns existed and that the originality of the prophets is creative in the sense of 'creative handling' rather than in the sense of *creation ex nihilo*. This is a matter which needs examination in the light of records of non-biblical prophecy.

27. H. Birkeland, *Zum hebräischen Traditionswesen: die Komposition der prophetis-chen Bücher des Alten Testaments*, Avhandlingen utg. av det Norske Videnskaps-Akademi i Oslo 1938, 15f.

28. We ought to consider that some at least of the prophets – and why not all? – were engaged in day-to-day consultations like that recorded of Samuel in I Samuel 9. One clear example is provided by Isaiah 38 (II Kings 20.1–11): here Isaiah is described both as speaking the divine oracle and as prescribing the medical treatment (Isa.38.21; II Kings 20.7). Probably this example is preserved because of its historical importance. Examples occur of political consultation (Isaiah 36–37 (II Kings 18–19), Jer.38.14ff.; 42), but Micah 3.5 indicates much more personal consultation, and Zech.7.3 (cf. also Hag.2.11–13) consultation on religious practice.

29. Cf. H. Riesenfeld, *The Gospel Tradition and its Beginnings*, Mowbray 1957; also in *Studia Evangelica. Papers presented to the International Congress on* 'The Four Gospels in 1957', Oxford 1957, ed. K. Aland et al. (TU 73), Akademie-Verlag, Berlin 1959, 43–65; and later in *The Gospel Tradition*, Blackwell, Oxford 1970, 1–29.

30. 'Instruction of the Vizier Ptah-Hotep', purporting to be by him (c. 2450 BC), though actual manuscripts are later. Cf. *ANET*, 412.

31. The function of Wisdom as the inculcator of order may here be clearly seen. Cf.G. von Rad, *Theologie des AT* I, ²1958, 426ff., ET, 421ff.

32. Cf.P.A.H. de Boer, 'The Counsellor', *VTS* 3, 1955, 42–71.

33. Cf. Prov.25.1 and R. B. Y. Scott, 'Solomon and the beginnings of wisdom in Israel', *VTS* 3, 1955, 262–79, see 272–9.

34. Köhler, *Hebrew Man*, 168, German 164.

35. There is here a reason for the difference between a vital preaching of the word of God which arises out of a perception of the significance of an occasion, and the casual moralizing use of a biblical text on which to hang a homily which has little realization of this historic aspect of the divine word.

36. Cf.D. R. Jones, art.cit., 238ff.

37. Cf. P. R. Ackroyd, art.cit. (n. 21 above), 153; and also commentary on Haggai and Zechariah in *New Peake Bible Commentary*, 643–55. [For fuller discussion, see R. J. Coggins, *Samaritans and Jews. The Origins of Samaritanism Reconsidered*, Blackwell, Oxford 1975.]

38. Cf. P. R. Ackroyd, *The Problem of Maccabean Psalms* (Diss., Cambridge 1945). Cf. art.cit. (n. 3 above.)
[While much has been written in the years following the publication of this article which extends the discussion of the topic, attention may be drawn particularly to:
E. W. Nicholson, *Preaching to the Exiles*, Blackwell, Oxford 1970, where this discussion is examined in some detail on pp. 5ff.;
J. Blenkinsopp, *Prophecy and Canon. A Contribution to the Study of Jewish Origins*, Notre Dame UP 1977;
M. Fishbane, *Biblical Interpretation in Ancient Israel*, Clarendon Press, Oxford 1985, for a much broader consideration of exegesis.]

6. *Isaiah 1–12: Presentation of a Prophet*
(Published in the Congress Volume, International Organization for the Study of the Old Testament (*VTS* 29), 1978, 16–48.)

1. H. Wildberger, *Jesaja 1–12* (BK), 1972.

2. James Barr, *Fundamentalism*, SCM Press 1977, ²1981, 157. The same phrase is used by R. F. Melugin, *The Formation of Isaiah 40–55* (BZAW 141), 1976, 176, in the context of some sensible concluding comments to his discussion of the structure of those particular chapters. Cf. also below.

3. For the quotation of critical scholars by fundamentalist writers, to undergird a position not intended by the scholar quoted, cf. e.g. R. K. Harrison, *Introduction to the Old Testament*, Eerdmans, Grand Rapids 1969, Tyndale Press 1970, and E. J. Young, *An Introduction to the Old Testament*, Tyndale Press and Eerdmans, Grand Rapids 1949, reissued 1960. Both books contain numerous examples of this procedure, designed to suggest that fundamentalist scholars take critical work seriously, and by implication that critical scholars do not trouble to read the fundamentalist works. At least Barr's volume gives the lie to the latter contention.

4. Cf. e.g. O. Kaiser, *Einleitung in das Alte Testament*, Mohn, Gütersloh 1969,

222–4; ³1975, 247f. [5th rev. ed., 1984, 280ff.]; ET by J. Sturdy, *Introduction to the Old Testament. A Presentation of its Results and Problems*, Blackwell, Oxford, 1976, 268–71.

5. Cf. e.g. C. C. Torrey, *The Second Isaiah*, Scribners, New York, and T. & T. Clark, Edinburgh 1928; J. D. Smart, *History and Theology in Second Isaiah: A Commentary on Isaiah 35, 40–66*, Westminster Press, Philadelphia 1965. [Cf. also O. H. Steck, *Bereitete Heimkehr. Jesaja 35 als redaktionelle Brücke zwischen dem Ersten und dem Zweiten Jesaja* (SBS 121), 1985; J. L. McKenzie, *Second Isaiah* (Anchor Bible 20), Doubleday, New York 1968.]

6. For the presence of elements in 1–39 akin to 40–55, cf. e.g. Kaiser, 175f.; ET 225f. The presence of other late elements is commonly assumed: cf. e.g. H. Barth (see n. 9 below), and G. Fohrer, 'The Origin, Composition and Tradition of Isaiah I–XXXIX', *ALUOS* 3, 1962, 3–38, see 6–23; German text 'Entstehung, Komposition und Überlieferung von Jes 1–39', *Studien zur alttestamentlichen Prophetie (1949–1965)* (BZAW 99), 1967, 113–47, see 117–34. More generally, cf. J. H. Eaton, 'The Origin of the Book of Isaiah', *VT* 9, 1959, 138–57. [Cf. also J. H. Eaton, 'The Isaiah Tradition' and J. F. A. Sawyer, 'A Change of Emphasis in the Study of the Prophets' in *Israel's Prophetic Tradition*, ed. R. J. Coggins et al., CUP 1982, 58–76, 233–49, including bibliographies.]

7. Cf. R. H. Pfeiffer, *Introduction to the Old Testament*, Harper, New York 1941, 447f.; O. Eissfeldt, *Einleitung in das Alte Testament*, Mohr, Tübingen ³1964 465f.; ET by P. R. Ackroyd, *The Old Testament: An Introduction*, Blackwell, Oxford and Harper, New York 1965, 346 – a view that Eissfeldt sets out but rejects as improbable.

8. Eissfeldt, 406, see also 466; ET, 302, 346.

9. H. Barth, *Israel und das Assyrerreich in den nichtjesajanischen Texten des Protojesajabuch* (Diss. Hamburg 1974). [Published in essentially the same form as *Die Jesaja-Werk in der Josiazeit. Israel und Assur als Thema einer produktiven Neuinterpretation der Jesajaüberlieferung* (WMANT 48), 1977.]

10. Cf. my 'Historians and Prophets', Essay 8, pp. 121–51, see pp. 137–50.

11. So A. van der Woude in the discussion of this paper, referring also to W. Rudolph, *Micha-Nahum-Habakuk-Zephanja* (KAT XIII/3), 1975, 255.

12. The proposed emendation of J. A. Bewer, *wā'eḥᵉzeh* (then I saw) would introduce the prophet here. [See also A. K. Jenkins, 'Isaiah 14.28–32 – An Issue of Life and Death', *Folio Orientalia* 21, 1980, 47–63.]

13. Cf. 36.3, 22; 37.2. The relationship between these passages and ch. 22 is by no means clear.

14. The reason for the addition of Jeremiah 52 is not at all clear.

15. Cf. e.g. B. S. Childs, *Isaiah and the Assyrian Crisis* (SBT 2.3) 1967, and my 'An Interpretation of the Babylonian Exile', Essay 9, pp. 152–71.

16. Cf. my 'Isaiah 36–39: Structure and Function' Essay 7, pp. 105–20. Cf. also Melugin, *The Formation of Isaiah 40–55*, 177.

17. 'A Judgment Narrative between Kings and Chronicles? An Approach to Amos 7.9–17', Essay 12, pp. 196–208. Reference may also be made to significantly placed narrative material in Hosea, Jeremiah, Ezekiel and Haggai.

18. Cf. I. L. Seeligmann, 'Die Auffassung von der Prophetie in der deuteronomischen und chronistischen Geschichtsschreibung', *VTS* 29, 1978, 254–84.

19. Cf. e.g. D. R. Jones, 'The Traditio of the Oracles of Isaiah of Jerusalem', *ZAW* 67, 1955, 226–46, see 245. I should express the relationship less precisely than in terms of knowledge on the part of Deutero-Isaiah of a definable Proto-Isaianic collection.

20. Cf. e.g. J. A. Soggin, *Introduction to the Old Testament*, ET by J. S. Bowden (OTL), 1976, rev. ed. 1980, 318f.; Eissfeldt, *Einleitung*, 466; ET, 346. Also J. Becker, *Isaias – der Prophet und sein Buch* (SBS 30), 1968, 33f.; L. J. Liebreich, 'The Compilation of the Book of Isaiah', *JQR*, NS 46, 1955/56, 259–77; 47, 1956/57, 114–38.

21. Cf. e.g. A. Weiser, *Das Buch Jeremia* (ATD 20/21), ⁶1969, 427. W. Rudolph, *Jeremia* (HAT 12), 1947, 256, suggests links with Isaiah 13–14 and notes *qᵉdôš yiśrā'ēl* (the Holy One of Israel, 50.29; 51.5) as Isaianic. It is, of course, frequent in later material in the book of Isaiah (see above).

22. G. Fohrer, *Einleitung in das Alte Testament*, Quelle und Meyer, Heidelberg 1965, 411; ET by D. Green, *Introduction to the Old Testament*, Abingdon, Nashville 1968, SPCK 1970, 375.

23. Cf. R. Fey, *Amos und Jesaja. Abhängigkeit und Eigenständlichkeit des Jesaja* (WMANT 12), 1963.

24. Cf. also the comments of H. W. Wolff, 'Wie verstand Micha von Moreschet sein prophetisches Amt?', VTS 29, 1978, 403–17 [= *Studien zum Prophetie*, Kaiser, Munich 1987, 79–92].

25. Cf. J. L. Mays, Micah (OTL), 1976, 148. Note also the extension of the Micah tradition implied in I Kings 22.28 which cites Micah 1.2, thus claiming identity for Micaiah and Micah, a point which might be linked to this curious element in Micah 6.16.

26. See my article 'A Judgment Narrative' (Essay 12, pp. 195–208).

27. See my article, 'An Interpretation of the Exile' (Essay 9, see p. 165).

28. R. P. Carroll, 'Prophecy, Dissonance and Jeremiah XXVI', *TGUOS* 25, 1973–74 (1976), 12–23; 'Ancient Israelite Prophecy and Dissonance Theory', *Numen* 24, 1977, 135–51. Dr Carroll has also kindly lent me the first draft of a chapter entitled 'Text and Interpretation' from a proposed book, provisionally entitled *Prophecy, Dissonance and Hermeneutic*, and I am glad here to acknowledge the stimulus of his discussion. [Published as *When Prophecy Failed*, SCM Press and Seabury, New York 1979.]

29. So Carroll, *TGUOS*, 19; *Numen*, 144. On the theme of repentance in Isaiah, cf. H. W. Hoffmann, *Die Intention der Verkündigung Jesajas* (BZAW 136), 1974.

30. Carroll, *Numen*, 144.

31. Ibid.

32. Or 'message', cf. H. M. I. Gevaryahu (see n. 34 below).

33. Cf. Wildberger, *Jesaja 1–12*, 345, who makes use of Eissfeldt's suggestion (*Der Beutel der Lebendigen* (BAL 105/6), 1960, 26f.) that the reference is to a bundle or bag tied up, amd hence a metaphor for preservation. This would in fact make it clear that there are here two distinct metaphors – the tied bag

and the sealed document – both emphasizing preservation intact. For other comments, cf. e.g. D. R. Jones, op. cit. (n. 19 above), 232ff. Cf. also 8.1 and 30.8 which indicate the actual writing of brief statements, though direct deductions cannot be made from this to the interpretation of 8.16.

34. Cf. e.g. S. Mowinckel, *Profeten Jesaja. En bibelstudiebok,* Aschehoug (Nygaard), Oslo 1925; *Jesaja-Disiplene. Profetien fra Jesaja til Jeremia,* Aschehoug (Nygaard), Oslo 1926; *Prophecy and Tradition* (ANVAO), 1946; D. R. Jones, op. cit.; and cf. his 'Exposition of Isaiah Chapter One Verses One to Nine', *SJT* 17, 1964, 463–7, see 465: '. . . the book of Isaiah . . . is the corpus of oracles of a school of prophets, brought into being by Isaiah ben Amoz and therefore standing under his name.' J. H. Eaton, op.cit. (n. 6 above); Eissfeldt, *Einleitung,* 466; ET, 346; J. Becker, op. cit. (n. 20 above), 40. For a similar attempt cf. also H. M. I. Gevaryahu, 'The School of Isaiah: "Biography", Transmission and Canonization of the Book of Isaiah', a lecture delivered at New York University, April 1976, of which the author has kindly lent me a copy. He hopes to publish this shortly [but I have no information about its date and place].

35. Cf. also the criticisms of Fohrer, *Einleitung,* 410; ET, 375, though these are weakened by his arbitrary excision of the word *belimmūdāy.*

36. The strength of the position maintained by Torrey and Smart (see n. 5 above) derives from their recognition of this relationship, though the arguments for a literary unity consisting of chs. (34) 35 and 40–66 are by no means strong. [Cf. also O. H. Steck and J. L. McKenzie (see n. 5).]

37. Cf. B. O. Banwell, 'A Suggested Analysis of Isaiah xl–lxvi', *ExpT* 76, 1964–65, 166, who proposes a division 40–48, 49–57, with 40 as introduction; and 58–66 as a third unit. Cf. F. Rückert, *Hebräische Propheten,* Weidmann, Leipzig 1831. (I have not been able to consult this, but cf. J. Muilenburg, 'Isaiah 40–66', *IB* 5, 1956, 384.) Cf. also A. Schoors, *Jesaja,* Romen und Zonen, Roermond 1972, ad loc., and especially 346: 'at a certain stage in the redaction, someone wished to articulate the point at 48.22 and 57.21 so as to anticipate 66.24. This last verse is differently formulated, but expresses the same idea in an even stronger form' (my translation). Cf. the further comment by Schoors on 391.

38. *maśśā'* occurs in 13.1; 14.28; 15.1; 17.1; 19.1; 21.1. 11, 13; 22.1; 23.1; also in 30.6. [*maśśā'* is a word meaning 'burden', but clearly here a technical term for an 'oracle' – possibly 'something lifted up', hence 'a solemn pronouncement'.] This last occurrence, introducing the oracle on Egypt of 30.6f., may point to a misplacement from the original context in 13–23, but it equally suggests the possibility that the arrangement of the whole complex from 13 to 33 is not simply to be understood in the neat subdivisions often proposed. On a link between 13–23 and 28–33, cf. O. Kaiser, *Der Prophet Jesaja, Kap. 13–39* (ATD 18), 1973, 3; ET by R. A. Wilson (OTL), 1974, xi.

39. So e.g. H. Barth, op. cit. (n. 9 above), 362 n.2, who accepts as assured the commonly held view (cf. B. Duhm, *Das Buch Jesaja,* Vandenhoeck und Ruprecht, Göttingen (1892) ⁵1968, 17, 64) that there are two Isaianic nuclei, 6.1–8.18* (9.6); 28(1)7b – 30.17. Even O. Kaiser (op.cit., 205f.; ET, 234–6), with his more radical critique of the Isaianic corpus, holds that the latter contains a nucleus of Isaianic sayings; Kaiser (*Introduction,* 224; cf. *Einleitung,*

[3]1975, 208) now holds that the former does 'not contain any geniune Isaianic material'. Cf. also O. Kaiser, 'Geschichtliche Erfahrung und eschatologische Erwartung. Ein Beitrag zur Geschichte der alttestamentlichen Eschatologie im Jesajabuch', *NZST* 15, 1973, 272–85. On this section, see some further comments below.

40. Cf. Fohrer, 'Jesaja 1 also Zusammenfassung der Verkündigung Jesajas', *ZAW* 74, 1962, 251–68, and further references there.

41. All the arguments adduced by Fohrer (see n. 40) to explain the content and arrangement of the material in this chapter appear to be equally valid to the view that this chapter, together with 2.2–5 as he believes to be proper – as I do also –, form a small coherent collection. It does not summarize the teaching of Isaiah as that was traditionally understood any more than the other small collections in 1–12 might be supposed to do; and it is introductory only in the sense that it stands first. For a presentation of Isa. 1.1–31 as a coherent structure, cf. A. Mattioli, 'Due schemi letterari negli oracoli d'introduzione al libro d'Isaia Is. 1, 1–31', *Rivista Biblica*, 14, 1966, 345–64; L. G. Rignell, 'Isaiah Chapter 1. Some exegetical remarks with special reference of the relationship between the text and the book of Deuteronomy', *StTh* 11, 1957, 140–58, affirming complete unity and close links especially with Deut. 28–32; R. J. Marshall, 'The Structure of Isaiah 1–12', *BiblRes* 7, 1962, 19–32, see p. 28 on 12–20.

42. There are many interesting comments on titles and colophons in H. M. I. Gevaryahu, 'Biblical Colophons: A Source for the "Biography" of Authors, Texts and Books", *VTS* 28, 1975, 42–59, and cf. also the lecture noted in n. 34. But the marked differences between the titles in the prophetic books and the colophons adduced as parallels, as well as the lack of real evidence of the transfer of 'colophons' to become 'superscriptions', make me very doubtful about the fuller extension of his investigations. Cf. the useful critical comments by G. M. Tucker, 'Prophetic Superscriptions and the Growth of a Canon' in *Canon and Authority: Essays in Old Testament Religion and Theology*, ed. George W. Coats and Burke O. Long, Fortress Press, Philadelphia 1977, 56–70, esp. 66f.

43. The variety of views here is considerable. Fohrer (in the article cited in n. 40, 252f.) allows for it having originally referred to 2–4 and subsequently, with the addition of 5–10, to 2–10. Wildberger, *Jesaja 1–12*, 81, leaves the question open, noting only that 13 begins a new collection. Kaiser (commentary, 17; ET, 23) considers that the agreement of content suggests that the collection contained the various sections of 5, 9.8–21 and 10.1–4, and even that it contained the substance of 10.5ff. and chs. 13–32. Schoors, 35f., thinks of chs. 2–12 or 2–10, but also suggests that the section originally belonged to 2–5, while 1.1 formed the original heading to 6 when, as he supposes, this chapter stood at the beginning of the book. But the arguments for this are not strong.

44. See my 'Note on Isaiah 2.1', *ZAW* 75, 1963, 320f. L. G. Rignell, op. cit. (n. 41 above), 141, considers that the title at 2.1 refers only to the prophecy which follows in that chapter, while treating 1.1 as title to 1–12. Cf. also R. B. Y. Scott, 'The Literary Structure of Isaiah's Oracles' in *Studies in Old Testament Prophecy presented to T. H. Robinson*, ed. H. H. Rowley, T. & T. Clark,

Edinburgh and Scribners, New York 1950, 175–86, see 177; Scott thinks it a possible view that 'the editor is claiming for Isaiah what he knows is also credited by others to Micah'.

45. But, as in Hos. 1.1, it can evidently denote a collection.

46. On the opening verses of ch.7, see below. The material which directly concerns Isaiah begins with verse 3, but it is evident that this does not mark the original opening of a narrative, since the unexplained presence of Isaiah's son Shear-jashub presupposes that some other account, offering an explanation of the origin of that evidently symbolic name, must originally have preceded this. It remains one of the unexplained oddities of the Isaianic material that this particular element has not survived.

47. F. E. Deist, 'Notes on the Structure of Isa.2.2–22', *Theologia Evangelica* 10/2–3, 1977, 1–6, attempts a structural analysis of the whole chapter, but in fact treats vv. 2–5 as a 'liturgical quotation', so that unity is only partially assumed. No relationship between vv. 2–5 and 6–22 is really established in either case. R. Lack, *La Symbolique du Livre d'Isaïe. Essai sur l'image littéraire comme élément de structuralisme* (AnalBibl 59), 1973, 36f., links 2.2–5 to 2.6–4.1 by the use of images. Cf. also J. Becker, op. cit. (n. 20 above), 46f.

48. Cf. also G. M. Tucker, op. cit. (n. 42 above), 70.

49. Against Schoors, op. cit. (n 37 above), 26, who argues that the title 'vision' is not suitable for the whole collection 1–12. 'The great vision of Isaiah is ch. 6. It is thus evident that this title originally introduced that chapter. Later, chs. 1–5 were inserted between the title and 6–12 so that 1.1 came to function for the whole of 1–12' (my translation). But this overlooks the point that whereas *ḥāzôn* is used in 1.1, as indeed it is used also in Obad. 1 and Nahum 1.1 and in II Chron. 32.32, of a total prophetic collection, the vision in ch. 6 is described with the use of *rā'āh*, not *ḥāzāh* [both meaning 'see'].

50. Cf. e.g. H. Barth, op. cit. (n. 9 above).

51. Deist (see n. 47 above) describes this verse as a concluding 'liturgical plea', but it appears to have a moralizing tone rather than a liturgical form.

52. An alternative approach is to treat the units in 1–12 as being 1–6 and 7–12, the latter sometimes being described as the 'book of Immanuel'. A recent study is that of E. Testa, 'L'Emmanuele e la Santa Sion', *Studii Biblici Franciscani Liber Annuus* 25, 1975, 171–92; but his analysis into Zion themes and David themes leaves considerable gaps in the material of these chapters. R. J. Marshall, op. cit. (n. 41 above) argues for a greater unity, noting correspondence between chs. 2, 4 (exaltation of Jerusalem and the temple) and 9.11 (the theme of David), and suggesting (p. 21) the insertion of chs. 6–8. He sees verbal links between 5.30*b* and 8.22 and notes also the link of *nēś* (signal, ensign) in 5.26; 11.10 and 11.12.

53. Cf. O. Procksch, *Jesaja I* (KAT 9), Deichert, Leipzig 1930, 161: 'It appears . . . that (Isaiah's) book is evaluated as a '*ma'yan hayyṣû'āh* [a source (spring) of salvation]'; L. Alonso Schökel, 'Is. 12: De duabus methodis pericopam explicandi', *VD* 24, 1956, 154–60, see 160; J. Steinmann, *Le Prophète Isaïe. Sa Vie, Son Oeuvre et Son Temps*, Gabalda, Paris 1950, 342f.; P. Auvray, *Isaïe 1–39*, Gabalda, Paris 1972. 149; J. Becker, op. cit., 52.

54. Alonso Schökel, 156, compares *'āmartā* with the use of comparable formulae in 24–27 (25.9; 26.1; 27.2) and suggests that the same redactor

might be responsible for the addition of this psalm as added psalm material there. But in fact only 25.9 is really comparable so far as formula is concerned.

55. Alonso Schökel finds the unity of the psalm by his 'artistic analysis'. His sensitive treatment of the literary structure and of the various motifs and their development contrasts very sharply with the view of the psalm as a 'mosaic' (so Duhm) and with that of Steinmann (op. cit., 342f.) who regards it as 'un type de prière passe-partout'.

56. The term is used loosely rather than precisely.

57. Links also with Ps.105.1; 148.13, Isa.35.10; 55.1 are suggested by Duhm; but it must be admitted that some of the links depend on common psalm phrases and others are not really very close.

58. On the text here, cf. S. Talmon, 'A Case of Abbreviation Resulting in Double Readings', *VT 4*, 1954, 206–8; 'Double Readings in the Massoretic Text', *Textus* 1, 1960, 144–84, see 163, comparing MT and 1QIsaᵃ for Isaiah 12, MT and Samaritan for Exodus 15.

59. Cf. Schoors, 96, who sees allusion to the theme of Yahweh as living water and to the stream in Jerusalem (cf. Isaiah 8 etc.).

60. Cf. S. Mowinckel, *Psalmenstudien* II (SNVAO), 1922, 100f.; *The Psalms in Israel's Worship*, translated by D. R. Ap-Thomas, Blackwell, Oxford 1962, I, 123 n. 58, 131, 187.

61. So Alonso Schökel, 159f.; R. Lack, 57, suggesting links of 12.2, 4, 5, to 2.6ff.; 12.3 to 8.6ff.; 12.6 to 6.11, 3. 25f.; and also clues here to chs. 24–27 and a link between 12.1 and 40.1.

62. Cf. R. J. Marshall, 24ff., on the process by which, with this psalm, the 'Jerusalem theology' of Isaiah is modified by references to 'covenant theology'.

63. Schoors, 97, states: 'Certain writers even contend that the frequent occurrence of *yᵉšûʿāh* in vv. 2f. contains an allusion to the name of Isaiah.' He refers only to Alonso Schökel, op. cit., who refers to Procksch. A similar point is made by Auvray, 151.

64. *TWAT* I, 1971, 786 (F. Stolz) notes 354 occurrences of the root, not including proper names: 136 in the Psalms, 56 in Isaiah, 22 in Judges, 20 each in I Samuel, II Samuel and Jeremiah. There are small numbers of occurrences in other books. For a much fuller discussion of *yšʿ* and related words, cf. J. F. A. Sawyer, *Semantics in Biblical Research. New Methods of Defining Hebrew Words for Salvation* (SBT 2.24), 1972.

65. II Samuel 22 (Psalm 18) contains a number of these.

66. The general significance of names is clear from many narratives of name-giving. In the case of Isaiah, there is the additional point that there are three symbolic names: 7.3, Shear-jashub, unexplained but reinterpreted in 10.21 as part of the unit 10.20–22(23), and there may be a further stage of reinterpretation in 11.11, 16, though the root *šûb* (return) is not used there; 7.14, Immanuel, reinterpreted in 8.10; 8.1, Mahershalal-hashbaz, not alluded to except in the short account of this symbolic naming. (Cf. R. Lack [see n. 47], 42–52, on 5.25–9.6 as a unit on this basis.) We may therefore consider it not improbable that such a reinterpretation also took place in relation to Isaiah's own name (cf. Alonso Schökel, 159, commenting on his view that chs. 7–12 are 'sub signo nominum', with the persons involved as signs (8.18), the interpretation of the sons of the prophet; 'yet, while all the names are

explained, the name of the prophet alone lacks an interpretation'. He notes also the emphasis on the name of God in v. 4, as also on the titles of the deity in v. 2). Name-interpretation is also marked in later material in the book, e.g. 60.14; 62.4. In relation to the root *yš'* we might also consider the possible degree to which the name *yᵉhôšūa'* (Joshua), in view of its links to exodus and land themes, might have contributed to the development of *yš'* usage in Isaiah 40–66, though the name of Joshua itself hardly occurs outside the books from Exodus to Joshua. A comparable link might be sought in the use of the root *ḥzq* (be strong) in relation to Ezekiel in 3.14, cf. also 3.7–9, 2.4, though the relatively frequent use of this root in other passages in the book, unrelated to the prophet himself, makes this much less striking.

67. Cf. also Ben Sira 48.20: *wayyôšî'ēm bᵉyad yᵉša'yāhû* [he delivered them by the hand (agency) of Isaiah].

68. So e.g. Schoors, 11–14. The title of Steinmann's volume (see n. 53 above) suggests a degree of knowledge that we do not possess.

69. The literature on this topic is immense, but I would refer here to B. O. Long, 'Reports of Visions among the Prophets', *JBL* 95, 1976, 353–65, see 360f., and his comment: 'The traditions and the literary form of vision-report work together to legitimate the claim of Isaiah to a prophetic office and to give a documentary explanation for his message of evil.' Also his 'Prophetic Authority as Social Reality' in *Canon and Authority* (see n. 42 above), 3–20, esp. 11–13.

70. I may here acknowledge that the stimulus for some elements in this discussion derives in part from A. Schoors, 'Isaiah, the Minister of Royal Anointment?', *Instruction and Interpretation* (OTS 20), 1977, 85–107. This was read at the joint meeting of the Dutch and British Old Testament Societies in Leuven in 1976. Dr Schoors kindly supplied me with a copy of the proof of this article which has enabled me to take more exact note of a number of the points which are relevant here. For the historical attachment, cf. his discussion on 99–101, and also his reference to H. Cazelles, 'Jesajas kallelse och kungaritualet', *SEÅ* 39, 1974, 38–58 (cf. L.-M. Dewailly, *RB* 82, 1975, 455). [See also Essay 7, p. 275, n. 9.] The association of ch. 6 with the anointing of Uzziah's successor by the prophet Isaiah is followed (102–6) with a consideration of wider Davidic elements in the following chapters.

71. Cf. Schoors, OTS 20, 99f.

72. Schoors, OTS 20, 92 n. 27, mentions my own conviction that ch. 6 is a complex structure, 'composite as to its literary origin'. Attempts at categorizing the chapter (see n. 69) suggest that it is by no means easy to find a satisfactory form-critical or literary analysis. If Schoors is right in contending that Isaiah is here presented as 'the minister of royal anointment', then it would hardly appear likely that the doom material of vv. 9–13 belongs originally to such an occasion. As the chapter now stands, the expected pronouncement of blessing and hoped for well-being appears to be lost, or replaced by words of doom; it might be found in 9.1–6, whether that is Isaianic or not, as a counter to the indications of unfaithfulness in the Davidic house in 7.1–8.23. Cf also below.

73. For the later stages, cf. my discussion in 'An Interpretation of the Exile'

(Essay 9, see pp. 152–71) with some reference to relevant rabbinic material.

74. Cf. Schoors, OTS 20, 102–6.

75. So too Fohrer, *ALUOS*, 8f. = BZAW 118f. (see n. 6), While 2.5 can be seen as a link phrase to 2.6ff. – and the verbal link of *bêt ya‘ᵃqōb* (house of Jacob) may be a factor in the present arrangement of the text – the parallel and significantly different text of Micah 4.5 strongly suggests that the form of the poem here used is designed to reach a climax in appeal to the whole community, *bēt ya‘ᵃqōb* understood as all Israel, to accept the way of true religion in allegiance to Yahweh.

76. Cf. L. J. Liebreich (see n. 20), *JQR* 46, 276f.; 47, 126f. In the latter passage, Liebreich also links ch. 65 with ch. 1.

77. The suggestion that 5.25–30 should be transposed to follow 5.4 (so e.g. BHS), or that 5.24f. should be so transposed (so e.g. NEB), is without textual basis. We have to accept that elements, probably of a long poem, have been used deliberately to underline the judgment theme of 5.1–22 and must be interpreted in their present context. Cf. D. R. Jones (n. 19 above), 244.

78. For fuller discussion, cf. H. Barth, op. cit. (n. 9 above).

79. Cf. e.g. D. R. Jones, 239f., and G. Fohrer, *ALUOS* (see n. 6), 6, and n. 9 (= BZAW, 116 and n. 9).

80. Cf. Cazelles, op. cit. (n. 70 above).

81. B. S. Childs, 'The Sensus Literalis of Scripture: An Ancient and Modern Problem' in *Beiträge zur alttestamentliche Theologie. Festschrift für Walther Zimmerli zum 70. Geburstag*, ed. H. Donner, E. Hanhart, R. Smend, Vandenhoeck & Ruprecht, Göttingen 1977, 70–93; see 89.

82. For a specific instance cf. R. P. Carroll, 'A Non-Cogent Argument in Jeremiah's Oracles against the Prophets', *StTh* 30, 1976, 43–51.

83. Cf. e.g. a number of recent studies by J. A. Sanders, 'Adaptable for Life: the Nature and Function of Canon', in *Magnalia Dei. The Mighty Acts of God. Essays on the Bible and Archaeology in Memory of G. Ernest Wright*, ed. F. M. Cross, W. E. Lemke and P. D. Miller, Doubleday, Garden City, New York 1976, 531–60; 'Hermeneutics in True and False Prophecy' in *Canon and Authority* (see n.42 above), 21–41; 'Biblical Criticism and the Bible as Canon', *USQR* 32/3–4, 1977, 157–65. Cf. also my 'Original Text and Canonical Text' (Essay 14, pp. 223–34).

7. *Isaiah 36–39: Structure and Function*
(Published in *Von Kanaan bis Kerala: Festschrift für J. P. M. van der Ploeg OP zur Vollendung des siebzigsten Lebensjahres am 4 Juli 1979*, ed. W. C. Delsman et al. (AOAT 211), 1982, 3–21.)

1. R. E. Clements, *Isaiah and the Deliverance of Jerusalem* (JSOT 13), 1980, discusses these same chapters, but primarily in relation to their function in the Deuteronomic History. Ch. III on 'The Isaiah Narratives' has particular relationship to matters discussed here, and I am indebted to Dr Clements for kindly lending me a copy of the manuscript before its publication.

2. So the Hebrew *bydw ‘md hšmš* (by his hand [agency] the sun stood still);

Greek ἐν ταῖς ἡμέραις αὐτοῦ (? *bymyw* sc. Hezekiah) ἀνεπόδισεν ὁ ἥλιος (in his days the sun stood still).

3. R. F. Melugin, *The Formation of Isaiah 40–55* (BZAW 41), 1976, 176–8.

4. Ibid., 177.

5. Ibid., 177 n. Cf my 'An Interpretation of the Babylonian Exile. A Study of II Kings 20, Isaiah 38–39' (Essay 9, pp. 152–71).

6. Cf. also B. S. Childs, 'The Canonical Shape of the Prophetic Literature', *Interpretation* 32, 1978, 46–55: 'drained of its historical particularity' (p. 50); and 'The Exegetical Significance of Canon for the Study of the Old Testament', *VTS* 29, 1978, 66–80.

7. Melugin, op. cit., 176.

8. Ibid., 87ff.

9. H. Cazelles, 'Jesajas kallelse och kungaritualet', *SEÅ* 39, 1974, 38–58; French version, 'La vocation d'Isaïe (ch. 6) et les rites royaux' in *Homenaje a Juan Prado*, Instituto 'Benito Arías Montano' de Estudios Hebraicos, Sefardíes y Oriente Próximo, Madrid 1975, 89–108, criticizes the view that Isaiah 6 does refer to the heavenly council, observing the absence of *šāmaim* (heaven) from the text (see p. 38, French 89f.). But this is surely to take too literalistic a view of the wording. It is true that the description of Isaiah 6 makes direct reference to the temple (so vv. 1, 4, 6), but the comparability of this description with that of I Kings 22. 10–22 makes it clear that the appearance of the enthroned deity is pictured in terms of the correlation between heavenly dwelling and earthly dwelling.

10. Cf. e.g. R. N. Whybray, *Isaiah 40–66* (New Century Bible), Oliphants 1975, 48.

11. MT *w'mr* (he said); 1QIs^a *w'wmrh* (I said). The often proposed acceptance of the first person form (supported by LXX (Vg) εἶπα) cannot be regarded as certain. MT may be treated as an indefinite form.

12. Cf. e.g. J. Barr, 'Theophany and Anthropomorphism in the Old Testament', *VTS* 7, 1960, 31–38.

13. Since ch. 6 clearly rests upon earlier material and is itself an elaborate construct, there seems to be no good reason for a merely literal reading of the text.

14. Again an oversimple reading of the text might seem to suggest that Isaiah responds to a wholly unexpected call; but the purificatory ritual already described implicitly designates the prophet as the chosen recipient of the divine command. This is surely the full significance of the analogies seen by I. Engnell, *The Call of Isaiah* (UUÅ 1949.4), 1949, 42, in the magical texts which he cites, but incompletely, from K. L. Tallqvist, *Die assyrische Beschwörungsserie Maqlû* (AASF 20.6), 1895.

15. The continuity of thought between vv. 1–2 and 3–5 strongly suggests that the opening words *qôl qôrē* in v. 3 should be seen as an underlining of the declaration, rather than as the designation of a new speaker.

16. Cf. ch. 6 too where the succeeding verses as they now stand draw out the wider implications of the divine message.

17. 'Isaiah 1–12: Presentation of a Prophet' (Essay 6, see pp. 79–104). Cf. also R. Lack, *La Symbolique du livre d'Isaïe. Essai sur l'image littéraire comme élément de structuralisme* (AnalBibl 59), 1973, 76. Lack treats 36–39 as an appendix

which may be left on one side in his discussion, though he notes in it themes of confidence (especially *bḥṭ*), Assyrian presumption (*šʾnn*), and Yahweh's protection of Zion and David. 'The failed siege of Sennacherib became in the Israelite tradition the concretization of the *Völkersturmmotiv* [the motif of the onslaught of the nations]. In the book of Isaiah, it is the paradigm of the inviolability of Zion' (my translation). On this point cf. R. E. Clements, see p. 274, n. 1. But such a comment invites us to ask whether 'appendix' is the appropriate term for so important a section.

18. While some reference is made in this discussion to the question of the relationship between these two closely similar but not identical texts, the major questions of a textual kind are not here considered.

19. Cf. my 'Historians and Prophets' (Essay 8, see pp. 121–51).

20. Cf. e.g. my 'A Judgment Narrative between Kings and Chronicles? An Approach to Amos 7.9–17' (Essay 12, pp. 196–208).

21. Cf. e.g. C. C. Torrey, *The Second Isaiah: A New Interpretation*, T. & T. Clark, Edinburgh, and Scribners, New York 1928; J. D. Smart, *History and Theology in Second Isaiah*, Westminster Press, Philadelphia 1965; J. L. McKenzie, *Second Isaiah* (Anchor Bible 20), Doubleday, New York 1968.

22. F. D. Hubmann, 'Der "Weg" zum Zion. Literatur- und stilkritische Beobachtungen zu Jes. 35,8–10' in *Memoria Jerusalem. Freundesgabe Franz Sauer zum 70. Geburtstag*, Akad. Druck- und Verlagsanstalt, Graz, 1977, 29–41. Some doubt must be expressed on this interpretation in view of the metrical structure of the verses; cf. also for a different view of the text, J. A. Emerton, 'A Note on Isaiah xxxv 9–10', *VT* 27, 1977, 488f. [Now also O. H. Steck, *Bereitete Heimkehr. Jesaja 35 als redaktionelle Brücke zwischen dem Ersten und dem Zweiten Jesaja* (SBS 121), 1985.]

23. Hubman, op. cit., 41.

24. Cf. e.g. McKenzie, op. cit., xxii.

25. Cf. e.g. O. Kaiser, *Der Prophet Jesaja Kapitel 13–39* (ATD 18), 1973, 187f.; ET, *Isaiah 13–39* (OTL), 1973, 234–6.

26. On the relation of Isaiah 33 to Psalm 46, cf. H. Gunkel, 'Jesaja 33, eine prophetische Liturgie', *ZAW* 42, 1924, 177–208, a theme further developed by R. Murray, 'Prophecy and the Cult', in *Israel's Prophetic Tradition*, ed. R. J. Coggins et al., CUP 1982, 200–16.

27. B. S. Childs, *Isaiah and the Assyrian Crisis* (SBT 2.3), 1967; and cf. Clements (see p. 274, n. 1 above).

28. A. K. Jenkins, 'Hezekiah's Fourteenth Year: A New Interpretation of 2 Kings xviii 13–xix 37', *VT* 26, 1976, 289–94.

29. R. E. Clements (see n. 1 above) devotes much attention to the impact of 701 BC on the ongoing interpretation of Judah's experience.

30. Cf. J. A. Montgomery, 'Archival Data in the Books of Kings', *JBL* 53, 1934, 46–52.

31. This must inevitably raise questions about the function of the corresponding section in II Kings 18–19 and about the underlying problem of how that particular section within the Deuteronomic History came into being. Cf. R. E. Clements' discussion (see p. 274, n. 1). The contacts with the wider Isaianic tradition and particularly with Deutero-Isaiah are more easily

intelligible in the context of the book of Isaiah; their significance for the Deuteronomic History is partly considered by Clements.

32. See Essay 9, pp. 152–71.

33. See Essay 9, and esp. pp. 157–60.

34. The Versions, especially the Targum, interpret the phrase as precative: so LXX[B] γενέσθω (LXX γενηθήτω) δὴ εἰρήνη; Vg. *sit pax et veritas in diebus meis* (let there be peace and truth in my days). The Isaiah text has *kî yihyeh šālôm weʾemet beyāmāy*, where *kî* may be understood as emphatic (there *will be* peace and truth in my days). II Kings has *haлôaʿ ʾim šālôm weʾemet yihyeh beyāmāy*, rendered literally by LXX[A] as Μὴ οὐκ ἐὰν εἰρήνη καὶ ἀλήθεια ἔσται ἐν ἡμέραις μου (shall there not be peace and truth in my days?).

35. For an explanation related to a view of the growth of the canon, cf. D. N. Freedman, 'The Law and the Prophets', *VTS* 9, 1962, 250–65, and more recently in 'Canon of the Old Testament', *IDBS*, 1976, 130–36, esp. 131–3. The view he propounds is inevitably almost entirely hypothetical.

36. Again this makes clear that the relationship of the two texts to one another and to their contexts raises difficult questions.

37. *Interpreter's One-Volume Commentary*, Abingdon, Nashville and New York 1971, 329–71, see 352f.

38. Cf. e.g. O. Kaiser, *Jesaja 13–39*, 291; ET, 367.

39. See Essay 6, pp. 79–104.

40. Cf. 'Historians and Prophets' (Essay 8, see pp. 125–34).

41. Cf. 'Historians and Prophets', pp. 142–47, on the presence in Jeremiah 37–44 of a text which is in some respects a variant form of the main part of II Kings 24–25. In the former, Jeremiah appears in some, though not in all, sections of the material; in the latter, there is no mention of the prophet. The absence of the Jeremiah material from II Kings could provide one pointer to a view somewhat like that of D. N. Freedman (see n. 35); if the prophetic corpus, eventually Isaiah-Malachi, was intended as a supplement to the narrative works, then there would be no need to include such a large body of prophetic material in II Kings. Freedman makes no use of this point. We should still, however, need to explain the presence of II Kings 18–20; Freedman's comment (*IDBS*, 132) that the overlap of II Kings 18–20/Isaiah 36–39; II Kings 24–25/Jeremiah 52 suggests 'that the two works were in some sense distinct' is too vague to be helpful.

42. This is the standard view of the relationship; often the texts are rearranged to bring the poem with refrain together, with 5.25–30 (or part of it) treated as the original final stanza. But may this not be too facile a view? The occurrence of the refrain – also rather oddly in 10.4 – does not prove that the passages belong together. The style of 5.25–30 is in a number of respects markedly different from that of 9.7–20.

43. The same problem appears in the woes as is raised in the previous note. Is 10.1–4 really another woe originally belonging with 5.8–24? Its opening may seem to support the view, but of greater interest is the marked shift in 10.3–4*a*. This looks like an exilic comment pointing to the relentlessness of doom and the inevitability of either submission (4*a* α) or death (4*a*β).

44. Should we also see in *ʿalmāh* (young woman, 7.14) a play on *maʿalāh* (7.11)? This would further emphasize the latter, and would raise some

interesting questions regarding the unending speculation about the identity of the *'almāh*. Could it be that *'almāh* was used simply to provide a wordplay?

45. Melugin, *The Formation of Isaiah 40–55*, 178.

46. I am indebted to my colleague R. J. Coggins for pointing this out.

47. So e.g. BHS ad loc.; J. H. Montgomery and H. S. Gehman, *The Books of Kings* (ICC), 1951, 512.

48. So in H. G. M. Williamson, *Israel in the Books of Chronicles*, CUP 1977, 114–18, on Ahaz, and 119–25, on Hezekiah. Williamson offers some criticism of the details of the earlier presentation of the theme by R. Mosis, *Untersuchungen zur Theologie des chronistischen Geschichtswerk* (Freiburger Theologische Studien 92), 1973. Mosis presents the contrast of the two rulers very forcibly (186–92); cf. also my discussion in *I and II Chronicles, Ezra, Nehemiah* (TBC), 1973, 174–96, esp. 179 [See also Essay 11, pp. 181–92].

49. 'An Interpretation of the Babylonian Exile', Essay 9, pp. 152–71. See also A. K. Jenkins, 'Isa. 14.28–32 – An Issue of Life and Death', *Folio Orientalia* 21, 1980, 47–63.

50. Cf. e.g. A. Schoors, 'Isaiah, the minister of royal anointment?' in *Instruction and Interpretation* (OTS 20), 1977, 85–107; and H. Cazelles, op. cit. (n. 9 above).

51. [Cf. also my 'Exile and Post-Exile: Continuity and Reformulation of the Davidic Theme', see p. 259, n. 19].

8. *Historians and Prophets*

1. The second part of this study: 'Jeremiah and the Fall of Jerusalem', was delivered as a lecture to the September 1968 meeting of the Uppsala Exegetiska Sällskap; the whole was delivered as two lectures in the Theological Faculty of the Åbo Akademi in the same month and published in *SEÅ* 33, 1968, 18–54.

2. Many examples might be given of this. It is very evident in the single narratives found only in the books of Judges, Samuel and Kings, i.e. narratives for which no duplicate form exists and no parallel in any other book.

3. John Bright, *A History of Israel*, Westminster Press, Philadelphia 1959; SCM Press 1960 [³1981].

4. Martin Noth, *Geschichte Israels*, Vandenhoeck & Ruprecht, Göttingen ²1955; ET, *The History of Israel*, rev. ed., A. and C. Black 1960.

5. Reference may also be made to the recent reappraisal of these questions in M. Weippert, *Die Landnahme der israelitischen Stämme in der neueren wissenschaftlichen Diskussion* (FRLANT 92), 1967 [ET, *The Settlement of the Israelite Tribes in Palestine* (SBT 2.21), 1971].

6. It is clear that if it could be proved that Ezekiel lived in the third century BC and not in the sixth – and I mean *proved*, not thought to be a reasonable hypothesis, proved by the discovery of whatever is the ancient world's equivalent of an authentic birth-certificate – then this would make a great deal of difference to certain aspects of the interpretation of the material which is associated with him. But if there were only a simple confirmation of what is generally believed – i.e. that he was in fact born in Jerusalem in the latter part of the seventh century – all that would have been gained would be the firm exclusion of all way-out hypotheses about his having been active at some

other time or about his being a creation of the poetic imagination of some fanciful writer.

7. [I would now qualify this statement. The material found only in Chronicles certainly needs to be fully and seriously evaluated: but it appears much less probable that this material rests on separate older sources, more probable that it derives from what we may properly call the Chronicler's creative handling of his material – which may not originally belong in the context in which he places it – and to his use of exegetical procedures in his explication of the text.]

8. No attempt has been made at doing this within the more narrowly defined limits of this present study.

9. Since no full commentary on the relevant sections is attempted here, it has not seemed necessary to cite detailed references to commentaries and other works in which these matters are given full treatment.

10. The singular form found in MT in Isa.7.1 is preferred here by some commentators. J. Gray, *I and II Kings* (OTL), 1964, 573 [³1977, 632], accepts this and renders: 'he could not fight for it'. But this decision begs the question. The point is further mentioned subsequently. We may, however, note that the interpretation of the various forms of the text is tied up with the historical problems. Gray's interpretation would suggest that Jerusalem was captured; for this there is no clear evidence one way or the other, but no statement is made anywhere to suggest that the allies were successful in replacing Ahaz by their own nominee. The Kings text suggests a real crisis, leading to an appeal to Assyria; the Isaiah text a situation of entirely unnecessary panic; the Chronicles text a quite different disastrous situation.

11. The tradition in Jeremiah 26 concerning Hezekiah's reform movement – laying stress on the influence of Micah – offers a quite different understanding of the period from that of II Kings 18.4–6. This provides another example of the same kind of diversity of presentation – one with a prophetic figure, the other without – as is to be seen in the examples here under discussion.

12. Cf. n. 10 above.

13. So 1QIsᵃ, LXX, Vg and II Kings.

14. Cf. the gloss in similar form to v. 17 and possibly also in 8.3.

15. His name is now overlaid with later derogatory interpretation, just as that of Rezin almost certainly conceals a form Rāṣōn which was avoided because of its theologically favourable overtones (how could such an opponent of Judah be named Rāṣōn, acceptability, with its strongly religious connotation?); presumably Tob'al (good for nothing) was originally named Tab'el or Tob'el (God is good). Who he was is a matter of speculation; the quotation of only the father's name is not necessarily to be taken as derogatory; it is more likely to indicate that he was a man of status, the successor to the office held by his father. The suggestion that here we have an ancestor of the later Tobiad line, influential in the time of Nehemiah and the time of Antiochus IV Epiphanes (B. Mazar, 'The Tobiads', *IEJ* 7, 1957, 137–45, 229–38) is very ingenious; it would be very understandable for the hostile kings to put on the throne a provincial governor of good family who would be acceptable to many in Judah, and whose anti-Assyrian policy must be assumed.

16. On this, cf. I. I. Scullion, 'An Approach to the Understanding of Isaiah 7: 10–17' *JBL* 87, 1968, 288–300.

17. Unless Egypt here is a much later gloss.

18. It does not have to be the case that prophets agree, even if they are both canonical; the emphasis of Micah may be seen to be much more severely negative, though as it is now presented it has been subjected to what we may term 'Isaianic' editorial process and has been dovetailed into a larger tradition, as appears in the reference in Jeremiah 26.

19. Cf. Micah 6.7 and references given above, p. 126.

20. It is not without interest to speculate that it was this story which provided the basis for the parable of the Good Samaritan.

21. [See the added note 7 above, p. 279].

22. A remarkable example is that in II Chron.20.20 where Jehoshaphat is permitted to quote allusively from Isa.7.9, the injunction to faith.

23. We might ask whether it is the Chronicler's presentation which reinterprets in terms of Damascus, or II Kings 16 which offers an interpretation of Damascus material in terms of Assyria.

24. This provides a link with the material of v. 5.

25. [See also Essay 11, pp. 181–92 for a fuller discussion of other aspects of the Ahaz material.]

26. The exception is in that narrative of the period of Hezekiah in which Isaiah features largely, a narrative which appears both in II Kings and in the book of Isaiah. The only other mention of a canonical prophet in the books of Kings is the mere reference to Jonah ben Amittai in II Kings 14; but the relationship of this to the prophetic 'novel' of the book of Jonah is of a quite different kind. Had we no such book, we should note the reference to Jonah as being comparable with those which are made to various figures of the ninth and eighth centuries about whom nothing else is known.

27. B. S. Childs, *Isaiah and the Assyrian Crisis* (SBT 2.3), 1967.

28. J. Bright, 'The Prophetic Reminiscence: Its Place and Function in the Book of Jeremiah', *Biblical Essays* (OTWSA), 1966, 11–30.

29. C. Rietzschel, *Das Problem den Urrolle*, Mohn, Gütersloh 1966.

30. We may note the complex structure of this section, clearly built out of various elements. We may observe in particular that II Kings 25.13–17 on the temple equipment appears to be an 'intrusive' element in the narratives of vv. 8–12 and 18–21.

31. *Exile and Restoration* (OTL), 1968, 78ff.

32. This hope is further expressed in the figure of Zerubbabel, and also in the Davidic genealogies of the Chronicler, though there with a refinement of hope into the non-political (cf. my 'History and Theology in the Writings of the Chronicler', *Concordia Theological Monthly* 38 1967, 501–15). [See also references in Essay 3, p. 259, n. 19].

33. We might well pose the questions: who made this 'extract' and on what basis did he make such a construction and on what basis was it used, by him or some other, to conclude the book of Jeremiah?

34. Cf. n. 30.

35. Cf. II Kings 19.2 = Isa.37.2. At a number of points similarities of structure or of motif appear in the Jeremiah and Isaiah traditions as presented

in Jeremiah 37–44 on the one hand and II Kings 18.13–20.19 = Isaiah 36–39 on the other. Do such similarities perhaps point to particular methods of compilation or to circles in which the elaboration of the tradition took place?

36. Again we may note how in the comparable Isaiah tradition in II Kings 18–20 and Isaiah 36–39 we have alternative versions of the same incident.

37. The theme is illustrated further by the use of the psalm motif of 38.22 (cf. Pss. 69.13ff.; 88; Job).

38. A note may be made here of the measure of difference and correspondence of these chapters with other comparable material in the book of Jeremiah. In Jer.21.1–10 we have an alternative and differently constructed presentation of like material. The same themes of relentlessness of judgment are utilized, though in detail the presentation is different. There is no mention of the Egyptian advance, but only of the impotence of the Judaean fighters against Babylonian might. The homiletic character of this passage in ch. 21 and its resemblance to Deuteronomic style, show the way in which similar elements in the Jeremiah tradition could be quite differently utilized in different contexts. Such divergent presentations provide another indication of the different character of the first part of the book from what follows. We may also note that a great deal of the content of chs. 26–36 is concentrated on the interpretation of the disaster; it too comments on the underlying nature of disobedience, and offers its clear and relentless explanation of what eventually must happen. In this it stands fittingly before the material of 37–44. But it is also self-contained, for it goes further towards illuminating the nature of restoration, both in oracular utterances in 30–31 and in the reinterpretation of doom in 32–33.

39. Cf. n. 30.

40. The quoting of the divine word by Nebuzaradan resembles the quoting of words by the Rabshakeh (cf. Isaiah 36).

41. For interesting comments on the words of blessing on Ebed-melech, Nebuzaradan (and Baruch), cf. O. Eissfeldt, 'Unheils– und Heilsweissagungen Jeremias als Vergeltung für ihm erwiesene Weh– und Wohltaten', *Wissenschaftliche Zeitschrift Halle-Wittenberg* 14, 1965, 181–6 [= *Kleine Schriften* 4, Mohr, Tübingen 1968, 181–92].

42. The balance of chs. 42–44 with 37–38 may be noted.

43. Cf. the similarly negative bias of such comparable passages as Deuteronomy 28 and Leviticus 26.

44. Cf. C. J. Labuschagne, 'The emphasising particle *gam* and its connotations', in *Studia Biblica et Semitica T. C. Vriezen dedicata*, ed. W. C. van Unnik and A. C. van der Woude, Wageningen 1966, 193–203, who does not mention this passage. But his interpretation offers a better sense than the common rendering 'also' (so RSV.).

45. On this passage, cf. *Exile and Restoration*, 239 ff.

46. On the interpretation of the exile, cf. my *Exile and Restoration*, 237–47 and 'The Interpretation of the Exile and Restoration', *Canadian Journal of Theology* 14, 1968, 3–12.

47. This is a significant point when we attempt to look behind this highly stylized presentation to see the prophet himself: as so often in Old Testament structures, the original material has been allowed to stand, and that original

material shows a Jeremiah for whom hope lay in Gedaliah, in continued submission to Babylon, in Palestine. That view has been largely obscured by the restructuring of the narrative. [Cf. K. F. Pohlmann, *Studien zum Jeremiabuch. Ein Beitrag zur Frage nach der Entstehung des Jeremiabuches* (FRLANT 118), 1978; and my 'Aspects of the Jeremiah Tradition', *IJT* 20, 1971, 1–12.]

48. A modern analogy may be seen in Lawrence Durrell, *Alexandria Quartet*, Faber, 1962, and in John Hopkins, *Talking to a Stranger*, Penguin Books, Harmondsworth 1967.

9. *An Interpretation of the Babylonian Exile: a study of II Kings 20, Isaiah 38–39*
(Published in the *Scottish Journal of Theology* 27, 1974, 329–52.)

1. Brevard S. Childs, *Isaiah and the Assyrian Crisis* (SBT 2.3), 1967.

2. Op. cit., 107, and bibliographical notes in n. 3 there. For some more recent references, cf. also B. S. Childs, 'Midrash and the Old Testament' in *Understanding the Sacred Text: Essays in honor of Morton S. Enslin on the Hebrew Bible and Christian Beginnings*, ed. J. Reumann, Judson Press, Valley Forge 1972, 45–59.

3. E.g. II Chron.10.15 with its reference to the Ahijah narrative of I Kings 11.29–39, and cf. below on the latter part of II Chronicles 32.

4. Isa.39.1 has a reading *wayyeḥᵉzāq* (and recovered) for II Kings 20.12 *ḥizqîyāhû* (Hezekiah), which adds emphasis to this linking.

5. Cf. e.g. A. L. Oppenheim in *IDB* 3, 355.

6. J. A. Brinkman, 'Sennacherib's Babylonian Problem: an Interpretation', *Journal of Cuneiform Studies* 25, 1973, 89–95, see 91.

7. [Cf. Essay 10, pp. 172–80, for discussion of this issue.]

8. Cf. p. 285, n. 33.

9. Cf. BHS comparing akk. *šapiru*; LXX in the Isaiah text offer both renderings: ἐπιστολάς καὶ πρέσβεις.

10. II Kings has a slip, reading *wayyiśmaʿ* (heard) for *wayyismaḥ* (rejoiced).

11. The Isaiah text omits *kol* (all).

12. Here II Kings omits *kol*.

13. The text as it stands has a double statement. ʼᵃšer yēṣ ᵉʼû mimmᵉkā: ᵃšer tôlîd. This could be a result of a double reading – (1) Your sons who have issued from you [(or as 1QIsᵃ has it 'from your loins' *(mmᵉykh)*] (2) Your sons whom you have engendered. The double expression, or even one part of it, following on the use of the word 'sons', underlines that the reference is specifically to members of the royal house, to the dynasty on which so many hopes and beliefs were centred. It is here that judgment falls.

14. The NAB has a similar rendering.

15. Cf. Gen.4.7 where *hᵃlōʼ ʼim* means: 'Is it not if', i.e. 'Is it not true that . . .'; cf. further C. J. Labuschagne, 'The Particles *hēn* and *hinnēh*', *Syntax and Meaning* (OTS 18), 1973, 1–14, see 3 n. 5. For the 'courtier' style of idiom used here, cf. A. van Selms, '*Hᵃlo* in the Courtier's Language in Ancient Israel', *Fourth World Congress of Jewish Studies, Papers*, vol. 1, 1967, 137–40.

16. Jer.46.27 *mērāḥôq* (from afar) paralleled by *mēʼereṣ šᵉbî* (from the land of captivity); Zech.6.15 *rᵉḥôqîm* (those far off); Isa.43.6 *bānay mērāḥôq* (sons from

afar); Jer.51.50 *mērāḥôq*; Ezek. 11.16 the hiph'il of the verb *rḥq*. Cf. also the probably more general exilic reference of *'ad rāḥôq* (to a distant place) in Micah 4.3. These passages do not support a claim that such expressions are only used of exile in Babylon; they suggest that, granted a reference to Babylon, the theme of exile is thus underlined.

17. Cf. J. Hempel in Pauly-Wissowa, *Realencyclopädie der classischen Altertumswissenschaft* 22.2, 1954, cols. 1963f. Without wishing to suggest that an even remoter analogy is of more than marginal interest, I may cite the following passage from A. W. Reed, *An Illustrated Encyclopaedia of Maori Life*, Wellington and Auckland 1963, 106: '. . . notable explorers (i.e. the leaders of the Maori settlers envisaged as coming in the original canoes) . . . claimed formal possession of the country by viewing it from advantageous points, but their claims were subsequently to be established by occupation. It then remained in the possession of the tribe from generation to generation by ancestral right . . .' The comment is further made that continued occupation was necessary for this to remain so, and that this occupation was deemed to be expressed by the continuous lighting of domestic fires.

18. David Daube, *Studies in Biblical Law*, CUP 1947, reprinted Ktav, New York 1969, 24ff.

19. Cf. E. A. Speiser, 'Of shoes and shekels', *BASOR* 77, 1940, 15–20 (= *Oriental and Biblical Studies*, ed. J. J. Finkelstein and M. Greenberg, University of Pennsylvania Press, Philadelphia, and OUP 1967, 151ff.), who also discusses the evidence for such a reference in I Sam. 12.3 and elsewhere.

20. Daube, 28, quotes a fragment of the *Digest*: 'If my vendor from my tower points out neighbouring land to me who have bought it, and says that he delivers vacant possession, I begin to possess no less than if I had set foot within its boundary.'

21. We may observe that this affects the interpretation of the parable. It is not to be understood as indicating trivial excuses, but valid ones: the man who has bought land must complete the transaction; the man who has married a wife must consummate the marriage, a point which is covered in the law of warfare in Deut. 24.5. If we have no immediate analogy for the buying and testing out of oxen, the second excuse, its position with the others strongly suggests either a case similar to the land, or an act involving putting into action what has clearly been expressed in intention. We may note too that the version in Matthew misses this point or deliberately suppresses it as irrelevant (Matt.22.5).

22. For a fuller comment, see my *I and II Chronicles, Ezra, Nehemiah* (TBC), 1973, 198. A similar collating of events and anticipation of exile and restoration may be seen in II Chronicles 12 where Shishak is said to have captured the fortified cities of Judah. Shishak's list of captured cities includes none in Judah proper, but only in the Negeb and Edom (in addition to his main campaign in Israel). Cf. M. Noth, *History of Israel*, ET 1960, 239f. and B. Mazar, 'The campaign of Pharaoh Shishak to Palestine', *VTS* 4, 1957, 57–66, esp. 64–66. It is Sennacherib's records which relate the capture of Judaean cities (cf. *ANET*, 288). A transfer of themes appears to have been made. It is then stated that the submission of King Rehoboam and his princes led to a divine promise that there would not be total destruction, but 'I will give them

deliverance in a short while' (v. 7). The comment of v. 8: 'For they shall be slaves to him, that they may know both my service and the service of alien rulers' provides a reflection which is in reality one upon the experience of the exile and after. (Cf my commentary noted above, 131f.)

23. Cf., e.g., Ahijah in I Kings 14, and certain of the Elijah and Elisha traditions.

24. The Isaiah form of the text has an important variant at this point, in that this theme is entirely lacking in the narrative proper, and may be found only in the form of an addendum in v. 21. It would appear that some later scribe, conscious that this element was missing, copied in here the relevant words from II Kings 20.7 and with them the opening of v. 8, in a slightly different and abbreviated form. It is unfortunate that the NEB and the NAB (cf. also BHS and some commentators) have chosen to insert vv. 21f. in the text of Isa. 38 after v. 6, and thereby attempt a harmonization of the two texts. It is much more satisfactory to see in this form of the text a different handling of the material in which various differences point to another style of interpretation. Thus here the departure of Isaiah from Hezekiah's presence is unmentioned (II Kings 20.4–5a); the divine word is portrayed as coming as an immediate answer to the king's prayer and distress; the granting of the sign – as the text stands, and surely significantly – is not in response to a request for a sign (as in II Kings), but is offered as an immediate token of assurance. The presence of vv. 21f. in the Isaiah text may be better seen as a scribal addition, amplifying the alternative presentation in Isaiah with a specific reminder of the other theme, which has not here been used at all. (Cf. further below on the significance of differences in the presentation in Isaiah 38.)

25. It is arbitrary to emend MT's *wayyᵉḥî* (he recovered) in order to obtain a link. The fact that LXX and Pesh. make such a link is to be seen as evidence of the harmonizing tendency (cf. previous note).

26. It seems possible, expecially now in the light of J. F. A. Sawyer's discussion of Josh. 10 (*PEQ* 104, 1972, 139–46), to see a miraculous element super-imposed on an original natural phenomenon. The comments of J. Gray, *I and II Kings*, ²1970, 699f. are very much to the point. To his comments may be added the observation that 'shadow' (*ṣēl*) is used in the Old Testament with two different types of metaphorical sense. The 'shadow' may be symbolic of what is ephemeral (e.g. Job 8.9); or it may express divine protection (e.g. Ps. 57.2, and note especially Lam. 4.20 where it is used of Yahweh's anointed in whom there was seen to be confidence for life).

27. Cf. further on this n. 36 below.

28. Cf. esp. Jer.38.1–13 for a narrative presentation of the theme and 38.22 for a psalm fragment. On these passages cf. my 'Aspects of the Jeremiah Tradition', *IJT* 21, 1971, 1–12, see 1f.; A. R. Johnson, *The Vitality of the Individual in the Thought of Ancient Israel*, University of Wales Press, Cardiff 1949, 92ff. and literature there.

29. E.g. Pss.22.31f.; 14.7; 51.20f.

30. Cf. H. W. F. Saggs, *Assyriology and the Study of the Old Testament* (Inaugural Lecture), University of Wales Press, Cardiff 1969, 17; ' "The Nimrud

Letters", 1952', *Iraq* 17, 1955, 21–56 and 126–60. This line of comment is followed by Childs, *Israel and the Assyrian Crisis*, 80ff., and by Gray, *Kings*, 664f.

31. E.g. Childs, op. cit., 82ff., 93; Gray, op, cit., 668.

32. Cf. my *I and II Chronicles, Ezra, Nehemiah* (TBC), 1973, 191f.

33. It is not my intention in this study to draw wider conclusions regarding the nature of the Deuteronomic editing of the whole work from Joshua to II Kings. The commonly held view is that we must distinguish two editions, one before the disaster of 587 (even perhaps before Josiah's death in 609), and the other after 587, with possibly an appendix after 562. But does this view do justice either to the complexity of the material or to the overall unified impact which it has upon the reader?

34. Cf. my 'Historians and Prophets' (Essay 8, pp. 121–51, see pp. 125ff.).

35. Cf. Justin Martyr, *Dialogue with Trypho*, 43.8, 67.1, 71.3, 77.1f.

36. Cf. D. Daube, *He that Cometh* (Oct. 1966 – a lecture delivered in St Paul's Cathedral, London), 1–6 and the references given there, and in particular Bab. Berakoth 28b 'prepare a chair (throne) for Hezekiah king of Judah who is coming'; Bab. Sanhedrin 94a which notes that God intended to make Hezekiah the Messiah; and the problematic saying attributed to Rabbi Hillel (Bab. Sanhedrin 99a) that there will be no Messiah for Israel since they had already eaten him up (? = enjoyed him) in the days of Hezekiah. I am indebted to Dr S. Lowry of the University of Leeds who first drew my attention to this. I subsequently discovered Daube's lecture on the whole theme.

10.   *The Death of Hezekiah: a Pointer to the Future?*
(Published in *De la Tôrah au Messie. Mélanges Henri Cazelles. Études d'exégèse et d'herméneutique bibliques offertes à Henri Cazelles pour ses 25 années d'enseignement à l'Institut Catholique de Paris (Octobre 1979)*, ed. M. Carrez et al., Desclée, Paris 1981, 219–26.)

1. See 'Isaiah 36–39: Structure and Function', Essay 7, pp. 105–20.

2. 'An Interpretation of the Babylonian Exile: A Study of II Kings 20, Isaiah 38–39', Essay 9 above, pp. 152–71.

3. Ibid., pp. 170f., with references to the texts.

4. Cf. n. 1 above.

5. See 'Historians and Prophets', Essay 8, pp. 121–51.

6. Ibid., pp. 142–50; H. G. M. Williamson, *Israel in the Books of Chronicles*, CUP 1977, 114–18.

7. See 'Historians and Prophets', pp. 142–50 above.

8. Cf. H. Cazelles, 'Jesajas kallelse och kungaritualet', *SEÅ* 39, 1974, 38–58 (= 'La vocaion d'Isaïe (ch. 6) et les rites royaux', *Homenaje a Juan Prado* Instituto 'Benito Arias Montano' de Estudios Hebraicos, Sefardíes y Oriente Próximo, Madrid 1975, 89–108). This study has provided much stimulus to my consideration of the Isaiah material, though I would wish to differ from Professor Cazelles at a number of points, particularly his rather negative view of Hezekiah (see 56, French 107), though this is qualified in some degree on the following page. Cf. also A. Schoors, 'Isaiah, the minister of royal anointment?', *Instruction and Interpretation* (OTS 20), 1977, 85–107 (see 102ff.).

9. Cf. Cazelles, op.cit., 47 (98). Also A. K. Jenkins, 'Isaiah 14:28–32 – An

Issue of Life and Death', *Folio Orientalia* 21, 1981, 47–63, who offers some valuable comments on the nature and function of these verses.

10. Cf. A. K. Jenkins, 'Hezekiah's Fourteenth Year: A new interpretation of 2 Kings 18.13 – 19.37', *VT* 26, 1976, 284–98, for interesting if rather speculative discussion of the historical problems, and also comments in the article mentioned in n. 9 for the relationship between chronological notes and the ordering of the Isaiah material.

11. Cf also Cazelles, op.cit., esp. 56f. (French 107f.), though he sees the absence of Hezekiah's name in 6.1 – 9.6 as indicative of a change in Isaiah's view to a negative evaluation of Hezekiah. I find this impossible to reconcile with the closely related presentation in Isaiah 36–39.

12. Cf. my discussion in Essay 9, esp. pp. 154–64.

13. Reference may be made here to a paper by R. F. Melugin, 'Isaiah 40.1–11 and the redaction of Isaiah', delivered at the New York meeting of SBL in November 1979. (See *SBL Abstracts* 1979, Nᴼ S278, p. 64.) The paper traced relationships between this passage and Isaiah 6.1 – 9.6, points both of comparison and contrast. The discussion was closely related to his *The Formation of Isaiah 40–55* (BZAW 141), 1976, esp. 176–8; cf. also 87ff.

14. But cf. now the discussion of possible earlier material in Isaiah 40–55 by J. M. Vincent, *Studien zur literarischen Eigenart und zur geistigen Heimat von Jesaja, Kap. 40–55* (BET 5), 1977.

15. The point here made, in question form, derives from my contribution to the discussion of Melugin's paper referred to in n. 13.

16. Cf. E. J. Smit, 'Death and Burial Formulas in Kings and Chronicles relating to the Kings of Judah', *Biblical Essays* (OTWSA), 1966, 173–7.

17. Cf. my comments in *I and II Chronicles, Ezra, Nehemiah* (TBC), 1973. 189ff., and also the discussion of the parallels between Hezekiah and Solomon set out by H. G. M. Williamson, op.cit., pp. 119–25.

18. KBL³, s.v., includes a second meaning 'storey', and this fits with K. Galling's view that the word here denotes 'upper storey, upper level' (so *Die Bücher der Chronik, Esra, Nehemia* (ATD 12), 1954, 166; BRL¹, col. 245, Abb., 9; BRL², 125, Abb. 14. S. Yeivin, 'The sepulchers of the kings of the house of Judah, *JNES* 7, 1948, 30–45, see p. 33 and n. 37: 'on the ascent to the sepulchers'. There is a curious coincidence in the use of this word with the repeated use of '*ālāh* and *maᶜᵃlôt* (5 times) in Isaiah 38. Is it possible that the Chronicler's introduction of this term – not elsewhere used in reference to a grave – is related to the II Kings 20, Isaiah 38 material? Cf. my discussion in Essay.

19. So NEB; cf. W. Rudolph. *Chronikbücher* (HAT 21), 1955, 314.

20. LXX in each case has *ekphora*, here clearly 'the carrying out of a corpse for burial'; this term is used in LXX only in these two passages. Has LXX possibly been influenced by the preceding description in II Chronicles 16.14, understanding *miškāb* as meaning bier?

21. Amos 6.10 has *misrᵉpô* (samek for *śin*). For a detailed discussion see W. Rudolph, *Joel, Amos, Obadja, Jona* (KAT 13/2), 1971, 222.

22. Cf. E. de Ward. 'Mourning Customs in 1,2 Samuel', *JJS* 23, 1972, 1–27, 145–66.' I am much indebted to Baroness de Ward both for this detailed

discussion of relevant material and for her valuable comments on earlier stages of the present article.

23. G. R. Driver, 'A Hebrew burial custom', *ZAW* NF 25, 1954, 314f.

24. J. F. A. Sawyer, 'Hebrew Words for the Resurrection of the Dead', *VT* 23, 1973, 218–34 (see 218, 226f.).

11. *The Biblical Interpretation of the Reigns of Ahaz and Hezekiah*
(Published in *In The Shelter of Elyon. Essays on Ancient Palestinian Life and Literature in Honor of G. W. Ahlström*, ed. W. Boyd Barrick and John R. Spencer (JSOTS 31), 1984, 247–59.)

1. So BHS. See also A. K. Jenkins, 'Hezekiah's Fourteenth Year: A New Interpretation of II Kings xviii 13 – xix 37', *VT*, 26 (1976), 289–94.

2. See again, BHS.

3. Y. Yadin, *'ma'alôt 'āḥāz'*, *Eretz Israel* 5, 1958, 91–96, 88*. However, Yadin's arguments do not really resolve the problems.

4. For some details of this, see 'Isaiah 36–39; Structure and Function' (Essay 7, pp. 105–20).

5. See BHS.

6. For some discussion of this issue, see 'An Interpretation of the Babylonian Exile: A Study of II Kings 20, Isaiah 38–39', (Essay 9, pp. 152–71).

7. For a discussion of the last two elements, see 'An Interpretation' (n. 6).

8. See 'The Death of Hezekiah – a pointer to the future?' (Essay 10, pp. 172–80.)

9. See, 'An Interpretation' (Essay 9) and references there.

10. See H. Tadmor and M. Cogan, 'Ahaz and Tiglath-Pileser in the Book of Kings: Historiographic Considerations', *Biblica* 60, 1979, 504.

11. The term *šōḥad* may be an appropriate technical term for such support of an appeal. To translate it as 'bribe' introduces a derogatory note, though this may have been intended by the narrator. On *šōḥad* see Tadmor and Cogan, 'Ahaz', 500–503, though their arguments do not appear to be conclusive.

12. So the MT, which would seem to mean 'took the people of Damascus into exile to Qir', but since *qîr (qîrāh)* means 'city' it is possible that this is really to be regarded as the object of the verb, as is implied in some Greek texts, suggesting the total removal of the city as a political entity.

13. Tadmor and Cogan, 'Ahaz', 505.

14. B. S. Childs, *Isaiah and the Assyrian Crisis* (SBT 2.3), 1967.

15. The text of 16.6 is problematical.

16. See II Chron. 28.17 for Edom and 28.18 for Philistia.

17. For this element, compare I Kings 14.24 and precisely, though in an extended form, II Kings 21.6.

18. See n. 11.

19. See comments below.

20. For a discussion of this passage, see J. W. McKay, *Religion in Judah under the Assyrians* (SBT 2.26), 5–12.

21. The account here includes the two technical terms *dᵉmût* and *tabnît*, perhaps indicating a design drawing and a description.

22. M. Cogan, *Imperialism and Religion* (SBLMS 19), Scholars Press, Missoula, Mont. 1974, 74; and Tadmor and Cogan, 'Ahaz', 506. See also McKay, *Religion in Judah*, 7f.

23. D. Daube, *Studies in Biblical Law* (Cambridge University Press, 1947), 24–39. See 'An Interpretation' (Essay 9, see pp. 161f.)

24. LXX has 'the foundation of the throne' (θεμέλιον τῆς καθέδρας) which suggests a Hebrew *mûsad haššebet*.

25. See 'Isaiah 36–39' (Essay 7, pp. 105–20).

26. II Chronicles 28 clearly offers a different view.

27. See Cogan, *Imperialism and Religion*, 73–75, for a fuller discussion.

28. See M. Cogan, 'The Ahaz Altar', in *The Proceedings of the Sixth World Congress of Jewish Studies* (Jerusalem: World Union of Jewish Studies, 1977); and McKay, *Religion in Judah*. It has not been possible in this study to take account of H. Spieckermann, *Juda unter Assur in der Sargonidenzeit* (FRLANT 129), 1982, see especially 307–72, who presents a close analysis of Assyrian texts and comes to different conclusions. If these conclusions are accepted, some modification of details in the present discussion would follow: the main argument, however, stands. In particular, Spieckermann's discussion of Ahaz (362–9) recognizes the king's political sagacity, though he offers a different explanation of II Kings 16.15*b* from that given here. [See also H. W. F. Saggs, *Assyriology and the Study of the Old Testament*, University of Wales Press, Cardiff 1969, esp. 21f.]

29. See the *'ammûd* for the king in II Kings 11.14; 23.3. It is perhaps a pillar but more probably a 'standing place', a 'station' for the king, the position occupied by him in the ritual.

30. 'An Interpretation' (Essay 9, pp. 152–71); and see, 'Isaiah 36–39' (Essay 7, pp. 105–20).

31. See the similar assessment of Gideon's ephod in Judges 8.27.

32. Perhaps it should be 'Tabeel'? Who he actually was is of no immediate consequence here.

33. For a view of this see Jenkins, 'Hezekiah's Fourteenth Year' (see n. 1).

34. For some relevant comments on the whole problem area, see R. E. Clements, *Isaiah and the Deliverance of Jerusalem* (JSOTS 13), 1980.

[Comparison may also be made with G. W. Ahlström, *Royal Administration and National Religion in Ancient Palestine* (Studies in the History of the Ancient Near East, 1, Brill, Leiden 1982), especially ch. 5 on Manasseh.]

12. *A Judgment Narrative between Kings and Chronicles? An Approach to Amos 7.9–17*

(Published in *Canon and Authority: Essays in Old Testament Religion and Theology*, ed. George W. Coats and Burke O. Long, Fortress Press, Philadelphia 1977, 71–87.)

1. For some observations of my own, see 'Historians and Prophets' (Essay 8, pp. 121–51, esp. pp. 137–51), and 'Aspects of the Jeremiah Tradition', *IJT* 20, 1971, 1–12.

2. For comments on some aspects of this, cf. my 'An Interpretation of

the Babylonian Exile: A Study of II Kings 20; Isaiah 38–39' (Essay 9, pp. 152–71).

3. Isaiah 7 has an example in which the annalistic material corresponds to II Kings 16. But where the latter has no mention of the prophet, the former subordinates the narrative content to the prophetic message. See my 'Historians and Prophets,' (pp. 125–34).

4. Were it not for v. 13 with its unusual indication of the direct sequel to an oracle (cf. Jer 28.17), this passage could as well be classified with other examples of oracles attached to a brief narrative or annalistic statement. The presentation of symbolic actions in the book of Ezekiel, as in Jeremiah, provides another genre, in which the narrative is purely in terms of the word of instruction to the prophet and the carrying out of that word, together with its interpretation (cf. also Hosea 1 and 3).

5. See W. A. M. Beuken, *Haggai-Sacharja 1–8* (Stud. Sem. Neerl. 101) Assen: Gorcum, 1967 for a full discussion, and R. A. Mason, 'The Purpose of the "Editorial Framework" of the Book of Haggai,' *VT* 27, 1977.

6. G. M. Tucker, 'Prophetic Authenticity. A Form-Critical Study of Amos 7:10–17,' *Interpretation* 27, 1973, 423–34; see 426–27 for a schematic presentation of the structure.

7. Ibid., 425.

8. So e.g. W. Rudolph, *Joel, Amos, Obadja, Jona* (KAT 13/2) 1971, 236–7, who treats it as an explanation of vv. 7–8, which then provides a link to what follows. Cf. S. Amsler, *Amos* (CAT 11) 1965, 227; J. L. Mays, *Amos* (OTL) 1969, 133.

9. So. e.g. H. W. Wolff, *Dodekapropheton Amos (BK* 14/2) 1969, 348. So also V. Maag, *Text, Wortschatz und Begriffswelt des Buches Amos*, Brill, Leiden 1951, 47–48, who describes it as 'Splitter eines Amoswortes,' owing its position to the compiler of the book. His proposed addition of an extra clause is unwarranted.

10. Note especially the application to the 'day' in clause *b*. The fifth vision, 9.1*a*, is quite different in structure from the other four, and it is difficult to see how it can be held to belong to an originally coherent series with them (*contra* Tucker 'Prophetic Authenticity,' 425, who cites the support of 'most commentators').

11. Cf. H. Graf Reventlow, 'Gattung und Überlieferung in der "Tempelrede Jeremias" ', *ZAW* 81, 1969, 342 n. 118.

12. Cf. J. van Seters, 'Confessional Reformulation in the Exilic Period,' *VT* 22, 1972, 448–59.

13. Only Josh.24.3–4 is non-formulaic, in a brief statement of patriarchal genealogy.

14. S. Terrien, 'Amos and Wisdom,' *Israel's Prophetic Heritage (Festschrift J. Muilenburg)*, ed. B. W. Anderson and W. Harrelson (Harper & Row, New York, and SCM Press 1962, 108–15, see 113–14, and Wolff, *Amos*, 356, suggest a link to the Beersheba references in 5.5 and 8.14, but this seems very far-fetched. Equally improbable is the suggestion of A. van Selms, 'Isaac in Amos,' *Studies on the Books of Hosea and Amos* (OTWSA), 1964–65, 157–66, that Isaac here indicates Transjordan, with particular reference to 'the temple

complex of Penuel-Mahanaim' (164). Van Selms offers useful comments on the probability that the *śîn* forms of name and verb (*śḥq*) are late.

15. Wolff, *Amos*, 355, explains it as due to the narrative having been composed in Judah after Amos' return. But this makes assumptions about the material which need examination (see below).

16. See also n. 23.

17. Cf. N. Lohfink, 'Isaias 8:12–14,' *BZ* 7, 1963, 98–104.

18. *qśr* in the sense of 'bind' occurs elsewhere, but this not relevant here. Ezek. 22.25 may well be corrupt, but if correct may stand with Jer.11.9 alongside the narrative books.

19. Of other forms of this root, only *pilpel* occurs in early material.

20. This sense belongs also to the *qal*, and some occurrences are probably early.

21. Cf. Wolff, *Amos*, 358; the use is mainly exilic and post-exilic.

22. I have examined all the evidence set out by Maag, *Wortschatz*, much of which contributes very little to our understanding of Amos. It could be argued that the sense of *lqḥ* (take, v. 15) is different from that appearing elsewhere; so too for *npl* (fall, v. 17), but perhaps for this cf. 5.2; 8.14.

23. I Sam.22.8, 13 (Saul. On the use of *qśr* as a theme word in I Sam.18.1; 22.8, 13, see my 'The Verb Love – *'āhēb* in the David-Jonathan Narratives', *VT* 25, 1975, 213f.). II Sam.15.12,31 (Absalom). I Kings 15.27; 16.9,16, 20 (Baasha, Zimri). II Kings 9.14; 10.9 (Jehu); 11.14 (II Chron. 23.13, against Athaliah); 12.20 (cf. II Chron.24.25f., against Joash). 14.19 (against Amaziah of Judah, son of Joash; cf. II Chron.25.27; and see below); 15.10, 15 (Shallum); 15.25 (Pekah); 15.30 (Hoshea); 17.4 (with *māṣā'*, find; cf. Jer.11.9, of Hoshea in relation to Assyria); 21.23f. (= II Chron. 33.24f., against Amon). Also Neh.4.2 (RSV = 4.8) of opponents to Nehemiah. Cf. further II Chron. 24.21, of conspiracy against Zechariah the son of Jehoiada the priest, in the context of the Joash conspiracy noted above, and cf. T. Willi, *Die Chronik als Auslegung* (FRLANT 106), 1972, 220 n. 20 on *qśr* as *Leitbegriff*.

24. F. Crüsemann, 'Kritik an Amos im Deuteronomistischen Geschichts-werk,' *Probleme biblischer Theologie (Festschrift G. von Rad)* ed. H. W. Wolff, C. Kaiser, Munich 1971, 57–63, argues that II Kings 14.27 is deliberately directed *against* the message of Amos. But it must be observed that there is nothing in the wording which corresponds precisely. Cf. further below.

25. On this, cf. 'Historians,' (pp. 137–51).

26. Even perhaps critical of him, if Crüsemann, 'Kritik an Amos,' is right.

27. H. Schmid, 'Nicht Prophet bin ich, nicht bin ich Prophetensohn,' *Judaica* 23, 1967, 68–74 observes the possible relationship between Amos 7 and the Jehu narrative of II Kings 9, particularly in the use of *qśr*. But he argues that the accusation of Amaziah derives from the supposition that Amos is just such another as Elisha, initiating rebellion, and that Amos' reply (see below) is directed toward denying such a view. In my view, Schmid is right in seeing a connection, but wrong in his interpretation of its nature.

28. There is a considerable literature on I Kings 13. The study by E. Würthwein, 'Die Erzählung vom Gottesmann aus Juda in Bethel. Zur Komposition von 1 Kön 13,' *Wort und Geschichte: Festschrift K. Elliger*; ed. H. Gese and H. P. Rüger (AOAT 18), and 1973, 181–90, provides both sufficient

bibliography and a useful analysis of the divergent traditions within this complex.

29. Cf. J. Bleek, *Einleitung in das AT*, 4th ed., ed. J. Wellhausen 4, Reimer, Berlin, 1878, 244; O. Eissfeldt, *Kleine Schriften*, Mohr, Tübingen, 1968, 137–42; especially 138–39 and bibliography, 138 n. 2. So too W. Rudolph, *Amos*, 100. J. L. Crenshaw, *Prophetic Conflict* (BZAW 124) 1971, 41–42, argues for general influence from Amos on I Kings 13, though noting important points of difference. The link has recently been denied by such scholars as M. Noth, *Könige* (BK 9) Neukirchen 1968, 295; and H. Jepsen, 'Gottesmann und Prophet, *Probleme biblischer Theologie* (see n. 24 above), 171–82; see 180 n. 15.

30. So Würthwein, 'Komposition,' 184.

31. Ibid., 182–5, who does not, however, discuss any possible source for the narrative.

32. Ibid., 185–7.

33. On Bethel and its significance, cf. Würthwein, 'Komposition,' especially 188f., and Jepsen, "Gottesmann," 174.

34. Cf. Tucker, 'Prophetic Authenticity,' 430, and see also below.

35. See n. 23.

36. The free translation is my own.

37. Cf. Tucker, 'Prophetic Authenticity,' 425.

38. Ibid., 426, citing T. H. Robinson, *Amos* (HAT 14 ³) 1964, 99; H. Grosch, *Der Prophet Amos* Mohn, Gütersloh 1969, 19.

39. Ibid., 429, citing T. H. Robinson, *Amos*, 99; J. D. W. Watts, *Vision and Prophecy in Amos*, Brill, Leiden, 1958, 2, 31; E. Hammershaimb, *The Book of Amos*, Blackwell, Oxford, 1970, 15, as upholders of the biographical view (cf. also A. Weiser, *Das Buch der Zwölf Kleinen Propheten I* (ATD 24) 1959, 165; J. L. Mays, *Amos*, 134); see E. Würthwein, 'Amos-Studien', *ZAW* 62, 1950, 10–52, especially 23–24, for criticism of it.

40. Many popular textbooks (and some more sophisticated commentaries) assume that Amos returned at this point to Judah, and, being unable to prophesy further in the North, gathered his message into written form there (see below). One might gain a little support for this view by adducing the II Chron.25.16 statement that 'the prophet ceased,' but this would be somewhat hazardous.

41. We may note that the study of the nature of this passage and of the parallels to it lends no support to the supposition that Amaziah was giving Amos a kindly warning to escape before any word came back from Jeroboam. (So Wolff, *Amos*, 358 tentatively; Würthwein, 'Amos-Studien,' 19–24. Cf. the sensible strictures of Tucker, 'Prophetic Authenticity,' 427.) Such a view depends in any case upon a very simplistic reading of the text.

42. So Hermann Schult, 'Amos 7:15a und die Legitimation des Aussenseiters,' *Probleme biblischer Theologie*, ed. Hans W. Wolff, C. Kaiser, Munich 1971, 462–78; especially 476, adducing a wide range of comparative material for this form.

43. Cf. the discussion with examples, by G. R. Driver, 'Affirmation by Exclamatory Negation,' *JANESCU* 5, 1973, 107–14 (*Festschrift M. Gaster*).

44. Cf. H. N. Richardson, 'A Critical Note on Amos 7, 14,' *JBL* 85, 1966,

89. Also J. Crenshaw, *Prophetic Conflict*, 67, and G. Ahlström, *Joel and the Temple Cult of Jerusalem* (*VTS* 21), 1971, 21 n. 2 and 96 n. 2 for further literature.

45. So Amsler, *Amos*, 230.

46. Richardson, 'Amos 7.14'; S. Cohen, 'Amos Was a Navi', *HUCA* 32, 1961, 175–78, especially 177; Schmid, 'Nicht Prophet,' 73, and Crenshaw (in an oral comment) would all maintain that the first phrase is emphatic: 'I certainly am a prophet,' but that the second is negative: 'but not a member of a guild.' This shift is extremely awkward. It is impossible here to attempt a discussion of the problematic passage in Zech. 13.5, with its apparent citation of the words of Amos: *lō' nābî' 'ānōkî*. The coincidence of the words cannot prove citation, although the degree to which earlier material is used in Zechariah 9–14 must make this probable. (Cf. R. A. Mason, '*The Use of Earlier Biblical Material in Zechariah IX-XIV: A Study in Inner Biblical Exegesis,*' Ph.D. Dissertation, London, 1973.) We cannot, however, argue from the meaning given to the words in their present context to their meaning in Amos, and the difficulty of their present context makes any firm decision impossible. Cf. Mason, *Zechariah*, 251f.; also P. D. Hanson, *The Dawn of Apocalyptic*, Fortress Press, Philadelphia. 1975, 367, and Crenshaw, *Prophetic Conflict*, 105f.

47. Crenshaw, *Prophetic Conflict*, 59, seems to miss the point when he describes this prophet as 'immoral,' 'expediently silent,' although he admits that the prophet does have the last word.

48. For this, cf. also Eissfeldt, *Kleine Schriften* 4, 139.

49. Cf. the comments of Crenshaw, *Prophetic Conflict*, 95. For the 'martyrdom of Amos,' cf. T. Schermann, *Prophetarum Vitae* Teubner, Leipzig 1907, and *Propheten- und Apostellegenden* (TU 31/3, Hinrichs, Leipzig) 1907, 51–53; C. C. Torrey, *The Lives of the Prophets* (SBLMS 1) Philadelphia, 1946, 26, 41. Cf the wider discussion of this whole theme in O. H. Steck, *Israel und das gewaltsame Geschick der Propheten* (WMANT 23) 1967, especially 249f. on Amos.

50. E.g., Jeremiah 1, Isaiah 6, Ezekiel 1–3 for the former, and Jeremiah 20, 26, 28 for the latter.

51. For a comparable instance, see my 'Babylonian Exile' Essay 9, pp. 152–71, and observe a possible link with the theme of 'unclean' in Ezek.4.13.

52. Cf. my 'The Chronicler as Exegete' in *JSOT* 2, 1977, 2–32.

53. Cf. my 'Babylonian Exile,' (pp. 169f.).

54. For some further comments on this theme, see my 'The Open Canon',' (Essay 13, pp. 209–24).

55. I am indebted to colleagues and others who have commented on the material for this discussion in earlier forms, and in particular to Burke O. Long for his discerning notes on an earlier draft of the text. Two articles by T. J. Wright, ('Amos and the "Sycomore fig" ', *VT* 26, 1976, 362–8 and 'Did Amos Inspect Livers?' *ABR* 23, 1975, 3–11), were available to me only after the completion of this article. They do not affect the issues considered here.

[For some of the problems raised by this passage in Amos, cf.Z. Zevit, 'A misunderstanding at Bethel. Amos VII 12–17', *VT* 25, 1975, 783–90; and the response to this by Y. Hoffmann, 'Did Amos regard himself as a Nābī?', *VT* 27, 1977, 209–12. Neither makes any use of my study.]

13.   *The Open Canon*
(Published in *Colloquium – The Australian and New Zealand Theological Review*, 3, 1970, 279–91.)

1. *Discoveries in the Judaean Desert of Jordan. IV. The Psalms Scroll of Qumran Cave 11* (11QPs[a]), OUP 1965; also *The Dead Sea Psalms Scroll*, Cornell UP and OUP 1967 (both ed. J. A. Sanders).

2. M. H. Goshen-Gottstein, 'The Psalms Scroll (11QPs[a]): A Problem of Canon and Text', *Textus* 5, 1966, 22–33; S. Talmon, 'Pisqah Be'emṣa' Pasuq and QPs[a]', ibid., 11–21, see p. 12 n. 9.

3. Cf. also J. van der Ploeg, 'Le Psaume XCI dans une recension de Qumran', *RB* 72, 1965, 210–17, who notes the existence of 11QPsAp containing apocryphal psalms and Psalm 91. One of the former is ascribed to David. This, in van der Ploeg's view, is also a liturgical collection (cf. p. 216). But the conclusion is by no means obvious.
[The discussion of this issue has been carried out much more fully now by G. H. Wilson, *The Editing of the Hebrew Psalter* (SBLDS 76), Scholars Press, Chico, Ca. 1985.]

4. See my article 'Some Notes on the Psalms', *JTS*, NS 17, 1966, 392–99, esp. 396–99.

5. Y. Yadin, 'Another Fragment (E) of the Psalms Scroll from Qumran Cave 11 (11QPs[a])', *Textus* 5, 1966, 1–10.

6. Cf. the edition by J. van der Ploeg already noted. On p. 217 he writes: 'It seems clear to me that the mss. 11QPs[a] and 11QPsAp present problems for the complex and little-known history of the canonization of the sacred books, but do not resolve those problems' (my translation).

7. It is of incidental interest to wonder whether the omission of the *nun*-verse in the MT in the alphabetical Psalm 145 occurred in such a refrain text, where its accidental omission could be much more readily explained than otherwise; for there seems no obvious reason for its omission between the *mem*- and *samek*-verses.

8. Two obvious examples of the analysis of such variant presentations may be found in my article, 'Historians and Prophets' (Essay 8, pp. 121–51), viz. the Isaiah/Ahaz tradition as it is found in II Kings 16, Isaiah 7–8 and II Chron. 28; and the fall of Jerusalem as it is found in II Kings 25, Jer. 52, Jer. 37–44 and II Chronicles 36. B. S. Childs, *Isaiah and the Assyrian Crisis* (SBT 2.3), 1967 also offers such an analysis.

9. Cf my *Continuity* (Essay 1, pp. 3–16) for some further comments on diversity in Old Testament thought. It might further be not unfairly said that some German research on the Old Testament suffers from the assumption that a selection of passages should be made from which a particular topic is to be investigated. The result is often extremely cogent, but may easily be very restricted. A different selection of passages could have led to a different set of conclusions.

10. Is the existence of the Qumran commentaries any guide to what was regarded as authoritative? If so, what do we say of the absence of Habakkuk 3? There appear to be other factors at work.

11. A. C. Sundberg, *The Old Testament of the Early Church* (Harvard Theological Studies 20) Harvard UP and OUP 1964.

12. Cf. J. Bowker, *The Targums and Rabbinic Literature*, CUP 1969, for a useful survey with much illustrative material.

13. G. A. F. Knight, *A Christian Theology of the Old Testament*, SCM Press 1959.

14. *The Documents of Vatican II*, ed. W. M. Abbott, S J, Herder & Herder, New York, and G. Chapman 1966, 116ff.

15. This has been carried much further by certain groups, e.g. the Swedenborgians, the Mormons and the Christian Scientists.

16. G. E. Wright has raised a number of the same problems as this discussion, with some difference of emphasis, in the final chapter of his study *The Old Testament and Theology*, Harper and Row, New York 1969, 166–85: 'The Canon as Theological Problem'. His discussion merits a fuller examination and correlation with what is said here.

[In relation to some of the questions raised here, reference may be made now to the very detailed discussion of the canon by R. Beckwith: *The Old Testament Canon of the New Testament* Church, SPCK 1985, though his confidence in precise results appears to be overstated. For wider issues, see C. F. Evans, *Is 'Holy Scripture' Christian? and other questions* SCM Press 1971. For matters raised in this final paragraph, see J. L. Houlden, *Connections. The Integration of Theology and Faith*, SCM Press 1986.]

14.   *Original Text and Canonical Text*
(Published in *USQR* 32/3–4, 1977, 166–73.)

1. 'A Judgment Narrative between King and Chronicles? An Approach to Amos 7.9–17', (Essay 12, pp. 196–208).

2. For discussion of these passages, cf. my 'Historians and Prophets', and 'An Interpretation of the Babylonian Exile: A Study of II Kings 20; Isaiah 38–39', (Essays 8 and 9, pp. 121–51, 152–71).

3. The proposal of F. Crüsemann, 'Kritik an Amos im deuteronomischen Geschichtswerk. Erwägungen zu 2 Könige 14:27', in *Probleme biblischer Theologie (Festschrift G. von Rad)* ed. H. W. Wolff. Kaiser, Munich 1971, 57–63, is difficult to maintain in view of the total lack of correspondence in the wording. Cf. my fuller discussion in the article cited in n. 1.

4. These are to be found in I Kings 13 and II Chronicles 25; see my discussion.

5. Cf. here the points made by J. A. Sanders, *Torah and Canon*, Fortress Press, Philadelphia, 1972, e.g., p. xvii, and B. S. Childs' review in *Interpretation* 27, 1973, 88–91.

6. Sid Z. Leiman, *The Canonization of Hebrew Scripture: The Talmudic and Midrashic Evidence*, Archon Books, Hamden, Conn. 1976, esp. 14–16 and 127–9.

7. So e.g., in the epilogue to the Code of Hammurabi, and probably also, though less clearly, in that to the earlier Lipit-Ishtar Lawcode in *ANET*, 178f., 161, and in Deut.4.2.

8. Cf. Leiman, *Canonization*, 51–53 for text, translation, and useful annotation.

9. The position accorded to such a book as Enoch in the Ethiopian Christian community (though not there alone) and the differing views of the status of the Apocrypha are two examples. Leiman, *Canonization*, 40–49 and notes, offers a discussion of the evidence, directed primarily toward the delineation of the Hebrew canon. [Cf. also 'The Open Canon', Essay 13, pp. 209–24].

10. MT here has a plural *'attem 'om⁽rîm* ('you are saying'); the context suggests that a singular form is needed and this appears in LXX. The judgment word being cited and corrected in v. 36 is, in fact, attributed to God in 36.28. MT's plural form may be seen as an exegetical shift by which what is at one point described as the divine word is now shown as being cited by 'you', i.e., the community, but its authority is challenged by the correction now provided. The passage contains other examples of the process, e.g., 32.43, 33.10, and yet others in which the same theme of modification or repeal of a divine word is expressed more directly, e.g., 33.12. Cf. comments in my 'Aspects of the Jeremiah Tradition', *IJT* 29, 1971, 1–12 esp. 8f.

11. The word is Morton Smith's in a review of the *Cambridge History of the Bible*, Volume 1 in the *American Historical Review* 77, February 1972, 95 n. 7. Smith's derogatory view of editors is characteristic of his attitudes in general. Such overly facile dismissal of the later stages in the formation of the biblical material would, if pressed, give authority or validity only to 'original' sayings, a view implied in many now dated books on the Old Testament, such as R. H. Pfeiffer's *Introduction to the Old Testament*, Harper, New York ²1952. See further below (pp. 230ff).

12. Cf. my brief discussion of the latter in 'An Authoritative Version of the Bible?', *ExpT* 85, 1973–74, 374–7.

13. One aspect of the problem is brought out in an illuminating manner by R. P. Carroll in his 'A Non-Cogent Argument in Jeremiah's Oracles against the Prophets', *StTh* 30, 1976, 43–51, though not all his arguments are satisfactory.

14. Cf. A. Fitzgerald, 'A Note on Psalm 29', *BASOR* 215, 1974, 61–63, and the comments of H. Ringgren and A. S. Kapelrud in *Tradition and Theology in the Old Testament*, ed. D. A. Knight, Fortress Press, Philadelphia 1977, 37, 39, 116.
[A full discussion is in J. L. Cunchillos, *Estudio del Salmo 29*, Institución San Jerónimo, Valencia 1976.]

15. On this cf. e.g. J. A. Wharton, 'The Secret of Yahweh: Story and Affirmation in Judges 13–16', *Interpretation* 27, 1973, 48–66.

16. James A. Sanders, 'Adaptable for Life: The Nature and Function of the Canon', *Magnalia Dei – The Mighty Acts of God: Essays on the Bible and Archaeology in Memory of G. Ernest Wright*, ed. F. M. Cross, W. E. Lemke and P. D. Miller, Jr., Doubleday, Garden City, New York 1976, 531–60. [Also T. Fornberg, 'Textual Criticism and Canon. Some Problems', *StTh* 40, 1986, 45–53.]

15.   *The Old Testament Religious Tradition: Unity and Change*
(Delivered as a lecture at Princeton Theological Seminary, November 1986)

1. Keith Whitelam, 'Recreating the history of Israel', *JSOT*, 35, 1986, 45–70.

2. Cf. J. A. Soggin, *A History of Israel*, SCM Press 1984, 32f.

3. J. H. Hayes and J. Maxwell Miller, *A History of Israel and Judah*, SCM Press and Westminster Press, Philadelphia 1986.

4. Cf. B. O. Long, 'Historical Narrative and the Fictionalizing Imagination', *VT* 35, 1965, 405–16.

5. See Soggin, op.cit., ch. 2, pp. 18–40.

6. See my 'Goddesses, Women and Jezebel', in *Images of Women in Antiquity*, ed. A. Cameron and A. Kuhrt, Croom Helm, London 1983, 245–59.

7. Cf. Morton Smith, *Palestinian Parties and Politics that shaped the Old Testament*, Columbia UP, New York and London 1971.

8. Another example of the effect of this attitude may perhaps be seen in the often oversimplified comments on loyalty and apostasy in the Hellenistic period. It is all too easy to take the tendentious comments of, for example, I Maccabees as pointing to an absolute abandonment of the religious tradition by some members of the community. The diversity of thought in the Graeco-Roman period, which provides the context for Qumran and Christianity, suggests that again a too easy assumption of the religious distinctiveness of Judaism and subsequently of Christianity may miss the real problems of religious thought and behaviour.

9. M. Fishbane, *Biblical Interpretation in Ancient Israel* OUP 1985.

10. Cf. e.g. the essays in *Holy Book and Holy Tradition*, ed. F. F. Bruce and E. G. Rupp, Manchester UP 1968.

11. The title of my *Exile and Restoration* (OTL), 1968, may properly be held to support this misleading effect, however much the argument of the book may provide a corrective.

12. Cf. Fishbane, op.cit., especially 265f. for a brief summary statement of the point.

INDEX OF MODERN AUTHORS

INDEX OF BIBLICAL REFERENCES

OLD TESTAMENT
(in the order of the Hebrew Bible)

300

APOCRYPHA AND PSEUDEPIGRAPHA

NEW TESTAMENT